World's Best Histories

GERMANY

FROM THE EARLIEST PERIOD

BY

WOLFGANG MENZEL

TRANSLATED FROM THE FOURTH GERMAN EDITION
BY MRS. GEORGE HORROCKS

WITH A SUPPLEMENTARY CHAPTER OF RECENT EVENTS
BY EDGAR SALTUS

IN FOUR VOLUMES
VOLUME FOUR

NEW YORK AND LONDON
THE CO-OPERATIVE PUBLICATION SOCIETY

HISTORY OF GERMANY

VOLUME FOUR

THE HISTORY OF GERMANY

PART XXI

THE RISE OF PRUSSIA

(*CONTINUED*)

CCXLIV. *Art and Fashion*

ALTHOUGH art had, under French influence, become unnatural, bombastical, in fine, exactly contrary to every rule of good taste, the courts, vain of their collections of works of art, still emulated each other in the patronage of the artists of the day, whose creations, tasteless as they were, nevertheless afforded a species of consolation to the people, by diverting their thoughts from the miseries of daily existence.

Architecture degenerated in the greatest degree. Its sublimity was gradually lost as the meaning of the Gothic style became less understood, and a tasteless imitation of the Roman style, like that of St. Peter's at Rome, was brought into vogue by the Jesuits and by the court architects, by whom the chateau of Versailles was deemed the highest chef-d'œuvre of art. This style of architecture was accompanied by a style of sculpture equally unmeaning and forced; saints and Pagan deities in theatrical attitudes, fat genii, and coquettish nymphs peopled the roofs of the churches and palaces, presided over bridges, fountains, etc. Miniature turnery-ware and microscopical sculpture also came into fashion. Such curiosities as, for instance, a cherry-stone, on which Pranner, the Carinthian, had carved upward of a hundred faces; a chessboard, the completion of which had occupied a Dutchman for eighteen years; golden carriages drawn by fleas; toys composed of porcelain or ivory in imitation of Chinese works of art; curious pieces of mechanism, musical clocks, etc., were industriously collected into the cabinets of the wealthy and powerful. This taste was, however, not utterly useless. The predilection for ancient gems promoted the study of the remains of antiquity, as Stosch, Lippert, and Winckelmann prove, and that of natural history was greatly facilitated by the collections of natural curiosities.

The style of painting was, however, still essentially German, although deprived by the Reformation and by French influence of its ancient sacred and spiritual character. Nature was now generally studied in the search after the beautiful. Among the pupils of Rubens, the great founder of the Dutch school, Jordaens was distinguished for brilliancy and force of execution, Van Dyck (1541), for grace and beauty, although principally a portrait painter and incapable of idealizing his subjects, in which Rembrandt (1674), who chose more extensive historical subjects, and whose coloring is remarkable for depth and effect, was equally deficient. Rembrandt's pupil, Gerhard Douw, introduced domestic scenes; his attention to the minutiæ of his art was such that he is said to have worked for three days at a broomstick, in order to represent it with perfect truth. Denner carried accuracy still further; in his portraits of old men every hair in the beard is carefully imitated. Francis and William[1] Mieris discovered far greater talent in their treatment of social and domestic groups; Terbourg and Netscher, on the other hand, delighted in the close imitation of velvet and satin draperies; and Schalken, in the effect of shadows and lamplight. Honthorst[2] attempted a higher style, but Van der Werf's small delicious nudities and Van

[1] Also his brother John, who painted with equal talent in the same style. —*Trans.*

[2] Called also Gerardo dalle Notti from his subjects, principally night-scenes and pieces illuminated by torch or candle-light. His most celebrated picture is that of Jesus Christ before the Tribunal of Pilate.—*Ibid.*

Loos's luxurious pastoral scenes were better adapted to the taste of the times. While these painters belonged to the higher orders of society, of which their works give evidence, numerous others studied the lower classes with still greater success. Besides Van der Meulen and Rugendas, the painters of battle-pieces, Wouvermann chiefly excelled in the delineation of horses and groups of horsemen, and Teniers, Ostade, and Jan Steen became famous for the surpassing truth of their peasants and domestic scenes. To this low but happily-treated school also belonged the cattle-pieces of Berchem and Paul de Potter, whose "Bull and Cows" were, in a certain respect, as much the ideal of the Dutch as the Madonna had formerly been that of the Italians or the Venus di Medici that of the ancients.

Landscape-painting alone gave evidence of a higher style. Nature, whenever undesecrated by the vulgarity of man, is ever sublimely simple. The Dutch, as may be seen in the productions of Breughel, called, from his dress, "Velvet Breughel," and in those of Elzheimer, termed, from his attention to minutiæ, the Denner of landscape-painting, were at first too careful and minute; but Paul Brill (1626) was inspired with finer conceptions and formed the link between preceding artists and the magnificent Claude Lorraine (so called from the place of his birth, his real name being Claude Gelee), who resided for a long time at Munich, and who first attempted to idealize nature as the Italian artists had formerly idealized man. Everdingen and Ruysdael, on the contrary, studied nature in her simple northern garb, and the sombre pines of the former, the cheerful woods of the latter, will ever be attractive, like pictures of a much-loved home, to the German. Bakhuysen's sea-pieces and storms are faithful representations of the Baltic. In the commencement of last century, landscape-painting also degenerated and became mere ornamental flower-painting, of which the Dutch were so passionately fond that they honored and paid the most skilful artists in this style like princes. The dull prosaic existence of the merchant called for relief. Huysum was the most celebrated of the flower-painters, with Rachel Ruysch, William von Arless, and others of lesser note. Fruit and kitchen pieces were also greatly admired. Hondekotter was celebrated as a painter of birds.

Painting was, in this manner, confined to a slavish imitation of nature, for whose lowest objects a predilection was evinced until the middle of the eighteenth century, when a style, half Italian, half antique, was introduced into Germany by the operas, by travellers, and more particularly by the galleries founded by the princes, and was still further promoted by the learned researches of connoisseurs, more especially by those of Winckelmann. Mengs, the Raphael of Germany, Oeser, Tischbein, the landscape-painters Seekatz, Hackert, Reinhardt, Koch, etc., formed the transition to the modern style. Frey, Chodowiecki, etc., gained great celebrity as engravers.

Architecture flourished during the Middle Ages, painting at the time of the Reformation, and music in modern times. The same spirit that spoke to the eye in the eternal stone now breathed in transient melody to the ear. The science of music, transported by Dutch artists into Italy, had been there assiduously cultivated; the Italians had speedily surpassed their masters, and had occupied themselves with the creation of a peculiar church-music and of the profane opera, while the Netherlands and the whole of Germany were convulsed by bloody religious wars. After the peace of Westphalia, the national music of Germany, with the exception of the choral music in the Protestant churches, was almost silent, and Italian operas were introduced at all the courts, where Italian chapel-masters, singers, and performers were patronized in imitation of Louis XIV., who pursued a similar system in France. German talent was reduced to imitate the Italian masters, and, in 1628, Sagittarius produced at Dresden the first German opera in imitation of the Italian, and Keyser published no fewer than one hundred and sixteen.

The German musicians were, nevertheless, earlier than the German poets, animated with a desire to extirpate the foreign and degenerate mode fostered by the vanity of the German princes, and to give free scope to their original and native talent. This regeneration was effected by the despised and simple organists of the Protestant churches. In 1717, Schroeder, a native of Hohenstein in Saxony invented the pianoforte and improved the organ. Sebastian Bach, in his colossal fugues, like to a pillared dome dissolved in melody,[1] raised music by his compositions to a height unattained by any of his successors. He was one of the most extraordinary geniuses that ever appeared on earth. Handel, whose glorious melodies entranced the senses, produced the grand oratorio of the "Messiah," which is still performed in both Protestant and Catholic cathedrals; and Graun, with whom Frederick the Great played the flute, brought private singing into vogue by his musical compositions. Gluck was the first composer who introduced the depth and pathos of more solemn music into the opera. He gained a complete triumph at Paris over Piccini, the celebrated Italian musician, in his contest respecting the comparative excellencies of the German and Italian schools. Haydn introduced the variety and melody of the opera into the oratorio, of which his "Creation" is a standing proof. In the latter half of the foregoing century, sacred music has gradually yielded to the opera. Mozart brought the operatic style to perfection in the wonderful compositions that eternalize his fame.

The German theatre was, owing to the Gallomania of the period, merely a bad imitation of the French stage. Gottsched,[2] who greatly contributed toward the reformation of German literature, still retained the stilted Alexandrine and the pseudo-Gallic imitation of the ancient dramatists to which Lessing put an end. Lessing wrote his "Dramaturgy" at Hamburg, recommended Shakespeare and other English authors as models, but more particularly nature. The celebrated Eckhof, the father of the German stage, who

---

[1] Gothic architecture has been likened to petrified music.

[2] He was assisted in his dramatic writings by his wife, a woman of splendid talents.—*Trans.*

at first travelled about with a company of actors and finally settled at Gotha, was the first who followed this innovation. He was succeeded by Schroeder in Hamburg, who was equally industrious as a poet, an actor, and a Freemason. In Berlin, where Fleck had already paved the way, Iffland, who, like Schroeder, was both a poet and an actor, founded a school, which in every respect took nature as a guide, and which raised the German stage to its well-merited celebrity.

At the close of the eighteenth century, men of education were seized with an enthusiasm for art, which showed itself principally in a love for the stage and in visits for the promotion of art to Italy. The poet and the painter, alike dissatisfied with reality, sought to still their secret longings for the beautiful amid the unreal creations of fancy and the records of classical antiquity.

Fashion, that masker of nature, that creator of deformity, had, in truth, arrived at an unparalleled pitch of ugliness. The German costume, although sometimes extravagantly curious during the Middle Ages, had nevertheless always retained a certain degree of picturesque beauty, nor was it until the reign of Louis XIV. of France that dress assumed an unnatural, inconvenient, and monstrous form. Enormous allonge perukes and ruffles, the fontange (high headdress), hoops, and high heels, rendered the human race a caricature of itself. In the eighteenth century, powdered wigs of extraordinary shape, hairbags, and queues, frocks and frills, came into fashion for the men; powdered headdresses an ell in height, diminutive waists, and patches for the women. The deformity, unhealthiness, and absurdity of this mode of attire were vainly pointed out by Salzmann, in a piece entitled, "Charles von Carlsberg, or Human Misery."

CCXLV. *Influence of the Belles-Lettres*

THE German, excluded from all participation in public affairs and confined to the narrow limits of his family circle and profession, followed his natural bent for speculative philosophy and poetical reverie; but while his thoughts became more elevated and the loss of his activity was, in a certain degree, compensated by the gentle dominion of the muses, the mitigation thus afforded merely aggravated the evil by rendering him content with his state of inaction. Ere long, as in the most degenerate age of ancient Rome, the citizen, amused by sophists and singers, actors and jugglers, lost the remembrance of his former power and rights and became insensible to his state of moral degradation, to which the foreign notions, the vain and frivolous character of most of the poets of the day, had not a little contributed.

After the thirty years' war, the Silesian poets became remarkable for Gallomania or the slavish imitation of those of France. Unbounded adulation of the sovereign, bombastical "carmina" on occasion of the birth, wedding, accession, victories, fêtes, treaties of peace, and burial of potentates, love-couplets equally strained, twisted compliments to female beauty, with pedantic, often indecent, citations from ancient mythology, chiefly characterized this school of poetry. Martin Opitz 1639, the founder of the first Silesian school,[1] notwithstanding the insipidity of the taste of the day, preserved the harmony of the German ballad. His most distinguished followers were Logau, celebrated for his Epigrams;[2] Paul Gerhard, who, in his fine hymns, revived the force and simplicity of Luther; Flemming, a genial and thoroughly German poet, the companion of Olearius[3] during his

---

[1] He was a friend of Grotius and is styled the father of German poetry. —*Trans.*

[2] Of which an edition, much esteemed, was published by Lessing and Ramler.

[3] Adam Œlschlager or Olearius, an eminent travelier and mathematician, a native of Anhalt. He became secretary to an embassy sent to Russia and Persia by the duke of Holstein. —*Trans.*

visit to Persia; the gentle Simon Dach, whose sorrowing notes bewail the miseries of the age. He founded a society of melancholy poets at Königsberg, in Prussia, the members of which composed elegies for each other; Tscherning and Andrew Gryphius, the Corneille of Germany, a native of Glogau, whose dramas are worthy of a better age than the insipid century in which they were produced. The life of this dramatist was full of incident. His father was poisoned; his mother died of a broken heart. He wandered over Germany during the thirty years' war, pursued by fire, sword, and pestilence, to the latter of which the whole of his relations fell victims. He travelled over the whole of Europe, spoke eleven languages, and became a professor at Leyden, where he taught history, geography, mathematics, physics, and anatomy. These poets were, however, merely exceptions to the general rule. In the poetical societies—the "Order of the Palm" or "Fructiferous Society," founded in 1617, at Weimar, by Caspar von Teutleben, the "Upright Pine Society," established by Rempler of Löwenthal at Strasburg, that of the "Roses," founded in 1643, by Philip von Zesen, at Hamburg, the "Order of the Pegnitz-shepherds," founded in 1644, by Harsdörfer, at Nuremberg—the spirit of the Italian and French operas and academies prevailed, and pastoral poetry, in which the god of Love was represented wearing an immense allonge peruke, and the coquettish immorality of the courts was glowingly described in Arcadian scenes of delight, was cultivated. The fantastical romances of Spain were also imitated, and the invention of novel terms was deemed the highest triumph of the poet. Every third word was either Latin, French, Spanish, Italian, or English. Francisci of Lübeck, who described all the discoveries of the New World in a colloquial romance contained in a thick folio volume, was the most extravagant of these scribblers. The romances of Antony Ulric, duke of Brunswick, who embraced Catholicism on the occasion of the marriage of his daughter with the emperor Charles VI., are equally bad. Lauremberg's satires, written in 1564, are excellent. He said with great truth that the French had deprived the German muse of her nose and had patched on another quite unsuited to her German ears. Moscherosch (Philander von Sittewald) wrote an admirable and cutting satire upon the manners of the age, and Greifenson von Hirschfeld is worthy of mention as the author of the first historical romance that gives an accurate and graphic account of the state of Germany during the thirty years' war.

This first school was succeeded by a second of surpassing extravagance. Hoffman von Hoffmannswaldau, 1679, the founder of the second Silesian school, was a caricature of Opitz, Lohenstein of Gryphius, Besser of Flemming, Talander and Ziegler of Zesen, and even Francisci was outdone by that most intolerable of romancers, Happel. This school was remarkable for the most extravagant license and bombastical nonsense, a sad proof of the moral perversion of the age. The German character, nevertheless, betrayed itself by a sort of naïve pedantry, a proof, were any wanting, that the ostentatious absurdities of the poets of Germany were but bad and paltry imitations. The French Alexandrine was also brought into vogue by this school, whose immorality was carried to the highest pitch by Günther, the lyric poet, who, in the commencement of the eighteenth century, opposed marriage, attempted the emancipation of the female sex, and, with criminal geniality, recommended his follies and crimes, as highly interesting, to the world. To him the poet, Schnabel, the author of an admirable romance, the "Island of Felsenburg," the asylum, in another hemisphere, of virtue, exiled from Europe, offers a noble contrast.

Three Catholic poets of extreme originality appear at the close of the seventeenth century, Angelus Silesius (Scheffler of Breslau), who gave to the world his devotional thoughts in German Alexandrines; Father Abraham a Sancta Clara (Megerle of Swabia), a celebrated Viennese preacher, who, with comical severity, wrote satires abounding with wit and humorous observations; and Balde, who wrote some fine Latin poems on God and nature. Prätorius, 1680, the first collector of the popular legendary ballads concerning Rübezahl and other spirits, ghosts and witches, also deserves mention. The Silesian, Stranizki, who, 1708, founded the Leopoldstadt theatre at Vienna, which afterward became so celebrated, and gave to it the popular comic style for which it is famous at the present day, was also a poet of extreme originality. Gottsched appeared as the hero of Gallomania, which was at that time threatened with gradual extinction by the Spanish and Hamburg romance and by Viennese wit. Assisted by Neuber, the actress, he extirpated all that was not strictly French, solemnly burned Harlequin in effigy at Leipzig in 1737, and laid down a law for German poetry, which prescribed obedience to the rules of the stilted French court-poetry, under pain of the critic's lash. He and his learned wife guided the literature of Germany for several years.

In the midst of these literary aberrations, during the first part of the foregoing century, Thomson, the English poet, Brokes of Hamburg, and the Swiss, Albert von Haller, gave their descriptions of nature to the world. Brokes, in his "Earthly Pleasures in God," was faithful, often Homeric, in his descriptions, while Haller depictured his native Alps with unparalleled sublimity. The latter was succeeded by a Swiss school, which imitated the witty and liberal-minded criticisms of Addison and other English writers, and opposed French taste and Gottsched. At its head stood Bodmer and Breitinger, who recommended nature as a guide, and instead of the study of French literature, that of the ancient classics and of English authors. It was also owing to their exertions that Müller published an edition of Rudiger Maness's collection of Swabian Minnelieder, the connecting link between modern and ancient German poetry. Still, notwithstanding their merit as critics, they were no poets, and merely opened to others the road to improvement. Hagedorn, although frivolous in his ideas, was graceful and easy in his versification; but the most eminent poet of the age was Gellert of Leipzig, 1769, whose tales, fables, and essays brought him into such note as to attract the attention of Frederick the Great, who, notwithstanding the contempt in which he held the poets of Germany, honored him with a personal visit.

Poets and critics now rose in every quarter and pitilessly assailed Gottsched, the champion of Gallomania. They were themselves divided into two opposite parties, into Anglomanists and Græcomanists, according to their predilection for modern English literature or for that of ancient Greece and Rome. England, grounded, as upon a rock, on her self-gained constitution, produced men of the rarest genius in all the higher walks of science and literature, and her philosophers, naturalists, historians, and poets exercised the happiest influence over their Teutonic brethren, who sought to regain from them the vigor of which they had been deprived by France. The power and national learning of Germany break forth in Klopstock, whose genius vainly sought a natural garb and was compelled to assume a borrowed form. He consecrated his muse to the service of religion, but, in so doing, imitated the Homeric hexameters of Milton; he sought to arouse the national pride of his countrymen by recalling the deeds of Hermann (Armin) and termed himself a bard, but, in the Horatian metre of his songs, imitated Ossian, the old Scottish bard, and was consequently labored and affected in his style. Others took the lesser English poets for their model, as, for instance, Kleist, who fell at Kunersdorf, copied Thomson in his "Spring"; Zachariä, Pope, in his satirical pieces; Hermes, in "The Travels of Sophia," the humorous romances of Richardson; Müller von Itzehoe, in his "Siegfried von Lindenberg," the comic descriptions of Smollett. The influence of the celebrated English poets, Shakespeare, Swift, and Sterne, on the tone of German humor and satire, was still greater. Swift's first imitator, Liscow, displayed considerable talent, and Rabener, a great part of whose manuscripts was burned during the siege of Dresden in the seven years' war, wrote witty, and at the same time instructive, satires on the manners of his age. Both were surpassed by Lichtenberg, the little hump-backed philosopher of Göttingen, whose compositions are replete with grace. The witty and amiable Thümmel was also formed on an English model, and Archenholz solely occupied himself with transporting the customs and literature of England into Germany. If Shakespeare has not been without influence upon Goethe and Schiller, Sterne, in his "Sentimental Journey," touched an echoing chord in the German's heart by blending pathos with his jests; Hippel was the first who, like him, united wit with pathos, mockery with tears.

In Klopstock, Anglo and Græcomania were combined. The latter had, however, also its particular school, in which each of the Greek and Roman poets found his imitator. Voss, for instance, took Homer for his model, Ramler, Horace, Gleim, Anacreon, Gessner, Theocritus, Cramer, Pindar, Lichtwer, Æsop, etc. The Germans, in the ridiculous attempt to set themselves up as Greeks, were, in truth, barbarians. But all was forced, unnatural, and perverted in this aping age. Wieland alone was deeply sensible of this want of nature, and hence arose his predilection for the best poets of Greece and France. The German muse, led by his genius, lost her ancient stiffness and acquired a pliant grace, to which the sternest critic of his too lax morality is not insensible. Some lyric poets, connected with the Græcomanists by the "Göttingen Hainbund," preserved a noble simplicity, more particularly Salis and Hòlty, and also Count Stolberg, wherever he has not been led astray by Voss's stilted manner. Matthison is, on the other hand, most tediously affected.

The German, never more at home than when abroad, boasted of being the cosmopolite he had become, made a virtue of necessity, and termed his want of patriotism, justice to others, humanity, philanthropy. Fortunately for him, there were, besides the French, other nations on which he could model himself, the ancient Greeks and the English, from each of whom he gathered something until he had converted himself into a sort of universal abstract. The great poets, who shortly before and after the seven years' war put an end to mere partial imitations, were not actuated by a reaction of nationality, but by a sentiment of universality. Their object was, not to oppose the German to the foreign, but simply the human to the single national element, and, although Germany gave them birth, they regarded the whole world equally as their country.

Lessing, by his triumph over the scholastic pedants, completed what Thomasius had begun, by his irresistible criticism drove French taste from the literary arena, aided Winckelmann to promote the study of the ancients and to foster the love of art, and raised the German theatre to an unprecedented height. His native language, in which he always wrote, breathes, even in his most trifling works, a free and lofty spirit, which, fascinating in every age, was more peculiarly so at that emasculated period. He is, however, totally devoid of patriotism. In his "Minna von Barnhelm," he inculcates the finest feelings of honor; his "Nathan" is replete with the wisdom "that cometh from above" and with calm dignity; and in "Emilia Galotti" he has been the first to draw the veil, hitherto respected, from scenes in real life. His life was, like his mind, independent. He scorned to cringe for favor, even disdained letters of recommendation when visiting Italy (Winckelmann had deviated from the truth for the sake of pleasing a patron), contented himself with the scanty lot of a librarian at Wolfenbüttel, and even preferred losing that appointment rather than subject himself to the censorship. He was the boldest, freest, finest spirit of the age.

Herder, although no less noble, was exactly his opposite. Of a soft and yielding temperament, unimaginative, and gifted with little penetration, but with a keen sense of the beautiful in others, he opened to his fellow countrymen with unremitting diligence the literary treasures of foreign nations, ancient classical poetry, that, hitherto unknown, of the East, and rescued from obscurity the old popular poetry of Germany. In his "Ideas of a Philosophical History of Mankind," he attempted to display in rich and manifold variety the moral character of every nation and of every age, and, while thus creating and improving the taste for poetry and history, ever, with childlike piety, sought for and revered God in all his works.

Goethe, with a far richer imagination, possessed the elegance but not the independence of Lessing, all the softness, pathos, and universality of Herder, without his faith. In the treatment and choice of his subjects he is indubitably the greatest poet of Germany, but he was never inspired with enthusiasm except for himself. His personal vanity was excessive. His works, like the lights in his apartment at Weimar, which were skilfully disposed so as to present him in the most favorable manner to his visitors, but artfully reflect upon self. The manner in which he palliated the weaknesses of the heart, the vain inclinations, shared by his contemporaries in common with himself, rendered him the most amiable and popular author of the day. French frivolity and license had long been practiced, but they had also been rebuked. Goethe was the first who gravely justified adultery, rendered the sentimental voluptuary an object of enthusiastic admiration, and deified the heroes of the stage, in whose imaginary fortunes the German forgot sad reality and the wretched fate of his country. His *fade* assumption of dignity, the art with which he threw the veil of mystery over his frivolous tendencies and made his commonplace ideas pass for something incredibly sublime, naturally met with astonishing success in his wonder-seeking times.

Rousseau's influence, the ideas of universal reform, the example of England, proud and free, but still more, the enthusiasm excited by the American war of independence, inflamed many heads in Germany and raised a poetical opposition, which began with the bold-spirited Schubart, whose liberal opinions threw him into a prison, but whose spirit still breathed in his songs and roused that of his great countryman, Schiller. The first cry of the oppressed people was, by Schiller, repeated with a prophet's voice. In him their woes found an eloquent advocate. Lessing had vainly appealed to the understanding, but Schiller spoke to the heart, and if the seed, sown by him, fell partially on corrupt and barren ground, it found a fostering soil in the warm, unadulterated hearts of the youth of both sexes. He recalled his fellow-men, in those frivolous times, to a sense of self-respect, he restored to innocence the power and dignity of which she had been deprived by ridicule, and became the champion of liberty, justice, and his country, things from which the love of pleasure and the aristocratic self-complacency, exemplified in Goethe, had gradually and completely weaned succeeding poets. Klinger, at the same time, coarsely portrayed the vices of the church and state, and Meyern extravagated in his romance "Dya-Na-Sore" on Utopian happiness. The poems of Muller, the painter, are full of latent warmth. Burger, Pfeffel, the blind poet, and Claudius, gave utterance, in Schubart's coarse manner, to a few trite truisms. Musæus was greatly admired for his amusing popular stories. As for the rest, it seemed as though the spiritless writers of that day had found it more convenient to be violent and savage in their endless chivalric pieces and romances than, like Schiller, steadily and courageously to attack the vices and evils of their age. Their fire but ended in smoke. Babo and Ziegler alone, among the dramatists, have a liberal tendency. The spirit that had been called forth also degenerated into mere bacchanalian license, and, in order to return to nature, the limits set by decency and custom were, as by Heinse, for instance, who thus disgraced his genius, wantonly overthrown.

In contradistinction to these wild spirits, which, whether borne aloft by their genius or impelled by ambition, quitted the narrow limits of daily existence, a still greater number of poets employed their talents in singing the praise of common life, and brought domesticity and household sentimentality into vogue. The very prose of life, so unbearable to the former, was by them converted into poetry. Although the ancient idyls and the family scenes of English authors were at first imitated, this style of poetry retained an essentially German originality; the hero of the modern idyl, unlike his ancient model, was a fop tricked out with wig and cane, and the domestic hero of the tale, unlike his English counterpart, was a mere political nullity. It is perhaps well when domestic comforts replace the want of public life, but these poets hugged the chain they had decked with flowers, and forgot the reality. They forgot that it is a misfortune and a disgrace for a German to be without a country, without a great national interest, to be the most unworthy descendant of the greatest ancestors, the prey and the jest of the foreigner; to this they were indifferent, insensible; they laid down the maxim that a German has nothing more to do than "to provide for" himself and his family, no other enemy to repel than domestic trouble, no other duty than "to keep his German wife in order," to send his sons to the university, and to marry his daughters. These commonplace private interests were withal merely adorned with a little sentimentality. No noble motive is discoverable in Voss's celebrated "Louisa" and Goethe's "Hermann and Dorothea." This style of poetry was so easy that hundreds of weak-headed men and women made it their occupation, and family scenes and plays speedily surpassed the romances of chivalry in number. The poet, nevertheless, exercised no less an influence, notwithstanding his voluntary renunciation of his privilege to elevate the sinking minds of his countrymen by the great memories of the past or by ideal images, and his degradation of poetry to a mere palliation of the weaknesses of humanity.

PART XXII

THE GREAT WARS WITH FRANCE

CCXLVI. *The French Revolution*

IN NO other European state had despotism arrived at such a pitch as in France; the people groaned beneath the heavy burdens imposed by the court, the nobility, and the clergy, and against these two estates there was no appeal, their tyranny being protected by the court, to which they had servilely submitted. The court had rendered itself not only unpopular, but contemptible, by its excessive license, which had also spread downward among the higher classes; the government was, moreover, impoverished by extravagance and weakened by an incapable administration, the helm of state, instead of being guided by a master-hand, having fallen under Louis XV. into that of a woman.

In France, where the ideas of modern philosophy emanated from the court, they spread more rapidly than in any other country among the tiers-etat, and the spirit of research, of improvement, of ridicule of all that was old, naturally led the people to inquire into the administration, to discover and to ridicule its errors. The natural wit of the people, sharpened by daily oppression and emboldened by Voltaire's unsparing ridicule of objects hitherto held sacred, found ample food in the policy pursued by the government, and ridicule became the weapon with which the tiers-etat revenged the tyranny of the higher classes. As learning spread, the deeds of other nations, who had happily and gloriously cast off the yoke of their oppressors, became known to the people. The names of the patriots of Greece and Rome passed from mouth to mouth, and their actions became the theme of the rising generation; but more powerful than all in effect, was the example of the North Americans, who, in 1783, separated themselves from their mother-country, England, and founded a republic. France, intent upon weakening her ancient foe, lent her countenance to the new republic, and numbers of her sons fought beneath her standard and bore the novel ideas of liberty back to their native land, where they speedily produced a fermentation among their mercurial countrymen.

Louis XV., a voluptuous and extravagant monarch, was succeeded by Louis XVI., a man of refined habits, pious and benevolent in disposition, but unpossessed of the moral power requisite for the extermination of the evils deeply rooted in the government. His queen, Marie Antoinette, sister to Joseph II., little resembled her brother or her husband in her tastes, was devoted to gayety, and, by her example, countenanced the most lavish extravagance. The evil increased to a fearful degree. The taxes no longer sufficed; the exchequer was robbed by privileged thieves; an enormous debt continued to increase; and the king, almost reduced to the necessity of declaring the state bankrupt, demanded aid from the nobility and clergy, who, hitherto free from taxation, had amassed the whole wealth of the empire.

The aristocracy, ever blind to their true interest, refused to comply, and, by so doing, compelled the king to have recourse to the tiers-etat. Accordingly, in 1789, he convoked a general assembly, in which the deputies sent by the citizens and peasant classes were not only numerically equal to those of the aristocracy, but were greatly superior to them in talent and energy, and, on the refusal of the nobility and clergy to comply with the just demands of the tiers-etat, or even to hold a common sitting with their despised inferiors, these deputies declared the national assembly to consist of themselves alone, and proceeded, on their own responsibility, to scrutinize the evils of the administration and to discuss remedial measures. The whole nation applauded the manly and courageous conduct of its representatives. The Parisians, ever in extremes, revolted, and murdered the unpopular public officers; the soldiers, instead of quelling the rebellion, fraternized with the people. The national assembly, emboldened by these first successes, undertook a thorough transformation of the state, and, in order to attain the object for which they had been assembled, that of procuring supplies, declared the aristocracy subject to taxation, and sold the enormous property belonging to the church. They went still further. The people was declared the only true sovereign, and the king the first servant of the state. All distinctions and privileges were abolished, and all Frenchmen were declared equal.

The nobility and clergy, infuriated by this dreadful humiliation, imbittered the people still more against them by their futile opposition, and, at length convinced of the hopelessness of their cause, emigrated in crowds and attempted to form another France on the borders of their country in the German Rhenish provinces. Worms and Coblentz were their chief places of resort. In the latter city, they continued their Parisian mode of life at the expense of the avaricious elector of Treves, Clement Wenzel, a Saxon prince, by whose powerful minister, Dominique, they were supported, and acted with unparalleled impudence. They were headed by the two brothers of the French king, who entered into negotiation with all the foreign powers, and they vowed to defend the cause of the sovereigns against the people. Louis, who for some time wavered between the national assembly and the emigrants, was at length persuaded by the queen to throw himself into the arms of the latter, and secretly fled, but was retaken and subjected to still more rigorous treatment. The emigrants, instead of saving, hurried him to destruction.

The other European powers at first gave signs of indecision. Blinded by a policy no longer suited to the times, they merely beheld in the French Revolution the ruin of a state hitherto inimical to them, and rejoiced at the event. The prospect of an easy conquest of the distracted country, however, ere long led to the resolution on their part of actively interfering with its affairs. Austria was insulted in the person of the French queen, and, as head of the empire, was bound to protect the rights of the petty Rhenish princes and nobility, who possessed property and ecclesiastical or feudal rights[1] on French territory, and had been injured by the new constitution. Prussia, habituated to despotism, came forward as its champion in the hope of gaining new laurels for her unemployed army. A conference took place at Pilnitz in Saxony, in 1791, between Emperor Leopold and King Frederick William, at which the Count D'Artois, the youngest brother of Louis XVI., was present, and a league was formed against the Revolution. The old ministers strongly opposed it. In Prussia, Herzberg drew upon himself the displeasure of his sovereign by zealously advising a union with France against Austria. In Austria, Kaunitz recommended peace, and said that were he allowed to act he would defeat the impetuous French by his "patience"; that, instead of attacking France, he would calmly watch the event and allow her, like a volcano, to bring destruction upon herself. Ferdinand of Brunswick, field-marshal of Prussia, was equally opposed to war. His fame as the greatest general of his time had been too easily gained, more by his manœuvres than by his victories, not to induce a fear on his side of being as easily deprived of it in a fresh war; but the

---

[1] To the archbishopric of Cologne belonged the bishopric of Strasburg, to the archbishopric of Treves, the bishoprics of Metz, Toul, Verdun, Nancy, St. Diez. Würtemberg, Baden, Darmstadt, Nassau, Pfalz-Zweibrücken, Leiningen, Salm-Salm, Hohenlohe-Bartenstein, Löwenstein, Wertheim, the Teutonic order, the knights of St. John, the immediate nobility of the empire, the bishop of Basel, etc., had, moreover, feudal rights within the French territory. The arch-chancellor, elector of Mayence, made the patriotic proposal to the imperial diet that the empire should, now that France had, by the violation of the conditions of peace, infringed the old and shameful treaties by which Germany had been deprived of her provinces, seize the opportunity also on her part to refuse to recognize those treaties, and to regain what she had lost. This sensible proposal, however, found no one capable of carrying it into effect.

proposal of the revolutionary party in France—within whose minds the memory of Rossbach was still fresh—mistrustful of French skill, to nominate him generalissimo of the troops of the republic, conspired with the incessant entreaties of the emigrants to reanimate his courage; and he finally declared that, followed by the famous troops of the great Frederick, he would put a speedy termination to the French Revolution.

Leopold II. was, as brother to Marie Antoinette, greatly imbittered against the French. The disinclination of the Austrians to the reforms of Joseph II. appears to have chiefly confirmed him in the conviction of finding a sure support in the old system; he consequently strictly prohibited the slightest innovation and placed a power hitherto unknown in the hands of the police, more particularly in those of its secret functionaries, who listened to every word and consigned the suspected to the oblivion of a dungeon. This mute terrorism found many a victim. This system was, on the death of Leopold II. in 1792[1] publicly abolished by his son and successor, Francis II., but was ere long again carried on in secret.

Catherine II., with the view of seizing the rest of Poland, employed every art in order to instigate Austria and Prussia to a war with France, and by these means fully to occupy them in the West. The Prussian king, although aware of her projects, deemed the French an easy conquest, and that in case of necessity his armies could without difficulty be thrown into Poland. He meanwhile secured the popular feeling in Poland in his favor by concluding, in 1790, an alliance with Stanislaus and giving his consent to the improved constitution established in Poland in 1791. Herzberg had even counselled an alliance with France and Poland—the latter was to be bribed with a promise of the annexation of Galicia—against Austria and Russia; this

---

[1] His sons were the emperor Francis II., Ferdinand, grandduke of Tuscany, the archduke Charles, celebrated for his military talents, Joseph, palatine of Hungary, Antony, grand-master of the Teutonic order, who died at Vienna in 1835, John, a general (he lived for many years in Styria), the present imperial vicar-general of Germany, and Rayner, viceroy of Milan.—*Trans.*

plan was, however, merely whispered about for the purpose of blinding the Poles and of alarming Russia.

The bursting storm was anticipated on the part of the French by a declaration of war in 1792, and while Austria still remained behind, for the purpose of watching Russia, Poland, and Turkey, and the unwieldy empire was engaged in raising troops, Ferdinand of Brunswick had already led the Prussians across the Rhine. He was joined by the emigrants under Condé, whose army almost entirely consisted of officers. The well-known manifesto, published by the duke of Brunswick on his entrance into France, and in which he declared his intention to level Paris with the ground should the French refuse to submit to the authority of their sovereign, was composed by Renfner, the counsellor of the embassy at Berlin. The emperor and Frederick William, persuaded that fear would reduce the French to obedience, had approved of this manifesto, which was, on the contrary, disapproved of by the duke of Brunswick, on account of its barbarity and its ill-accordance with the rules of war.[1] He did not, however, withdraw his signature on its publication. The effect of this manifesto was that the French, instead of being struck with terror, were maddened with rage, deposed their king, proclaimed a republic, and flew to arms in order to defend their cities against the barbarians threatening them with destruction. The Orleans party and the Jacobins, who were in close alliance with the German Illuminati, were at that time first able to gain the mastery and to supplant the noble-spirited constitutionists. A Prussian baron, Anacharsis Cloots,[2] was even elected in the na-

---

[1] Gentz, who afterward wrote so many manifestoes for Austria, practically remarks that this celebrated manifesto was in perfect conformity with the intent, and that the only fault committed was the non-fulfilment of the threats therein contained.

[2] From Cleve. He compared himself with Anacharsis the Scythian, a barbarian, who visited Greece for the sake of learning. He sacrificed the whole of his property to the Revolution. Followed by a troop of men dressed in the costumes of different nations, of whom they were the pretended representatives, he appeared before the convention, from which he demanded the liberation of the whole world from the yoke of kings and priests. He became president of the

tional convention of the French republic, where he appeared as the advocate of the whole human race. These atheistical babblers, however, talked to little purpose, but the national pride of the troops, hastily levied and sent against the invaders, effected wonders.

The delusion of the Prussians was so complete that Bischofswerder said to the officers, "Do not purchase too many horses, the affair will soon be over"; and the duke of Brunswick remarked, "Gentlemen, not too much baggage, this is merely a military trip."

The Prussians, it is true, wondered that the inhabitants did not, as the emigrants had alleged they would, crowd to meet and greet them as their saviors and liberators, but at first they met with no opposition. The noble-spirited Lafayette, who commanded the main body of the French army, had at first attempted to march upon Paris for the purpose of saving the king, but the troops were already too much republicanized and he was compelled to seek refuge in the Netherlands, where he was, together with his companions, seized by command of the emperor of Austria, and thrown into prison at Olmütz, where he remained during five years under the most rigorous treatment merely on account of the liberality of his opinions, because he wanted a constitutional king, and notwithstanding his having endangered his life and his honor in order to save his sovereign. Such was the hatred with which high-minded men of strict principle were at that period viewed, while at the same time a negotiation was carried on with Dumouriez,[1] a characterless Jacobin intriguant, who had succeeded Lafayette in the command of the French armies.

Ferdinand of Brunswick now became the dupe of Du-

---

great Jacobin club, and it was principally owing to his instigations that the French, at first merely intent upon defence, were roused to the attack and inspired with the desire for conquest.

[1] Dumouriez proposed as negotiator John Müller, who was at that time teaching at Mayence, and who was in secret correspondence with him. Vide Memoirs of a Celebrated Statesman, edited by Rüder. Rüder remarks that John Müller is silent in his autobiography concerning his correspondence with the Jacobins, for which he might, under a change of circumstances, have had good reason.

mouriez, as he had formerly been that of the emigrants. In the hope of a counter-revolution in Paris, he procrastinated his advance and lost his most valuable time in the siege of fortresses. Verdun fell: three beautiful citizens' daughters, who had presented bouquets to the king of Prussia, were afterward sent to the guillotine by the republicans as traitoresses to their country. Ferdinand, notwithstanding this success, still delayed his advance in the hope of gaining over the wily French commander and of thus securing beforehand his triumph in a contest in which his ancient fame might otherwise be at stake. The impatient king, who had accompanied the army, spurred him on, but was, owing to his ignorance of military matters, again pacified by the reasons alleged by the cautious duke. Dumouriez, consequently, gained time to collect considerable reinforcements and to unite his forces with those under Kellermann of Alsace. The two armies came within sight of each other at Valmy; the king gave orders for battle, and the Prussians were in the act of advancing against the heights occupied by Kellermann, when the duke suddenly gave orders to halt and drew off the troops under a loud *vivat* from the French, who beheld this movement with astonishment. The king was at first greatly enraged, but was afterward persuaded by the duke of the prudence of this extraordinary step. Negotiations were now carried on with increased spirit. Dumouriez, who, like Kaunitz, said that the French, if left to themselves, would inevitably fall a prey to intestine convulsions, also contrived to accustom the king to the idea of a future alliance with France. The result of these intrigues was an armistice and the retreat of the Prussian army, which dysentery, bad weather, and bad roads rendered extremely destructive.

Austria was now, owing to the intrigues of the duke of Brunswick and the credulity of Frederick William, left unprotected. As early as June, old Marshal Lukner invaded Flanders, but, being arrested on suspicion, was replaced by Dumouriez, who continued the war in the Netherlands and defeated the stadtholder, Albert, duke of Saxon-Teschen (son-in-law to Maria Theresa, in consideration of which he had been endowed with the principality of Teschen and the stadtholdership at Brussels), at Jemappes, and the whole of the Netherlands fell into the hands of the Jacobins, who, on the 14th of November, entered Brussels, where they proclaimed liberty and equality. A few days later (19th of November) the national convention at Paris proclaimed liberty and equality to all nations, promised their aid to all those who asserted their liberty, and threatened to compel those who chose to remain in slavery to accept of liberty. As a preliminary, however, the Netherlands, after being declared free, were ransacked of every description of movable property, of which Pache, a native of Freiburg in Switzerland, at that time the French minister of war, received a large share. The fluctuations of the war, however, speedily recalled the Jacobins. Another French army under Custines, which had marched to the Upper Rhine, gained time to take a firm footing in Mayence.

CCXLVII. *German Jacobins*

In Lorraine and Alsace, the Revolution had been hailed with delight by the long-oppressed people. On the 10th of July, 1789, the peasants destroyed the park of the bishop, Rohan, at Zabern, and killed immense quantities of game. The chateaux and monasteries throughout the country were afterward reduced to heaps of ruins, and, in Suntgau, the peasants took especial vengeance on the Jews, who had, in that place, long lived on the fat of the land. Mulhausen received a democratic constitution and a Jacobin club. In Strasburg, the town-house was assailed by the populace,[1] notwithstanding which, order was maintained by the mayor, Dietrich. The unpopular bishop, Rohan, was replaced by Brendel, against whom the people of Colmar revolted, and even assaulted him in the church for having taken the oath imposed by the French republic, and which was rejected by all good Catholics. Dietrich, aided by the great majority of the citizens of Strasburg, long succeeded in keeping the sans culottes at bay, but was at length overcome, deprived of his office, and guillotined at Paris, while Eulogius Schneider, who had formerly been a professor at Bonn, then court preacher to the Catholic duke, Charles of Wurtemberg,[2] became the tyrant of Strasburg, and, in the character of public accuser before the revolutionary tribunal, conducted the executions. The national convention at Paris nominated as

---

[1] Oberlin, the celebrated philologist, an ornament to German learning, a professor at Strasburg, rescued, at the risk of his life, a great portion of the ancient city archives, which had been thrown out of the windows, by re-collecting the documents with the aid of the students. On account of this sample of old German pedantry he pined, until 1793, in durance vile at Metz, and narrowly escaped being guillotined.

[2] At Bonn he had the impudence to say to the elector, "I cannot pay you a higher compliment than by asserting you to be no Catholic."—*Van Alpen, History of Rhenish Franconia.*

his colleague Monet, a man twenty-four years of age, totally ignorant of the German language, and who merely made himself remarkable for his open rapacity.[1] This was, however, a mere prelude to far greater horrors. Two members of the convention, St. Just and Lebas, unexpectedly appeared at Strasburg, declared that nothing had as yet been done, ordered the executions to take place on a larger scale, and, in 1793, imposed a fine of nine million livres on the already plundered city. The German costume and mode of writing were also prohibited; every sign, written in German, affixed to the houses, was taken down; and, finally, the whole of the city council and all the officers of the national guard were arrested and either exiled or guillotined, notwithstanding their zealous advocacy of revolutionary principles—on the charge of an understanding with Austria, without proof, on a mere groundless suspicion, without being permitted to defend themselves—for the sole purpose of removing them out of the way in order to replace them with trueborn Frenchmen, a Parisian mob, who established themselves in the desolate houses. Schneider and Brendel continued to retain their places by means of the basest adulation. On the 21st of November, a great festival was solemnized in the Minster, which had been converted into a temple of Reason. The bust of Marat, the most loathsome of all the monsters engendered by the Revolution, was borne in solemn procession to the cathedral, before whose portals an immense fire was fed with pictures and images of the saints, crucifixes, priests' garments, and sacred vessels, among which Brendel hurled his mitre. Within the cathedral walls, Schneider delivered a discourse in controversion of the Christian religion, which he concluded by solemnly renouncing; a number of Catholic ecclesiastics followed his example. All the statues and ecclesiastical symbols were piled in a rude heap at the

[1] He mulcted the brewers to the amount of 255,000 livres, "on account of their well-known avarice," the bakers and millers to that of 314,000, a publican to that of 40,000, a baker to that of 30,000, "because he was an enemy of mankind," etc.—*Vide Friese's History of Strasburg.*

foot of the great tower, which it was also attempted to pull down for the promotion of universal equality; an attempt which the extraordinary strength of the building and the short reign of revolutionary madness fortunately frustrated. All the more wealthy citizens had, meanwhile, been consigned either to the guillotine or to prison, and their houses filled with French bandits, who revelled in their wealth and dishonored their wives and daughters. Eulogius Schneider was compelled to seek at midnight for a wife, suspicion having already attached to him on account of his former profession. It was, however, too late. On the following morning, he was seized and sent to Paris, where he was guillotined. All ecclesiastics, all schoolmasters, even the historian, Friese, were, without exception, declared suspected and dragged to the prisons of Besançon, where they suffered the harshest treatment at the hands of the commandant, Prince Charles of Hesse. In Strasburg, Neumann, who had succeeded Schneider as public accuser, raged with redoubled fury. The guillotine was ever at work, was illuminated during the night time, and was the scene of the orgies of the drunken bandits. On the advance of the French armies to the frontiers, the whole country was pillaged.[1]

In other places, where the plundering habits of the French had not cooled the popular enthusiasm, it still rose high, more particularly at Mayence. This city, which had been rendered a seat of the Muses by the elector, Frederick Charles, was in a state of complete demoralization. On the loss of Strasburg, Mayence, although the only remaining bulwark of Germany, was entirely overlooked. The war had already burst forth; no imperial army had as yet been levied, and the fortifications of Mayence were in the most shameful state of neglect. Magazines had been established by the imperial troops on the left bank of the Rhine, seemingly for the mere purpose of letting them fall into the hands

[1] It was asserted that the Jacobins had formed a plan to depopulate the whole of Alsace, and to partition the country among the bravest soldiers belonging to the republican armies.

of Custine: but eight hundred Austrians garrisoned Mayence; the Hessians, although numerically weak, were alone sincere in their efforts for the defence of Germany. Custine's advanced guard no sooner came in sight than the elector and all the higher functionaries fled to Aschaffenburg. Von Gymnich, the commandant of Mayence, called a council of war and surrendered the city, which was unanimously declared untenable by all present with the exception of Eikenmaier, who, notwithstanding, went forthwith over to the French, and of Andujar, the commander of the eight hundred Austrians, with whom he instantly evacuated the place. The Illuminati, who were here in great number, triumphantly opened the gates to the French in 1792. The most extraordinary scenes were enacted. A society, the members of which preached the doctrines of liberty and equality, and at whose head stood the professors Blau, Wedekind, Metternich, Hoffmann, Forster, the eminent navigator, the doctors Böhmer and Stamm, Dorsch of Strasburg, etc., chiefly men who had formerly been Illuminati, was formed in imitation of the revolutionary Jacobin club at Paris.[1] These people committed unheard-of follies. At first, notwithstanding their doctrine of equality, they were distin-

---

[1] John Müller played a remarkable part. This thoroughly deceptive person had, by his commendation of the ancient Swiss in his affectedly written History of Switzerland, gained the favor of the friends of liberty, and, at the same time, that of the nobility by his encomium on the degenerate Swiss aristocracy. While with sentimental phrases and fine words he pretended to be one of the noblest of mankind, he was addicted to the lowest and most monstrous vices. His immorality brought him into trouble in Switzerland, and the man, who had been, apparently, solely inspired with the love of republican liberty, now paid court, for the sake of gain, to foreign princes; the adulation that had succeeded so well with all the lordlings of Switzerland was poured into the ears of all the potentates of Europe. He even rose to great favor at Rome by his flattery of the pope in a work entitled "The Travels of the Popes." He published the most virulent sophisms against the beneficial reforms of the emperor Joseph, and cried up the League, for which he was well paid. He contrived, at the same time, to creep into favor with the Illuminati. He was employed by the elector of Mayence to carry on negotiations with Dumouriez, got into office under the French republic, and afterward revisited Mayence for the express purpose of calling upon the citizens, at that time highly dissatisfied with the conduct of the French, to unite themselves with France. Vide Forster's Correspondence. Dumouriez shortly afterward went over to the Austrians, and Müller suddenly appeared at Vienna, adorned with a title and in the character of an Aulic councillor.

guished by a particular ribbon; the women, insensible to shame, wore girdles with long ends, on which the word "liberty" was worked in front, and the word "equality" behind. Women, girt with sabres, danced franticly around tall trees of liberty, in imitation of those of France, and fired off pistols. The men wore monstrous mustaches in imitation of those of Custine, whom, notwithstanding their republican notions, they loaded with servile flattery. As a means of gaining over the lower orders among the citizens, who with plain good sense opposed their apish tricks, the clubbists demolished a large stone, by which the Archbishop Adolphus had formerly sworn, "You, citizens of Mayence, shall not regain your privileges until this stone shall melt." This, however, proved as little effective as did the production of a large book, in which every citizen, desirous of transforming the electorate of Mayence into a republic, was requested to inscribe his name. Notwithstanding the threat of being treated, in case of refusal, as slaves, the citizens and peasantry, plainly foreseeing that, instead of receiving the promised boon of liberty, they would but expose themselves to Custine's brutal tyranny, withheld their signatures, and the clubbists finally established a republic under the protection of France without the consent of the people, removed all the old authorities, and, at the close of 1792, elected Dorsch, a remarkably diminutive, ill-favored man, who had formerly been a priest, president.

The manner in which Custine levied contributions in Frankfort on the Maine[1] was still less calculated to render the French popular in Germany. Cowardly as this general was, he, nevertheless, told the citizens of Frankfort a truth that time has, up to the present period, confirmed. "You have beheld the coronation of the emperor of Germany? Well! you will not see another."

Two Germans, natives of Colmar in Alsace, Rewbel and

---

[1] While in his proclamations he swore by all that was sacred (what was so to a Frenchman?) to respect the property of the citizens and that France coveted no extension of territory.

Hausmann, and a Frenchman, Merlin, all three members of the national convention, came to Mayence for the purpose of conducting the defence of that city. They burned symbolically all the crowns, mitres, and escutcheons of the German empire, but were unable to induce the citizens of Mayence to declare in favor of the republic. Rewbel, infuriated at their opposition, exclaimed that he would level the city with the ground, that he should deem himself dishonored were he to waste another word on such slaves. A number of refractory persons were expelled the city,[1] and, on the 17th of March, 1793, although three hundred and seventy of the citizens alone voted in its favor, a Teuto-Rhenish national convention, under the presidency of Hoffmann, was opened at Mayence and instantly declared in favor of the union of the new republic with France. Forster, in other respects a man of great elevation of mind, forgetful, in his enthusiasm, of all national pride, personally carried to Paris the scandalous documents in which the French were humbly entreated to accept of a province of the German empire. The Prussians, who had remained in Luxemburg (without aiding the Austrians), meanwhile advanced to the Rhine, took Coblentz, which Custine had neglected to garrison (a neglect for which he afterward lost his head), repulsed a French force under Bournonville, when on the point of forming a junction with Custine, at Treves, expelled Custine from Frankfort,[2] and closely besieged Mayence, which, after making a valiant defence, was compelled to capitulate in July.

Numbers of the clubbists fled, or were saved by the

---

[1] Forster was so blinded at that time by his enthusiasm that he wrote, "all of those among us who refuse the citizenship of France are to be expelled the city, even if complete depopulation should be the result." He relates: "I summoned, at Grünstadt, the Counts von Leiningen to acknowledge themselves citizens of France. They protested against it, caballed, instigated the citizens and peasantry to revolt; one of my soldiers was attacked and wounded. I demanded a reinforcement, took possession of both the castles, and placed the counts under guard. To-day I sent them with an escort to Landau. This has been a disagreeable duty, but we must reduce every opponent of the good cause to obedience."

[2] Where the weak garrison left by the French was disarmed by the workmen.

French, when evacuating the city, in the disguise of soldiers. Others were arrested and treated with extreme cruelty. Every clubbist, or any person suspected of being one, received five and twenty lashes in the presence of Kalkreuth, the Prussian general. Metternich was, together with numerous others, carried off, chained fast between the horses of the hussars, and, whenever he sank from weariness, spurred on at the sabre point. Blau had his ears boxed by the Prussian minister, Stein.[1] A similar reaction took place at Worms,[2] Spires, etc.

The German Jacobins suffered the punishment amply deserved by all those who look for salvation from the foreigner. Those who had barely escaped the vengeance of the Prussian on the Rhine were beheaded by their pretended good friends in France. Robespierre, an advocate, who, at that period, governed the convention, sent every foreigner who had enrolled himself as a member of the Jacobin club to the guillotine, as a suspicious person, a bloody but instructive lesson to all unpatriotic German Gallomanists.[3]

The victims who fell on this occasion were a prince of Salm-Kyrburg, who had voluntarily republicanized his petty territory, Anacharsis Cloots,[4] and the venerable Trenk, who

---

[1] Either the Prussian minister who afterward gained such celebrity or one of his relations.

[2] Where Skekuly forced the German clubbists, with the lash, to cut down the tree of liberty.

[3] Forster wrote from Paris, "Suspicion hangs over every foreigner, and the essential distinctions which ought to be made in this respect are of no avail." Thus did nature, by whom nations are eternally separated, avenge herself on the fools who had dreamed of universal equality.

[4] Cloots had incessantly preached war, threatened all the kings of the earth with destruction, and, in his vanity, had even set a price upon the head of the Prussian monarch. His object was the union of the whole of mankind, the abolition of nationality. The French were to receive a new name, that of "Universel." He preached in the convention: "I have struggled during the whole of my existence against the powers of heaven and earth. There is but one God, Nature, and but one sovereign, mankind, the people, united by reason in one universal republic. Religion is the last obstacle, but the time has arrived for its destruction. J'occupe la tribune de l'univers. Je le repète, le genre humain est Dieu, le *Peuple Dieu.* Quiconque a la débilité de croire en Dieu ne sauroit avoir la sagacité de connaitre le genre humain, le souverain unique," etc.—*Moniteur of* 1793, No. 120. He also subscribed himself the "personal enemy of Jesus of Nazareth."

had so long pined in Frederick's prisons. Adam Lux, a friend of George Forster, was also beheaded for expressing his admiration of Charlotte Corday, the murderess of Marat. Marat was a Prussian subject, being a native of Neufchâtel. Göbel von Bruntrut, uncle to Rengger,[1] a celebrated character in the subsequent Swiss revolution, vicar-general of Basel, a furious revolutionist, who had on that account been appointed bishop of Paris, presented himself, on the 6th of November, 1793, at the bar of the convention as an associate of Cloots, Hebert, Chaumette, etc., cast his mitre and other insignia of office to the ground, and placing the bonnet rouge on his head, solemnly renounced the Christian faith and proclaimed that of "liberty and equality." The rest of the ecclesiastics were compelled to imitate his example; the Christian religion was formally abolished and the worship of Reason was established in its stead. Half-naked women were placed upon the altars of the desecrated churches and worshipped as "goddesses of Reason." Göbel's friend, Pache, a native of Freiburg, a creature abject as himself, was particularly zealous, as was also Proli, a natural son of the Austrian minister, Kaunitz. Prince Charles of Hesse, known among the Jacobins as Charles Hesse, fortunately escaped. Schlaberndorf,[2] a Silesian count, who appears to have been a mere spectator, and Oelsner, a distinguished author, were equally fortunate. These two latter remained in Paris. Reinhard, a native of Wurtemberg, secretary to the celebrated Girondin, Vergniaud, whom he is said to have aided in the composition of his eloquent speeches, remained in the service of France, was afterward ennobled and raised to the ministry. Felix von Wimpfen, whom the faction of the Gironde (the moderates who opposed the savage Jaco-

---

[1] Whose nephew, the celebrated traveller, Rengger, was, with Bonpland, so long imprisoned in Paraguay.

[2] He had been already imprisoned and was ordered to the guillotine, but not being able to find his boots quickly enough, his execution was put off until the morrow. During the night, Robespierre fell, and his life was saved. He continued to reside at Paris, where he never quitted his apartment, cherished his beard, and associated solely with ecclesiastics.

bins) elected their general, and who, attempting to lead a small force from Normandy against Paris, was defeated and compelled to seek safety by flight. The venerable Lukner, the associate of Lafayette, who had termed the great Revolution merely "a little occurrence in Paris," was beheaded. The unfortunate George Forster perceived his error and died of sorrow.[1] Among the other Rhenish Germans of distinction, who had at that time formed a connection with France, Joseph Görres brought himself, notwithstanding his extreme youth, into great note at Coblentz by his superior talents. He went to Paris as deputy of Treves and speedily became known by his works (Rubezahl and the Red Leaf). He also speedily discovered the immense mistake made by the Germans in resting their hopes upon France. It was indeed a strange delusion to suppose the vain and greedy Frenchman capable of being inspired with disinterested love for all mankind, and it was indeed a severe irony, that, after such repeated and cruel experience, after having for centuries seen the French ever in the guise of robbers and pillagers, and after breathing such loud complaints against the princes who had sold Germany to France, that the warmest friends of the people should on this occasion be guilty of similar treachery, and, like selecting the goat for a gardener, intrust the weal of their country to the French.

The people in Germany too little understood the real motives and object of the French Revolution, and were too soon provoked by the predatory incursions of the French troops, to be infected with revolutionary principles. These merely fermented among the literati; the Utopian idea of universal fraternization was spread by Freemasonry; numbers at first cherished a hope that the Revolution would preserve a pure moral character, and were not a little astonished on beholding the monstrous crimes to which it gave

---

[1] After an interview with his wife, Theresa (daughter to the great philologist, Heyne of Göttingen), on the French frontier, he returned to Paris and killed himself by drinking aquafortis. Vide Crome's Autobiography. Theresa entered into association with Huber, the journalist, whom she shortly afterward married. She gained great celebrity by her numerous romances.

birth. Others merely rejoiced at the fall of the old and insupportable system, and numerous anonymous pamphlets in this spirit appeared in the Rhenish provinces. Fichte, the philosopher, also published an anonymous work in favor of the Revolution. Others again, as, for instance, Reichard, Girtanner, Schirach, and Hoffmann, set themselves up as informers, and denounced every liberal-minded man to the princes as a dangerous Jacobin. A search was made for Crypto-Jacobins, and every honest man was exposed to the calumny of the servile newspaper editors. French republicanism was denounced as criminal, notwithstanding the favor in which the French language and French ideas were held at all the courts of Germany. Liberal opinions were denounced as criminal, notwithstanding the example first set by the courts in ridiculing religion, in mocking all that was venerable and sacred. Nor was this reaction by any means occasioned by a burst of German patriotism against the tyranny of France, for the treaty of Basel speedily reconciled the self-same newspaper editors with France. It was mere servility; and the hatred which, it may easily be conceived, was naturally excited against the French as a nation, was vented in this mode upon the patient Germans,[1] who were, unfortunately, ever doomed, whenever their neighbors were visited with some political chronic convulsion, to taste the bitter remedy. But few of the writers of the day took a historical view of the Revolution and weighed its irremediable results in regard to Germany, besides Gentz, Rehberg, and the Baron von Gagern, who published an "Address to his Countrymen," in which he started the painful question, "Why are we Germans disunited?" The whole of these contending opinions of the learned were, however, equally erroneous. It was as little possible to preserve the Revolution from blood and immorality, and to extend the boon of

---

[1] The popular work "Huergelmer" relates, among other things, the conduct of the Margrave of Baden toward Lauchsenring, his private physician, whom he, on account of the liberality of his opinions, delivered over to the Austrian general, who sentenced him to the bastinado.

liberty to the whole world, as it was to suppress it by force, and, as far as Germany was concerned, her affairs were too complicated and her interests too scattered for any attempt of the kind to succeed. A Doctor Faust, at Buckeburg, sent a learned treatise upon the origin of trousers to the national convention at Paris, by which Sansculottism had been introduced; an incident alone sufficient to show the state of feeling in Germany at that time.

The revolutionary principles of France merely infected the people in those parts of Germany where their sufferings had ever been the greatest, as, for instance, in Saxony, where the peasantry, oppressed by the game laws and the rights of the nobility, rose, after a dry summer by which their misery had been greatly increased, to the number of eighteen thousand, and sent one of their class to lay their complaints before the elector (1790). The unfortunate messenger was instantly consigned to a madhouse, where he remained until 1809, and the peasantry were dispersed by the military. A similar revolt of the peasantry against the tyrannical nuns of Wormelen, in Westphalia, merely deserves mention as being characteristic of the times. A revolt of the peasantry, of equal unimportance, also took place in Buckeburg, on account of the expulsion of three revolutionary priests, Froriep, Meyer, and Rauschenbusch. In Breslau, a great émeute, which was put down by means of artillery, was occasioned by the expulsion of a tailor's apprentice in 1793.

In Austria, one Hebenstreit formed a conspiracy, which brought him to the gallows, in 1793. That formed by Martinowits, for the establishment of the sovereignty of the people in Hungary and for the expulsion of the magnates, was of a more dangerous character. Martinowits was beheaded, in 1793, with four of his associates.[1] These at-

[1] Schneller says: "The first great conspiracy was formed in the vicinity of the throne in 1793. The chief conspirator was Hebenstreit, the commandant, who held, by his office, the keys to the arsenal, and had every place of importance in his power. His fellow conspirators were Prandstätter, the magistrate and poet, who, by his superior talents, led the whole of the magistracy, and

tempts so greatly excited the apprehensions of the government that the reaction, already begun on the death of Joseph II., was brought at once to a climax; Thugut, the minister, established an extremely active secret police and a system of surveillance, which spread terror throughout Austria and was utterly uncalled for, no one, with the exception of a few crack-brained individuals, being in the slightest degree infected with the revolutionary mania.[1]

---

possessed great influence in the metropolis, Professor Riedl, who possessed the confidence of the court, which he frequented for the purpose of instructing some of the principal personages, and Häckel, the merchant, who had the management of its pecuniary affairs. The rest of the conspirators belonged to every class of society and were spread throughout every province of the empire. The plan consisted in the establishment of a democratic constitution, the first step to which appears to have been an attempt against the life of the imperial family. The signal for insurrection was to be given by firing the immense wood-yards. The hearts of the people were to be gained by the destruction of the government accounts. The discovery was made through a conspiracy formed in Denmark. The chief conspirator was seized and sent to the gallows. The rest were exiled to Munkatch, where several of them had succumbed to the severity of their treatment and of the climate when their release was effected by Bonaparte by the peace of Campo Formio, which gave rise to the supposition that the Hebenstreit conspiracy was connected with the French republicans and Jacobins. —The second conspiracy was laid in Hungary, by the bishop and abbot, Josephus Ignatius Martinowits, a man whom the emperors Joseph, Leopold, and Francis had, on account of his talent and energy, loaded with favors. The plan was an *actionalis conspiratio*, for the purpose of contriving an attempt against the sacred person of his Majesty the king, the destruction of the power of the privileged classes in Hungary, the subversion of the administration, and the establishment of a democracy. The means for the execution of this project were furnished by two secret societies." Huergelmer relates: "A certain Dr. Plank somewhat thoughtlessly ridiculed the institution of the jubilee; in order to convince him of its utility, he was sent as a recruit to the Italian army, an act that was highly praised by the newspapers." On the 22d of July, 1795, a Baron von Riedel was placed in the pillory at Vienna for some political crime, and was afterward consigned to the oblivion of a dungeon; the same fate, some days later, befell Brandstetter, Fellesneck, Billeck, Ruschitiski (Ephemeridæ of 1795). A Baron Taufner was hanged at Vienna as a traitor to his country (E. of 1796).

[1] "The increase of crime occasioned by the artifices of the police, who thereby gained their livelihood, rendered an especial statute, prohibitory of such measures, necessary in the new legislature. Even the passing stranger perceived the disastrous effect of their intrigues upon the open, honest character and the social habits of the Viennese. The police began gradually to be considered as a necessary part of the machine of government, a counterbalance to or a remedy for the faults committed by other branches of the administration. Large sums, the want of which was heavily felt in the national education and in the army, were expended on this arsenal of poisoned weapons."—*Hormayr's Pocket-Book*, 1832. Thugut is described as a diminutive, hunchbacked old man, with a face resembling the mask of a fawn and with an almost satanic expression.

It may be recorded as a matter of curiosity that, during the bloodstained year of 1793, the petty prince of Schwarzburg-Rudolstadt held, as though in the most undisturbed time of peace, a magnificent tournament, and the fetes customary on such an occasion.

CCXLVIII. *Loss of the Left Bank of the Rhine*

The object of the Prussian king was either to extend his conquests westward or, at all events, to prevent the advance of Austria. The war with France claimed his utmost attention, and, in order to guard his rear, he again attempted to convert Poland into a bulwark against Russia.

His ambassador, Lucchesini, drove Stackelberg, the Russian envoy, out of Warsaw, and promised mountains of gold to the Poles, who dissolved the perpetual council associated by Russia with the sovereign; freed themselves from the Russian guarantee; aided by Prussia, compelled the Russian troops to evacuate the country; devised a constitution, which they laid before the cabinets of London and Berlin; concluded an offensive and defensive alliance with Prussia on the 29th of March, 1790, and, on the 3d of May, 1791, carried into effect the new constitution ratified by England and Prussia, and approved of by the emperor Leopold. During the conference, held at Pilnitz, the indivisibility of Poland was expressly mentioned. The constitution was monarchical. Poland was, for the future, to be a hereditary instead of an elective monarchy, and, on the death of Poniatowsky, the crown was to fall to Saxony. The modification of the peasants' dues and the power conceded to the serf of making a private agreement with his lord also gave the monarchy a support against the aristocracy.

Catherine of Russia, however, no sooner beheld Prussia and Austria engaged in a war with France, than she commenced her operations against Poland, declared the new Polish constitution French and Jacobinical, notwithstanding its abolition of the liberum veto and its extension of the prerogatives of the crown, and, taking advantage of the king's absence from Prussia, speedily regained possession of the country. What was Frederick William's policy in this dilemma? He was strongly advised to make peace with France, to throw himself at the head of the whole of his forces into Poland, and to set a limit to the insolence of the autocrat; but—he feared, should he abandon the Rhine, the extension of the power of Austria in that quarter, and—calculating that Catherine, in order to retain his friendship, would cede to him a portion of her booty,[1] unhesitatingly broke the faith he had just plighted with the Poles, suddenly took up Catherine's tone, declared the constitution he had so lately ratified Jacobinical, and despatched a force under Möllendorf into Poland in order to secure possession of his stipulated prey. By the second partition of Poland, which took place as rapidly, as violently, and, on account of the assurances of the Prussian monarch, far more unexpectedly than the first, Russia received the whole of Lithuania, Podolia, and the Ukraine, and Prussia, Thorn and Dantzig, besides Southern Prussia (Posen and Calisch). Austria, at that time fully occupied with France, had no participation in this robbery, which was, as it were, committed behind her back.

Affairs had worn a remarkably worse aspect since the campaign of 1792. The French had armed themselves with all the terrors of offended nationalism and of unbounded, intoxicating liberty. All the enemies of the Revolution within the French territory were mercilessly exterminated, and hundreds of thousands were sacrificed by the guillotine, a machine invented for the purpose of accelerating the mode of execution. The king was beheaded in this manner in the January of 1793, and the queen shared a similar fate in the ensuing October.[2] While Robespierre directed the execu-

---

[1] Prussia chiefly coveted the possession of Dantzig, which the Poles refused to give or the English to grant to him, and which he could only seize by the aid of Russia.

[2] After having been long retained in prison, ill fed and ill clothed, after supporting, with unbending dignity, the unmanly insults of the republican mob be-

tions, Carnot undertook to make preparations for war, and, in the very midst of this immense fermentation, calmly converted France into an enormous camp, and more than a million Frenchmen, as if summoned by magic from the clod, were placed under arms.

The sovereigns of Europe also prepared for war, and, 1793, formed the first great coalition, at whose head stood England, intent upon the destruction of the French navy. The English, aided by a large portion of the French population devoted to the ancient monarchy, attacked France by sea, and made a simultaneous descent on the northern and southern coasts. The Spanish and Portuguese troops crossed the Pyrenees; the Italian princes invaded the Alpine boundary; Austria, Prussia, Holland, and the German empire threatened the Rhenish frontier, while Sweden and Russia stood frowning in the background. The whole of Christian Europe took up arms against France, and enormous armies hovered, like vultures, around their prey.

The duke of Coburg commanded the main body of the Austrians in the Netherlands, where he was at first merely opposed by the old French army, whose general, Dumouriez, after unsuccessfully grasping at the supreme power, entered into a secret agreement with the coalition, allowed himself to be defeated at Aldenhoven[1] and Neerwinden, and finally deserted to the Austrians. At this moment, when the French army was dispirited by defeat and without a leader, Coburg, who had been reinforced by the English and Dutch under the duke of York, might, by a hasty advance, have taken Paris by surprise, but both the English and Austrian generals solely owed the command, for which they were totally unfit, to their high birth, and Colonel Mack, the most prominent character among the officers of the staff, was a mere theoretician, who could cleverly enough conduct a campaign

---

fore whose tribunal she was dragged. The young dauphin expired under the ill-treatment he received from his guardian, a shoemaker. His sister, the present Duchess d'Angouleme, was spared.

[1] Where the peasantry, infuriated at the depredations of the French, cast the wounded and the dead indiscriminately into a trench.—*Benzenberg's Letters.*

—upon paper. Clairfait, the Austrian general, beat the disbanded French army under Dampiere at Famars, but temporized instead of following up his victory. Coburg, in the hope of the triumph of the moderate party, the Girondins, published an extremely mild and peaceable proclamation, which, on the fall of the Gironde, was instantly succeeded by one of a more threatening character, which his want of energy and decision in action merely rendered ridiculous. No vigorous attack was made, nor was even a vigorous defence calculated upon, not one of the frontier forts in the Netherlands, demolished by Joseph II., having been rebuilt. The coalition foolishly trusted that the French would be annihilated by their inward convulsions, while they were in reality seizing the opportunity granted by the tardiness of their foes to levy raw recruits and exercise them in arms. The principal error, however, lay in the system of conquest pursued by both Austria and England. Conde, Valenciennes, and all towns within the French territory taken by Coburg, were compelled to take a formal oath of allegiance to Austria, and England made, as the condition of her aid, that of the Austrians for the conquest of Dunkirk. The siege of this place, which was merely of importance to England in a mercantile point of view, retained the armies of Coburg and York, and the French were consequently enabled, in the meantime, to concentrate their scattered forces and to act on the offensive. Ere long, Houchard and Jourdan pushed forward with their wild masses, which, at first undisciplined and unsteady, were merely able to screen themselves from the rapid and sustained fire of the British by acting as tirailleurs (a mode of warfare successfully practiced by the North Americans against the serried ranks of the English), became gradually bolder, and finally, by their numerical strength and republican fury, gained a complete triumph. Houchard, in this manner, defeated the English at Hondscoten (September 8th), and Jourdan drove the Austrians off the field at Wattignies on the 16th of October, the day on which the French queen was beheaded. Coburg, although the Austrians had maintained their ground on every other point, resolved to retreat, notwithstanding the urgent remonstrances of the youthful archduke, Charles, who had greatly distinguished himself. During the retreat, an unimportant victory was gained at Menin by Beaulieu, the imperial general.[1] His colleague, Wurmser, nevertheless maintained with extreme difficulty the line extending from Basel to Luxemburg, which formed the Prussian outposts. A French troop under Delange advanced as far as Aix-la-Chapelle, where they crowned the statue of Charlemagne with a bonnet rouge.

Mayence was, during the first six months of this year, besieged by the main body of the Prussian army under the command of Ferdinand, duke of Brunswick. The Austrians, when on their way past Mayence to Valenciennes with a quantity of heavy artillery destined for the reduction of the latter place (which they afterward compelled to do homage to the emperor), refusing the request of the king of Prussia for its use *en passant* for the reduction of Mayence, greatly displeased that monarch, who clearly perceived the common intention of England and Austria to conquer the north of France to the exclusion of Prussia, and consequently revenged himself by privately partitioning Poland with Russia, and refusing his assistance to General Wurmser in the Vosges country. The dissensions between the allies again rendered their successes null. The Prussians, after the conquest of Mayence, in 1793, advanced and beat the fresh masses led against them by Moreau at Pirmasens, but Frederick William, disgusted with Austria and secretly far from disinclined to peace with France, quitted the army (which he maintained in the field, merely from motives of honor, but allowed to remain in a state of inactivity), in order to visit his newly acquired territory in Poland.

The gallant old Wurmser was a native of Alsace, where

---

[1] The Hanoverian general, Hammerstein, and his adjutant Scharnhorst, who afterward became so noted, made a gallant defence. When the city became no longer tenable, they boldly sallied forth at the head of the garrison and escaped.

he had some property, and fought meritoriously for the German cause, while so many of his countrymen at that time ranged themselves on the side of the French.[1] His position on the celebrated Weissenburg line was, owing to the non-assistance of the Prussians, replete with danger, and he consequently endeavored to supply his want of strength by striking his opponents with terror. His Croats, the notorious Rothmäntler, are charged with the commission of fearful deeds of cruelty. Owing to his system of paying a piece of gold for every Frenchman's head, they would rush, when no legitimate enemy could be encountered, into the first large village at hand, knock at the windows and strike off the heads of the inhabitants as they peeped out. The petty principalities on the German side of the Rhine also complained of the treatment they received from the Austrians. But how could it be otherwise? The empire slothfully cast the whole burden of the war upon Austria. Many of the princes were terror-stricken by the French, while others meditated an alliance with that power, like that formerly concluded between them and Louis XIV. against the empire. Bavaria alone was, but with great difficulty, induced to furnish a contingent. The weak imperial free towns met with most unceremonious treatment at the hands of Austria. They were deprived of their artillery and treated with the utmost contempt. It often happened that the aristocratic magistracy, as, for instance, at Ulm, sided with the soldiery against the citizens. The slothful bishops and abbots of the empire were, on the other hand, treated with the utmost respect by the Catholic soldiery. The infringement

[1] Rewbel, one of the five directors of the great French republic, and several of the most celebrated French generals, Germany's unwearied foes, were natives of Alsace, as, for instance, the gallant Westermann, one of the first leaders of the republican armies; the intrepid Kellermann, the soldiers' father; the immortal Kleber, generalissimo of the French forces in Egypt, who fell by the dagger of a fanatical Mussulman; and the undaunted Rapp, the hero of Dantzig. The lion-hearted Ney, justly designated by the French as the bravest of the brave, was a native of Lorraine. These were, one and all, men of tried metal, but whose German names induce the demand, "Why did they fight for France?" Wurmser belonged to the same old Strasburg family which had given birth to Wurmser, the celebrated court-painter of the emperor, Charles IV.

of the law of nations by the arrest of Semonville, the French ambassador to Constantinople, and of Maret, the French ambassador to Naples, and the seizure of their papers on neutral ground, in the Valtelline, by Austria, created a far greater sensation.

The duke of Brunswick, who had received no orders to retreat, was compelled, bongré-malgré, to hazard another engagement with the French, who rushed to the attack. He was once more victorious, at Kaiserslautern, over Hoche, whose untrained masses were unable to withstand the superior discipline of the Prussian troops. Wurmser took advantage of the moment when success seemed to restore the good humor of the allies to coalesce with the Prussians, dragging the unwilling Bavarians in his train. This junction, however, merely had the effect of disclosing the jealousy rankling on every side. The greatest military blunders were committed and each blamed the other. Landau ought to and might have been rescued from the French, but this step was procrastinated until the convention had charged Generals Hoche and Pichegru, "Landau or death." These two generals brought a fresh and numerous army into the field, and, in the very first engagements, at Worth and Froschweiler, the Bavarians ran away and the Austrians and Prussians were signally defeated. The retreat of Wurmser, in high displeasure, across the Rhine afforded a welcome pretext to the duke of Brunswick to follow his example and even to resign the command of the army to Mollendorf. In this shameful manner was the left bank of the Rhine lost to Germany.

In the spring of the ensuing year, 1794, the emperor Francis II. visited the Netherlands in person, with the intent of pushing straight upon Paris. This project, practicable enough during the preceding campaign, was, however, now utterly out of the question, the more so on account of the retreat of the Prussians. The French observed on this occasion with well-merited scorn: "The allies are ever an idea, a year and an army behindhand." The Austrians, nevertheless, attacked the whole French line in March and were at first victorious on every side, at Catillon, where Kray and Wernek distinguished themselves, and at Landrecis, where the Archduke Charles made a brilliant charge at the head of the cavalry. Landrecis was taken. But this was all. Clairfait, whose example might have animated the inactive duke of York, being left unsupported by the British, was attacked singly at Courtray by Pichegru and forced to yield to superior numbers. Coburg fought an extremely bloody but indecisive battle at Doornik (Tournay), where Pichegru ever opposed fresh masses to the Austrian artillery. Twenty thousand dead strewed the field. The youthful emperor, discouraged by the coldness displayed by the Dutch, whom he had expected to rise en masse in his cause, returned to Vienna. His departure and the inactivity of the British commander completely dispirited the Austrian troops, and on the 26th of June, 1794,[1] the duke of Coburg was defeated at Fleurus by Jourdan, the general of the republic. This success was immediately followed by that of Pichegru, not far from Breda, over the inefficient English general,[2] who consequently evacuated the Netherlands, which were instantly overrun by the pillaging French. And thus had the German powers, notwithstanding their well-disciplined armies and their great plans, not only forfeited their military honor, but also drawn the enemy, and, in his train, anarchy with its concomitant horrors, into the empire. The Austrians had rendered themselves universally unpopular by their arbitrary measures, and each province remained stu-

[1] The Austrian generals Beaulieu, Quosdanowich, and the Archduke Charles, who, at that period, laid the foundation to his future fame, had pushed victoriously forward and taken Fleurus, when the ill-timed orders, as they are deemed, of the generalissimo Coburg compelled them to retreat. Quosdanowich dashed his sabre furiously on the ground and exclaimed, "The army is betrayed, the victory is ours, and yet we must resign it. Adieu, thou glorious land, thou garden of Europe, the house of Austria bids thee eternally adieu!" The French had, before and during the action, made use of a balloon for the purpose of watching the movements of the enemy.

[2] The worst spirit prevailed among the British troops; the officers were wealthy young men, who had purchased their posts and were, in the highest degree, licentious. Vide Dietfurth's Hessian Campaigns.

pidly indifferent to the threatened pillage of its neighbor by the victorious French. Jourdan but slowly tracked the retreating forces of Coburg, whom he again beat at Sprimont, where he drove him from the Maese, and at Aldenhoven, where he drove him from the Roer. Frederick, Landgrave of Hesse-Cassel, capitulated at Maestricht, with ten thousand men, to Kléber; and the Austrians, with the exception of a small corps under the Count von Erbach, stationed at Düsseldorf, completely abandoned the Lower Rhine.

The disasters suffered by the Austrians seem at that time to have flattered the ambition of the Prussians, for Mollendorf suddenly recrossed the Rhine and gained an advantage at Kaiserslautern, but was, in July, 1794, again repulsed at Trippstadt, notwithstanding which he once more crossed the Rhine in September, and a battle was won by the Prince von Hohenlohe-Ingelfingen at Fischbach, but, on the junction of Jourdan with Hoche, who had until then singly opposed him, Mollendorf again, and for the last time, retreated across the Rhine. The whole of the left bank of the Rhine, Luxemburg and Mayence alone excepted, were now in the hands of the French. Resius, the Hessian general, abandoned the Rheinfels with the whole garrison, without striking a blow in its defence. He was, in reward, condemned to perpetual imprisonment.[1] Jourdan converted the fortress into a ruined

---

[1] Peter Hammer, in his "Description of the Imperial Army," published in 1796, at Cologne, graphically depictures the sad state of the empire. The imperial troops consisted of the dregs of the populace, so variously arranged as to justify the remark of Colonel Sandberg of Baden that the only thing wanting was their regular equipment as jack-puddings. A monastery furnished two men; a petty barony, the ensign; a city, the captain. The arms of each man differed in calibre. No patriotic spirit animated these defenders of the empire. An anonymous author remarks: "For love of one's country to be felt, there must, first of all, be a country; but Germany is split into petty useless monarchies, chiefly characterized by their oppression of their subjects, by pride, slavery, and unutterable weakness. Formerly, when Germany was attacked, each of her sons made ready for battle, her princes were patriotic and brave. Now, may Heaven have pity on the land; the princes, the counts, and nobles march hence and leave their country to its fate. The Margrave of Baden—I do not speak of the prince bishop of Spires and of other spiritual lords whose profession forbids their laying hand to sword—the Landgrave of Darmstadt and other nobles fled on the mere report of an intended visit from the French, by which

heap. The whole of the fortifications on the Rhine were yielded for the sake of saving Mannheim from bombardment.

In the Austrian Netherlands, the old government had already been abolished, and the whole country been transformed into a Belgian republic by Dumouriez. The reform of all the ancient evils, so vainly attempted but a few years before by the noble-spirited emperor, Joseph II., was successfully executed by this insolent Frenchman, who also abolished with them all that was good in the ancient system. The city deputies, it is true, made an energetic but futile resistance.[1] After the flight of Dumouriez, fresh depredations were, with every fresh success, committed by the French. Liege was reduced to the most deplorable state of desolation, the cathedral and thirty splendid churches were

---

they plainly intimated that they merely held sovereign rule for the purpose of being fattened by their subjects in time of peace. Danger no sooner appears than the miserable subject is left to his own resources. *Germany is divided into too many petty states.* How can an elector of the Pfalz, or indeed any of the still lesser nobility, protect the country? Unity, moreover, is utterly wanting. The Bavarian regards the Hessian as a stranger, not as his countryman. Each petty territory has a different tariff, administration, and laws. The subject of one petty state cannot travel half a mile into a neighboring one without leaving behind him great part of his property. The bishop of Spires strictly forbids his subjects to intermarry with those of any other state. And patriotism is expected to result from these measures! The subject of a despot, whose revenues exceed those of his neighbors by a few thousand florins, looks down with contempt on the slave of a poorer prince. Hence the boundless hatred between the German courts and their petty brethren, hence the malicious joy caused by the mishaps of a neighboring dynasty." Hence the wretchedness of the troops. "With the exception of the troops belonging to the circle there were none to defend the frontiers of the empire. Grandes battues, balls, operas, and mistresses, swallowed up the revenue, not a farthing remained for the erection of fortresses, the want of which was so deeply felt for the defence of the frontiers."

[1] "How can France, with her solemn assurances of liberty, arbitrarily interfere with the government of a country already possessing a representative elected by the people? How can she proclaim us as a free nation, and, at the same moment, deprive us of our liberty? Will she establish a new mythology of nations, and divide the different peoples on the face of the earth, according to their strength, into nations and demi-nations?"—*Protest of the Provisional Council of the City of Brussels. The President, Theodore Dotrenge.* "Every free nation gives to itself laws, does not receive them from another."—*Protest of the City of Antwerp. President of the Council, Van Dun.* "You confiscate alike public and private property. That have even our former tyrants never ventured to do when declaring us rebels, and you say that you bring to us liberty."—*Protest of the Hennegau.* The most copious account of the revolutionizing of the Netherlands is contained in Rau's History of the Germans in France, and of the French in Germany. Frankfort on the Maine, 1794 and 1795.

levelled with the ground by the ancient enemies of the bishop. Treves was also mercilessly sacked and converted into a French fortress.

CCXLIX. *The Defection of Prussia—The Archduke Charles*

Frederick William's advisers, who imagined the violation of every principle of justice and truth an indubitable proof of instinctive and consummate prudence, unwittingly played a high and hazardous game. Their diplomatic absurdity, which weighed the fate of nations against a dinner, found a confusion of all the solid principles on which states rest as stimulating as the piquant ragouts of the great Ude Lucchesini, under his almost intolerable airs of sapience, as artfully veiled his incapacity in the cabinet as Ferdinand of Brunswick did his in the field, and to this may be ascribed the measures which but momentarily and seemingly aggrandized Prussia and prepared her deeper fall. Each petty advantage gained by Prussia but served to raise against her some powerful foe, and finally, when placed by her policy at enmity with every sovereign of Europe, she was induced to trust to the shallow friendship of the French republic.

The Poles, taken unawares by the second partition of their country, speedily recovered from their surprise and collected all their strength for an energetic opposition. Kosciuszko, who had, together with Lafayette, fought in North America in the cause of liberty, armed his countrymen with scythes, put every Russian who fell into his hands to death, and attempted the restoration of ancient Poland. How easily might not Prussia, backed by the enthusiasm of the patriotic Poles, have repelled the Russian colossus, already threatening Europe! But the Berlin diplomatists had yet to learn the homely truth, that "honesty is the best policy." They aided in the aggrandizement of Russia, drew down a nation's curse upon their heads for the sake of an addition to the territory of Prussia, the maintenance of which cost more than its revenue, and violated the Divine commands during a period of storm and convulsion, when the aid of Heaven was indeed required. The ministers of Frederick William II. were externally religious, but those of Frederick William I., by whom the Polish question had been so justly decided, were so in reality.

The king led his troops in person into Poland. In June, 1794, he defeated Kosciuszko's scythemen at Szczekociny, but met with such strenuous opposition in his attack upon Warsaw as to be compelled to retire in September.[1] On the retreat of the Prussian troops, the Russians, who had purposely awaited their departure in order to secure the triumph for themselves, invaded the country in great force under their bold general, Suwarow, who defeated Kosciuszko, took him prisoner, and besieged Warsaw, which he carried by storm. On this occasion, termed by Reichardt "a peaceful and merciful entry of the clement victor," eighteen thousand of the inhabitants of every age and sex were cruelly put to the sword. The result of this success was the third partition or utter annihilation of Poland. Russia took possession of the whole of Lithuania and Volhynia, as far as the Riemen and the Bug; Prussia, of the whole country west of the Riemen, including Warsaw; Austria, of the whole country south of the Bug, in 1795. An army of German officials, who earned for themselves not the best of reputations, settled in the Prussian division: they were ignorant of the language of the country, and enriched themselves by tyranny and oppression. Von Treibenfeld, the counsellor to the forest-board, one of Bischofswerder's friends, bestowed a number of confiscated lands upon his adherents.

The ancient Polish feof of Courland was, in consequence

---

[1] The following trait proves the complete stagnation of chivalric feeling in the army. Szekuli, colonel of the Prussian hussars, condemned several patriotic ladies, belonging to the highest Polish families at Znawrazlaw, to be placed beneath the gallows, in momentary expectation of death, until it, at length, pleased him to grant a reprieve, couched in the most offensive and indecent terms.

of the annihilation of Poland, incorporated with the Russian empire, Peter, the last duke, the son of Biron, being compelled to abdicate in 1795.

Pichegru invaded Holland late in the autumn of 1794. The duke of York had already returned to England. A line of defence was, nevertheless, taken up by the British under Wallmoden, by the Dutch under their hereditary stadtholder, William V. of Orange, and by an Austrian corps under Alvinzi; the Dutch were, however, panic-struck, and negotiated a separate treaty with Pichegru,[1] who, at that moment, solely aimed at separating the Dutch from their allies; but when, in December, all the rivers and canals were suddenly frozen, and nature no longer threw insurmountable obstacles in his path, regardless of the negotiations then pending in Paris, he unexpectedly took up arms, marched across the icebound waters, and carried Holland by storm. With him marched the anti-Orangemen, the exiled Dutch patriots, under General Daendels and Admiral de Winter, with the pretended view of restoring ancient republican liberty to Holland and of expelling the tyrannical Orange dynasty.

The British (and some Hessian troops) were defeated at Thiel on the Waal; Alvinzi met with a similar fate at Pondern, and was compelled to retreat into Westphalia. Some English ships, which lay frozen up in the harbor, were captured by the French hussars. A most manly resistance was made; but no aid was sent from any quarter. Prussia, who so shortly before had ranged herself on the side of the stadtholder against the people, was now an indifferent spectator. William V. was compelled to flee to England. Holland was transformed into a Batavian republic. Hahn, Hoof, etc., were the first furious Jacobins

---

[1] A most disgraceful treaty. William's enemies, the fugitive patriots, had promised the French, in return for their aid, sixty million florins of the spoil of their country. William, upon this, promised to pay to France a subsidy of eighty millions, in order to guarantee the security of his frontier, but was instantly outbid by the base and self-denominated patriots, who offered to France a hundred million florins in order to induce her to invade their country.

by whom everything was there formed upon the French model. The Dutch were compelled to cede Maestricht, Venloo, and Vliessingen; to pay a hundred millions to France, and, moreover, to allow their country to be plundered, to be stripped of all the splendid works of art, pictures, etc. (as was also the case in the Netherlands and on the Rhine), and even of the valuable museum of natural curiosities collected by them with such assiduity in every quarter of the globe. These depredations were succeeded by a more systematic mode of plunder. Holland was mercilessly drained of her enormous wealth. All the gold and silver bullion was first of all collected; this was followed by the imposition of an income-tax of six per cent, which was afterward repeated, and was succeeded by an income-tax on a sliding scale from three to thirty per cent. The British, at the same time, destroyed the Dutch fleet in the Texel commanded by de Winter, in order to prevent its capture by the French, and seized all the Dutch colonies, Java alone excepted. The flag of Holland had vanished from the seas.

In August, 1794, the reign of terror in France reached its close. The moderate party which came into power gave hopes of a general peace, and Frederick William II. without loss of time negotiated a separate treaty, suddenly abandoned the monarchical cause which he had formerly so zealously upheld, and offered his friendship to the revolutionary nation, against which he had so lately hurled a violent manifesto. The French, with equal inconsistency on their part, abandoned the popular cause, and, after having murdered their own sovereign and threatened every European throne with destruction, accepted the alliance of a foreign king. Both parties, notwithstanding the contrariety of their principles and their mutual animosity, were conciliated by their political interest. The French, solely bent upon conquest, cared not for the liberty of other nations; Prussia, intent upon self-aggrandizement, was indifferent to the fate of her brother sovereigns. Peace was concluded between France and Prussia at Basel, April 5, 1795. By a secret article of this treaty, Prussia confirmed the French republic in the possession of the whole of the left bank of the Rhine, while France in return richly indemnified Prussia at the expense of the petty German states. This peace, notwithstanding its manifest disadvantages, was also acceded to by Austria, which, on this occasion, received the unfortunate daughter of Louis XVI. in exchange for Semonville and Maret, the captive ambassadors of the republic, and the members of the convention seized by Dumouriez. Hanover[1] and Hesse-Cassel participated in the treaty and were included within the line of demarcation, which France, on her side, bound herself not to transgress.

The countries lying beyond this line of demarcation, the Netherlands, Holland, and Pfalz-Juliers, were now abandoned to France, and Austria, kept in check on the Upper Rhine, was powerless in their defence. In this manner fell Luxemburg and Düsseldorf. All the Lower Rhenish provinces were systematically plundered by the French under pretext of establishing liberty and equality.[2] The Batavian republic was permitted to subsist, but dependent upon France; Belgium was annexed to France in 1795.

---

[1] Von Berlepsch, the councillor of administration, proposed to the Calemberg diet to declare their neutrality in defiance of England, and, in case of necessity, to place "the Calemberg Nation" under the protection of France.—*Havemann.*

[2] "Wherever these locusts appear, everything, men, cattle, food, property, etc., is carried off. These thieves seize everything convertible into money. Nothing is safe from them. At Cologne, they filled a church with coffee and sugar. At Aix-la-Chapelle, they carried off the finest pictures of Rubens and Van Dyck, the pillars from the altar, and the marble slab from the tomb of Charlemagne, all of which they sold to some Dutch Jews."—*Posselt's Annals of 1796.* At Cologne, the nuns were instantly emancipated from their vows, and one of the youngest and most beautiful afterward gained great notoriety as a bar-maid at an inn. This scandalous story is related by Klebe in his Travels on the Rhine. In Bonn, Gleich, a man who had formerly been a priest, placed himself at the head of the French rabble and planted trees of liberty. He also gave to the world a decade, as he termed his publication.—*Müller, History of Bonn.* "The French proclaimed war against the palaces and peace to the huts, but no hut was too mean to escape the rapacity of these birds of prey. The first-fruits of liberty was the pillage of every corner."—*Schwaben's History of Siegburg.* The brothers Boisserée afterward collected a good many of the church pictures, at that period carried away from Cologne and more particularly from the Lower Rhine. They now adorn Munich and form the best collection of old German paintings now existing.

On the retreat of the Prussians, Mannheim was surrendered without a blow by the electoral minister, Oberndorf, to the French. Wurmser arrived too late to the relief of the city. Quosdanowich, his lieutenant-general, nevertheless, succeeded in saving Heidelberg by sheltering himself behind a great abatis at Handschuchsheion, whence he repulsed the enemy, who were afterward almost entirely cut to pieces by General Klenau, whom he sent in pursuit with the light cavalry. General Boros led another Austrian corps across Nassau to Ehrenbreitstein, at that time besieged by the French under their youthful general, Marceau, who instantly retired. Wurmser no sooner arrived in person than, attacking the French before Mannheim, he completely put them to the rout and took General Oudinot prisoner. Clairfait, at the same time, advanced unperceived upon Mayence, and unexpectedly attacking the besieging French force, carried off one hundred and thirty-eight pieces of heavy artillery. Pichegru, who had been called from Holland to take the command on the Upper Rhine, was driven back to the Vosges. Jourdan advanced to his aid from the Lower Rhine, but his vanguard under Marceau was defeated at Kreuznach and again at Meissenheim. Mannheim also capitulated to the Austrians. The winter was now far advanced; both sides were weary of the campaign, and an armistice was concluded. Austria, notwithstanding her late success, was, owing to the desertion of Prussia, in a critical position. The imperial troops also refused to act. The princes of Southern Germany longed for peace. Even Spain followed the example of Prussia and concluded a treaty with the French republic.

The consequent dissolution of the coalition between the German powers had at least the effect of preventing the formation of a coalition of nations against them by the French. Had the alliance between the sovereigns continued, the French would, from political motives, have used their utmost endeavors to revolutionize Germany; this project was rendered needless by the treaty of Basel, which broke up the coalition and confirmed France in the undisturbed possession of her liberties; and thus it happened that Prussia unwittingly aided the monarchical cause by involuntarily preventing the promulgation of the revolutionary principles of France.

Austria remained unshaken, and refused either to betray the monarchical cause by the recognition of a revolutionary democratical government, or to cede the frontiers of the empire to the youthful and insolent generals of the republic. Conscious of the righteousness of the cause she upheld, she intrepidly stood her ground and ventured her single strength in the mighty contest, which the campaign of 1796 was to decide. The Austrian forces in Germany were commanded by the emperor's brother, the Archduke Charles; those in Italy, by Beaulieu. The French, on the other hand, sent Jourdan to the Lower Rhine, Moreau to the Upper Rhine, Bonaparte to Italy, and commenced the attack on every point with their wonted impetuosity.

The Austrians had again extended their lines as far as the Lower Rhine. A corps under Prince Ferdinand of Würtemberg was stationed in the Bergland, in the narrow corner still left between the Rhine and the Prussian line of demarcation. Marceau forced him to retire as far as Altenkirchen, but the Archduke Charles hastening to his assistance encountered Jourdan's entire force on the Lahn near Kloster Altenberg, and, after a short contest, compelled it to give way. A great part of the Austrian army of the Rhine under Wurmser having been, meanwhile, drawn off and sent into Italy, the archduke was compelled to turn hastily from Jourdan against Moreau, who had just despatched General Ferino across the Lake of Constance, while he advanced upon Strasburg. A small Swabian corps under Colonel Raglowich made an extraordinary defence in Kehl (the first instance of extreme bravery given by the imperial troops at that time), but was forced to yield to numbers. The Austrian general, Sztarray, was, notwithstanding the gallantry displayed on the occasion, also repulsed at Sasbach; the

Wurtemberg battalion was also driven from the steep pass of the Kniebes,[1] across which Moreau penetrated through the Black Forest into the heart of Swabia, and had already reached Freudenstadt, when the Austrian general, Latour, marched up the Murg. He was, however, also repulsed. The Archduke Charles now arrived in person in the country around Pforzheim (on the skirts of the Black Forest), and sent forward his columns to attack the French in the mountains, but in vain; the French were victorious at Rothensol and at Wildbad. The archduke retired behind the Neckar to Cannstadt; his rearguard was pursued through the city of Stuttgard by the vanguard of the French. After a short cannonade, the archduke also abandoned his position at Cannstadt. The whole of the Swabian circle submitted to the French. Wurtemberg was now compelled to make a formal cession of Mumpelgard, which had been for some time garrisoned by the French,[2] and, moreover, to pay a contribution of four million livres; Baden was also mulcted two millions, the other states of the Swabian circle twelve millions, the clergy seven millions, altogether twenty-five million livres, without reckoning the enormous requisition of provisions, horses, clothes, etc. The archduke, in the meantime, deprived the troops belonging to the Swabian circle of their arms at Biberach, on account of the peace concluded by their princes with the French, and retired behind the Danube by Donauwœrth. Ferino had, meanwhile, also advanced from Huningen into the Breisgau and to the Lake of Constance, had beaten the small corps under General Fröhlick at Herbolsheim and the remnant of the French

---

[1] "Had Würtemberg possessed but six thousand well-organized troops, the position on the Roszbuhl might have been maintained, and the country have been saved. The millions since paid by Würtemberg, and which she may still have to pay, would have been spared."—*Appendix to the History of the Campaign of 1796.*

[2] The duke, Charles, had, in 1791, visited Paris, donned the national cockade, and bribed Mirabeau with a large sum of money to induce the French government to purchase Mümpelgard from him. The French, however, were quite as well aware as the duke that they would ere long possess it gratis.

emigrants under Conde at Mindelheim,[1] and joined Moreau in pursuit of the archduke. His troops committed great havoc wherever they appeared.[2]

Jourdan had also again pushed forward. The archduke had merely been able to oppose to him on the Lower Rhine thirty thousand men under the Count von Wartensleben, who, owing to Jourdan's numerical superiority, had been repulsed across both the Lahn and Maine. Jourdan took Frankfort by bombardment and imposed upon that city a contribution of six millions. The Franconian circle also submitted and paid sixteen millions, without reckoning the requisition of natural productions and the merciless pillage.[3]

The Archduke Charles, too weak singly to encounter the armies of Moreau and Jourdan, had, meanwhile, boldly resolved to keep his opponents as long as possible separate,

---

[1] Moreau generously allowed all his prisoners, who, as ex-nobles, were destined to the guillotine, to escape.

[2] Armbruster's "Register of French Crime" contains as follows: "Here and there, in the neighboring towns, there were certainly symptoms of an extremely favorable disposition toward the French, which would ill deserve a place in the annals of German patriotism and of—German good sense. This disposition was fortunately far from general. The appearance of the French in their real character, and the barbarous excesses and heavy contributions by which they rendered the people sensible of their presence, speedily effected their conversion." The French, it is true, neither murdered the inhabitants nor burned the villages as they had during the previous century in the Pfalz, but they pillaged the country to a greater extent, shamefully abused the women, and desecrated the churches. Their license and the art with which they extorted the last penny from the wretched people surpassed all belief. "Not satisfied with robbing the churches, they especially gloried in giving utterance to the most fearful blasphemies, in destroying and profaning the altars, in overthrowing the statues of saints, in treading the host beneath their feet or casting it to dogs.—At the village of Berg in Weingarten, they set up in the holy of holies the image of the devil, which they had taken from the representation of the temptation of the Saviour in the wilderness. In the village of Boos, they roasted a crucifix before a fire."—*Vide Hurter's Memorabilia, concerning the French allies in Swabia, who attempted to found an Alemannic Republic. Schaffhausen, 1840.* Moreau reduced them to silence by declaring, "I have no need of a revolution to the rear of my army."

[3] Notwithstanding Jourdan's proclamation, promising protection to all private property, Würzburg, Schweinfurt, Bamberg, etc., were completely pillaged. The young girls fled in hundreds to the woods. The churches were shamelessly desecrated. When mercy in God's name was demanded, the plunderers replied, "God! we are God!" They would dance at night-time around a bowl of burning brandy, whose blue flames they called their être suprême.—*The French in Franconia, by Count Soden.*

and, on the first favorable opportunity, to attack one with the whole of his forces, while he kept the other at bay with a small division of his army. In pursuance of this plan, he sent Wartensleben against Jourdan, and, meanwhile, drew Moreau after him into Bavaria, where, leaving General Latour with a small corps to keep him in check at Rain on the Lech, he recrossed the Danube at Ingolstadt with the flower of his army and hastily advanced against Jourdan, who was thus taken unawares. At Teiningen, he surprised the French avant-garde under Bernadotte, which he compelled to retire. At Amberg, he encountered Jourdan, whom he completely routed (1796). The French retreated through the city, on the other side of which they formed an immense square against the imperial cavalry under Wernek; it was broken on the third charge, and a terrible slaughter took place, three thousand of the French being killed and one thousand taken prisoner. The peasantry had already flown to arms, and assisted in cutting down the fugitives. Jourdan again made a stand at Wurzburg, where Wernek stormed his batteries at the head of his grenadiers and a complete rout ensued, September 3. The French lost six thousand dead and two thousand prisoners. The peasantry rose en masse, and hunted down the fugitives.[1] On the Upper Rhone, Dr. Röder placed himself at the head of the peasantry, but, encountering a superior French corps at Mellrichstadt, was defeated and killed. The French suffered most in the Spessart, called by them, on that account, La petite Vendee. The peasantry were here headed by an aged forester named Philip Witt, and, protected by their forests, exterminated numbers of the flying foe. The imperial troops were also unremitting in their pursuit, again defeated Bernadotte at Aschaffenburg and chased Jourdan through Nassau across

---

[1] "They deemed the assassination of a foreigner a meritorious work."—*Ephemeridæ of 1797*. "The peasantry, roused to fury by the disorderly and cruel French, whose excesses exceeded all belief, did not even extend mercy to the wounded; and the French, with equal barbarity, set whole villages on fire."—*Appendix to the Campaign of 1796*.

the Rhine. Marceau, who had vainly besieged Mayence, again made stand at Allerheim, where he was defeated and killed.[1]

Moreau, completely deceived by the archduke, had, meanwhile, remained in Bavaria. After defeating General Latour at Lechhausen, instead of setting off in pursuit of the archduke and to Jourdan's aid, he was, as the archduke had foreseen, attracted by the prospect of gaining a rich booty, in an opposite direction, toward Munich. Bavaria submitted to the French, paid ten millions, and ceded twenty of the most valuable pictures belonging to the Dusseldorf and Munich galleries. The news of Jourdan's defeat now compelled Moreau to beat a rapid retreat in order to avoid being cut off by the victorious archduke. Latour set off vigorously in pursuit, came up with him at Ulm and again at Ravensberg, but was both times repulsed, owing to his numerical inferiority. A similar fate awaited the still smaller imperial corps led against the French by Nauendorf at Rothweil and by Petrosch at Villingen, and Moreau led the main body of his army in safety through the deep narrow gorges of the Hollenthal in the Black Forest to Freiburg in the Breisgau, where he came upon the archduke, who, amid the acclamations of the armed peasantry (by whom the retreating French[2] were, as in the Spessart, continually harassed in their passage through the Black Forest), had hurried, but too late, to his encounter. Moreau had already sent two divisions of his army, under Ferino and Desaix, across the

---

[1] When scarcely in his twenty-seventh year. He was one of the most distinguished heroes of the Revolution, and as remarkable for his generosity to his weaker foes as for his moral and chivalric principles. The Archduke Charles sent his private physicians to attend upon him, and, on the occasion of his burial, fired a salvo simultaneously with that of the French stationed on the opposite bank of the Rhine.—*Mussinan.*

[2] The peasants of the Artenau and the Kinzigthal were commanded by a wealthy farmer, named John Baader. Besides several French generals, Hausmann, the commissary of the government, who accompanied Moreau's army, was taken prisoner.—*Mussinan, History of the French War of 1796,* etc. A decree, published on the 18th of September by Frederick Eugene, Duke of Würtemberg, in which he prohibited his subjects from taking part in the pursuit of the French, is worthy of remark.

Rhine at Huningen and Breisach, and covered their retreat with the third by taking up a strong position at Schliesgen, not far from Freiburg, whence, after braving a first attack, he escaped during the night to Huningen. This retreat, in which he had saved his army with comparatively little loss, excited general admiration, but in Italy there was a young man who scornfully exclaimed, "It was, after all, merely a retreat!"

CCL. *Bonaparte*

THIS youth was Napoleon Bonaparte, the son of a lawyer in the island of Corsica, a man of military genius, who, when a mere lieutenant, had raised the siege of Toulon, had afterward served the Directory by dispersing the old Jacobins with his artillery in the streets of Paris, and had been intrusted with the command of the army in Italy. Talents, that under a monarchy would have been doomed to obscurity, were, under the French republic, called into notice, and men of decided genius could, amid the general competition, alone attain to power or retain the reins of government.

Bonaparte was the first to take the field. In the April of 1796, he pushed across the Alps and attacked the Austrians. Beaulieu, a good general, but too old for service (he was then seventy-two, Napoleon but twenty-seven), had incautiously extended his lines too far, in order to preserve a communication with the English fleet in the Mediterranean. Bonaparte defeated his scattered forces at Montenotte and Millesimo, between the 10th and 15th of April, and, turning sharply upon the equally scattered Sardinian force, beat it in several engagements, the principal of which took place at Mondovi, between the 19th and 22d of April. An armistice was concluded with Sardinia, and Beaulieu, who vainly attempted to defend the Po, was defeated on the 7th and 8th of May, at Fombio. The bridge over the Adda at Lodi, three hundred paces in length, extremely narrow and to all appearance impregnable, defended by his lieutenant Sebottendorf, was carried by storm, and, on the 15th of May, Bonaparte entered Milan. Beaulieu took up a position behind the Mincio, notwithstanding which, Bonaparte carried the again ill-defended bridge at Borghetto by storm. While in this part of the country, he narrowly escaped being taken prisoner by a party of skirmishers, and was compelled to fly half-naked, with but one foot booted, from his night quarters at St. Georgio.

Beaulieu now withdrew into the Tyrol. Sardinia made peace, and terms were offered by the pope and by Naples. Leghorn was garrisoned with French troops; all the English goods lying in this harbor, to the value of twelve million pounds, were confiscated. The strongly fortified city of Mantua, defended by the Austrians under their gallant leader, Canto d'Irles, was besieged by Bonaparte. A fresh body of Austrian troops under Wurmser crossed the mountains to their relief; but Wurmser, instead of advancing with his whole force, incautiously pressed forward with thirty-two thousand men through the valley of the Adige, while Quosdanowich led eighteen thousand along the western shore of the Lake of Garda. Bonaparte instantly perceived his advantage, and, attacking the latter, defeated him on the 3d of August, at Lonato. Wurmser had entered Mantua unopposed on the 1st, but, setting out in search of the enemy, was unexpectedly attacked, on the 5th of August, by the whole of Bonaparte's forces at Castiglione, and compelled, like Quosdanowich, to seek shelter in the Tyrol. This senseless mode of attack had been planned by Weirotter, a colonel belonging to the general staff. Wurmser now received reinforcements, and Laner, the general of the engineers, was intrusted with the projection of a better plan. He again weakened the army by dividing his forces. In the beginning of September, Davidowich penetrated with twenty thousand men through the valley of the Adige and was defeated at Roveredo, and Wurmser, who had, meanwhile, advanced with an army of twenty-six thousand men through the valley of the Brenta, met with a similar fate at Bassano. He, nevertheless, escaped the pursuit of the victorious French by making a circuit, and threw himself by a forced march into Mantua, where he was, however, unable to make a lengthy resistance, the city being overpopulated and provisions scarce. A fresh army of twenty-eight thousand men, under Alvinzi, sent to his relief[1] through the valley of the Brenta, was attacked in a strong position at Arcole, on the river Alpon. Two dams protected the bank and a narrow bridge, which was, on the 15th of November, vainly stormed by the French, although General Augereau and Bonaparte, with the colors in his hand, led the attack. On the following day, Alvinzi foolishly crossed the bridge and took up an exposed position, in which he was beaten, and, on the third day, he retreated. Davidowich, meanwhile, again advanced from the Tyrol and gained an advantage at Rivoli, but was also forced to retreat before Bonaparte. Wurmser, when too late, made a sally, which was, consequently, useless. The campaign was, nevertheless, for the fifth time, renewed. Alvinzi collected reinforcements and again pushed forward into the valley of the Adige, but speedily lost courage and suffered a fearful defeat, in which twenty thousand of his men were taken prisoners, on the 14th and 15th of January, 1797, at Rivoli. Provera, on whom he had relied for assistance from Padua, was cut off and taken prisoner with his entire corps. Wurmser capitulated at Mantua with twenty-one thousand men.

The spring of 1797 had scarcely commenced when Bonaparte was already pushing across the Alps toward Vienna. Hoche, at the same time, again attacked the Lower and Moreau the Upper Rhine. Bonaparte, the nearest and most dangerous foe, was opposed by the archduke, whose army, composed of the remains of Alvinzi's disbanded and discouraged troops, called forth the observation from Bonaparte,

---

[1] Clausewitz demands, with great justice, why the Austrians so greatly divided their forces on this occasion for the sake of saving Italy, as they had only to follow up their successes vigorously on the Rhine in order to gain, in that quarter. far more than thev could lose on the Po.

"Hitherto I have defeated armies without generals, now I am about to attack a general without an army!" A battle took place at Tarvis, amid the highest mountains, whence it was afterward known as "the battle above the clouds." The archduke, with a handful of Hungarian hussars, valiantly defended the pass against sixteen thousand French under Massena, nor turned to fly until eight only of his men remained. Generals Bayalich and Ocskay, instead of supporting him, had yielded. The archduke again collected five thousand men around him at Glogau and opposed the advance of the immensely superior French force until two hundred and fifty of his men alone remained. The conqueror of Italy rapidly advanced through Styria upon Vienna. Another French corps under Joubert had penetrated into the Tyrol, but had been so vigorously assailed at Spinges by the brave peasantry[1] as to be forced to retire upon Bonaparte's main body, with which he came up at Villach, after losing between six and eight thousand men during his retreat through the Pusterthal. The rashness with which Bonaparte, leaving the Alps to his rear and regardless of his distance from France, penetrated into the enemy's country, had placed him in a position affording every facility for the Austrians, by a bold and vigorous stroke, to cut him off and take him prisoner. They had garrisoned Trieste and Fiume on the Adriatic and formed an alliance with the republic of Venice, at that time well supplied with men, arms, and gold. A great insurrection of the peasantry, infuriated by the pillage of the French troops, had broken out at Bergamo. The

[1] At Absom, in the valley of the Inn, a peasant girl had, at that time, discovered a figure of the Virgin in one of the panes of glass in her chamber window. This appearance being deemed miraculous by the simple peasantry, the authorities of the place investigated the matter, had the glass cleaned and scraped, etc., and at length pronounced the indelible figure to be simply the outline of an old colored painting. The peasantry, however, excited by the appearance of the infidel French, persisted in giving credence to the miracle and set up the piece of glass in a church, which was afterward annually visited by thousands of pilgrims. In 1407, the celebrated pilgrimage to Waldrast, in the Tyrol, had been founded in a similar manner by the discovery of a portrait of the Virgin which had been grown up in a tree, by two shepherd lads.

gallant Tyrolese, headed by Count Lehrbach, and the Hungarians, had risen en masse. The victorious troops of the Archduke Charles were en route from the Rhine, and Mack had armed the Viennese and the inhabitants of the thickly-populated neighborhood of the metropolis. Bonaparte was lost should the archduke's plan of operations meet with the approbation of the Viennese cabinet, and, perfectly aware of the fact, he made proposals of peace under pretence of sparing unnecessary bloodshed. The imperial court, stupefied by the late discomfiture in Italy, instead of regarding the proposals of the wily Frenchman as a confession of embarrassment, and of assailing him with redoubled vigor, acceeded to them, and, on the 18th of April, Count Cobenzl, Thugut's successor, concluded the preliminaries of peace at Leoben, by which the French, besides being liberated from their dangerous position, were recognized as victors. The negotiations of peace were continued at the château of Campo Formio, where the Austrians somewhat regained courage, and Count Cobenzl[1] even ventured to refuse some of the articles proposed. Bonaparte, irritated by opposition, dashed a valuable cup, the gift of the Russian empress, violently to the ground, exclaiming, "You wish for war? Well! you shall have it, and your monarchy shall be shattered like that cup." The armistice was not interrupted. Hostilities were even suspended on the Rhine. The archduke had, before quitting that river, gained the *têtes de pont* of Strasburg (Kehl) and of Huningen, besides completely clearing the right bank of the Rhine of the enemy. The whole of these advantages were again lost on his recall to take the field against Napoleon. The Saxon troops, which had, up to this period, stead-

---

[1] Cobenzl was a favorite of Kaunitz and a thorough courtier. At an earlier period, when ambassador at Petersburg, he wrote French comedies, which were performed at the Hermitage in the presence of the empress Catherine. The arrival of an unpleasant despatch being ever followed by the production of some amusing piece as an antidote to care, the empress jestingly observed, "that he was no doubt keeping his best piece until the news arrived of the French being in Vienna." He expired in the February of 1809 a year pregnant with fate for Austria.

ily sided with Austria, were recalled by the elector. Swabia, Franconia, and Bavaria were intent upon making peace with France. Baron von Fahnenberg, the imperial envoy at Ratisbon, bitterly reproached the Protestant estates for their evident inclination to follow the example of Prussia by siding with the French and betraying their fatherland to their common foe, but, on applying more particularly for aid to the spiritual princes, who were exposed to the greatest danger, he found them equally lukewarm. Each and all refused to furnish troops or to pay a war tax. The imperial troops were, consequently, compelled to enforce their maintenance, and naturally became the objects of popular hatred. In this wretched manner was the empire defended! The petty imperial corps on the Rhine were, meanwhile, compelled to retreat before an enemy vastly their superior in number. Wernek, attempting with merely twenty-two thousand men to obstruct the advance of an army of sixty-five thousand French under Hoche, was defeated at Neuwied and deprived of his command.[1] Sztarray, who charged seven times at the head of his men, was also beaten by Moreau at Kehl and Diersheim. At this conjuncture, the armistice of Leoben was published.

A peace, based on the terms proposed at Leoben, was formally concluded at Campo Formio, October 17, 1797. The triumph of the French republic was confirmed, and ancient Europe received a new form. The object for which the sovereigns of France had for centuries vainly striven was won by the monarchless nation; France gained the preponderance in Europe. Italy and the whole of the left bank of the Rhine were abandoned to her arbitrary rule, and this fearful loss, far from acting as a warning to Germany and promoting her unity, merely increased her internal dissensions and offered to the French republic an opportunity for intervention, of which it took advantage for purposes of gain and pillage.

---

[1] He indignantly refused the stipend offered to him on this occasion and protested against the injustice of his condemnation.

The principal object of the policy of Bonaparte and of the French Directory, at that period, was, by rousing the ancient feelings of enmity between Austria and Prussia, to eternalize the disunion between those two monarchies. Bonaparte, after effectuating the peace by means of terror, loaded Austria with flattery. He flattered her religious feelings by the moderation of his conduct in Italy toward the pope, notwithstanding the disapprobation manifested by the genuine French republicans, and her interests by the offer of Venice in compensation for the loss of the Netherlands, and, making a slight side-movement against that once powerful and still wealthy republic, reduced it at the first blow, nay, by mere threats, to submission; so deeply was the ancient aristocracy here also fallen. The cession of Venice to the emperor was displeasing to the French republicans. They were, however, pacified by the delivery of Lafayette, who had been still detained a prisoner in Austria after the treaty of Basel. Napoleon said in vindication of his policy, "I have merely lent Venice to the emperor, he will not keep her long." He, moreover, gratified Austria by the extension of her western frontier, so long the object of her ambition, by the possession of the archbishopric of Salzburg and of a part of Bavaria with the town of Wasserburg.[1] The sole object of these concessions was provisionally to dispose Austria in favor of France,[2] and to render Prussia's ancient jealousy of Austria implacable.[3] Hence the secret articles

---

[1] Bavaria regarded these forced concessions as a bad reward for her fidelity to Austria. Napoleon appears to have calculated upon relighting by this means the flames of discord, whence he well knew how to draw an advantage, between Bavaria and Austria.

[2] "Thus the emperor also now abandoned the empire by merely bargaining with the enemy to quit his territories, and leaving the wretched provinces of the empire a prey to war and pillage. And if the assurances of friendship, of confidence, and of affection between Austria and Venice are but recalled to mind, the contrast was indeed laughable when the emperor was pleased to allow that loyal city to be ceded to him. The best friend was in this case the cloth from which the emperor cut himself an equivalent."—*Huergelmer.*

[3] A curious private memoir of Talleyrand says: "J'ai la certitude que Berlin est le lieu, où le traité du 26 Vendémiaire (the reconciliation of Austria with France at Campo Formio), aura jetté le plus d'etonnement, d'embarras et de crainte." He then explains that, now that the Netherlands no longer belong to Austria,

of peace by which France and Austria bound themselves not to grant any compensation to Prussia. Prussia was on her part, however, resolved not to be the loser, and, in the summer of 1797, took forcible possession of the imperial free town of Nuremberg, notwithstanding her declaration made just three years previously through Count Soden to the Franconian circle, "that the king had never harbored the design of seeking a compensation at the expense of the empire, whose constitution had ever been sacred in his eyes!" and to the empire, "He deemed it beneath his dignity to refute the reports concerning Prussia's schemes of aggrandizement, oppression, and secularization." Prussia also extended her possessions in Franconia[1] and Westphalia, and Hesse-Cassel imitated her example by the seizure of a part of Schaumburg-Lippe. The diet energetically remonstrated, but in vain. Pamphlets spoke of the Prussian reunion-chambers opened by Hardenberg in Franconia. An attempt was, however, made to console the circle of Franconia by depicturing the far worse sufferings of that of Swabia under the imperial contributions. The petty Estates of the empire stumbled, under these circumstances, upon the unfortunate idea "that the intercession of the Russian court should be requested for the maintenance of the integrity of the German empire and for that of her constitution"; the intercession of the Russian court, which had so lately annihilated Poland!

Shortly after this (1797), Frederick William II., who had,

---

and that Austria and France no longer come into collision, both powers would be transformed from natural foes into natural friends and would have an equal interest in weakening Prussia. Should Russia stir, the Poles could be roused to insurrection, etc.

[1] "Exactly at this period, when the empire's common foe was plundering the Franconian circle, when deeds of blood and horror, when misery and want had reached a fearful height, the troops of the Elector of Brandenburg overran the cities and villages. The inhabitants were constrained to take the oath of fealty, the public officers, who refused, were dragged away captive, etc. Ellingen, Stopfenheim, Absperg, Eschenbach, Nüremberg, Postbaur, Virnsperg, Oettingen, Dinkelspühl, Ritzenhausen, Gelchsheim, were scenes of brutal outrage."—*The History of the Usurpation of Brandenburg, A.D. 1797*, with the original Documents, published by the Teutonic Order.

on his accession to the throne, found seventy-two millions of dollars in the treasury, expired, leaving twenty-eight millions of debts. His son, Frederick William III., placed the Countess Lichtenau under arrest, banished Wollner, and abolished the unpopular monopoly in tobacco, but retained his father's ministers and continued the alliance, so pregnant with mischief, with France.—This monarch, well-meaning and destined to the severest trials, educated by a peevish valetudinarian and ignorant of affairs, was first taught by bitter experience the utter incapacity of the men at that time at the head of the government, and after, as will be seen, completely reforming the court, the government, and the army, surrounded himself with men, who gloriously delivered Prussia and Germany from all the miseries and avenged all the disgrace, which it is the historian's sad office to record.

Austria, as Prussia had already done by the treaty of Basel, also sacrificed, by the peace of Campo Formio, the whole of the left bank of the Rhine and abandoned it to France, the loss thereby suffered by the Estates of the empire being indemnified by the secularization of the ecclesiastical property in the interior of Germany and by the prospect of the seizure of the imperial free towns. Mayence was ceded without a blow to France. Holland was forgotten. The English, under pretext of opposing France, destroyed, in 1797, the last Dutch fleet, in the Texel, though not without a heroic and determined resistance on the part of the admirals de Winter and Reintjes, both of whom were severely wounded, and the latter died in captivity in England. Holland was formed into a Batavian, Genoa into a Ligurian, Milan with the Valtelline (from which the Grisons was severed) into a Cisalpine, republic. Intrigues were, moreover, set on foot for the formation of a Roman and Neapolitan republic in Italy and of a Rhenish and Swabian one in Germany, all of which were to be subordinate to the mother republic in France. The proclamation of a still-born Cisrhenish republic (it not having as yet been constituted when it was swallowed up in the great French republic), in the masterless Lower Rhenish provinces in the territory of Treves, Aix-la-Chapelle, and Cologne, under the influence of the French Jacobins and soldiery, was, however, all that could at first be done openly.

The hauteur with which Bonaparte, backed by his devoted soldiery, had treated the republicans, and the contempt manifested by him toward the citizens, had not failed to rouse the jealous suspicions of the Directory, the envy of the less successful generals, and the hatred of the old friends of liberty, by whom he was already designated as a tyrant. The republican party was still possessed of considerable power, and the majority of the French troops under Moreau, Jourdan, Bernadotte, etc., were still ready to shed their blood in the cause of liberty. Bonaparte, compelled to veil his ambitious projects, judged it more politic, after sowing the seed of discord at Campo Formio, to withdraw a while in order to await the ripening of the plot and to return to reap the result. He, accordingly, went meantime, in 1798, with a small but well-picked army to Egypt, for the ostensible purpose of opening a route overland to India, the sea-passage having been closed against France by the British, but, in reality, for the purpose of awaiting there a turn in continental affairs, and, moreover, by his victories over the Turks in the ancient land of fable to add to the wonder it was ever his object to inspire. On his way thither he seized the island of Malta and compelled Baron Hompesch, the grand-master of the order of the Knights of Malta, to resign his dignity, the fortress being betrayed into his hands by the French knights.

At Rastadt, near Baden, where the compensation mentioned in the treaty of Campo Formio was to be taken into consideration, the terrified Estates of the empire assembled for the purpose of suing the French ambassadors for the lenity they had not met with at the hands of Austria and Prussia.—The events that took place at Rastadt are of a description little calculated to flatter the patriotic feelings of the German historian. The soul of the congress was Charles Maurice Talleyrand-Perigord, at one time a bishop, at the present period minister of the French republic. His colloquy with the German ambassadors resembled that of the fox with the geese, and he attuned their discords with truly diabolical art. While holding Austria and Prussia apart, instigating them one against the other, flattering both with the friendship of the republic and with the prospect of a rich booty by the secularization of the ecclesiastical lands, he encouraged some of the petty states with the hope of aggrandizement by an alliance with France,[1] and, with cruel contempt, allowed others a while to gasp for life before consigning them to destruction. The petty princes, moreover, who had been deprived of their territory on the other side of the Rhine, demanded lands on this side in compensation; all the petty princes on this side consequently trembled lest they should be called upon to make compensation, and each endeavored, by bribing the members of the congress, Talleyrand in particular, to render himself an exception. The French minister was bribed not by gold alone; a considerable number of ladies gained great notoriety by their liaison with the insolent republican, from whom they received nothing, the object for which they sued being sold by him sometimes even two or three times. Momus, a satirical production of this period, relates numerous instances of crime and folly that are perfectly incredible. The avarice manifested by the French throughout the whole of the negotiations was only surpassed by the brutality of their language and behavior. Roberjot, Bonnier, and Jean de Bry, the dregs of the French nation, treated the whole of the German empire on this occasion en canaille, and, while picking the pockets of the Germans, were studiously coarse and brutal; still the trifling opposition they encountered, and the total want of spirit in the representatives of the great German empire,

---

[1] His secret memoirs, even at that period, designate Baden, Würtemberg, and Darmstadt as states securely within the grasp of France.

whom it must, in fact, have struck them as ridiculous to see thus humbled at their feet, forms an ample excuse for their demeanor.

Gustavus Adolphus IV., who mounted the throne of Sweden in 1796, distinguished himself at that time among the Estates of the empire, when Duke of Pomerania and Prince of Rugen, by his solemn protest against the depredations committed by France, and by his summons to every member of the German empire to take the field against their common foe. Hesse-Cassel was also remarkable for the warlike demeanor and decidedly anti-Gallic feeling of her population; and Wurtemberg, for being the first of the German states that gave the example of making concessions more in accordance with the spirit of the times. By the abolition of ancient abuses alone could the princes meet the threats used on every occasion by the French at Rastadt to revolutionize the people unless their demands were fully complied with. In Wurtemberg, the duke, Charles, had been succeeded, in 1793, by his brother, Louis Eugène, who banished license from his court, but, a foe to enlightenment, closed the Charles college, placed monks around his person, was extremely bigoted, and a zealous but impotent friend to France. He expired in 1795, and was succeeded by the third brother, Frederick Eugène, who had been during his youth a canon at Salzburg, but afterward became a general in the Prussian service, married a princess of Brandenburg, and educated his children in the Protestant faith in order to assimilate the religion of the reigning family with that of the people. His mild government terminated in 1797. Frederick, his talented son and successor, mainly frustrated the projected establishment of a Swabian republic, which was strongly supported by the French, by his treatment of the provincial Estates, the modification of the rights of chase, etc., on which occasion he took the following oath: "I repeat the solemn vow, ever to hold the constitution of this country sacred, and to make the weal of my subjects the aim of my life." He nevertheless appears, by the magnificent fetes, masquerades, and pastoral festivals given by him, as if in a time of the deepest peace, at Hohenheim, to have trusted more to his connection with England, by his marriage with the princess royal, Matilda,[1] with Russia, and with Austria (the emperor Paul, Catherine's successor, having married the princess Maria of Wurtemberg, and the emperor Francis II., her sister Elisabeth), than to the constitution, which he afterward annihilated.

The weakness displayed by the empire and the increasing disunion between Austria and Prussia encouraged the French to further insolence. Not satisfied with garrisoning every fortification on the left bank of the Rhine, they boldly attacked, starved to submission, and razed to the ground, during peace time, the once impregnable fortress of Ehrenbreitstein, on the right bank of the Rhine, opposite Coblentz.[2] Not content with laying the Netherlands and Holland completely waste, they compelled the Hanse towns to grant them a loan of eighteen million livres. Lubeck refused, but Hamburg and Bremen, more nearly threatened and hopeless of aid from Prussia, were constrained to satisfy the demands of the French brigands. In the Netherlands, the German faction once more rose in open insurrection; in 1798, the young men, infuriated by the conscription and by their enrolment into French regiments, flew to arms, and torrents of blood were shed in the struggle, in which they were unaided by their German brethren, before they were again reduced to submission. The English also landed at Ostend, but for the sole purpose of destroying the sluices of the canal at Bruges.

The French divided the beautiful Rhenish provinces, yielded to them almost without a blow by Germany, into four departments: First, Roer, capital Aix-la-Chapelle; be-

---

[1] He fled on Moreau's invasion to England, where he formed this alliance. There was at one time a project of creating him elector of Hanover and of partitioning Würtemberg between Bavaria and Baden.

[2] The commandant, Faber, defended the place for fourteen months with a garrison of 2,000 men. During the siege, the badly-disciplined French soldiery secretly sold provisions at an exorbitant price to the starving garrison.

sides Cologne and Cleves. Secondly, Donnersberg, capital Mayence; besides Spires and Zweibrucken. Thirdly, Saar, capital Treves. Fourthly, Rhine and Moselle, capital Coblentz; besides Bonn. Each department was subdivided into cantons, each canton into communes. The department was governed by a perfect, the canton by a sub-prefect, the commune by a mayor. All distinction of rank, nobility, and all feudal rights were abolished. Each individual was a citizen, free and equal. All ecclesiastical establishments were abandoned to plunder, the churches alone excepted, they being still granted as places of worship to believers, notwithstanding the contempt and ridicule into which the clergy had fallen. The monasteries were closed. The peasantry, more particularly in Treves, nevertheless, still manifested great attachment to Popery. Guilds and corporations were also abolished. The introduction of the ancient German oral law formerly in use throughout the empire, the institution of trial by jury, which, to the disgrace of Germany, the Rhenish princes, after the lapse of a thousand years, learned from their Gallic foe, was a great and signal benefit.

Liberality, equality, and justice were, at that period, in all other respects, mere fictions. The most arbitrary rule in reality existed, and the new provinces were systematically drained by taxes of every description, as, for instance, register, stamp, patent, window, door, and land taxes: there was also a tax upon furniture and upon luxuries of every sort; a poll-tax, a percentage on the whole assessment, etc.; besides extortion, confiscation, and forced sales. And woe to the new citizen of the great French republic if he failed in paying more servile homage to its officers, from the prefect down to the lowest underling, than had ever been exacted by the princes![1] Such was the liberty bestowed by

[1] Klebe gave an extremely detailed account of the French government: "It is, for instance, well known that a pastry cook was nominated lord high warden of the forests over a whole department, and a jeweller was raised to the same office in another.—The documents proving the cheating and underselling carried

republican France! Thus were her promises fulfilled! The German Illuminati were fearfully undeceived, particularly on perceiving how completely their hopes of universally revolutionizing Germany were frustrated by the treaty of Basel. The French, who had proclaimed liberty to all the nations of the earth, now offered it for sale. The French character was in every respect the same as during the reign of Louis XIV. The only principle to which they remained ever faithful was that of robbery.—Switzerland was now, in her turn, attacked, and vengeance thus overtook every province that had severed itself from the empire, and every part of the once magnificent empire of Germany was miserably punished for its want of unity.

---

on by Pioc, the lord high warden of the forests, and by his assistant, Gauthier, in all the forests in the department of the Rhine and Moselle, are detailed at full length in 'Rübezahl,' a sort of monthly magazine. It is astonishing to see with what boundless impudence these people have robbed the country.—Still greater rascalities were carried on on the right bank of the Rhine. Gauthier robbed from Coblentz down to the Prussian frontiers." These allegations are confirmed by Görres in a pamphlet, "Results of my Mission to Paris," in which he says, "The Directory had treated the four departments like so many Pashalics, which it abandoned to its Janissaries and colonized with its favorites. Every petition sent by the inhabitants was thrown aside with revolting contempt; everything was done that could most deeply wound their feelings in regard to themselves or to their country." "The secret history of the government of the country between the Rhine and the Moselle," sums up as follows: "All cheated, all thieved, all robbed. The cheating, thieving, and robbing were perfectly terrible, and not one of the cheats, thieves, or robbers seemed to have an idea that this country formed, by the decree of union, a part of France." A naïve confession! The French, at all events, acted as if conscious that the land was not theirs. The Rhenish Jews, who, as early as the times of Louis XIV., had aided the French in plundering Germany, again acted as their bloodhounds, and, by accepting bills in exchange for their real or supposed loans, at double the amount, on wealthy proprietors, speedily placed themselves in possession of the finest estates. Vide Reichardt's Letters from Paris.

CCLI. *The Pillage of Switzerland*

PEACE had reigned throughout Switzerland since the battle of Villmergen, in 1712, which had given to Zurich and Berne the ascendency in the confederation. The popular discontent caused by the increasing despotism of the aristocracy had merely displayed itself in petty conspiracies, as, for instance, that of Henzi in 1749, and in partial insurrections. In all the cantons, even in those in which the democratic spirit was most prevalent, the chief authority had been seized by the wealthier and more ancient families. All the offices were in their hands, the higher posts in the Swiss regiments raised for the service of France were monopolized by the younger sons of the more powerful families, who introduced the social vices of France into their own country, where they formed a strange medley in conjunction with the pedantry of the ancient oligarchical form of government. In the great canton of Berne, the council of two hundred, which had unlimited sway, was solely composed of seventy-six reigning families. In Zurich, the one thousand nine hundred townsmen had unlimited power over the country. For one hundred and fifty years no citizen had been enrolled among them, and no son of a peasant had been allowed to study for, or been nominated to, any office, even to that of preacher. In Solothurn, but one-half of the eight hundred townsmen were able to carry on the government. Lucerne was governed by a council of one hundred, so completely monopolized by the more powerful families that boys of twenty succeeded their fathers as councillors. Basel was governed by a council of two hundred and eighty, which was entirely formed out of seventy wealthy mercantile families. Seventy-one families had usurped the authority at Freiburg: similar oligarchical government prevailed at St. Gall and Schaffhausen. The Junker, in the latter place, rendered themselves especially ridiculous by the innumerable offices and chambers in which they transacted their useless and prolix affairs. In all these aristocratic cantons, the peasantry were cruelly harassed, oppressed, and, in some parts, kept in servitude, by the provincial governors. The wealthy provincial governments were monopolized by the great aristocratic families.[1] Even in the pure democracies, the provincial communes were governed by powerful peasant families, as, for instance, in Glarus, and the tyranny exercised by these peasants over the territory beneath their sway far exceeded that of the aristocratic burgesses in their provincial governments. The Italian valleys groaned beneath the yoke of the original cantons, particularly under that of Uri,[2] the seven provincial governments in Unterwallis under that of Oberwallis, the countship of Werdenberg under that of the Glarner, the Valtelline under that of the Grisons.[3] The princely abbot of St. Gall was unlimited sovereign over his territory. Separate monasteries, for instance, Engelberg, had feudal sway over their vassals.

Enlightenment and liberal opinions spread also gradually over Switzerland, and twenty years after Henzi's melancholy death, a disposition was again shown to oppose the tyranny of the oligarchies. In 1792, Lavater and Fuszli were banished Zurich for venturing to complain of the arbitrary conduct of one of the provincial governors;[4] in 1779, a curate

---

[1] "The peasant, when summoned into the presence of a governor, lord of the council, head of a guild, or preacher, stood there, not as a free Swiss, but as a criminal trembling before his judge."—*Lehmann on the imaginary Freedom of the Swiss. 1799.*

[2] "The important office of provincial secretary was, in this manner, hereditary in the family of the Beroldingen of Uri."—*Lehmann.*

[3] "In the Grisons, the constitution was extremely complicated. The lordships of Meyenfeld and Aspermont were, for instance, subject to the three confederated cantons and under the control of the provincial governors nominated by them; they were at the same time members of the whole free state, and, as such, had a right of lordship over the subject provinces, over which they, in their turn, appointed a governor."—*Meyer von Knonau's Geography.*

[4] The best information concerning the authority held by the provincial governors, who enjoyed almost unlimited sway over their districts, is to be met with in the excellent biography of Solomon Landolt, the provincial governor of Zurich, by David Hesz. Landolt was the model of an able but extremely

named Waser, a man of talent and a foe to the aristocracy, was beheaded on a false charge of falsifying the archives;[1] in 1794, the oppressed peasantry of Lucerne revolted against the aristocracy; in the same year, the peasantry in Schwyz, roused by the insolence of the French recruiting officers, revolted, and, in the public provincial assembly, enforced the recall of all the people of Schwyz in the French service, besides imposing a heavy fine upon General Reding on his return. In 1781, a revolt of the Freiburg peasantry, occasioned by the tyranny of the aristocracy, was quelled with the aid of Berne; in 1784, Suter, the noble-spirited Landammann of Appenzell, fell a sacrifice to envy. His mental and moral superiority to the rest of his countrymen inspired his rival, Geiger, with the most deadly hatred, and he persecuted him with the utmost rancor. He was accused of being a free-thinker; documents and protocols were falsified; the stupid populace was excited against him, and, after having been exposed on the pillory, publicly whipped, and tortured on the rack, he was beheaded, and all intercession on his behalf was prohibited under pain of death. Solothurn, on the other hand, was freed from feudal servitude in 1785. The popular feeling at that time prevalent throughout Switzerland was, however, of far greater import than these petty events. The oligarchies had everywhere suppressed public opinion; the long peace had slackened the martial ardor of the people; the ridiculous affectation of ancient heroic lan-

---

tyrannical governor (he ruled over Greisensee and Eglisau) and gained great note by his Salomonic judgments and by his quaint humor. He founded the Swiss rifle clubs and introduced that national weapon into modern warfare. He was also a painter and had the whim, notwithstanding the constant triumph of the French, ever to represent them in his pictures as the vanquished party.

[1] Hirzel wrote at that time, in his "Glimpses into the History of the Confederation," that Captain Henzi had been deprived of his head because he was the only man in the country who had one. Zimmerman says in his "National Pride," "A foreign philosopher visited Switzerland for the purpose of settling in a country where thought was free; he remained ten days at Zurich and then went to—Portugal." In 1774, the clocks at Basel, which, since the siege of Rudolph of Habsburg, had remained one hour behindhand, were, after immense opposition, regulated like those in the rest of the world. Two factions sprang up on this occasion, that of the Spieszburghers or Lalleburghers (the ancient one), and that of the Francemen or new-modellers (the modern one).

guage brought into vogue by John Muller rendered the contrast yet more striking, and, on the outburst of the French Revolution, the tyrannized Swiss peasantry naturally threw themselves into the arms of the French, the aristocracy into those of the Austrians.

The oppressed peasantry revolted as early as 1790 against the ruling cities, the vassal against the aristocrat, in Schaffhausen, on account of the tithes; in Lower Valais, on account of the tyranny of one of the provincial governors. These petty outbreaks and an attempt made by Laharpe to render the Vaud independent of Berne[1] were suppressed in 1791. The people remained, nevertheless, in a high state of fermentation. The new French republic at first quarrelled with the ancient confederation for having, unmindful of their origin, descended to servility. The Swiss guard had, on the 16th of August, 1792, courageously defended the palace of the unfortunate French king and been cut to pieces by the Parisian mob. At a later period, the Austrians had seized the ambassadors of the French republic, Semonville and Maret, in the Valtelline, in the territory of the Grisons. The Swiss patriots, as they were called, however, gradually fomented an insurrection against the aristocrats and called the French to their aid. In 1793, the vassals of the bishop of Basel at Pruntrut had already planted trees of liberty and placed the bishopric, under the name of a Rauracian republic, under the protection of France, chiefly at the instigation of Gobel, who was, in reward, appointed bishop of Paris, and whose nephew, Rengger, shortly afterward became a member of the revolutionary government in Berne. In Geneva, during the preceding year, the French faction had gained the upper hand. The fickleness of the war kept the rest of the patriots in a state of suspense, but, on the seizure of the left bank of the Rhine by the French, the movements in Switzerland assumed a more serious char-

---

[1] Laharpe was at the same time a demagogue in the Vaud and tutor to the emperor Alexander at Petersburg.

acter. The abbot, Beda, of St. Gall, 1795, pacified his subjects by concessions, which his successor, Pancras, refusing to recognize, he was, in consequence, expelled. The unrelenting aristocracy of Zurich, upon this, took the field against the restless peasantry, surrounded the patriots in Stäfa, threw the venerable Bodmer and a number of his adherents into prison, and inflicted upon them heavy fines or severe corporeal chastisement.

The campaign of 1796 had fully disclosed to Bonaparte the advantage of occupying Switzerland with his troops, whose passage to Italy or Germany would be thereby facilitated, while the line of communication would be secured, and the danger to which he and Moreau had been exposed through want of co-operation would at once be remedied. He first of all took advantage of the dissensions in the Grisons to deprive that republic of the beautiful Valtelline,[1] and, even at that time, demanded permission from the people of Valais to build the road across the Simplon, which he was, however, only able to execute at a later period. On his return to Paris from the Italian expedition, he passed through Basel,[2] where he was met by Talleyrand. Peter Ochs, the chief master of the corporation, was, on this occasion, as he himself relates in his History of Basel, won over, as the acknowledged chief of the patriots, to revolutionize Switzerland and to enter into a close alliance with France. The base characters, at that time the tools of the French Directory, merely acceded to the political plans of Bonaparte and

---

[1] Valtelline with Chiavenna and Bormio (Cleves and Worms) were ill-treated by the people of the Grisons. Offices and justice were regularly jobbed and sold to the highest bidder. The people of Valtelline hastily entered into alliance with France, while the oppressed peasantry in the Grisons rebelled against the ruling family of Salis, which had long been in the pay of the French kings, and had, since the revolution, sided with Austria. John Müller appeared at Basel as Thugut's agent for the purpose of inciting the confederation against France.—*Ochs' History of Basel.*

[2] While here, he gave Fesch, the pastry-cook, whose brother, a Swiss lieutenant, was the second husband of Bonaparte's maternal grandmother, a very friendly reception. The offspring of this second marriage was the future Cardinal Fesch, Letitia's half-brother and Napoleon's uncle, whom Napoleon attempted to create primate of Germany and to raise to the pontifical throne.

Talleyrand in the hope of reaping a rich harvest by the plunder of the federal cantons, and the Swiss expedition was, consequently, determined upon. The people of Valais, whose state of oppression served as a pretext for interference, revolted, under Laharpe, against Berne, 1798, and demanded the intervention of the French republic, as heir to the dukes of Savoy, on the strength of an ancient treaty, which had, for that purpose, been raked up from the ashes of the past. Nothing could exceed the miserable conduct of the diet at that conjuncture. After having already conceded to France her demand for the expulsion of the emigrants and having exposed its weakness by this open violation of the rights of hospitality, it discussed the number of troops to be furnished by each of the cantons, when the enemy was already in the country. Even the once haughty Bernese, who had set an army, thirty thousand strong, on foot, withdrew, under General Wysz, from Valais to their metropolis, where they awaited the attack of the enemy. There was neither plan[1] nor order; the patriots rose in every quarter and struck terror into the aristocrats, most of whom were now rather inclined to yield and impeded by their indecision the measures of the more spirited party. In Basel, Ochs deposed the oligarchy; in Zurich, the government was induced, by intimidation, to restore Bodmer and his fellow-prisoners to liberty. In Freiburg, Lucerne, Schaffhausen, and St. Gall, the oligarchies resigned their authority; Constance asserted its independence.

Within Berne itself, tranquillity was with difficulty preserved by Steiger, the venerable mayor, a man of extreme firmness of character. A French force under Brune had already overrun Vaud, which, under pretext of being delivered from oppression, was laid under a heavy contribution; the ancient charnel-house at Murten was also destroyed, because the French had formerly been beaten on this spot by

---

[1] Some of the cantons imagined that France merely aspired to the possession of Valais, and, jealous of the prosperity and power of Berne, willingly permitted her to suffer this humiliation.—*Meyer von Knonau.*

the Germans. But few of the Swiss marched to the aid of Berne; two hundred of the people of Uri, arrayed in the armor of their ancestors, some of the peasantry of Glarus, St. Gall, and Freiburg.[1] A second French force under Schauenburg entered Switzerland by Basel, defeated the small troops of Bernese sent to oppose it at Dornach and Langnau, and took Solothurn, where it liberated one hundred and eighty self-styled patriots imprisoned in that place. The patriots, at this conjuncture, also rose in open insurrection in Berne, threw everything into confusion, deposed the old council, formed a provisional government, and checked all the preparations for defence. The brave peasantry, basely betrayed by the cities, were roused to fury. Colonels Ryhiner, Stettler, Crusy, and Goumores were murdered by them upon mere suspicion (their innocence was afterward proved), and boldly following their leader, Grafenried, against the French, they defeated and repulsed the whole of Brune's army and captured eighteen guns at the bridge of Neuenegg. But a smaller Bernese corps which, under Steiger, the mayor, opposed the army of Schauenburg in the Grauen Holz, was routed after a bloody struggle, and, before Erlach, the newly-nominated generalissimo, could hurry back to Berne with the victors of Neuenegg, the patriots, who had long been in the pay of France, threw wide the gates to Schauenburg. All was now lost. Erlach fled to Thun, in order to place himself at the head of the people of the Oberland, who descended in thick masses from the mountains; but, on his addressing the brave Senn peasantry in French, according to the malpractice of the Bernese, they mistook him for a French spy and struck him dead in his carriage. The loss of Berne greatly dispirited them and they desisted from further and futile opposition. Steiger escaped. Hotze, a gallant Austrian general, who, mindful of his Swiss origin, had attempted to place himself at the head of his countrymen, was compelled

[1] Two Bernese, condemned to work in the trenches at Yferten, on being liberated by the French, returned voluntarily to Berne, in order to aid in the defence of the city. A rare trait, in those times, of ancient Swiss fidelity.

to retrace his steps. In Berne, the French meanwhile pillaged the treasures of the republic.[1] Besides the treasury and the arsenal, estimated at twenty-nine million livres, they levied a contribution of sixteen million. Brune planted a tree of liberty, and Frisching, the president of the provisional government, had the folly to say, "Here it stands! may it bear good fruit! Amen!"

Further bloodshed was prevented by the intervention of the patriots. The whole of Switzerland, Schwyz, Upper Valais, and Unterwalden alone excepted, submitted, and, on the 12th of April, the federal diet at Aarau established, in the stead of the ancient federative and oligarchical government, a single and indivisible Helvetian republic, in a strictly democratic form, with five directors, on the French model. Four new cantons, Aargau, Leman (Vaud), the Bernese Oberland, and Constance, were annexed to the ancient ones. Schwyz, Uri, Unterwalden, and Zug were, on the other hand, to form but one canton. Rapinat, a bold bad man, Rewbel's brother-in-law, who was at that time absolute in Switzerland, seized everything that had escaped the pillage of the soldiery in Berne and Zurich, sacked Solothurn, Lucerne, Freiburg, etc., and hunted out the hidden treasures of the confederation, which he sent to France. The protestations of the directors, Bay and Pfyffer, were unheeded; Rapinat deposed them by virtue of a French warrant and nominated Ochs and Dolder in their stead. The patriotic feelings of the Swiss revolted at this tyranny; Schwyz rose in open insurrection; the peasantry, headed by Aloys Reding, seized and garrisoned Lucerne and called the whole country to arms against the French invader. The peasantry of the free cantons also marched against Aarau, but were defeated by Schauenburg at Häcklingen; two hundred of their number fell, among others a priest bearing the colors. Schauenburg then attacked the people of Schwyz at

---

[1] A good deal of it was spent by Bonaparte during his expedition into Egypt, and, even at the present day, the Bernese bear is to be seen on coins still in circulation on the banks of the Nile.—*Meyer von Knonau.*

Richtenschwyl, where, after a desperate combat that lasted a whole day, he at length compelled them to give way. They, nevertheless, speedily rallied, and two engagements of equal obstinacy took place on the Schindeleggy and on the mountain of Etzel. The flight of Herzog, the pastor of Einsiedeln, was the sole cause of the discomfiture of the Swiss. Reding, however, reassembling his forces at the Red Tower, in the vicinity of the old battlefield of Morgarten, the French, unable to withstand their fury, were repulsed with immense loss. They also suffered a second defeat at Arth, at the foot of the Rigi. The Swiss, on their part, on numbering their forces after the battle, found their strength so terribly reduced that, although victors, they were unable to continue the contest, and voluntarily recognized the Helvetian republic. The rich monastery of Einsiedeln was plundered and burned; the miraculous picture of the Virgin was, however, preserved. Upper Valais also submitted, after Sion and the whole of the valley had been plundered and laid waste. The peasantry defended themselves here for several weeks at the precipice of the Dala. Unterwalden offered the most obstinate resistance. The peasantry of this canton were headed by Lüssi. The French invaded the country simultaneously on different sides, by water, across the lake of the four cantons, and across the Brünig from the Haslithal; in the Kernwald they were victorious over the masses of peasantry, but a body of three or four thousand French, which had penetrated further down the vale, was picked off by the peasantry concealed in the woods and behind the rocks. A rifleman, stationed upon a projecting rock, shot more than a hundred of the enemy one after another, his wife and children, meanwhile, loading his guns. Both of the French corps coalesced at Stanz, but met with such obstinate resistance from the old men, women and girls left there, that, after butchering four hundred of them, they set the place in flames.[1] The sturdy mountaineers, al-

[1] The venerable Pestalozzi assembled the orphans and founded his celebrated model academy at Stanz. Seventy-nine women and girls were found among

though numerically weak, proved themselves worthy of their ancient fame.—The four Waldstätte were thrown into one canton, Waldstätten; Glarus and Toggenburg into another, Linth; Appenzell and St. Gall into that of Säntis. The old Italian prefectures, with the exception of the Valtelline, were formed into two cantons, Lugano and Bellinzona (afterward the canton of Tessin). The canton of Vaud also finally acceded to this arrangement, but was shortly afterward, as well as the former bishopric of Basel, Pruntrut,[1] and the city and republic of Genoa, incorporated with France.

The levy of eighteen thousand men (the Helvetlers, Galloschwyzers or eighteen batzmen) for the service of the Helvetian republic occasioned fresh disturbances in the beginning of 1799. The opposition was so great that the recruits were carried in chains to Berne. The Bernese Oberland, the peasantry of Basel, Solothurn, Toggenburg, Appenzell, and Glarus rose in open insurrection, but were again reduced to submission by the military. The spirit of the mountaineers was, however, less easily tamed. In April, 1799, the people of Schwyz took four hundred French prisoners; those of Uri, under their leader, Vincenz Schmid, stormed and burned Altorf, the seat of the French and their adherents; those of Valais, under the youthful Count Courten, drove the French from their valleys, and those of the Grisons surprised and cut to pieces a French squadron at Dissentis. General Soult took the field with a strong force against them in May and reduced them one after the other, but with great loss on his side, to submission. Twelve hundred French fell in Valais, which was completely laid waste by fire and sword; in Uri, stones and rocks were hurled upon them by the infuriated peasantry as they defiled through the narrow gorges; Schmid was, however, taken and shot;

---

the slain. A story is told of a girl who, being attacked, in a lonely house, by two Frenchmen, knocked their heads together with such force that they dropped down dead.

[1] Not far from Pruntrut is the hill of Terri, said to have been formerly occupied by one of Cæsar's camps. The French named it *Mont Terrible* and created a *department du Mont Terrible.* Vide Meyer von Knonau's Geography.

Schwyz was also reduced to obedience; in the Grisons, upward of a thousand French fell in a bloody engagement at Coire, and the magnificent monastery of Dissentis was, in revenge, burned to the ground. The beautiful Bergland was reduced to an indescribable state of misery. The villages lay in ashes; the people, who had escaped the general massacre, fell victims to famine. In this extremity, Zschokke, at that time Helvetic governor of the Waldstätte, proposed the complete expulsion of the ancient inhabitants and the settlement of French colonists in the fatherland of William Tell.[1]

The imperial free town of Muhlhausen in the Suntgau, the ancient ally of Switzerland, fell, like her, into the hands of the French. Unable to preserve her independence, she committed a singular political suicide. The whole of the town property was divided among the citizens. A girl, attired in the ancient Swiss costume, delivered the town keys to the French commissioner; the city banner and arms were buried with great solemnity.[2]

The French had also shown as little lenity in their treatment of Italy. Rome was entered and garrisoned with French troops; the handsome and now venerable puppet, Pope Pius VI., was seized, robbed, and personally maltreated (his ring was even torn from his hand), and dragged a prisoner to France, where he expired in the August of 1799.

---

[1] In his "Political Remarks touching the Canton of Waldstätten," dated the 23d of June, 1799, he says: "Let us imitate the political maxims of the conquerors of old, who drove the inhabitants most inimical to them into foreign countries and established colonies, composed of families of their own kin, in the heart of the conquered provinces." His proposal remaining unseconded, he sought to obliterate the bad impression it had made, by publishing a proclamation, calling upon the charitably inclined to raise a subscription for the unfortunate inhabitants of the Waldstätte.

[2] Vide Graf's History of Mühlhausen.

CCLII. *The Second Coalition*

PRUSSIA looked calmly on, with a view of increasing her power by peace while other states ruined themselves by war, and of offering her arbitration at a moment when she could turn their mutual losses to advantage. Austria, exposed to immediate danger by the occupation of Switzerland by the French, remained less tranquil and hastily formed a fresh coalition with England and Russia. Catherine II. had expired, 1796. Her son, Paul I., cherished the most ambitious views. His election as grand-master of the Maltese order dispersed by Napoleon had furnished him with a sort of right of interference in the affairs of the Levant and of Italy. On the 1st of March, 1799, the Ionian Islands, Corfu, etc., were occupied by Russian troops, and a Russian army, under the terrible Suwarow, moved, in conjunction with the troops of Austria, upon Italy. The project of the Russian czar was, by securing his footing on the Mediterranean and at the same time encircling Turkey, to attack Constantinople on both sides, on the earliest opportunity. Austria was merely to serve as a blind tool for the attainment of his schemes. Mack was despatched to Naples for the purpose of bringing about a general rising in Southern Italy against the French, and England lavished gold. The absence of Bonaparte probably inspired several of the allied generals with greater courage, not the French, but he, being the object of their dread. The conduct of the French at Rastadt had revolted every German and had justly raised their most implacable hatred, which burst forth during a popular tumult at Vienna, when the tricolor, floating from the palace of General Bernadotte, the French ambassador, was torn down and burned. The infamous assassination of the French ambassadors at Rastadt also took place during this agitated period. Bonnier, Roberjot, and Jean de Bry quitted Rastadt on the breaking out of war, and were attacked and cut to pieces by some Austrian hussars in a wood close to the city gate. Jean de Bry alone escaped, although dangerously wounded, with his life. This atrocious act was generally believed to have been committed through private revenge, or, what is far more probable, for the purpose of discovering by the papers of the ambassadors the truth of the reports at that time in circulation concerning the existence of a conspiracy and projects for the establishment of republics throughout Germany. The real motive was, however, not long ago,[1] unveiled. Austria had revived her ancient projects against Bavaria, and, as early as 1798, had treated with the French Directory for the possession of that electorate in return for her toleration of the occupation of Switzerland by the troops of the republic. The venerable elector, Charles Theodore, who had been already persuaded to cede Bavaria and to content himself with Franconia, dying suddenly of apoplexy while at the card-table, was succeeded by his cousin, Maximilian Joseph of Pfalz-Zweibrucken, from whom, on account of his numerous family, no voluntary cession was to be expected either for the present or future. Thugut and Lehrbach, the rulers of the Viennese cabinet, in the hope of compromising and excluding him, as a traitor to the empire, from the Bavarian succession, by the production of proofs of his being the secret ally of France, hastily resolved upon the assassination of the French ambassadors at Rastadt, on the bare supposition of their having in their possession documents in the handwriting of the elector. None were, however, discovered, the French envoys having either taken the precaution of destroying them or of committing them to the safe-keeping of the Prussian ambassador. This crime was, as Hormayr observes, at the same time, a political blunder. This horrible act was perpetrated on the 28th of April, 1799.

The campaign had, a month anterior to this event, been opened by the French, who had attacked the Austrians in

---

[1] Scenes during the War of Liberation.

their still scattered positions. Disunion prevailed as usual in the Austrian military council. The Archduke Charles proposed the invasion of France from the side of Swabia. The occupation of Switzerland by the troops of Austria was, nevertheless, resolved upon, and General Auffenberg, accordingly, entered the Grisons. The French instantly perceived and hastened to anticipate the designs of the Austrian cabinet. Auffenberg was defeated by Massena on the St. Luciensteig and expelled the Grisons, while Hotze on the Vorarlberg and Bellegarde in the Tyrol looked calmly on at the head of fifteen thousand men. The simultaneous invasion of Swabia by Jourdan now induced the military council at Vienna to accede to the proposal formerly made by the Archduke Charles, who was despatched with the main body of the army to Swabia, where, on the 25th of March, 1799, he gained a complete victory over Jourdan at Ostrach and Stockach.[1] The Grisons were retaken in May by Hotze, and, in June, the archduke joining him, Massena was defeated at Zurich, and the steep passes of Mont St. Gothard were occupied by Haddik. Massena was, however, notwithstanding the immense numerical superiority of the archduke's forces, which could easily have driven him far into France, allowed to remain undisturbed at Bremgarten. The French, under Scherer, in Italy, had, meanwhile, been defeated, in April, by Kray, at Magnano. This success was followed by the arrival of Melas from Vienna, of Bellegarde from the Tyrol, and lastly, by that of the Russian vanguard under Suwarow, who took the chief command and beat the whole of the French forces in Italy; Moreau, at Cassano and Marengo, in May; Macdonald, on his advance from Lower Italy, on the Trebbia, in June; and finally, Joubert, in the great battle of Novi, in which Joubert was killed, August the 15th, 1799. Dissensions now broke out among the victors. A fourth of the forces in Italy belonged to Aus-

---

[1] Jourdan might easily have been annihilated during his retreat by the imperial cavalry, twenty-seven thousand strong, had his strength and position been better known to his pursuers.

tria, merely one-fifth to Russia; the Austrians, consequently, imagined that the war was merely carried on on their account. The Austrian forces were, against Suwarow's advice, divided, for the purpose of reducing Mantua and Alessandria and of occupying Tuscany. The king of Sardinia, whom Suwarow desired to restore to his throne, was forbidden to enter his states by the Austrians, who intended to retain possession of them for some time longer. The whole of Italy, as far as Ancona and Genoa, was now freed from the French, whom the Italians, imbittered by their predatory habits, had aided to expel, and Suwarow received orders to join his forces with those under Korsakow, who was then on the Upper Rhine with thirty thousand men. The archduke might, even without this fresh reinforcement, have already annihilated Massena had he not remained during three months, from June to August, in a state of complete inactivity; at the very moment of Suwarow's expected arrival he allowed the important passes of the St. Gothard to be again carried by a coup de main by the French under General Lecourbe, who drove the Austrians from the Simplon, the Furca, the Grimsel, and the Devil's bridge. The archduke, after an unsuccessful attempt to push across the Aar at Dettingen, suddenly quitted the scene of war and advanced down the Rhine for the purpose of supporting the English expedition under the Duke of York against Holland. This unexpected turn in affairs proceeded from Vienna. The Viennese cabinet was jealous of Russia. Suwarow played the master in Italy, favored Sardinia at the expense of the house of Habsburg, and deprived the Austrians of the laurels and of the advantages they had won. The archduke, accordingly, received orders to remain inactive, to abandon the Russians, and finally to withdraw to the north; by this movement Suwarow's triumphant progress was checked, he was compelled to cross the Alps to the aid of Korsakow, and to involve himself in a mountain warfare ill-suited to the habits of his soldiery.[1] Korsakow, whom Bavaria had been

[1] Scenes during the War of Liberation.

bribed with Russian gold to furnish with a corps one thousand strong, was solely supported by Kray and Hotze with twenty thousand men. Massena, taking advantage of the departure of the archduke and the non-arrival of Suwarow, crossed the Limmat at Dietikon and shut Korsakow, who had imprudently stationed himself with his whole army in Zurich, so closely in, that, after an engagement that lasted two days, from the 15th to the 17th of September, the Russian general was compelled to abandon his artillery and to force his way through the enemy. Ten thousand men were all that escaped.[1] Hotze, who had advanced from the Grisons to Schwyz to Suwarow's rencounter, was, at the same time, defeated and killed at Schännis. Suwarow, although aware that the road across the St. Gothard was blocked by the lake of the four cantons, on which there were no boats, had the folly to attempt the passage. In Airolo, he was obstinately opposed by the French under Lecourbe, and, although Schweikowski contrived to turn this strong position by scaling the pathless rocks, numbers of the men were, owing to Suwarow's impatience, sacrificed before it. On the 24th of September, 1799, he at length climbed the St. Gothard, and a bloody engagement, in which the French were worsted, took place on the Oberalpsee. Lecourbe blew up the Devil's bridge, but, leaving the Urnerloch open, the Russians pushed through that rocky gorge, and, dashing through the foaming Reuss, scaled the opposite rocks and drove the French from their position behind the Devil's bridge. Altorf on the lake was reached in safety by the Russian general, who was compelled, owing to the want of boats, to seek his way through the valleys of Shächen and Muotta, across the almost impassable rocks, to Schwyz. The heavy rains rendered the undertaking still more arduous; the Russians, owing to the badness of the road, speed-

---

[1] The celebrated Lavater was, on this occasion, mortally wounded by a French soldier. The people of Zurich were heavily mulcted by Massena for having aided the Austrians to the utmost in their power. Zschokke, who was at that time in the pay of France, wrote against the "Imperialism" of the Swiss. Vide Haller and Landolt's Life by Hess.

ily became barefoot; the provisions were also exhausted. In this wretched state they reached Muotta on the 29th of September and learned the discouraging news of Korsakow's defeat. Massena had already set off in the hope of cutting off Suwarow, but had missed his way. He reached Altorf, where he joined Lecourbe on the 29th, when Suwarow was already at Muotta, whence Massena found on his arrival he had again retired across the Bragelberg, through the Klonthal. He was opposed on the lake of Klonthal by Molitor, who was, however, forced to retire by Auffenberg, who had joined Suwarow at Altorf and formed his advanced guard, Rosen, at the same time, beating off Massena with the rearguard, taking five cannons and one thousand of his men prisoners. On the 1st of October, Suwarow entered Glarus, where he rested until the 4th, when he crossed the Panixer mountains through snow two feet deep to the valley of the Rhine, which he reached on the 10th, after losing the whole of his beasts of burden and two hundred of his men down the precipices; and here ended his extraordinary march, which had cost him the whole of his artillery, almost all his horses, and a third of his men.

The archduke had, meanwhile, tarried on the Rhine, where he had taken Philippsburg and Mannheim, but had been unable to prevent the defeat of the English expedition under the Duke of York by General Brune at Bergen, on the 19th of September. The archduke now, for the first time, made a retrograde movement, and approached Korsakow and Suwarow. The different leaders, however, merely reproached each other, and the czar, perceiving his project frustrated, suddenly recalled his troops and the campaign came to a close. The archduke's rearguard was defeated in a succession of petty skirmishes at Heidelberg and on the Neckar by the French, who again pressed forward.[1] These

---

[1] Concerning the wretched provision for the Austrian army, the embezzlement of the supplies, the bad management of the magazines and hospitals, see "Representation of the Causes of the Disasters suffered by the Austrians," etc. 1802.

disasters were counterbalanced by the splendid victory gained by Melas in Italy, at Savigliano, over Championnet, who attempted to save Genoa.

Austria was no sooner deprived in Suwarow of the most efficient of her allies than she was attacked by her most dangerous foe. Bonaparte returned from Egypt. The news of the great disasters of the French in Italy no sooner arrived, than he abandoned his army and hastened, completely unattended, to France, through the midst of the English fleet, then stationed in the Mediterranean. His arrival in Paris was instantly followed by his public nomination as generalissimo. He alone had the power of restoring victory to the standard of the republic. The ill success of his rivals had greatly increased his popularity; he had become indispensable to his countrymen. His power was alone obnoxious to the weak government, which, aided by the soldiery, he dissolved on the 9th of November (the 18th Brumaire, by the modern French calendar); he then bestowed a new constitution upon France and placed himself, under the title of First Consul, at the head of the republic.

In the following year, 1800, Bonaparte made preparations for a fresh campaign against Austria, under circumstances similar to those of the first. But this time he was more rapid in his movements and performed more astonishing feats. Suddenly crossing the St. Bernard, he fell upon the Austrian flank. Genoa, garrisoned by Massena, had just been forced by famine to capitulate. Ten days afterward, on the 14th of June, Bonaparte gained such a decisive victory over Melas, the Austrian general, at Marengo,[1] that he and the remainder of his army capitulated on the ensuing day. The whole of Italy fell once more into the hands of the French. Moreau had, at the same time, invaded Ger-

---

[1] The contest lasted the whole day: the French already gave way on every side, when Desaix led the French centre with such fury to the charge that the Austrians, surprised by the suddenness of the movement, were driven back and thrown into confusion, and the French, rallying at that moment, made another furious onset and tore the victory from their grasp.

many and defeated the Austrians under Kray in several engagements, principally at Stockach and Moskirch,[1] and again at Biberach and Hochstädt, laid Swabia and Bavaria under contribution, and taken Ratisbon, the seat of the diet. An armistice, negotiated by Kray, was not recognized by the emperor, and he was replaced in his command by the Archduke John (not Charles), who was, on the 3d of December, totally routed by Moreau's manœuvres during a violent snowstorm, at Hohenlinden. A second Austrian army, despatched into Italy, was also defeated by Brune on the Mincio. These disasters once more inclined Austria to peace, which was concluded at Luneville, on the 9th of February, 1801. The Archduke Charles seized this opportunity to propose the most beneficial reforms in the war administration, but was again treated with contempt. In the ensuing year, 1802, England also concluded peace at Amiens.

The whole of the left bank of the Rhine was, on this occasion, ceded to the French republic. The petty republics, formerly established by France in Italy, Switzerland, and Holland, were also renewed and were recognized by the allied powers. The Cisalpine republic was enlarged by the possessions of the grandduke of Tuscany and of the duke of Modena, to whom compensation in Germany was guaranteed. Suwarow's victories had, in the autumn of 1799, rendered a conclave, on the death of the captive pope, Pius VI., in France, possible, for the purpose of electing his successor, Pius VII., who was acknowledged as such by Bonaparte, whose favor he purchased by expressing his approbation of the seizure of the property of the church during the French Revolution, and by declaring his readiness to agree to the secularization of church property, already determined upon, in Germany.

---

[1] The impregnable fortress of Hohentwiel, formerly so gallantly defended by Widerhold, was surrendered without a blow by the cowardly commandant, Bilfinger. Rotenburg on the Tauber, on the contrary, wiped off the disgrace with which she had covered herself during the thirty years' war. A small French skirmishing party demanded a contribution from this city; the council yielded, but the citizens drove off the enemy with pitchforks.

The Helvetian Directory fell, like that of France, and was replaced by an administrative council, composed of seven members, in 1800. The upholders of ancient cantonal liberty, now known under the denomination of Federalists, gained the upper hand, and Aloys Reding, who had, shortly before, been denounced as a rebel, became Landammann of Switzerland. Bonaparte even invited him to Paris in order to settle with him the future fate of Switzerland. Reding, however, showing an unexpected degree of firmness, and unmoved by either promises or threats, obstinately refusing to permit the annexation of Valais to France, Bonaparte withdrew his support and again favored the Helvetlers. Dolder and Savari, who had long been the creatures of France, failing in their election, were seated by Verninac, the French ambassador, in the senate of the Helvetian republic, and Reding, who was at that moment absent, was divested of his office as Landammann. Reding protested against this arbitrary conduct and convoked a federal diet to Schwyz.

Andermatt, general of the Helvetian republic, attempted to seize Zurich, which had joined the federalists, but was compelled to withdraw, covered with disgrace. An army of federalists under General Bachmann repulsed the Helvetlers in every direction and drove them, together with the French envoys, across the frontier. Bonaparte, upon this, sent a body of thirty to forty thousand men, under Ney, into Switzerland, which met with no opposition, the federalists being desirous of avoiding useless bloodshed and being already acquainted with Bonaparte's secret projects. He would not tolerate opposition on their part, like that of Reding: he had resolved upon getting possession of Valais at any price, on account of the road across the Simplon, so important to him as affording the nearest communication between Paris and Milan: in all other points, he perfectly coincided with the federalists and was willing to grant its ancient independence to every canton in Switzerland, where disunion and petty feuds placed the country the more securely in his hands. With feigned commiseration for the ineptitude of the Swiss to settle their own disputes, he invited deputies belonging to the various factions and cantons to Paris, lectured them like schoolboys, and compelled them by the Act of Mediation, under his intervention, to give a new constitution to Switzerland. Valais was annexed to France in exchange for the Austrian Frickthal. Nineteen cantons were created.[1] Each canton again administered its internal affairs. Bonaparte was never weary of painting the happy lot of petty states and the delights of petty citizenship. "But ye are too weak, too helpless, to defend yourselves; cast yourselves therefore into the arms of France, ready to protect you while, free from taxation, and from the burdensome maintenance of an army, ye dwell free and independent in your native vales." The Swiss, although no longer to have a national army, were, nevertheless, compelled to furnish a contingent of eighteen thousand men to that of France, and, while deluded by the idea of their freedom from taxation, the fifteen millions of French *bons* given in exchange for the numerous Swiss loans were cashiered by Bonaparte, under pretext of the Swiss having been already sufficiently paid by their deliverance from their enemies by the French.[2] The real Swiss patriots implored the German powers to protect their country, the bulwark of Germany

---

[1] The ancient ones, Berne, Zurich, Basel, Solothurn, Freiburg, Lucerne, Schaffhausen; the re-established ones, Uri, Schwyz, Unterwalden, Zug, Glarus, Appenzell, St. Gall (instead of Waldstätten, Linth, and Säntis), Valais (instead of Leman), Aargau, Constance, Grisons, Tessin (instead of Lugano and Bellinzona). The Bernese Oberland again fell to Berne. The ambassador, attempting to preserve its independence, was asked by Napoleon: "Where do you take your cattle, your cheese, etc.?" "À Berne," was the reply. "Whence do you get your grain, cloth, iron, etc.?" "De Berne." "Well," continued Napoleon, "de Berne, à Berne, you consequently belong to Berne."—The Bernese were highly delighted at the restoration of their independence, and the re-erection of the ancient arms of Berne became a joyous fête. A gigantic black bear that was painted on the broad walls of the castle of Trachselwald was visible far down the valley.

[2] Murald, in his life of Reinhard, records an instance of shameless fraud, the attempt made during a farewell banquet at Paris to cozen the Swiss deputies out of a million. After plying them well with wine, an altered document was offered them for signature; Reinhard, the only one who perceived the fraud, frustrated the scheme.

against France; but Austria was too much weakened by her own losses, and Prussia handed the letters addressed to her from Switzerland over to the First Consul.

The melancholy business, commenced by the empire at the congress of Rastadt, and which had been broken off by the outbreak of the war, had now to be recommenced. Fresh compensations had been rendered necessary by the robberies committed upon the Italian princes. The church property no longer sufficed to satisfy all demands, and fresh seizures had become requisite. A committee of the diet was intrusted with the settlement of the question of compensation, which was decided on the 25th of February, 1803, by a decree of the imperial diet. All the great powers of Germany had not suffered; all had not, consequently, a right to demand compensation, but, in order to appease their jealousy, all were to receive a portion of the booty. The three spiritual electorates, Mayence, Treves, and Cologne, were abolished, their position on the other side of the Rhine including them within the French territory. The archbishop of Mayence alone retained his dignity, and was transferred to Ratisbon. The whole of the imperial free cities were moreover deprived of their privileges, six alone excepted, Lubeck, Hamburg,[1] Bremen, Frankfort, Augsburg, and Nuremberg. The unsecularized bishoprics and abbeys were abolished. The petty princes, counts and barons, and the Teutonic order, were still allowed to exist, in order ere long to be included in the general ruin.

Prussia retained the bishoprics of Hildesheim and Paderborn, a part of Munster, numerous abbeys and imperial free towns in Westphalia and Thuringia, more particularly Erfurt. Bavaria had ever suffered on the conclusion of peace between France and Austria; in 1797, she had ceded the Rhenish Pfalz to France and a province on the Inn to Austria; by the treaty of Luneville she had been, moreover,

---

[1] Hamburg was, however, compelled to pay to the French 1,700,000 marcs banco, and to allow Rumbold, the English agent, to be arrested by them within the city walls.

compelled to raze the fortress of Ingolstadt.[1] The inclination for French innovations displayed by the reigning duke, Maximilian Joseph, who surrounded himself with the old Illuminati, caused her, on this occasion, by Bonaparte's aid, to be richly compensated by the annexation of the bishoprics of Bamberg, Wurzburg, Augsburg, and Freisingen, with several small towns, etc.; all the monasteries were abolished. Bavaria had formerly supported the institutions of the ancient church of Rome more firmly than Austria, where reforms had already been begun in the church by Joseph II. Hanover received Osnabruck; Baden, the portion of the Pfalz on this side the Rhine, the greater part of the bishoprics of Constance, Basel, Strasburg, and Spires, also on this side the Rhine; Wurtemberg, both Hesses (Cassel and Darmstadt); and Nassau, all the lands in the vicinity formerly belonging to the bishopric of Mayence, to imperial free towns and petty lordships. Ferdinand, grandduke of Tuscany, younger brother to the emperor Francis II., was compelled to relinquish his hereditary possessions in Italy,[2] and received in exchange Salzburg, Eichstädt, and Passau. Ferdinand, duke of Modena, uncle to the emperor Francis II. and younger brother to the emperors Leopold II. and Joseph II., also resigned his duchy,[3] for which he received the Breisgau in exchange. William V., hereditary stadtholder of Holland, who had been expelled his states, also received, on this occasion, in compensation for his son of like name (he was himself already far advanced in years), the rich abbey of Fulda, which was created the principality of Orange-Fulda.[4]

---

[1] The university had been removed, in 1800, to Landshut.

[2] Bonaparte transformed them into a kingdom of Etruria, which he bestowed upon a Spanish prince, Louis of Parma, who shortly afterward died and his kingdom was annexed to France.

[3] He was son-in-law to Hercules, the last duke of Modena, who still lived, but had resigned his claims in his favor. This duke expired in 1805.

[4] Which he speedily lost by rejoining Napoleon's adversaries. Adalbert von Harstall, the last princely abbot of Fulda, was an extremely noble character; he is almost the only one among the princes who remained firmly by his subjects when all the rest fled and abandoned theirs to the French. After the edict of secularization he remained firmly at his post until compelled to resign it by the Prussian soldiery.

The electoral dignity was at the same time bestowed upon the Archduke Ferdinand, the Landgrave of Hesse-Cassel, the duke of Wurtemberg, and the Margrave of Baden.

Submission, although painful, produced no opposition. The power of the imperial free cities had long passed away,[1] and the spiritual princes no longer wielded the sword. The manner in which the officers of the princes took possession, the insolence with which they treated the subject people, the fraud and embezzlement that were openly practiced, are merely excusable on account of the fact that Germany was, notwithstanding the peace, still in a state of war. The decree of the imperial diet can scarcely be regarded as the ignominious close of a good old time, but rather as a violent but beneficial incisure in an old and rankling sore. With the petty states, a mass of vanity and pedantry disappeared on the one side, pusillanimity and servility on the other; the ideas of the subjects of a large state have naturally a wider range; the monasteries, those dens of superstition, the petty princely residences, those hotbeds of French vice and degeneracy, the imperial free towns, those abodes of petty burgher prejudice, no longer existed. The extension of the limits of the states rendered the gradual introduction of a better administration, the laying of roads, the foundation of public institutions of every description, and social improvement, possible. The example of France, the ever-renewed warfare, and the conscriptions, created, moreover, a martial spirit among the people, which, although far removed from patriotism, might still, when compared with the spirit for-

---

[1] The citizens of Esslingen were shortly before at law with their magistrate on account of his nepotism and tyranny without being able to get a decision from the supreme court of judicature.—Quedlinburg had also not long before sent envoys to Vienna with heavy complaints of the insolence of the magistrate, and the envoys had been sent home without a reply being vouchsafed and were threatened with the house of correction in case they ventured to return. Vide Hess's Flight through Germany, 1793.—Wimpfen also carried on a suit against its magistrate. In 1784, imperial decrees were issued against the aristocracy of Ulm. In 1786, the people of Aix-la-Chapelle rose against their magistrate. Nuremberg repeatedly demanded the production of the public accounts from the aristocratic town-council. The people of Hildesheim also revolted against their council. Vide Schlözer, State Archives.

merly pervading the imperial army, be regarded as a first step from effeminacy, cowardice, and sloth, toward true, unflinching, manly courage.

CCLIII. *Fall of the Holy Roman-Germanic Empire*

A GREAT change had, meanwhile, taken place in France. The republic existed merely in name. The first consul, Bonaparte, already possessed regal power. The world beheld with astonishment a nation that had so lately and so virulently persecuted royalty, so dearly bought and so strictly enforced its boasted liberty, suddenly forget its triumph and restore monarchy. Liberty had ceased to be in vogue, and had yielded to a general desire for the acquisition of fame. The equality enforced by liberty was offensive to individual vanity, and the love of gain and luxury opposed republican poverty. Fame and wealth were alone to be procured by war and conquest. France was to be enriched by the plunder of her neighbors. Bonaparte, moreover, promoted the prosperity and dignity of the country by the establishment of manufactures, public institutions, and excellent laws. The awe with which he inspired his subjects insured their obedience; he was universally feared and reverenced. In whatever age this extraordinary man had lived, he must have taken the lead and have reduced nations to submission. Even his adversaries, even those he most deeply injured, owned his influence. His presence converted the wisdom of the statesman, the knowledge of the most experienced general, into folly and ignorance; the bravest armies fled panic-struck before his eagles; the proudest sovereigns of Europe bowed their crowned heads before the little hat of the Corsican. He was long regarded as a new savior, sent to impart happiness to his people, and, as though by magic, bent the blind and pliant mass to his will. But philanthropy, Christian wisdom, the virtues of the Prince of peace, were not his. If he bestowed excellent laws upon his people, it was merely with the view of increasing the power of the state for military purposes. He was ever possessed and tormented by the demon of war.

On the 18th of May, 1804, Bonaparte abolished the French republic and was elected hereditary emperor of France. On the 2d of December, he was solemnly anointed and crowned by the pope, Pius VII., who visited Paris for that purpose. The ceremonies used at the coronation of Charlemagne were revived on this occasion. On the 15th of March, 1805, he abolished the Ligurian and Cisalpine republics, and set the ancient iron crown of Lombardy on his head, with his own hand, as king of Italy. He made a distinction between la France and l'empire, the latter of which was, by conquest, to be gradually extended over the whole of Europe, and to be raised by him above that of Germany, in the same manner that the western Roman-Germanic empire had formerly been raised by Charlemagne above the eastern Byzantine one.

The erection of France into an empire was viewed with distrust by Austria, whose displeasure had been, moreover, roused by the arbitrary conduct of Napoleon in Italy. Fresh disputes had also arisen between him and England; he had occupied the whole of Hanover, which Wallmoden's[1] army had been powerless to defend, with his troops, and violated the Baden territory by the seizure of the unfortunate Duc d'Enghien, a prince of the house of Bourbon, who was carried into France and there shot. Prussia offered no interference, in the hope of receiving Hanover in reward for her neutrality.[2] Austria, on her part, formed a third coalition

---

[1] He capitulated at Suhlingen on honorable terms, but was deceived by Mortier, the French general, and Napoleon took advantage of a clause not to recognize all the terms of capitulation. The Hanoverian troops, whom it was intended to force to an unconditional surrender to the French, sailed secretly and in separate divisions to England, where they were formed into the German Legion.

[2] England offered the Netherlands instead of Hanover to Prussia; to this Russia, however, refused to accede. Prussia listened to both sides, and acted with such duplicity that Austria was led, by the false hope of being seconded by her, to a too early declaration of war.—*Scenes during the War of Liberation.*

with England, Russia, and Sweden.[1] Austria acted, undeniably, on this occasion, with impolitic haste; she ought rather to have waited until Prussia and public opinion throughout Germany had been ranged on her side, as sooner or later must have been the case, by the brutal encroachments of Napoleon. Austria, unaided by Prussia, could scarcely dream of success.[2] But England, at that time fearful of Napoleon's landing on her coast, lavished her all-persuasive gold.

The Archduke Ferdinand was placed at the head of the Austrian troops in Germany; the Archduke Charles, of those in Italy. Ferdinand commanded the main body and was guided by Mack, who, without awaiting the arrival of the Russians, advanced as far as Ulm, pushed a corps, under Jellachich, forward to Lindau, and left the whole of his right flank exposed. He, nevertheless, looked upon Napoleon's defeat and the invasion of France by his troops as close at hand. He was in ill-health and highly irritable. Napoleon, in order to move with greater celerity, sent a part of his troops by carriage through Strasburg, declared to the Margrave of Baden, the duke of Wurtemberg, and the elector of Bavaria, his intention not to recognize them as neutral powers, that they must be either against him or with him, and made them such brilliant promises (they were, moreover, actuated by distrust of Austria), that they ranged themselves on his side. Napoleon instantly sent orders to General Bernadotte, who was at that time stationed in Hanover, to cross the neutral Prussian territory of Anspach,[3]

---

[1] Gustavus Adolphus IV. of Sweden, who had wedded a princess of Baden, was at Carlsruhe at the very moment that the Duc d'Enghien was seized as it were before his eyes. This circumstance and the ridicule heaped upon him by Napoleon, who mockingly termed him the Quixote of the North, roused his bitter hatred.

[2] Bulow wrote in his remarkable criticism upon this war: "The hot coalition party—that of the ladies—of the empress and the queen of Naples—removed Prince Charles from the army and called Mack from oblivion to daylight; Mack, whose name in the books of the prophets in the Hebrew tongue signifies defeat."

[3] Napoleon gained almost all his victories either by skilfully separating his opponents and defeating them singly with forces vastly superior in number, or by creeping round the concentrated forces of the enemy and placing them between two fires.

without demanding the permission of Prussia, to Mack's rear, in order to form a junction with the Bavarian troops. Other corps were at the same time directed by circuitous routes upon the flanks of the Austrian army, which was attacked at Memmingen by Soult, and was cut off to the north by Ney, who carried the bridge of Elchingen[1] by storm. Mack had drawn his troops together, but had, notwithstanding the entreaties of his generals, refused to attack the separate French corps before they could unite and surround him. The Archduke Ferdinand alone succeeded in fighting his way with a part of the cavalry through the enemy.[2] Mack lost his senses and capitulated on the 17th of October, 1805. With him fell sixty thousand Austrians, the elite of the army, into the hands of the enemy. Napoleon could scarcely spare a sufficient number of men to escort this enormous crowd of prisoners to France. Wernek's corps, which had already been cut off, was also compelled to yield itself prisoner at Trochtelfingen, not far from Heidenheim.

Napoleon, while following up his success with his customary rapidity and advancing with his main body straight upon Vienna, despatched Ney into the Tyrol, where the peasantry, headed by the Archduke John, made a heroic defence. The advanced guard of the French, composed of the Bavarians under Deroy, were defeated at the Strub pass, but, notwithstanding this disaster, Ney carried the Schaarnitz by storm and reached Innsbruck. The Archduke John was compelled to retire into Carinthia in order to form a junction with his brother Charles, who, after beating Massena at Caldiero, had been necessitated by Mack's defeat to hasten from Italy for the purpose of covering Austria. Two corps, left in the hurry of retreat too far westward, were cut off and taken prisoner, that under Prince Rohan at

---

[1] Ney was, for this action, created Duke of Elchingen.

[2] Klein, the French general, also a German, allowed himself to be kept in conversation by Prince, afterward field-marshal Schwarzenberg, who had been sent to negotiate terms with him, until the Austrians had reached a place of safety.—*Prokesch, Schwarzenberg's Memorabilia.*

Castellfranco, after having found its way from Meran into the Venetian territory, and that under Jellachich on the Lake of Constance; Kinsky's and Wartenleben's cavalry threw themselves boldly into Swabia and Franconia, seized the couriers and convoys to the French rear, and escaped unhurt to Bohemia.

Davoust had, in the meanwhile, invaded Styria and defeated a corps under Meerveldt at Mariazell. In November, Napoleon had reached Vienna, neither Linz nor any other point having been fortified by the Austrians. The great Russian army under Kutusow appeared at this conjuncture in Moravia. The czar, Alexander I., accompanied it in person, and the emperor, Francis II., joined him with his remaining forces. A bloody engagement took place between Kutusow and the French at Durrenstein on the Danube, but, on the loss of Vienna, the Russians retired to Moravia. The sovereigns of Austria and Russia loudly called upon Prussia to renounce her alliance with France, and, in this decisive moment, to aid in the annihilation of a foe, for whose false friendship she would one day dearly pay. The violation of the Prussian territory by Bernadotte had furnished the Prussian king with a pretext for suddenly declaring against Napoleon. The Prussian army was also in full force. The British and the Hanoverian legion had landed at Bremen and twenty thousand Russians on Rugen; ten thousand Swedes entered Hanover; electoral Hesse was also ready for action. The king of Prussia, nevertheless, merely confined himself to threats, in the hope of selling his neutrality to Napoleon for Hanover, and deceived the coalition.[1] The emperor Alexander visited Berlin in person for the purpose of rousing Prussia to war, but had no sooner returned to Austria in order to rejoin his army than Count Haugwitz, the Prussian minister, was despatched to Napoleon's camp

[1] "Prussia made use of the offers made by England (and Russia) to stipulate terms with France exactly subversive of the object of the negotiations of England (and Russia)."—*The Manifest of England against Prussia. Allgemeine Zeitung, No. 132.*

with express instructions not to declare war. The famous battle, in which the three emperors of Christendom were present, took place, meanwhile, at Austerlitz, not far from Brunn, on the 2d of December, 1805, and terminated in one of Napoleon's most glorious victories.[1] This battle decided the policy of Prussia, and Haugwitz confirmed her alliance with France by a treaty, by which Prussia ceded Cleves, Anspach, and Neufchâtel to France in exchange for Hanover.[2] This treaty was published with a precipitation equalling that with which it had been concluded, and seven hundred Prussian vessels, whose captains were ignorant of the event, were seized by the enraged English either in British harbors or on the sea. The peace concluded by Austria, on

---

[1] On the 4th of December, Napoleon met the emperor Francis in the open street in the village of Nahedlowitz. That the impression made by the former upon the latter was far from favorable is proved by the emperor's observation, "Now that I have seen him, I shall never be able to endure him!" On the 5th of December, the Bavarians under Wrede were signally defeated at Iglau by the Archduke Ferdinand.

[2] "After the commission of such numerous mistakes, I must nevertheless praise the minister, Von Haugwitz, for having, in the first place, evaded a war unskilfully managed, and, in the second, for having annexed Hanover to Prussia, although its possession, it must be confessed, is somewhat precarious. Here, however, I hear it said that the commission of a robbery at another's suggestion is, in the first place, the deepest of degradations, and, in the second place, unparalleled in history."—*Von Bulow, The Campaign of 1805.* It has been asserted that Haugwitz had, prior to the battle of Austerlitz, been instructed to declare war against Napoleon in case the intervention of Prussia should be rejected by him. Still, had Haugwitz overstepped instructions of such immense importance, he would not immediately afterward, on the 12th of January, 1806, have received, as was actually the case, fresh instructions, in proof that he had in no degree abused the confidence of his sovereign. Haugwitz, by not declaring war, husbanded the strength of Prussia and gained Hanover; and, by so doing, he fulfilled his instructions, which were to gain Hanover without making any sacrifice. His success gained for him the applause of his sovereign, who intrusted him, on account of his skill as a diplomatist, with the management of other negotiations. Prussia at that time still pursued the system of the treaty of Basel, was unwilling to break with France, and was simply bent upon selling her neutrality to the best advantage. Instead, however, of being able to prescribe terms to Napoleon, she was compelled to accede to his. Napoleon said to Haugwitz, "Jamais on n'obtiendra de moi ce qui pourrait blesser ma gloire." Haugwitz had been instructed through the duke of Brunswick: "Pour le cas que vos soins pour rétablir la paix échouent, pour le cas où l'apparition de la Prusse sur le théâtre de la guerre soit jugée inévitable, mettez tous vos soins pour conserver à la Prusse l'épée dans le fourreau jusqu'au 22 Décembre, et s'il se peut jusqu'à un terme plus reculé encore."—*Extract from the Memoirs of the Count von Haugwitz.*

the 26th of December, at Presburg, was purchased by her at an enormous sacrifice. Napoleon had, in the opening of the campaign, when pressing onward toward Austria, compelled Charles Frederick, elector of Baden,[1] Frederick, elector of Wurtemberg, and Maximilian Joseph, elector of Bavaria (in whose mind the memory of the assassination of the ambassadors at Rastadt, the loss of Wasserburg, the demolition of Ingolstadt, etc., still rankled), to enter into his alliance; to which they remained zealously true on account of the immense private advantages thereby gained by them, and of the dread of being deprived by the haughty victor of the whole of their possessions on the first symptom of opposition on their part. Napoleon, with a view of binding them still more closely to his interests by motives of gratitude, gave them on the present occasion an ample share in the booty. Bavaria was erected into a kingdom,[2] and received, from Prussia, Anspach and Baireuth; from Austria, the whole of the Tyrol, Vorarlberg and Lindau, the Margraviate of Burgau, the dioceses of Passau, Eichstädt, Trent, and Brixen, besides several petty lordships. Wurtemberg was raised to a monarchy and enriched with the bordering Austrian lordships in Swabia. Baden was rewarded with the Breisgau, the Ortenau, Constance, and the title of grandduke. Venice was included by Napoleon in his kingdom of Italy, and, for all these losses, Austria was merely indemnified by the possession of Salzburg. Ferdinand, elector of Salzburg, the former grandduke of Tuscany, was transferred to Wurzburg. Ferdinand of Modena lost the whole of his possessions.

The imperial crown, so well maintained by Napoleon, now shone with redoubled lustre. The petty republics and

---

[1] He married a Mademoiselle von Geyer. His children had merely the title of Counts von Hochberg, but came, in 1830, on the extinction of the Agnati, to the government.

[2] On the 1st of January, 1806; the Bavarian state newspaper announced it at New Year with the words, "Long live Napoleon, the restorer of the kingdom of Bavaria!" Bavarian authors, more particularly Pallhausen, attempted to prove that the Bavarians had originally been a Gallic tribe under the Gallic kings. It was considered a dishonor to belong to Germany.

the provinces dependent upon the French empire were erected into kingdoms and principalities and bestowed upon his relatives and favorites. His brother Joseph was created king of Naples; his brother Louis, king of Holland; his stepson Eugene Beauharnais, viceroy of Italy; his brother-in-law Murat, formerly a common horse-soldier, now his best general of cavalry, grandduke of Berg; his first adjutant, Berthier, prince of Neufchâtel; his uncle, Cardinal Fesch, was nominated successor to the elector of Mayence, then resident at Ratisbon. In order to remove the stigma attached to him as a parvenu, Napoleon also began to form matrimonial alliances between his family and the most ancient houses of Europe. His handsome stepson, Eugene, married the Princess Augusta, daughter to the king of Bavaria; his brother Jerome, Catherine, daughter to the king of Wurtemberg; and his niece, Stephanie, Charles, hereditary prince of Baden. All the new princes were vassals of the emperor Napoleon, and, by a family decree, subject to his supremacy. All belonged to the great empire. Switzerland was also included, and but one step more was wanting to complete the incorporation of half the German empire with that of France.

On the 12th of July, 1806, sixteen princes of Western Germany concluded, under Napoleon's direction, a treaty, according to which they separated themselves from the German empire and founded the so-called Rhenish Alliance, which it was their intention to render subject to the supremacy of the emperor of the French.[1] On the 1st of August,

[1] In 1797, the anonymous statesman, in the dedication "to the congress of Rastadt," foretold the formation of the Rhenish alliance as a necessary result of the treaty of Basel. "The electors of Brandenburg, Hanover, Hesse-Cassel, and all the princes, who defended themselves behind the line of demarcation against their obligations to the empire, and tranquilly awaited the issue of the contest between France and that part of the empire that had taken up arms; all those princes to whom their private interests were dearer than those of the empire, who, devoid of patriotism, formed a separate party against Austria and Southern Germany, from which they severed and isolated themselves, could, none of them, arrogate to themselves a voice in the matter, if Southern Germany, abandoned by them, concluded treaties for herself as her present and future interests demanded."

Napoleon declared that he no longer recognized the empire of Germany! No one ventured to oppose his omnipotent voice. On the 6th of August, 1806, the emperor, Francis II., abdicated the imperial crown of Germany and announced the dissolution of the empire in a touching address, full of calm dignity and sorrow. The last of the German emperors had shown himself, throughout the contest, worthy of his great ancestors, and had, almost alone, sacrificed all in order to preserve the honor of Germany, until abandoned by the greater part of the German princes, he was compelled to yield to a power superior to his. The fall of the empire that had stood the storms of a thousand years, was, however, not without dignity. A meaner hand might have levelled the decayed fabric with the dust, but fate, that seemed to honor even the faded majesty of the ancient Cæsars, selected Napoleon as the executioner of her decrees. The standard of Charlemagne, the greatest hero of the first Christian age, was to be profaned by no hand save that of the greatest hero of modern times.

Ancient names, long venerated, now disappeared. The holy Roman-German emperor was converted into an emperor of Austria, the electors into kings or granddukes, all of whom enjoyed unlimited sovereign power and were free from subjection to the supremacy of the emperor. Every bond of union was dissolved with the diet of the empire and with the imperial chamber. The barons and counts of the empire and the petty princes were mediatized; the princes of Hohenlohe, Oettingen, Schwarzenberg, Thurn and Taxis, the Truchsess von Waldburg, Furstenberg, Fugger, Leiningen, Lowenstein, Solms, Hesse-Homburg, Wied-Runkel, and Orange-Fulda became subject to the neighboring Rhenish confederated princes. Of the remaining six imperial free cities, Augsburg and Nuremberg fell to Bavaria; Frankfort, under the title of grandduchy, to the ancient elector of Mayence, who was again transferred thither from Ratisbon. The ancient Hanse towns, Hamburg, Lubeck and Bremen, alone retained their freedom.

The Rhenish confederation now began its wretched existence. It was established on the basis of the Helvetian republic. The sixteen confederated princes were to be completely independent, and to exercise sovereign power over the internal affairs of their states, like the Swiss cantons, but were, in all foreign affairs, dependent upon Napoleon as their protector.[1] The whole Rhenish confederation became a part of the French empire. The federal assembly was to sit at Frankfort, and Dalberg, the former elector of Mayence, now grandduke of Frankfort, was nominated by Napoleon, under the title of Prince Primate, president. Napoleon's uncle, and afterward his stepson, Eugene Beauharnais, were his destined successors, by which means the control was placed entirely in the hands of France. To this confederation there belonged two kings, those of Bavaria and Wurtemberg, five grandukes, those of Frankfort, Wurzburg, Baden, Darmstadt, and Berg, and ten princes, two of Nassau, two of Hohenzollern, two of Salm, besides those of Aremberg, Isenburg, Lichtenstein and Leyen. Every trace of the ancient free constitution of Germany, her provincial Estates, was studiously annihilated. The Wurtemberg Estates, with a spirit worthy of their ancient fame, alone made an energetic protest, by which they merely succeeded in saving their honor, the king, Frederick, dissolving them by force and closing their chamber.[2] An ab-

---

[1] "Oldenburg affords a glaring proof of the insecurity and meanness characteristic of the Rhenish alliance. The relation even with Bavaria was not always the purest, and I have sometimes caught a near glimpse of the claws."—*Gagern's Share in Politics.*

[2] No diet had, since 1770, been held in Würtemberg, only the committee had continued to treat secretly with the duke. In 1797, Frederick convoked a fresh diet and swore to hold the constitution sacred. Some modern elements appeared in this diet; the old opposition was strengthened by men of the French school. Disputes, consequently, ere long arose between it and the duke, a man of an extremely arbitrary disposition. The Estates discovered little zeal for the war with France, attempted to economize in the preparations, etc., while the duke made great show of patriotism as a prince of the German empire, nor gave the slightest symptom of his one day becoming an enemy to his country, a member of the Rhenish alliance, and the most zealous partisan of France. Moreau, however, no sooner crossed the Rhine than the duke fled, abandoned his states, and afterward not only refused to bear the smallest share of the contributions levied

solute, despotic form of government, similar to that existing in France under Napoleon, was established in all the confederated states. The murder of the unfortunate bookseller, Palm of Nuremberg, who was, on the 25th of August, 1806, shot by Napoleon's order, at Braunau, for nobly refusing to give up the author of a patriotic work published by him, directed against the rule of France, and entitled, "Germany in her deepest Degradation," furnished convincing proof, were any wanting, of Napoleon's supremacy.

CCLIV. *Prussia's Declaration of War and Defeat*

PRUSSIA, by a timely declaration of war against France before the battle of Austerlitz, might have turned the tide against Napoleon, and earned for herself the glory and the gain, instead of being, by a false policy, compelled, at a later period, to make that declaration under circumstances of extreme disadvantage. Her maritime commerce suffered extreme injury from the attacks of the English and Swedes. War was unavoidable, either for or against France. The decision was replete with difficulty. Prussia, by continuing to side with France, was exposed to the attacks of England, Sweden, and probably Russia; it was, moreover, to be feared that Napoleon, who had more in view the diminution of the power of Prussia than that of Austria, might delay his aid. During the late campaign, the Prussian territory had been violated and the fortress of Wesel seized by Napoleon, who had also promised the restoration of Hanover to England as a condition of peace. He had invited Prussia to found, be-

---

upon the country by the French, but also seized the subsidies furnished by England. The duke, shortly after this, quarrelling with his eldest son, William, the Estates sided with the latter and supplied him with funds, at the same time refusing to grant any of the sums demanded by the duke, who, on his part, omitted the confirmation of the new committee and ordered Grosz, the councillor, Stockmaier, the secretary of the diet, and several others, besides Batz, the agent of the diet at Vienna, to be placed under arrest, their papers to be seized, and a sum of money to be raised from the church property, 1805. Not long after this, rendered insolent by the protection of the great despot of France, he utterly annihilated the ancient constitution of Würtemberg.

sides the Rhenish, a northern confederation, and had, at the same time, bribed Saxony with a promise of the royal dignity, and Hesse with that of the annexation of Fulda, not to enter into alliance with Prussia. Prussia saw herself scorned and betrayed by France. A declaration of war with France was, however, surrounded with tenfold danger. The power of France, unweakened by opposition, had reached an almost irresistible height. Austria, abandoned in every former campaign and hurried to ruin by Prussia, could no longer be reckoned on for aid. The whole of Germany, once in favor of Prussia, now sided with the foe. Honor at length decided. Prussia could no longer endure the scorn of the insolent Frenchman, his desecration of the memory of the great Frederick, or, with an army impatient for action, tamely submit to the insults of both friend and foe. The presence of the Russian czar, Alexander, at Berlin, his visit to the tomb of Frederick the Great, rendered still more popular by an engraving, had a powerful effect upon public opinion. Louisa, the beautiful queen of Prussia and princess of Mecklenburg, animated the people with her words and roused a spirit of chivalry in the army, which still deemed itself invincible. The younger officers were not sparing of their vaunts, and Prince Louis vented his passion by breaking the windows of the minister Haugwitz. John Muller, who, on the overthrow of Austria, had quitted Vienna and had been appointed Prussian historiographer at Berlin, called upon the people, in the preface to the "Trumpet of the Holy War," to take up arms against France.

War was indeed declared, but with too great precipitation. Instead of awaiting the arrival of the troops promised by Russia or until Austria had been gained, instead of manning the fortresses and taking precautionary measures, the Prussian army, in conjunction with that of Saxony, which lent but compulsory aid, and with those of Mecklenburg and Brunswick, its voluntary allies, took the field without any settled plan, and suddenly remained stationary in the Thuringian forest, like Mack two years earlier at Ulm, waiting for the appearance of Napoleon, 1806. The king and the queen accompanied the army, which was commanded by Ferdinand, duke of Brunswick, a veteran of seventy-two, and by his subordinate in command, Frederick Louis, prince of Hohenlohe-Ingelfingen, who constantly opposed his measures. In the general staff the chief part was enacted by Colonel Massenbach, a second Mack, whose counsels were rarely followed. All the higher officers in the army were old men, promotion depending not upon merit but upon length of service. The younger officers were radically bad, owing to their airs of nobility and licentious garrison life; their manners and principles were equally vulgar. Women, horses, dogs, and gambling formed the staple of their conversation; they despised all solid learning, and, when decorated on parade, in their enormous cocked hats and plumes, powdered wigs and queues, tight leather breeches and great boots, they swore at and cudgelled the men, and strutted about with conscious heroism. The arms used by the soldiery were heavy and apt to hang fire, their tight uniform was inconvenient for action and useless as a protection against the weather, and their food, bad of its kind, was stinted by the avarice of the colonels, which was carried to such an extent that soldiers were to be seen, who, instead of a waistcoat, had a small bit of cloth sewn on to the lower part of the uniform where the waistcoat was usually visible. Worst of all, however, was the bad spirit that pervaded the army, the enervation consequent upon immorality. Even before the opening of the war, Lieutenant Henry von Bulow, a retired officer, the greatest military genius at that period in Germany, and, on that account, misunderstood, foretold the inevitable defeat of Prussia, and, although far from being a devotee, declared, "The cause of the national ignorance lies chiefly in the atheism and demoralization produced by the government of Frederick II. The enlightenment, so highly praised in the Prussian states, simply consists in a loss of energy and power."

The main body of the Prussian army was stationed around

Weimar and Jena, a small corps under General Tauenzien was pushed forward to cover the rich magazines at Hof, and a reserve of seventeen thousand men under Eugene, duke of Wurtemberg, lay to the rear at Halle. It was remarked that this position, in case of an attack being made by Napoleon, was extremely dangerous, the only alternatives left for the Prussian army being either to advance, form a junction with the gallant Hessians and render the Rhine the seat of war, or to fall back upon the reserve and hazard a decisive battle on the plains of Leipzig. That intriguing impostor, Lucchesini, the oracle of the camp, however, purposely declared that *he* knew Napoleon, that Napoleon would most certainly not attempt to make an attack. A few days afterward Napoleon, nevertheless, appeared, found the pass at Kosen open, cut off the Prussian army from the right bank of the Saal, from its magazines at Hof and Naumburg, which he also seized, from the reserve corps stationed at Halle, and from Prussia. Utterly astounded at the negligence of the duke of Brunswick, he exclaimed, while comparing him with Mack, "Les Prussiens sont encore plus stupides que les Autrichiens!" On being informed by some prisoners that the Prussians expected him from Erfurt when he was already at Naumberg, he said, "Ils se tromperont furieusement, ces perruques." He would, nevertheless, have been on his part exposed to great peril had the Prussians suddenly attacked him with their whole force from Weimar, Jena, and Halle, or had they instantly retired into Franconia and fallen upon his rear; but the idea never entered the heads of the Prussian generals, who tranquilly waited to be beaten by him one after the other.

After Tauenzien's repulse, a second corps under Prince Louis of Prussia, which had been pushed forward to Saalfeld, imprudently attempting to maintain its position in the narrow valley, was surrounded and cut to pieces. The prince refused to yield, and, after a furious defence, was killed by a French horse-soldier. The news of this disaster speedily reached the main body of the Prussians. The duke of Brunswick, at that time holding a military council in the castle of Weimar, so entirely lost his presence of mind as to ask in the hearing of several young officers, and with embarrassment depicted on his countenance, "What are we to do?" This veteran duke would with painful slowness write down in the neatest hand the names of the villages in which the various regiments were to be quartered, notwithstanding which, it sometimes happened that, owing to his topographical ignorance, several regiments belonging to different corps d'armee were billeted in the same village and had to dispute its possession. He would hesitate for an hour whether he ought to write the name of a village Munchenholzen or Munchholzen.

The Prussian army was compared to a ship with all sail spread lying at anchor. The duke was posted with the main body not far from Weimar, the Saxons at the Schnecke on the road between Weimar and Jena, the prince of Hohenlohe at Jena. Mack had isolated and exposed his different corps d'armee in an exactly similar manner at Ulm. Hohenlohe again subdivided his corps and scattered them in front of the concentrated forces of the enemy. Still, all was not yet lost, the Prussians being advantageously posted in the upper valley, while the French were advancing along the deep valleys of the Saal and its tributaries. But, on the 13th of October, Tauenzien retired from the vale, leaving the steeps of Jena, which a hundred students had been able to defend simply by rolling down the stones there piled in heaps, open, and, during the same night, Napoleon sent his artillery up and posted himself on the Landgrafenberg. There, nevertheless, still remained a chance; the Dornberg, by which the Landgrafenberg was commanded, was still occupied by Tauenzien, and the Windknollen, a still steeper ascent, whence Hohenlohe, had he not spent the night in undisturbed slumbers at Capellendorf, might have utterly annihilated the French army, remained unoccupied. The thunder of the French artillery first roused Hohenlohe from his couch, and, while he was still under the hands of his barber, Tauenzien was driven from the Dornberg. The duties of the toilet at length concluded, Hohenlohe led his troops up the hillside with a view of retaking the position he had so foolishly lost; but his serried columns were exposed to the destructive fire of a body of French tirailleurs posted above, and were repulsed with immense loss. General Ruchel arrived, with his corps that had been uselessly detached, too late to prevent the flight of the Hohenlohe corps, and, making a brave but senseless attack, was wounded and defeated. A similar fate befell the unfortunate Saxons at the Schnecke and the duke of Brunswick at Auerstädt. The latter, although at the head of the strongest division of the Prussian army, succumbed to the weakest division of the French army, that commanded by Davoust, who henceforward bore the title of duke of Auerstadt, and was so suddenly put to the rout that a body of twenty thousand Prussians under Kalkreuth never came into action. The duke was shot in both eyes. This incident was, by his enemies, termed fortune's revenge, "as he never would see when he had his eyes open."[1]

Napoleon followed up his victory with consummate skill. The junction of the retreating corps d'armee and their flight by the shortest route into Prussia were equally prevented. The defeated Prussian army was in a state of indescribable confusion. An immensely circuitous march lay before it ere Prussia could be re-entered. A number of the regiments disbanded, particularly those whose officers had been the first to take to flight or had crept for shelter behind hedges and walls. An immense number of officers' equipages, provided with mistresses, articles belonging to the toilet, and epicurean delicacies, fell into Napoleon's hands. Wagons laden with poultry, complete kitchens on wheels, wine casks, etc., had followed this luxurious army. The scene

[1] On the 14th of October. On this unlucky day, Frederick the Great had, in 1758, been surprised at Hochkirch, and Mack, in 1805, at Ulm. On this day, the peace of Westphalia was, in 1648, concluded at Osnabrück, and, in 1809, that of Vienna. It was, however, on this day that the siege of Vienna was, in 1529, raised, and that, in 1813, Napoleon was shut up at Leipzig.

presented by the battlefield of Jena widely contrasted with that of Rossbach, whose monument was sent by Napoleon to Paris as the most glorious part of the booty gained by his present easy victory.[1]

The fortified city of Erfurt was garrisoned with fourteen thousand Prussians under Mollendorf, who, on the first summons, capitulated to Murat, the general of the French cavalry. The hereditary Prince of Orange was also taken prisoner on this occasion. Von Hellwig, a lieutenant of the Prussian hussars, boldly charged the French guard escorting the fourteen thousand Prussian prisoners of war from Erfurt, at the head of his squadron, at Eichenrodt in the vicinity of Eisenach, and succeeded in restoring them to liberty. The liberated soldiers, however, instead of joining the main body, dispersed. Eugene, duke of Wurtemberg, was also defeated at Halle, and, throwing up his command, withdrew to his states. History has, nevertheless, recorded one trait of magnanimity, that of a Prussian ensign fifteen years of age, who, being pursued by some French cavalry not far from Halle, sprang with the colors into the Saal and was crushed to death by a mill-wheel.

Kalkreuth's corps, that had not been brought into action and was the only one that remained entire, being placed under the command of the prince of Hohenlohe, its gallant commander, enraged at the indignity, quitted the army. Hohenlohe's demand, on reaching Magdeburg, for a supply of ammunition and forage, was refused by the commandant, Von Kleist, and he hastened helplessly forward in the hope of reaching Berlin, but the route was already blocked by the enemy, and he was compelled to make a fatiguing and circuitous march to the west through the sandy March. Magdeburg, although garrisoned with twenty-two thousand Prussians, defended by eight hundred pieces of artillery

---

[1] The whole of these disasters had been predicted by Henry von Bülow, whose prophecies had brought him into a prison. On learning the catastrophe of Jena, he exclaimed, "That is the consequence of throwing generals into prison and of placing idiots at the head of the army!"

and almost impregnable fortifications, capitulated on the 11th of November to Ney, on his appearance beneath the walls with merely ten thousand men and a light field-battery. Kleist, in exculpation of his conduct, alleged his expectation of an insurrection of the citizens in case of a bombardment. Magdeburg contained at that time three thousand unarmed citizens. It is not known whether Kleist had been bribed, or whether he was simply infected with the cowardice and stupidity by which the elder generals of that period were distinguished; it is, however, certain that among the numerous younger officers serving under his command not one raised the slightest opposition to this disgraceful capitulation.[1]

The Hohenlohe corps, which consisted almost exclusively of infantry, was accompanied in its flight by Blucher, the gallant general of the hussars, with the élite of the remaining cavalry. Blucher had, however, long borne a grudge against his pedantic companion, and, mistrusting his guidance, soon quitted him. Being surrounded by a greatly superior French force under Klein,[2] he contrived to escape by asserting with great earnestness to that general that an armistice had just been concluded. When afterward urgently entreated by Hohenlohe to join him with his troops, he procrastinated too long, it may be owing to his desire to bring Hohenlohe, who, by eternally retreating, completely disheartened his troops, to a stand, or owing to the impossibility of coming up with greater celerity.[3] He had, indubitably, the intention to join Hohenlohe at Prenzlow, but

---

[1] The young "vons," on the contrary, capitulated with extreme readiness, in order to return to their pleasurable habits. Several of them set a great shield over their doors, with the inscription, "Herr von N. or M., prisoner of war on parole." In all the capitulations, the commandants and officers merely took care of their own persons and equipages and sacrificed the soldiery. Napoleon, who was well aware of this little weakness, always offered them the most flattering personal terms.

[2] The same man who had been imposed upon by a similar ruse at Ulm by the Archduke Ferdinand. Napoleon dismissed him the service.

[3] Massenbach published an anonymous charge against Blücher, which that general publicly refuted.

unfortunately arrived a day too late, the prince, whose ammunition and provisions were completely spent, and who, owing to the stupidity of Massenbach, who rode up and down the Ucker without being able to discover whether he was on the right or left bank, had missed the only route by which he could retreat, having already fallen, with twelve thousand men, into the enemy's hands. This disaster was shortly afterward followed by the capture of General Hagen with six thousand men at Pasewalk and that of Bila with another small Prussian corps not far from Stettin. Blucher, strengthened by the corps of the duke of Weimar and by numerous fugitives, still kept the field, but was at length driven back to Lubeck, where he was defeated, and, after a bloody battle in the very heart of the terror-stricken city, four thousand of his men were made prisoners. He fled with ten thousand to Radkan, where, finding no ships to transport him across the Baltic, he was forced to capitulate.

The luckless duke of Brunswick was carried on a bier from the field of Jena to his palace at Brunswick, which he found deserted. All belonging to him had fled. In his distress he exclaimed, "I am now about to quit all and am abandoned by all!" His earnest petition to Napoleon for protection for himself and his petty territory was sternly refused by the implacable victor, who replied that he knew of no reigning duke of Brunswick, but only of a Prussian general of that name, who had, in the infamous manifest of 1792, declared his intention to destroy Paris and was undeserving of mercy. The blind old man fled to Ottensen, in the Danish territory, where he expired.

Napoleon, after confiscating sixty millions worth of English goods on his way through Leipzig, entered Berlin on the 17th of October, 1806. The defence of the city had not been even dreamed of; nay, the great arsenal, containing five hundred pieces of artillery and immense stores, the sword of Frederick the Great, and the private correspondence of the reigning king and queen, were all abandoned to the victor.[1] Although the citizens were by no means martially disposed, the authorities deemed it necessary to issue proclamations to the people, inculcatory of the axiom, "Tranquillity is the first duty of the citizen." Napoleon, on his entry into Berlin, was received, not as at Vienna, with mute rage, but with loud demonstrations of delight. Individuals belonging to the highest class stationed themselves behind the crowd and exclaimed, "For God's sake, give a hearty hurrah! Cry Vive l'empereur! or we are all lost." On a demand, couched in the politest terms, for the peaceable delivery of the arms of the civic guard, being made by Hulin, the new French commandant, to the magistrate, the latter, on his own accord, ordered the citizens to give up their arms "under pain of death." Numerous individuals betrayed the public money and stores, that still remained concealed, to the French. Hulin replied to a person who had discovered a large store of wood, "Leave the wood untouched; your king will want a good deal to make gallows for traitorous rogues." Napoleon's reception struck him with such astonishment that he declared, "I know not whether to rejoice or to feel ashamed." At the head of his general staff, in full uniform and with bared head, he visited the apartment occupied by Frederick the Great at Sans Souci, and his tomb. He took possession of Frederick's sword and declared in the army bulletin, "I would not part with this weapon for twenty millions." Frederick's tomb afforded him an opportunity for giving vent to the most unbecoming expressions of contempt against his unfortunate descendant. He publicly aspersed the fame of the beautiful and noble-hearted Prussian queen, in order to deaden the enthusiasm she sought to

---

[1] While the unfortunate Henry von Bülow, whose wise counsels had been despised, was torn from his prison to be delivered to the Russians, whose behavior at Austerlitz he had blamed. On his route he was maliciously represented as a friend to the French and exposed to the insults of the rabble, who bespattered him with mud, and to such brutal treatment from the Cossacks that he died of his wounds at Riga. Never had a prophet a more ungrateful country. He was delivered by his fellow-citizens to an ignominious death for attempting their salvation, for pointing out the means by which alone their safety could be insured, and for exposing the wretches by whom they were betrayed.

raise. But he deceived himself. Calumny but increased the esteem and exalted the enthusiasm with which the people beheld their queen and kindled a feeling of revenge in their bosoms. Napoleon behaved, nevertheless, with generosity to another lady of rank. Prince Hatzfeld, the civil governor of Berlin, not having quitted that city on the entry of Napoleon, had been discovered by the spies and been condemned to death by a court-martial. His wife, who was at that time enceinte, threw herself at Napoleon's feet. With a smile, he handed to her the paper containing the proof of her husband's guilt, which she instantly burned, and her husband was restored to liberty. John Muller was among the more remarkable of the servants of the state who had remained at Berlin. This sentimental parasite, the most despicable of them all, whose pathos sublimely glossed over each fresh treason, was sent for by Napoleon, who placed him about his person. Among other things, he asked him, "Is it not true the Germans are somewhat thick-brained?" to which the fawning professor replied with a smile. In return for the benefits he had received from the royal family of Prussia, he delivered, before quitting Berlin, an academical lecture upon Frederick the Great, in the presence of the French general officers, in which he artfully (the lecture was of course delivered in the French language) contrived to flatter Napoleon at the expense of that monarch.[1] Prince Charles of Isenberg raised, in the very heart of Berlin, a regiment, composed of Prussian deserters, for the service of France.[2]

The Prussian fortresses fell, meanwhile, one after the

---

[1] In the "Trumpet of the Holy War," he had summoned the nation to take up arms against the heathens (the French). He breathed war and flames. In his address to the king, he said, "The idle parade of the ruler during a long peace has never maintained a state!" He excited the hatred of the people against the French, telling them to harbor "such hatred against the enemy, like men who knew how to hate!' After thus aiding to kindle the flames of war, he went over to the French and wrote the letter to Bignon which that author has inserted in his History of France: "Like Ganymede to the seat of the gods, have I been borne by the eagle to Fontainebleau, there to serve a god."

[2] The conduct of these deserters, how, decorated with the French cockade, they treated the German population with unheard-of insolence, is given in detail by Seume.

other, during the end of autumn and during the winter, some from utter inability, on account of their neglected state, to maintain themselves, but the greater part owing to their being commanded by old villains, treacherous and cowardly as the commandant of Magdeburg. The strong fortress of Hameln was in this manner yielded by a Baron von Schöler, Plassenburg by a Baron von Becker, Nimburg on the Weser by a Baron von Dresser, Spandau by a Count von Benkendorf. The citadel of Berlin capitulated without a blow, and Stettin, although well provided with all the *materiel* of war, was delivered up by a Baron von Romberg. Custrin, one of the strongest fortified places, was commanded by a Count von Ingersleben. The king visited the place during his flight and earnestly recommended him to defend it to the last. This place, sooner than yield, had, during the seven years' war, allowed itself to be reduced to a heap of ruins. When standing on one of the bastions, the king inquired its name. The commandant was ignorant of it. Scarcely had the king quitted the place than a body of French hussars appeared before the gates, and Ingersleben instantly capitulated.

Silesia, although less demoralized than Berlin, viewed these political changes with even greater apathy. This fine province had, during the reign of Frederick the Great, been placed under the government of the minister, Count Hoym, whose easy disposition had, like insidious poison, utterly enervated the people. The government officers, as if persuaded of the reality of the antiquarian whim which deduced the name of Silesia from Elysium, dwelt in placid self-content, unmoved by the catastrophes of Austerlitz or Jena. No measures were, consequently, taken for the defence of the country, and a flying corps of Bavarians, Wurtembergers, and some French under Vandamme, speedily overran the whole province, notwithstanding the number of its fortresses. At Glogau, the commandant, Von Reinhardt, unhesitatingly declared his readiness to capitulate and excluded the gallant Major von Putlitz, who insisted upon making an obstinate defence, "as a revolutionist," from the military council. Being advised by one of the citizens to fire upon the enemy, he rudely replied, "Sir, you do not know what one shot costs the king." In Breslau, the Counts von Thiele and Lindner made a terrible fracas, burned down the fine faubourgs, and blew up the powder-magazine, merely in order to veil the disgrace of a hasty capitulation, which enraged the soldiery to such a pitch that, shattering their muskets, they heaped imprecations on their dastard commanders, and, in revenge, plundered the royal stores. Brieg was ceded after a two days' siege, by the Baron von Cornerut. The defence of the strong fortress of Schweidnitz, of such celebrated importance during the seven years' war, had been intrusted to Count von Haath, a man whose countenance even betokened imbecility. He yielded the fortress without a blow, and, on the windows of the apartment in which he lodged in the neighboring town of Jauer being broken by the patriotic citizens, he went down to the landlord, to whom he said, "My good sir, you must have some enemies!" The remaining fortresses made a better defence. Glatz was taken by surprise, the city by storm. The fortress was defended by the commandant, Count Gotzen, until ammunition sufficient for twelve days longer alone remained. Neisse capitulated from famine; Kosel was gallantly defended by the commandant, Neumann; and Silberberg, situated on an impregnable rock, refused to surrender.

The troops of the Rhenish confederation, encouraged by the bad example set by Vandamme and by several of the superior officers, committed dreadful havoc, plundered the country, robbed and barbarously treated the inhabitants. It was quite a common custom among the officers, on the conclusion of a meal, to carry away with them the whole of their host's table-service. The filthy habits of the French officers were notorious. Their conduct is said to have been not only countenanced but commanded by Napoleon, as a sure means of striking the enervated population with the profoundest terror; and the panic in fact almost amounted to absurdity, the inhabitants of this thickly-populated province nowhere venturing to rise against the handful of robbers by whom they were so cruelly persecuted. A Baron von Puckler offered an individual exception: his endeavors to rouse the inert masses met with no success, and, rendered desperate by his failure, he blew out his brains. When too late a prince of Anhalt-Pless assembled an armed force in Upper Silesia and attempted to relieve Breslau, but Thiele neglecting to make a sally at the decisive moment, the Poles in Prince of Pless's small army took to flight, and the whole plan miscarried. A small Prussian corps, amounting to about five hundred men, commanded by Losthin, afterward infested Silesia, surprised the French under Lefebvre at Kanth and put them to the rout, but were a few days after this exploit taken prisoners by a superior French force.

Attempts at reforms suited to the spirit of the age had, even before the outbreak of war, been made in Prussia by men of higher intelligence; Menken, for instance, had labored to effect the emancipation of the peasantry, but had been removed from office by the aristocratic party. During the war, the corruption pervading every department of the government, whether civil or military, was fully exposed, and Frederick William III. was taught by bitter experience to pursue a better system, to act with decision and patient determination. The Baron von Stein, a man of undoubted talent, a native of Nassau, was placed at the head of the government; two of the most able commanders of the day, Gneisenau and Scharnhorst, undertook the reorganization of the army. On the 1st of December, 1806, the king cashiered every commandant who had neglected to defend the fortress intrusted to his care and every officer guilty of desertion or cowardly flight, and the long list of names gave disgraceful proof of the extent to which the nobility were compromised. One of the first measures taken by the king was, consequently, to throw open every post of distinction in the army to the citizens. The old inconvenient uniform and firearms were at the same time improved, the queue was cut off, the cane abandoned. The royal army was indeed scanty in number, but it contained within itself germs of honor and patriotism that gave promise of future glory.

The reform, however, but slowly progressed. Ferdinand von Schill, a Prussian lieutenant, who had been wounded at Jena, formed, in Pomerania, a guerilla troop of disbanded soldiery and young men, who, although indifferently provided with arms, stopped the French convoys and couriers. His success was so extraordinary that he was sometimes enabled to send sums of money, taken from the enemy, to the king. Among other exploits, he took prisoner Marshal Victor, who was exchanged for Blucher. Blucher assembled a fresh body of troops on the island of Rugen. Schill, being afterward compelled to take refuge from the pursuit of the French in the fortress of Colberg, the commandant, Loucadou, placed him under arrest for venturing to criticise the bad defence of the place.

The king of Sweden, Gustavus Adolphus IV., might with perfect justice have bitterly reproached Prussia and Austria for the folly with which they had, by their disunion, contributed to the aggrandizement of the power of France. He acted nobly by affording a place of refuge to the Prussians at Stralsund and Rugen.

Colberg was, on Loucadou's dismissal, gloriously defended by Gneisenau and by the resolute citizens, among whom Nettelbek, a man seventy years of age, chiefly distinguished himself. Courbiere acted with equal gallantry at Graudenz. On being told by the French that Prussia was in their hands and that no king of Prussia was any longer in existence, he replied, "Well, be it so! but I am king at Graudenz." Pillau was also successfully defended by Herrmann.[1] Polish Prussia naturally fell off on the advance of the French. Calisch rose in open insurrection; the Prussian authorities were everywhere compelled to save themselves

[1] Courbiere, Herrmann, and Neumann of Cosel were bourgeois: the commandants of the other fortresses, so disgracefully ceded, were, without exception, nobles.

by flight from the vengeance of the people. Poland had been termed the Botany Bay of Prussia, government officers in disgrace for bad conduct being generally sent there by way of punishment. No one voluntarily accepted an appointment condemning him to dwell amid a population inspired by the most ineradicable national hatred, glowing with revenge, and unable to appreciate the benefits bestowed upon them in their ignorance and poverty by the wealthier and more civilized Prussians.

The king had withdrawn with the remainder of his troops, which were commanded by the gallant L'Estoc, to Kœnigsberg, where he formed a junction with the Russian army, which was led by a Hanoverian, the cautious Bennigsen, and accompanied by the emperor Alexander in person. Napoleon expected that an opportunity would be afforded for the repetition of his old manœuvre of separating and falling singly upon his opponents, but Bennigsen kept his forces together and offered him battle at Eylau, in the neighborhood of Kœnigsberg; victory still wavered, when the Prussian troops under L'Estoc fell furiously upon Marshal Ney's flank, while that general was endeavoring to surround the Russians, and decided the day. It was the 8th of February, and the snow-clad ground was stained with gore. Napoleon, after this catastrophe, remained inactive, awaiting the opening of spring and the arrival of reinforcements. Dantzig, exposed by the desertion of the Poles, fell, although defended by Kalkreuth, into his hands, and, on the 14th of June, 1807, the anniversary, so pregnant with important events, of the battle of Marengo, he gained a brilliant victory at Friedland, which was followed by General Ruchel's abandonment of Kœnigsberg with all its stores.

The road to Lithuania now lay open to the French, and the emperor Alexander deemed it advisable to conclude peace. A conference was held at Tilsit on the Riemen between the sovereigns of France, Russia, and Prussia, and a peace, highly detrimental to Germany, was concluded on the 9th of July, 1807. Prussia lost half of her territory, was restricted to the maintenance of an army merely amounting to forty-two thousand men, was compelled to pay a contribution of one hundred and forty millions of francs to France, and to leave her most important fortresses as security for payment in the hands of the French. These grievous terms were merely acceded to by Napoleon "out of esteem for his Majesty the emperor of Russia," who, on his part, deprived his late ally of a piece of Prussian-Poland (Bialystock) and divided the spoil of Prussia with Napoleon.[1] Nay, he went, some months later, so far in his—generosity, as, on an understanding with Napoleon and without deigning any explanation to Prussia, arbitrarily to cancel an article of the peace of Tilsit, by which Prussia was indemnified for the loss of Hanover with a territory containing four hundred thousand souls.

The Prussian possessions on the left bank of the Elbe, Hanover, Brunswick, and Hesse-Cassel,[2] were converted by Napoleon into the new kingdom of Westphalia, which he bestowed upon his brother Jerome and included in the Rhenish confederation. East Friesland was annexed to Holland. Poland was not restored, but a petty grandduchy of Warsaw

---

[1] Bignon remarks that the queen, Louisa, who left no means untried in order to save as much as possible of Prussia, came somewhat too late, when Napoleon had already entered into an agreement with Russia. Hence Napoleon's inflexibility, which was the more insulting owing to the apparently yielding silence with which, from a feeling of politeness, he sometimes received the personal petitions of the queen, to which he would afterward send a written refusal. The part played in this affair by Alexander was far from honorable, and Bignon says with great justice, "The emperor of Russia must at that time have had but little judgment, if he imagined that taking Prussia in such a manner under his protection would be honorable to the protector." With a view of appeasing public opinion in Germany and influencing it in favor of the alliance between France and Russia, Zschokke, who was at that time in Napoleon's pay, published a mean-spirited pamphlet, entitled, "Will the human race gain by the present political changes?"

[2] The elector, William, who had solicited permission to remain neutral, having made great military preparations and received the Prussians with open arms, was, in Napoleon's twenty-seventh bulletin, deposed with expressions of the deepest contempt. "The house of Hesse-Cassel has for many years past sold its subjects to England, and by this means has the elector collected his immense wealth. May this mean and avaricious conduct prove the ruin of his house." —Louis, Landgrave of Hesse-Darmstadt, was threatened with similar danger for inclining on the side of Prussia but perceived his peril in time to save himself from destruction.

was erected, which Frederick Augustus, elector of Saxony, received, together with the royal dignity. Prussia, already greatly diminished in extent, was to be still further encroached upon and watched by these new states. The example of electoral Saxony was imitated by the petty Saxon princes, and Anhalt, Lippe, Schwarzburg, Reuss, Mecklenburg and Aldenburg joined the Rhenish confederation. Dantzig became a nominal free town with a French garrison.[1]

The brave Hessians resisted this fresh act of despotism. The Hessian troops revolted, but were put down by force, and their leader, a sergeant, rushed frantically into the enemy's fire. The Hessian peasantry also rose in several places. The Hanse towns, on the contrary, meekly allowed themselves to be pillaged and to be robbed of their stores of English goods.

Gustavus Adolphus IV. of Sweden, who had neglected to send troops at an earlier period to the aid of Prussia, now offered the sturdiest resistance and steadily refused to negotiate terms of peace or to recognize Napoleon as emperor. His generals, Armfeldt[2] and Essen, made some successful inroads from Stralsund, and, in unison with the English, might have effected a strong diversion to Napoleon's rear, had their movements been more rapid and combined. On the conclusion of the peace of Tilsit, a French force under Mortier appeared, drove the Swedes back upon Stralsund, and compelled the king, in the August of 1807, to abandon that city, which the new system of warfare rendered no longer tenable.

---

[1] Marshal Lefebvre, who had taken the city, was created duke of Dantzig. The city, however, did not belong to him, but became a republic; notwithstanding which, it was at first compelled to pay a contribution, amounting to twenty million francs, to Napoleon, to maintain a strong French garrison at its expense, and was fleeced in every imaginable way. A stop was consequently put to trade, the wealthiest merchants became bankrupt, and Napoleon's satraps established their harems and celebrated their orgies in their magnificent houses and gardens, and, by their unbridled license, demoralized to an almost incredible degree the staid manners of the quondam pious Lutheran citizens. Vide Blech, The Miseries of Dantzig, 1815.

[2] One of the handsomest men of his time and the Adonis of many a princely dame.

CCLV. *The Rhenish Confederation*

THE whole of western Europe bent in lowly submission before the genius of Napoleon; Russia was bound by the silken chains of flattery; England, Turkey, Sweden, and Portugal, alone bade him defiance. England, whose fleets ruled the European seas, who lent her aid to his enemies, and instigated their opposition, was his most dangerous foe. By a gigantic measure, known as the continental system, he sought to undermine her power. The whole of the continent of Europe, as far as his influence was felt, was, by an edict, published at Berlin on the 21st of November, 1806, closed against British trade; nay, he went so far as to lay an embargo on all English goods lying in store and to make prisoners of war of all the English at that time on the continent. All intercourse between England and the rest of Europe was prohibited. But Napoleon's attempt to ruin the commerce of England was merely productive of injury to himself; the promotion of every branch of industry on the continent could not replace the loss of its foreign trade; the products of Europe no longer found their way to the more distant parts of the globe, to be exchanged for colonial luxuries, which, with the great majority of the people, more particularly with the better classes, had become necessaries, and numbers who had but lately lauded Napoleon to the skies regarded him with bitter rage on being compelled to relinquish their wonted coffee and sugar.

Napoleon, meanwhile, undeterred by opposition, enforced his continental system. Russia, actuated by jealousy of England and flattered by the idea, with which Napoleon had, at Tilsit, inspired the emperor Alexander, of sharing with him the empire of a world, aided his projects. The first step was to secure to themselves possession of the Baltic; the king of Sweden, Napoleon's most implacable foe, was to be dethroned, and Sweden to be promised to Frederick, prince-regent of Denmark, in order to draw him into the interests of the allied powers of France and Russia. The scheme, however, transpired in time to be frustrated. An English fleet, with an army, among which was the German Legion, composed of Hanoverian refugees, on board, attacked, and, after a fearful bombardment, took Copenhagen, and either destroyed or carried off the whole of the Danish fleet, September, 1807.[1] The British fleet, on its triumphant return through the Sound, was saluted at Helsingfors by the king of Sweden, who invited the admirals to breakfast. The island of Heligoland, which belonged to Holstein and consequently formed part of the possessions of Denmark, and which carried on a great smuggling trade between that country and the continent, was at that time also seized by the British.

Napoleon revenged himself by a bold stroke in Spain. He proposed the partition of Portugal to that power, and, under that pretext, sent troops across the Pyrenees. The licentious queen of Spain, Maria Louisa Theresa of Parma, and her paramour, Godoy, who had, on account of the treaty between France and Spain, received the title of Prince of Peace, reigned at that time in the name of the imbecile king, Charles IV. His son, Ferdinand, placed himself at the head of the democratic faction, by which Godoy was regarded with the most deadly hatred. Both parties, however, conscious of their want of power, sought aid from Napoleon, who flattered each in turn, with a view of rendering the one a tool for the destruction of the other. The Prince of Peace was overthrown by a popular tumult; Ferdinand VII. was proclaimed king, and his father, Charles IV., was compelled to abdicate. These events were apparently countenanced by Napoleon, who invited the youthful sovereign to an interview; Ferdinand, accordingly, went to

---

[1] See accounts of this affair in the Recollections of a Legionary, Hanover, 1826, and in Beamisch's History of the Legion.

Bayonne and was—taken prisoner. The Prince of Peace, on the eve of flying from Spain, where his life was no longer safe, with his treasures and with the queen, persuaded the old king, Charles, also to go to Bayonne, where his person was instantly seized. Both he and his son were compelled to renounce their right to the throne of Spain and to abdicate in favor of Joseph, Napoleon's brother, the 5th of May, 1808. The elevation of Joseph to the Spanish throne was followed by that of Murat to the throne of Naples. The haughty Spaniard, however, refused to be trampled under foot, and his proud spirit disdained to accept a king imposed upon him by such unparalleled treachery. Napoleon's victorious troops were, for the first time, routed by peasants, an entire army was taken prisoner at Baylen, and another, in Portugal, was compelled to retreat. Napoleon's veterans were scattered by monks and peasants, a proof, to the eternal disgrace of every subject people, that the invincibility of a nation depends but upon its will.

Napoleon did not conduct the war in Spain in person during the first campaign; the tranquillity of the North had first to be secured. For this purpose, he held a personal conference, in October, 1808, with the emperor Alexander at Erfurt, whither the princes of Germany hastened to pay their devoirs, humbly as their ancestors of yore to conquering Attila. The company of actors brought in Napoleon's train from Paris boasted of gaining the plaudits of a royal parterre, and a French sentinel happening to call to the watch to present arms to one of the kings there dancing attendance was reproved by his officer with the observation, "Ce n'est qu un roi."[1] Both emperors, for the purpose of

---

[1] A graphic description of these times is to be met with in Joanna Schopenhauer's Tour on the Lower Rhine. The kings of Bavaria, Wurtemberg, Westphalia, Saxony, the prince primate, the hereditary prince of Baden and of Mecklenburg-Strelitz, the duke of Weimar, the princes of Hohenzollern, Hesse-Rotenburg, and Hesse-Philippsthal, were present. No one belonging to the house of Austria was there: of that of Prussia there was Prince William, the king's brother. The Allgemeine Zeitung of that day wrote: "The fact of Napoleon's sending for the privy-councillor, Von Goethe, into his cabinet, and conversing with him for upward of an hour, appears to us well worthy of mention. What

offering a marked insult to Prussia, attended a great hare-hunt on the battlefield of Jena. It was during this conference that Napoleon and Alexander divided between themselves the sovereignty of Europe, Russia undertaking the subjugation of Sweden and the seizure of Finland, France the conquest of Spain and Portugal.

The period immediately subsequent to the fall of the ancient empire forms the blackest page in the history of Germany. The whole of the left bank of the Rhine was annexed to France. The people, notwithstanding the improvement that took place in the administration under Bon Jean St. André, groaned beneath the exorbitant taxes and the conscription. The commerce on the Rhine had almost entirely ceased.[1]—The grandduchy of Berg was, until 1808, governed with great mildness by Avar, the French minister.—Holland had, since 1801, remained under the administration of her benevolent governor, Schimmelpenninck, but had been continually drained by the imposition of additional income taxes, which, in 1804, amounted to six per cent on the capital in the country. Commerce had entirely ceased, smuggling alone excepted. In 1806, the Dutch were commanded

---

German would not rejoice that the great emperor should have entered into such deep conversation with such a fitting representative of our noblest, and now, alas, sole remaining national possession, our art and learning, by whose preservation alone can our nationality be saved from utter annihilation." Notwithstanding which the company of actors belonging to the theatre at Weimar, which was close at hand and had been under Goethe's instruction, was not once allowed to perform on the Erfurt stage, which Napoleon had supplied with actors from Paris. Wieland was also compelled to remain standing for an hour in Napoleon's presence, and when, at length, unable, owing to the weakness of old age, to continue in that position, he ventured to ask permission to retire, Napoleon is said to have considered the request an unwarrantable liberty. The literary heroes of Weimar took no interest in the country from which they had received so deep a tribute of admiration. Not a patriotic sentiment escaped their lips. At the time when the deepest wound was inflicted on the Tyrol, Goethe gave to the world his frivolous "Wahlverwandschaften," which was followed by a poem in praise of Napoleon, of whom he says:

"Doubts, that have baffled thousands, *he* has solved;
Ideas, o'er which centuries have brooded,
His giant mind intuitively compassed."

[1] The great and dangerous robber bands of the notorious Damian Hessel, and of Schinderhannes, afford abundant proof of the demoralized condition of the people.

to entreat Napoleon to grant them a king in the person of his brother Louis, who fixed his residence in the venerable council-house at Amsterdam, and, it must be confessed, endeavored to promote the real interests of his new subjects.[1]

The Swiss, with characteristic servility, testified the greatest zeal on every occasion for the emperor Napoleon, celebrated his fete-day, and boasted of his protection,[2] and of the freedom they were still permitted to enjoy. Freedom of thought was expressly prohibited. Sycophants, in the pay of the foreign ruler, as, for instance, Zschokke, alone guided public opinion. In Zug, any person who ventured to speak disparagingly of the Swiss in the service of France was declared an enemy to his country and exposed to severe punishment.[3] The Swiss shed their blood in each and all of Napoleon's campaigns, and aided him to reduce their kindred nations to abject slavery.[4]

The Rhenish confederation shared the advantages of French influence to the same degree in which it, in common with the old states on the left bank of the Rhine, was subject to ecclesiastical corruption or to the upstart vanity incidental to petty states. Wherever enlightenment and liberty had formerly existed, as in Protestant and constitutional Würtemberg, the violation of the ancient rights of the people was deeply felt, and the new aristocracy, modelled on that of France, appeared as unbearable to the older inhabitants of Würtemberg as did the loss of their ancient inde-

---

[1] On the 12th of January, 1807, a ship laden with four hundred quintals of gunpowder blew up in the middle of the city of Leyden, part of which was thereby reduced to ruins, and one hundred and fifty persons, among others the celebrated professors Luzac and Kleit, were killed.

[2] On the opening of the federal diet in 1806, the Landammann lauded "the omnipotent benevolence of the gracious mediator." In earlier times, the Swiss would, on the contrary, have boasted of their affording protection to, not of receiving protection from, France.

[3] In order to prove of what importance they considered the benevolent protection of Napoleon the Great.—*Allgemeine Zeitung of 1810, No. 190.*

[4] Their general, Von der Wied, who was taken prisoner at Talavera in Spain and died shortly afterward of a pestilential disease, had done signal service to France, in 1798 in Switzerland, in 1792 in Italy, in 1805 in Austria, in 1806 in Prussia, and finally in Spain.—*Allgemeine Zeitung of 1811, No. 46.*

pendence to the mediatized princes and lordlings. King Frederick, notwithstanding his refusal to send troops into Spain, was compelled to furnish an enormous contingent for the wars in eastern Europe; the conscription and taxes were heavily felt, and the peasant was vexed by the great hunts, celebrated by Matthisson, the court-poet, as festivals of Diana.[1] In Bavaria, the administration of Maximilian Joseph and of his minister, Montgelas, although arbitrary in its measures, promoted, like that of Frederick II. and Joseph II., the advance of enlightenment and true liberty. The monasteries were closed, the punishment of the rack was abolished, unity was introduced in the administration of the state; the schools, the police, and the roads were improved, toleration was established; in a word, the dreams of the Illuminati, thirty years before this period, were, in almost every respect, realized. But, on the other hand, patriotism was here more unknown than in any other part of Germany. Christopher von Aretin set himself up as an apparitor to the French police, and, in 1810, published a work against the few German patriots still remaining, whom he denounced, in the fourteenth number of the Literary Gazette of Upper Germany, as "Preachers of Germanism, criminals and traitors,

---

[1] Personal freedom was restricted by innumerable decrees. Freedom of speech, formerly great in Würtemberg, was strictly repressed; all social confidence was annihilated. A swarm of informers insnared those whom the secret police were unable to entrap. The secrecy of letters was violated. Trials in criminal cases were no longer allowed to be public. The sentence passed upon the accused was, particularly in cases of the highest import, not delivered by the judge as dictated by the law, but by the despot's caprice.—The conscription was enforced with increased severity and tyranny.—The natural right of emigration was abolished.—The people were disarmed, and not even the inhabitants of solitary farms and hamlets were allowed to possess arms in order to defend themselves against wolves and robbers. A man was punished for killing a mad dog, because the gun used for that purpose had been illegally secreted. Pass-tickets were given to and returned by all desirous of passing the gates of the pettiest town. The members of the higher aristocracy were compelled, under pain of being deprived of the third of their income, to spend three months in the year at court.—The citizen was oppressed by a variety of fresh taxes, by the newly-created monopolies of tobacco, salt, etc., and colonial imposts, by the tenfold rise of the excise and custom-house dues, etc. Vide Zahn in the Würtemberg Annual. Zschokke, meanwhile, in his pamphlet already mentioned, "Will the human race gain," etc., advocated republican equality and liberty under a monarchical constitution.

by whom the Rhenish confederation was polluted." The crown prince of Bavaria, who deeply lamented the rule of France and the miseries of Germany, offers a contrary example. A constitution, naturally a mere tool in the hand of the ministry, was bestowed, in 1808, upon Bavaria.

The government of Charles von Dalberg, the prince primate and grandduke of Frankfort, was one of the most despicable of those composing the Rhenish confederation. Equally insensible to the duties attached to his high name and station,[1] he flattered the foreign tyrant to an extent unsurpassed by any of the other base sycophants at that time abounding in the empire; with folded hands would he at all times invoke the blessing of the Most High on the head of the almighty ruler of the earth, and celebrate each of his victories with hymns of gratitude and joy, while his ministers misruled and tyrannized over the country,[2] whose freedom they loudly vaunted.[3]—In Würzburg, the French ambassador reigned with the despotism of an Eastern satrap.[4] Saxe-Coburg[5] and Anhalt-Gotha,[6] where the native tyrant was

---

[1] The Von Dalbergs of Franconia were the first hereditary barons of the holy Roman empire, and one of their race was dubbed knight at each imperial coronation. Hence the demand of the imperial herald, "Is no Dalberg here?" And a Dalberg it was, who, in Napoleon's name, declared to the German emperor that he no longer recognized an emperor of Germany.—In 1797, Dalberg had, at the diet, and again in 1805, expressed himself with great zeal against France; on the present occasion he was Napoleon's first satrap.

[2] They sold the demesnes of Hanau and Fulda and received the sums produced by the sale in gift from the grandduke.—*Görres' Rhenish Mercury, A.D. 1814, No. 168.*

[3] They were barefaced enough to bestow a constitution, and, in 1810, to open a diet at Hanau, although all the newspapers had, five days previously, been suppressed, and orders had been issued that the editor of the only newspaper permitted for the future was to be appointed by the police.—*Allgemeine Zeitung, No. 294.*

[4] Count Montholon-Semonville sold justice and mercy. Vide Brockhaus' Deutsche Blätter, 1814, No. 101.

[5] The duke, Francis, allowed the country to be mercilessly drained and impoverished by the minister, Von Kretschmann. He lived on extremely bad terms with his uncle, Frederick Josias, duke of Coburg, the celebrated Austrian general. Francis died in 1806. Ernest, his son and successor, delivered the country, in 1809, from Kretschmann's tyranny, and, in 1811, bestowed upon it a constitution, which was, nevertheless, merely an imitation of that of Westphalia.

[6] The prince, Augustus Christian Frederick, contracted debts to an enormous amount, completely drained his petty territory, and even seized bail-money. Mili-

sheltered beneath the wing of Napoleon, were in the most lamentable state.—In Saxony, the government remained unaltered. Frederick Augustus, filled with gratitude for the lenity with which he had been treated after the war and for the grant of the royal dignity, remained steadily faithful to Napoleon, but introduced no internal innovations into the government. The adhesion of Saxe-Weimar to the Rhenish confederation was of deplorable consequence to Germany, the great poets assembled there by the deceased Duchess Amalia also scattering incense around Napoleon.

The kingdom of Westphalia was doomed to taste to the dregs the bitter cup of humiliation. The new king, Jerome, who declared, "Je veux qu'on respecte la dignite de l'homme et du citoyen," bestowed, it is true, many and great benefits upon his subjects; the system of flogging, so degrading to the soldier, was abolished, the judicature was improved, the administration simplified, and the German in authority, notwithstanding his traditionary gruffness, became remarkable for urbanity toward the citizens and peasants. But Napoleon's despotic rule ever demanded fresh sacrifices of men and money and increased severity on the part of the police, in order to quell the spirit of revolt. Jerome, conscious of being merely his brother's representative, consoled himself for his want of independence in his gay court at Cassel.[1] He had received but a middling education, and had, at one period, held a situation in the marine at Baltimore in North America. While still extremely young, placed unexpectedly upon a throne, more as a splendid puppet than as an independent sovereign, he gave way to excesses, natural, and, under the circumstances, almost excusable. It would be

---

tary amusements, drunkenness and other gross excesses, the preservation of enormous herds of deer which destroyed the fields of the peasantry, formed the pleasures of this prince.—*Stenzel's History of Anhalt.*

[1] Napoleon nicknamed him *roi de coulisses*, and gave him a guardian in his ambassador, Reinhard, a person of celebrity during the Revolution. Jerome's first ministers were friends of his youth; the Creole, Le Camus, who was created Count Fürstenstein, and Malchus, whose office it was to fill a bottomless treasury. Vide Hormayr, Archive 5, 458, and the Secret History of the Court of Westphalia, 1814.

ungenerous to repeat the sarcasms showered upon him on his expulsion. The execrations heaped, at a later period, upon his head, ought with far greater justice to have fallen upon those of the Germans themselves, and more particularly upon those of that portion of the aristocracy that vied with the French in enriching the chronique scandaleuse of Cassel, and upon those of the citizens who, under Bongars, the head of the French police, acted the part of spies upon and secret informers against their wretched countrymen.—The farcical donation of a free constitution to the people put a climax to their degradation. On the 2d of July, 1808, Jerome summoned the Westphalian Estates to Cassel and opened the servile assembly, thus arbitrarily convoked, with extreme pomp. The unfortunate deputies, who had, on the conclusion of the lengthy ceremonial, received an invitation *assister au rêpas* at the palace and had repaired thither, their imaginations, whetted by hunger, revelling in visions of gastronomic delight, were sorely discomfited on discovering that they were simply expected "to look on while the sovereign feasted." The result of this assembly was, naturally, a unanimous tribute of admiration and an invocation of blessings on the head of the foreign ruler, the principal part in which was played by John Müller, who attempted to convince his fellow countrymen that by means of the French usurpation they had first received the boon of true liberty. This cheaply-bought apostate said, in his usual hyperbolical style, "It is a marked peculiarity of the northern nations, more especially of those of German descent, that, whenever God has, in His wisdom, resolved to bestow upon them a new kind or a higher degree of civilization, the impulse has ever been given from without. This impulse was given to us by Napoleon, by him before whom the earth is silent, God having given the whole world into his hand, nor can Germany at the present period have a wish ungratified, Napoleon having reorganized her as the nursery of European civilization. Too sublime to condescend to every-day polity, he has given durability to Germany!

Happy nation! what an interminable vista of glory opens to thy view!" Thus spoke John Müller. Thousands of Germans had been converted into abject slaves, but none other than he was there ever found, with sentimental phrases to gild the chains of his countrymen, to vaunt servility as liberty and dishonor as glory.[1] John Müller's unprincipled address formed, as it were, the turning-point of German affairs. Self-degradation could go no further. The spirit of the sons of Germany henceforward rose, and, with manly courage, they sought, by their future actions, to wipe off the deep stain of their former guilt and dishonor.

---

[1] Vide Strombeck's Life and the Allgemeine Zeitung of September, 1808. Besides John Müller and Aretin, mention may, with equal justice, be made of Crome of Geissen and Zschokke, a native of Magdeburg naturalized in Switzerland, who, in 1807, ventured to declare in public that Napoleon had done more for Swiss independence than William Tell five hundred years ago; who, paid by Napoleon, defamed the noble-spirited Spaniards and Tyrolese in 1815, decried the enthusiastic spirit animating Germany, and afterward whitewashed himself by his liberal tirades. With these may also be associated Murhard, the publisher of the *Moniteur Westphalien*, K. J. Schültz, the author of a work upon Napoleon, the Berlinese Jew, Saul Asher, the author of a scandalous work, entitled "Germanomanie," and of a slanderous article in Zschokke's Miscellanies against Prussia, Kosegarten the poet, who, in 1809, delivered a speech in eulogy of Napoleon, far surpassing all in bombast and mean adulation. Benturini, at that time, also termed Napoleon the emanation of the universal Spirit, a second incarnation of the Deity, a second savior of the world. In Posselt's European Annals of 1807, a work by a certain W. upon the political interests of Germany appeared, and concluded as follows: "Let us raise to him (Napoleon) a national monument, worthy of the first and only benefactor of the nations of Germany. Let his name be engraved in gigantic letters of shining gold on Germany's highest and steepest pinnacle, whence, lighted by the effulgent rays of morn, it may be visible far over the plains on which he bestowed a happier futurity!" This writer also drew a comparison between Napoleon and Charlemagne, in which he designated the latter a barbarous despot and the former the new savior of the world. He says, "Napoleon first solved the enigma of equality and liberty—his chief aim was the prevention of despotism—his chief desire, to eternalize the dominion of virtue." In the course of 1808, it was said in the essay, "On the Regeneration of Germany," that the Germans were still children whom it was solely possible for the French to educate: "Our language is also not logical like French—if we intend to attain unity, we must adhere with heart and soul to him who has smoothed the path to it, to him, our securest support, to him, whose name outshines that of Charlemagne—foreign princes in German countries are no proof of subjection, they, on the contrary, most surely warrant our continued existence as a nation." In France sixty authors dedicated their works, within the space of a year, to the emperor Napoleon—in Germany, ninety.

CCLVI. *Resuscitation of Patriotism Throughout Germany—Austria's Demonstration*

THE general slavery, although most severely felt in Eastern Germany, bore there a less disgraceful character. Austria and Prussia had been conquered, pillaged, reduced in strength and political importance, while the Rhenish states, forgetful that it is ever less disgraceful to yield to an overpowering enemy than voluntarily to lend him aid, had shared in and profited by the triumph of the empire's foe. Austria and Prussia suffered to a greater extent than the Rhenish confederation, but they preserved a higher degree of independence. Prussia, although almost annihilated by her late disasters,[1] still dreamed of future liberation. Austria had, notwithstanding her successive and numerous defeats, retained the greater share of independence, but her subjection, although to a lesser degree, was the more disgraceful on account of her former military glory and her preponderance as a political power in Germany. With steady perseverance and unfaltering courage she opposed the attacks of the for-

[1] The whole of the revenues of Prussia were confiscated by the French until 1808. The contribution of one hundred and forty millions was, nevertheless, to be paid, and the French garrisons in the Prussian fortresses of Glogau, Küstrin, and Stettin were to be maintained at the expense of Prussia. The suppression of the monasteries in Silesia was far from lucrative, the commissioners, who were irresponsible, carrying on a system of pillage, and landed property having greatly fallen in value. The most extraordinary imposts of every description were resorted to for the purpose of raising a revenue, among other means, a third of all the gold and silver in the country was called in. A coinage, still more debased, was issued, and one more inferior still was smuggled into the country by English coiners. In 1808, silver money fell two-thirds of its current value and was even refused acceptance at that price.—The French, moreover, lorded over the country with redoubled insolence, broke every treaty, increased their garrisons, and occasionally laid the most inopportune commands, in the form of a request, upon the king; as, for instance, to lay under embargo and deliver up to them a number of English merchantmen that had been driven into the Prussian harbors by a dreadful storm. Blücher, at that time governor of Pomerania, restrained his fiery nature and patiently endured their insolence, while silently brooding over deep and implacable revenge.

eign tyrant against the empire, and, France's first and last antagonist, the most faithful champion of the honor of Germany, she rose, with redoubled vigor, after each successive defeat, to renew the unequal struggle.

Prussia had been overcome, because, instead of uniting with the other states of Germany, she had first abandoned them to be afterward deserted by them in her turn, and because, instead of arming her warlike people against every foreign foe, she had habituated her citizens to unarmed effeminacy and had rested her sole support on a mercenary army, an artificial and spiritless automaton, separated from and unsympathizing with the people. The idea that the salvation of Prussia could now alone be found in her reconciliation with the neighboring powers of Germany, in a general confederation, in the patriotism of her armed citizens, had already arisen. But, in order to inspire the citizen with enthusiasm, he must first, by the secure and free possession of his rights and by his participation in the public weal, be deeply imbued with a consciousness of freedom. The slave has no country; the freeman alone will lay down his life in its defence. In those times of Germany's deepest degradation and suffering, men for the first time again heard speak of a great and common fatherland, of national fame and honor; and liberty, that glorious name, was uttered not only by those who groaned beneath the rule of the despotic foreigner, but even by those who deplored the loss of the internal liberty of their country, the gradual subjection of the proud and free-spirited German to native tyranny. The king of Prussia, not content with morally reorganizing his army, also bestowed wise laws, which restored the citizen and the peasant to their rights, to their dignity as men, of which they had for so long been deprived by the nobility, the monopolizers of every privilege. The emancipation of the peasant essentially consisted in the abolition of feudal servitude and forced labor; that of the citizen, in the donation of a free municipal constitution, of self-administration, and freedom of election. The nobility were, at the same time, despoiled of the exclusive appointment to the higher civil and military posts and of the exclusive possession of landed property. Each citizen possessed the right, hitherto strictly prohibited, of purchasing baronial estates, and the nobility were, on their part, permitted to exercise trades, which a miserable prejudice had hitherto deemed incompatible with noble birth. These new institutions date from 1808 and are due to the energy of the minister, Stein.

This noble-spirited German was the founder of a secret society, the Tugendbund, by which a general insurrection against Napoleon was silently prepared throughout Germany. Among its members were numerous statesmen, officers, and literati. Among the latter, Arndt gained great note by his popular style, Jahn by his influence over the rising generation. Jahn reintroduced gymnastics, so long neglected, into education, as a means of heightening moral courage by the increase of physical strength.[1] Scharnhorst, meanwhile, although restricted to the prescribed number of troops, created a new army by continually exchanging trained soldiers for raw recruits, and secretly purchased an immense quantity of arms, so that a considerable force could, in case of necessity, be speedily assembled. He also had all the brass battery guns secretly converted into field-pieces and replaced by iron guns. Napoleon's spies, however, came upon the trace of the Tugendbund. Stein, exposed by an intercepted letter, was outlawed[2] by Napoleon and compelled to quit Prussia. He was succeeded by Hardenberg, by whom the treaty of Basel had formerly been con-

---

[1] When marching with his pupils out of Berlin, he would ask the fresh ones as he passed beneath the Bradenburg gate, "What are you thinking of now?" If the boy did not know what to answer, he would give him a box on the ear, saying as he did so, "You should think of this, how you can bring back the four fine statues of horses that once stood over this gate and were carried by the French to Paris."

[2] Decree of 16th December, 1808: "A certain Stein, who is attempting to create disturbances, is herewith declared the enemy of France; his property shall be placed under sequestration, and his person shall be secured." The Allgemeine Zeitung warns, at the same time, in its 330th number, all German savants not to give way to patriotic enthusiasm and to follow in John Müller's footsteps.

cluded and whose nomination was publicly approved of by Napoleon. Scharnhorst and Julius Gruner, the head of the Berlin police, were also deprived of their offices. The Berlin university, nevertheless, continued to give evidence of a better spirit. Enlightenment and learning, on their decrease at Frankfort on the Oder, here found their headquarters. Halle had become Westphalian, and the universities of Rinteln and Helmstädt had, from a similar cause, been closed.

Austria also felt her humiliation too deeply not to be inspired, like Prussia, with an instinct of self-preservation. The imperial dignity and catholicism were here closely associated with the memory of the Middle Ages, whose magnificence and grandeur were once more disclosed to the people in the masterly productions of the writers of the day. Hence the unison created by Frederick Schlegel between the romantic poets and antiquarians of Germany and Viennese policy. The predilection for ancient German art and poetry had, in the literary world, been merely produced by the reaction of German intelligence against foreign imitation; this literary reaction, however, happened coincidently with and aided that in the political world. The Nibelungen, the Minnesingers, the ancient chronicles, became a popular study. The same enthusiasm inspired the liberal-spirited poets, Tieck, Arnim, and Brentano; Fouqué charmed the rising generation and the multitude with his extravagant descriptions of the age of chivalry; the learned researches of Grimm, Hagen, Busching, Gräter, etc., into German antiquity, at that time excited general interest, but the glowing colors in which Joseph Gorres, himself a former Jacobin, and amid the half Gallicized inhabitants of Coblentz, revived, as if by magic, the Middle Age on the ruin-strewed banks of the Rhine caused the deepest delight. Two men, Stein, now a refugee in Austria, and Count Munster, first of all Hanoverian minister and afterward English ambassador at Petersburg, who kept up a constant correspondence with Stein and conducted the secret negotiations in the name of Great Britain, were unwearied in their endeavors to forge arms against Napoleon. In Austria, Count John Philip von Stadion, who had, since the December of 1805, been placed at the head of the ministry, had both the power and the will to repair the blunders committed by Thugut and Cobenzl.

The Russo-gallic alliance was viewed with terror by Austria. Europe had, to a certain degree, been partitioned at Erfurt, by Napoleon and Alexander. Fresh sacrifices were evidently on the eve of being extorted from Germany. Russia had resolved at any price to gain possession of either the whole or a part of Turkey, and offered to confirm Napoleon in that of Bohemia, on condition of being permitted to seize Moldavia and Wallachia.[1] The danger was urgent. Austria, sold by Russia to France, could alone defend herself against both her opponents by an immense exertion of the national power of Germany. The old and faulty system had been fearfully revenged. The disunion of the German princes, the despotism of the aristocratic administrations, the estrangement of the people from all public affairs, had all conduced to the present degradation of Germany. Necessity now induced an alteration in the system of government and an appeal to the German people, whose voice had hitherto been vainly raised. The example set by Spain was to be followed. Stein, who was at that time at Vienna, kindled the glowing embers to a flame. The military reforms begun at an earlier period by the Archduke Charles were carried out on a wider basis. A completely new institution, that of the Landwehr or armed citizens, in contradistinction with the mercenary soldiery, was set on foot. Enthusiasm and patriotism were not wanting. The circumstance of the pope's imprisonment in Rome by Napoleon sufficed to rouse the Catholics. Everything was hoped for from a general rising throughout Germany against the French. Precipitation, however, ruined all. Prussia was still too much weakened, her fortresses were still in the hands of the French,

[1] Bignon's History of France.

and Austria inspired but little confidence, while the Rhenish confederation solely aimed at aggrandizing itself by fresh wars at the expense of that empire, and, notwithstanding the inclination to revolt evinced by the people in different parts of Germany, more particularly in Westphalia, the terror inspired by Napoleon kept them, as though spellbound, beneath their galling yoke.

While Napoleon was engaged in the Peninsula, Austria levied almost the whole of her able-bodied men and equipped an army, four hundred thousand strong, at the head of which no longer foreign generals, but the princes of the house of Habsburg, were placed. The Archduke Charles[1] set off, in 1809, for the Rhine, John for Italy, Ferdinand for Poland. The first proclamation, signed by Prince Rosenberg and addressed to the Bavarians, was as follows: "You are now beginning to perceive that we are Germans like yourselves, that the general interest of Germany touches you more nearly than that of a nation of robbers, and that the German nation can alone be restored to its former glory by acting in unison. Become once more what you once were, brave Germans! Or have you, Bavarian peasants and citizens, gained aught by your prince being made into a king? by the extension of his authority over a few additional square miles? Have your taxes been thereby decreased? Do you enjoy greater security in your persons and property?" The proclamation of the Archduke Charles "to the German nation," declared: "We have taken up arms to restore independence and na-

[1] He undertook the chief command with extreme unwillingness and had long advised against the war, the time not having yet arrived, Prussia being still adverse, Germany not as yet restored to her senses, and experience having already proved to him how little he could act as his judgment directed. How often had he not been made use of and then suddenly neglected, been restrained, in the midst of his operations, by secret orders, been permitted to conduct the first or only the second part of a campaign, been placed in a subaltern position when the chief command was rightfully his, or been forced to accept of it when all was irremediably lost. Even on this occasion the first measure advised by him, that of pushing rapidly through Bohemia and Franconia, met with opposition. On the Maine and on the Weser alone was there a hope of inspiring the people with enthusiasm, not in Bavaria, where the hatred of the Austrians was irradicably rooted. It, nevertheless, pleased the military advisers of the emperor at Vienna to order the army to advance slowly through Bavaria.

tional honor to Germany. Our cause is the cause of Germany. Show yourselves deserving of our esteem! The German, forgetful of what is due to himself and to his country, is our only foe." An anonymous but well-known proclamation also declared: "Austria beheld—a sight that drew tears of blood from the heart of every true-born German—you, O nations of Germany! so deeply debased as to be compelled to submit to the legislation of the foreigner and to allow your sons, the youth of Germany, to be led to war against their still unsubdued brethren. The shameful subjection of millions of once free-born Germans will ere long be completed. Austria exhorts you to raise your humbled necks, to burst your slavish chains!" And in another address was said: "How long shall Hermann mourn over his degenerate children? Was it for this that the Cherusci fought in the Teutoburg forest? Is every spark of German courage extinct? Does the sound of your clanking chains strike like music on your ears? Germans, awake! shake off your death-like slumber in the arms of infamy! Germans! shall your name become the derision of after ages?"

The Austrian army, instead of vigorously attacking and disarming Bavaria, but slowly advanced, and permitted the Bavarians to withdraw unharassed for the purpose of forming a junction with the other troops of the Rhenish confederation under Napoleon, who had hastened from Spain on the first news of the movements of Austria. The hopes of the German patriots could not have been more fearfully disappointed or the German name more deeply humiliated than by the scorn with which Napoleon, on this occasion, placed himself at the head of the nations of western Germany, by whose arms alone, for he had but a handful of French with him, he overcame their eastern brethren at a moment in which the German name and German honor were more loudly invoked. "I have not come among you," said Napoleon smilingly to the Bavarians, Wurtembergers, etc., by whom he was surrounded, "I am not come among you as the emperor of France, but as the protector of your country and of the German confederation. No Frenchman is among you; *you alone* shall beat the Austrians."[1] The extent of the blindness of the Rhenish confederation[2] is visible in their proclamations. The king of Saxony even called Heaven to his aid, and said to his soldiers, "Draw your swords against Austria with full trust in the aid of Divine providence!"[3]

In the April of 1809, Napoleon led the Rhenish confederated troops, among which the Bavarians under General Wrede chiefly distinguished themselves, against the Austrians, who had but slowly advanced, and defeated them in

---

[1] "None of my soldiers accompany me. You will know how to value this mark of confidence."—*Napoleon's Address to the Bavarians. Bölderndorf's Bavarian Campaigns.* "I am alone among you and have not a Frenchman around my person. This is an unparalleled honor paid by me to you."—*Napoleon's Address to the Würtemberg troops.* Arndt wrote at that time:

"By idle words and dastard wiles
Hath he the mastery gained;
He holds our sacred fatherland
In slavery enchained.
Fear hath rendered truth discreet,
And Honor croucheth at his feet.

Is this his work? ah no! 'tis *thine!*
This *thou* alone hast done.
For him thy banner waved, for him
Thy sword the battle won.

By thy disputes he gaineth strength,
By thy disgrace full honor,
And 'neath the German hero's arm
His weakness doth he cover:
Glittering erewhile in borrowed show,
The Gallic cock doth proudly crow."

[2] The states of Würtemberg imparted, among other things, the following piece of information to the house of Habsburg: "That the heads of a democratical government should spread principles destructive to order among its neighbors was easily explicable, but that Austria should take advantage of the war to derange the internal mechanism of neighboring states was inexcusable."—*Allgemeine Zeitung, No. 113.* The Bavarian proclamation (*Allgemeine Zeitung, No. 135*) says, "Princes of the blood royal unblushingly subscribed to proclamations placing them on an equality with the men of the Revolution of 1793." The *Moniteur*, Napoleon's Parisian organ, said in August, 1809, after the conclusion of the war, "The mighty hand of Napoleon has snatched Germany from the revolutionary abyss about to engulf her."

[3] Posselt's Political Annals at that time contained an essay, in which the attempt made by the Austrian cabinet to call the Germans to arms was designated as a "crime" against the sovereigns "among whom Germany was at that period partitioned, and in whose hearing it was both foolish and dangerous to speak of Germany." Derision has seldom been carried to such a pitch.

five battles, on five successive days, the most glorious triumph of his surpassing tactics, at Pfaffenhofen, Thann, Absenberg, Landshut, Eckmuhl, and Ratisbon. The Archduke Charles retired into Bohemia in order to collect reinforcements, but General Hiller was, on account of the delay in repairing the fortifications of Linz, unable to maintain that place, the possession of which was important on account of its forming a connecting point between Bohemia and the Austrian Oberland. Hiller, however, at least saved his honor by pushing forward to the Traun, and, in a fearfully bloody encounter at Ebelsberg, capturing three French eagles, one of his colors alone falling into the enemy's hands. He was, nevertheless, compelled to retire before the superior forces of the French, and Napoleon entered Vienna unopposed. A few balls from the walls of the inner city were directed against the faubourg in his possession, but he no sooner began to bombard the palace than the inner city yielded. The Archduke Charles arrived, when too late, from Bohemia. Both armies, separated by the Danube, stood opposed to one another in the vicinity of the imperial city. Napoleon, in order to bring the enemy to a decisive engagement, crossed the river close to the great island of Lobau. He was received on the opposite bank near Aspern and Esslingen by the Archduke Charles, and, after a dreadful battle, that was carried on with unwearied animosity for two days, the 21st and 22d of May, 1809, was for the first time completely beaten[1] and compelled to fly for refuge to the island of Lobau. The rising stream had, meanwhile, carried away the bridge, Napoleon's sole chance of escape to the opposite bank. For two days he remained on the island

---

[1] The finest feat of arms was that performed by the Austrian infantry, who repulsed twelve French regiments of cuirassiers. This picked body of cavalry was mounted on the best and strongest horses of Holstein and Mecklenburg (for Napoleon overcame Germany principally by means of Germany), and bore an extremely imposing appearance. The Austrian infantry coolly stood their charge and allowed them to come close upon them before firing a shot, when, taking deliberate aim at the horses, they and their riders were rolled in confused heaps on the ground. Three thousand cuirasses were picked up by the victors after the battle.

with his defeated troops, without provisions, and in hourly expectation of being cut to pieces; the Austrians, however, neglected to turn the opportunity to advantage and allowed the French leisure to rebuild the bridge, a work of extreme difficulty. During six weeks afterward the two armies continued to occupy their former positions under the walls of Vienna on the right and left banks of the Danube, narrowly watching each other's movements and preparing for a final struggle.

The Archduke John had successfully penetrated into Italy, where he had defeated the viceroy, Eugene, at Salice and Fontana fredda. Favored by the simultaneous revolt of the Tyrolese, his success appeared certain, when the news of his brother's disaster compelled him to retreat. He withdrew into Hungary,[1] whither he was pursued by Eugene, by whom he was, on the 14th of June, defeated at Raab. The Archduke Ferdinand, who had advanced as far as Warsaw, had been driven back by the Poles under Poniatowski and by a Russian force sent by the emperor Alexander to their aid, which, on this success, invaded Galicia. Napoleon rewarded the Poles for their aid by allowing Russia to seize Wallachia and Moldavia.

The fate of Austria now depended on the issue of the struggle about to take place on the Danube. The archduke's troops were still elate with recent victory, but Napoleon had been strongly reinforced and again began the attack at Wagram, not far from the battleground of Aspern. The contest lasted two days, the 5th and 6th of July. The Austrians fought with great personal gallantry, lost one of their colors, but captured twelve golden eagles and standards of the enemy; but the reserve body, intended to protect their left wing, failing to make its appearance on the field, they were outflanked by Napoleon and driven back upon Moravia. Every means of conveyance in Vienna was put

[1] Napoleon proclaimed independence to the Hungarians, but was unable to gain a single adherent among them.

into requisition for the transport of the forty-five thousand men, wounded on this occasion, to the hospitals, and this heartrending scene indubitably contributed to strengthen the general desire for peace. An armistice was, on the 12th of July, concluded at Znaym, and, after long negotiation, was followed, on the 10th of October, by the treaty of Vienna. Austria was compelled to cede Carniola, Trieste, Croatia, and Dalmatia to Napoleon, Salzburg, Berchtoldsgaden, the Innviertel, and the Hausruckviertel to Bavaria, a part of Galicia to Warsaw and another part to Russia. Count Stadion lost office and was succeeded by Clement, Count von Metternich.—Frederick Stabs, the son of a preacher of Naumburg on the Saal, formed a resolution to poniard Napoleon at Schönbrunn, the imperial palace in the neighborhood of Vienna. Rapp's suspicions became roused, and the young man was arrested before his purpose could be effected. He candidly avowed his intention. "And if I grant you your life?" asked Napoleon. "I would merely make use of the gift to rob you, on the first opportunity, of yours," was the undaunted reply. Four-and-twenty hours afterward the young man was shot.[1] The ancient German race of Gotscheer in Carniola and the people of Istria rose in open insurrection against the French and were only put down by force.

Although Prussia had left Austria unsuccored during this war, many of her subjects were animated with a desire to aid their Austrian brethren. Schill, unable to restrain his impetuosity, quitted Berlin on the 28th of April, for that purpose, with his regiment of hussars. His conduct, although condemned by a sentence of the court-martial, was universally applauded. Dornberg, an officer of Jerome's

---

[1] Aretin about this time published a "Representation of the Patriots of Austria to Napoleon the Great," in which that great sovereign was entreated to bestow a new government upon Austria and to make that country, like the new kingdom of Westphalia, a member of his family of states. A fitting pendant to John Müller's state speech, and so much the more uncalled-for as it was exactly the Austrians who, during this disastrous period, had, less than any of the other races of Germany, lost their national pride.

guard, revolted simultaneously in Hesse, but was betrayed by a false friend at the moment in which Jerome's person was to have been seized, and was compelled to fly for his life. Schill merely advanced as far as Wittenberg and Halberstadt, was again driven northward to Wismar, and finally to Stralsund, by the superior forces of Westphalia and Holland. In a bloody street-fight at Stralsund he split General Carteret's, the Dutch general's head, and was himself killed by a cannon-ball. Thus fell this young hero, true to his motto, "Better a terrible end than endless terror." The Dutch cut off his head, preserved it in spirits of wine, and placed it publicly in the Leyden library, where it remained until 1837, when it was buried at Brunswick in the grave of his faithful followers. Five hundred of his men, under Lieutenant Brunow, escaped by forcing their way through the enemy. Of the prisoners taken on this occasion, eleven officers were, by Napoleon's command, shot at Wesel, fourteen subalterns and soldiers at Brunswick, the rest, about six hundred in number, were sent in chains to Toulon and condemned to the galleys.[1] Dörnberg fled to England. Katt, another patriot, assembled a number of veterans at Stendal and advanced as far as Magdeburg, but was compelled to flee to the Brunswickers in Bohemia. What might not have been the result had the plan of the Archduke Charles to march rapidly through Franconia been followed on the opening of the campaign?

William, duke of Brunswick, the son of the hapless Duke Ferdinand, had quitted Oels, his sole possession, for Bohemia, where he had collected a force two thousand strong, known as the black Brunswickers on account of the color of their uniform and the death's head on their helmets, with which he resolved to avenge his father's death. Victorious in petty engagements over the Saxons at Zittau and over the French under Junot at Berneck, he refused to recognize the armis-

---

[1] They were afterward condemned to hard labor in the Hieres Isles, nor was it until 1814 that the survivors, one hundred and twenty in number, were restored to their homes.—*Allgemeine Zeitung, 1814. Appendix 91.*

tice between Austria and France, and, fighting his way through the enemy, surprised Leipzig by night and there provided himself with ammunition and stores. He was awaited at Halberstadt by the Westphalians under Wellingerode, whom, notwithstanding their numerical superiority, he completely defeated during the night of the 30th of July. Two days later he was attacked in Brunswick, in his father's home, by an enemy three times his superior, by the Westphalians under Rewbel, who advanced from Celle while the Saxons and Dutch pursued him from Erfurt. Aided by his brave citizens, many of whom followed his fortunes, he was again victorious and was enabled by a speedy retreat, in which he broke down all the bridges to his rear, to escape to Elsfleth, whence he sailed to England.

In August, an English army, forty thousand strong, landed on the island of Walcheren and attempted to create a diversion in Holland, but its ranks were speedily thinned by disease, it did not venture up the country and finally returned to England. The English, nevertheless, displayed henceforward immense activity in the Peninsula, where, aided by the brave and high-spirited population,[1] they did great detriment to the French. In the English army in the Peninsula were several thousand Germans, principally Hanoverian refugees. There were also numerous deserters from the Rhenish confederated troops, sent by Napoleon into Spain.

During the war in June, the king of Wurtemberg took possession of Mergentheim, the chief seat of the Teutonic order, which had, up to the present period, remained unsecularized. The surprised inhabitants received the new Protestant authorities with demonstrations of rage and revolted. They were the last and the only ones among all the secularized or mediatized Estates of the empire that boldly attempted opposition. They were naturally overpowered without much difficulty and were cruelly punished. About

---

[1] Vide Napier's Peninsular War for an account of the military achievements of the Spaniards.—*Trans.*

thirty of them were shot by the soldiery; six were executed; several wealthy burgesses and peasants were condemned as criminals to work in chains in the new royal gardens at Stuttgard. Thus miserably terminated the celebrated Teutonic order.

CCLVII. *Revolt of the Tyrolese*

THE Alps of the Tyrol had for centuries been the asylum of liberty. The ancient German communal system had there continued to exist even in feudal times. Exactly at the time when the house of Habsburg lost its most valuable possessions in Switzerland, at the time of the council of Constance, Duke Frederick, surnamed Friedel with the empty purse, was compelled by necessity and for the sake of retaining the affection of the Tyrolese, to confirm them by oath in the possession of great privileges, which his successors, owing to a wholesome dread of exciting the anger of the sturdy mountaineers, prudently refrained from violating. The Tyrol was externally independent and was governed by her own diet. No recruits were levied in that country by the emperor, excepting those for the rifle corps, which elected its own commanders and wore the Tyrolean garb. The imposts were few and trifling in amount, the administration was simple. The free-born peasant enjoyed his rights in common with the patriarchal nobility and clergy, who dwelt in harmony with the people; in several of the valleys the public affairs were administered by simple peasants; each commune had its peculiar laws and customs.

The first invasion of the Tyrol, in 1703, by the Bavarians, was successfully resisted. The Bavarians were driven, with great loss on their side, out of the country. A somewhat similar spirit animated the Tyrolese in 1805, and their anger was solely appeased by the express remonstrances of the Archduke John, whom the inhabitants of the Austrian Tyrol treated with the veneration due to a father. They now fell under the dominion of Bavaria, whose benevolent sovereign, Maximilian Joseph, promised, under the act dated the 14th of January, 1806, "not only strongly to uphold the constitution of the country and the well-earned rights and privileges of the people, but also to promote their welfare"; but, led astray by his, certainly noble, enthusiasm for the rescue of his Bavarian subjects from Jesuit obscurantism, he imagined that similar measures might also be advantageously taken in the Tyrol, where the mountaineers, true to their ancient simplicity, were revolted by the severity of the cure, attempted too by a physician of whose intentions they were mistrustful. Bavaria was overrun with rich monasteries; the Tyrol, less fertile, possessed merely a patriarchal clergy, less numerous, more moral and active. There was no motive for interference. The conscription that, by converting the idle youth of Bavaria into disciplined soldiery, was a blessing to the martial-spirited and improvident population, was impracticable amid the well-trained Tyrolese, and, although the control exercised by a well-regulated bureaucracy might be beneficial when viewed in contradistinction with the ancient complicated system of government and administration of justice during the existence of the division into petty states and the manifold contradictory privileges, it was utterly uncalled for in the simple administration of the Tyrol. For what purpose were mere presumptive ameliorations to be imposed upon a people thoroughly contented with the laws and customs bequeathed by their ancestors? The attempt was nevertheless made, and ancient Bavarian official insolence leagued with French frivolity of the school of Montgelas to vex the Tyrolese and to violate their most sacred privileges. The numerous chapels erected for devotional purposes were thrown down amid marks of ridicule and scorn; the ignorance and superstition of the old church was at one blow to yield to modern enlightenment.[1]

---

[1] Without any attempt being made on the part of the government to prepare the minds of the people by proper instruction, the children were taken away by force in order to be inoculated for the smallpox. The mothers, under an idea that their infants were being bewitched or poisoned, trembled with rage and fear, while the Bavarian authorities and their servants mocked their dismay.

The people shudderingly beheld the crucifixes and images of saints, so long the objects of their deepest veneration, sold to Jews. Notwithstanding the late assurances of the Bavarian king, the Tyrolean diet was, moreover, not only dissolved, but the country was deprived of its ancient name and designated "Southern Bavaria," and the castle of the Tyrol, that had defied the storms of ages, and whose possessor, according to a sacred popular legend, had alone a right to claim the homage of the country, was sold by auction. The national pride of the Tyrolese was deeply and bitterly wounded, their ancient rights and customs were arbitrarily infringed, and, instead of the great benefits so recently promised, eight new taxes were levied, and the tax-gatherers not infrequently rendered themselves still more obnoxious by their brutality. Colonel Dittfurt, who, during the winter of 1809, acted with extreme inhumanity in the Fleimserthal, where the conscription had excited great opposition, and who publicly boasted that with his regiment alone he would keep the whole of the beggarly mountaineers in subjection, drew upon himself the greatest share of the popular animosity.

Austria, when preparing for war in 1809, could therefore confidently reckon upon a general rising in the Tyrol. Andrew Hofer, the host of the Sand at Passeyr (the Sandwirth), went to Vienna, where the revolt was concerted.[1] A con-

[1] Hofer was, in 1790, as the deputy of the Passeyrthal, a member of the diet at Innsbruck which so zealously opposed the reforms attempted by Joseph II.; he had fought, as captain of a rifle corps, against the French in 1796, and, in 1805, when bidding farewell to the Archduke John on the enforced cession of the Tyrol by Austria to Bavaria, had received a significant shake of the hand with an expressed hope of seeing him again in better times. Hofer traded in wine, corn and horses, was well known and highly esteemed as far as the Italian frontier. He had a Herculean form and was remarkably good-looking. He wore a low-crowned, broad-brimmed black Tyrolean hat, ornamented with green ribbons and the feathers of the capercailzie. His broad chest was covered with a red waistcoat, across which green braces, a hand in breadth, were fastened to black chamois-leather knee-breeches. His knees were bare, but his well-developed calves were covered with red stockings. A broad black leathern girdle clasped his muscular form. Over all was thrown a short green coat without buttons. His long dark-brown beard, that fell in rich curls upon his chest, added dignity to his appearance. His full, broad countenance was expressive of good-humor and honesty. His small, penetrating eyes sparkled with vivacity.

spiracy was entered into by the whole of the Tyrolese peasantry. Sixty thousand men, on a moderate calculation, were intrusted with the secret, which was sacredly kept, not a single townsman being allowed to participate in it. Kinkel, the Bavarian general, who was stationed at Innsbruck and narrowly watched the Tyrol, remained perfectly unconscious of the mine beneath his feet. Colonel Wrede, his inferior in command, had been directed to blow up the important bridges in the Pusterthal at St. Lorenzo, in order to check the advance of the Austrians, in case of an invasion. Several thousand French were expected to pass through the Tyrol on their route from Italy to join the army under Napoleon. No suspicion of the approach of a popular outbreak existed. On the 9th of April, the signal was suddenly given; planks bearing little red flags floated down the Inn; on the 10th, the storm burst. Several of the Bavarian sappers sent at daybreak to blow up the bridges of St. Lorenzo being killed by the bullets of an invisible foe, the rest took to flight. Wrede, enraged at the incident, hastened to the spot at the head of two battalions, supported by a body of cavalry and some field-pieces. The whole of the Pusterthal had, however, already risen at the summons of Peter Kemnater, the host of Schabs,[1] in defence of the bridges. Wrede's artillery was captured by the enraged peasantry and cast, together with the artillerymen, into the river. Wrede, after suffering a terrible loss, owing to the skill of the Tyrolean riflemen, who never missed their aim, was completely put to rout, and, although he fell in with a body of three thousand French under Brisson on their route from Italy, resolved, instead of returning to the Pusterthal, to withdraw with the French to Innsbruck. The passage through the valley of the Eisack had, however, been already closed against them by the host of Lechner, and the fine old Roman bridge at Laditsch been blown up. In the pass of the Brixen, where

---

[1] A youth of two-and-twenty, slight in person and extremely handsome, at that time a bridegroom, and inspired by the deepest hatred of the Bavarians, by whose officers he had been personally insulted.

the valley closes, the French and Bavarians suffered immense loss; rocks and trees were rolled on the heads of the appalled soldiery, numbers of whom were also picked off by the unerring rifles of the unseen peasantry. Favored by the open ground at the bridge of Laditsch, they constructed a temporary bridge, across which they succeeded in forcing their way on the 11th of April. Hofer had, meanwhile, placed himself, early on the 10th, at the head of the brave peasantry of Passeyr, Algund, and Meran, and had thrown himself on the same road, somewhat to the north, near Sterzing, where a Bavarian battalion was stationed under the command of Colonel Bärnklau, who, on being attacked by him, on the 11th, retreated to the Sterzinger Moos, a piece of tableland, where, drawn up in square, he successfully repulsed every attempt made to dislodge him until Hofer ordered a wagon, loaded with hay and guided by a girl,[1] to be pushed forward as a screen, behind which the Tyrolese advancing, the square was speedily broken and the whole of Bärnklau's troop was either killed or taken prisoner.

The whole of the lower valley of the Inn had, on the selfsame day, been raised by Joseph Speckbacher, a wealthy peasant of Rinn, the greatest hero called into existence by this fearful peasant war. The alarm-bell pealed from every church tower throughout the country. A Bavarian troop, at that time engaged in levying contributions at Axoms as a punishment for disobedience, hastily fled. The city of Hall was, on the ensuing night, taken by Speckbacher, who, after lighting about a hundred watch-fires in a certain quarter, as if about to make an attack on that side, crept, under cover of the darkness, to the gate on the opposite side, where, as a common passenger, he demanded permission to enter, took possession of the opened gate, and seized the four hundred Bavarians stationed in the city. On the 12th, he appeared before Innsbruck. Kinkel was astounded at the au-

---

[1] The daughter of a tailor, named Camper. As the balls flew around her, she shouted, "On with ye! who cares for Bavarian dumplings!"

dacity of the peasants, whom Dittfurt glowed with impatience to punish. But the people, shouting "Vivat Franzl! Down with the Bavarians!" again rushed upon the guns and turned them upon the Bavarians, who were, moreover, exposed to a murderous fire poured upon them from the windows and towers by the citizens, who had risen in favor of the peasantry. The people of the upper valley of the Inn, headed by Major Teimer, also poured to the scene of carnage. Dittfurt performed prodigies of valor, but every effort was vain. Scornfully refusing to yield to the canaille, he continued, although struck by two bullets, to fight with undaunted courage, when a third stretched him on the ground; again he started up and furiously defended himself until a fourth struck him in the head. He died four days afterward in a state of wild delirium, cursing and swearing. Kinkel and the whole of the Bavarian infantry yielded themselves prisoners. The cavalry attempted to escape, but were dismounted with pitchforks by the peasantry, and the remainder were taken prisoners before Hall.

Wrede and Brisson, meanwhile, crossed the Brenner. At Sterzing, every trace of the recent conflict had been carefully obliterated, and Wrede vainly inquired the fate of Bärnklau. He entered the narrow pass, and Hofer's riflemen spread death and confusion among his ranks. The strength of the allied column, nevertheless, enabled it to force its way through, and it reached Innsbruck, where, completely surrounded by the Tyrolese, it, in a few minutes, lost several hundred men, and, in order to escape utter destruction, laid down its arms. The Tyrolese entered Innsbruck in triumph, preceded by the military band belonging to the enemy, which was compelled to play, followed by Teimer and Brisson in an open carriage, and with the rest of their prisoners guarded between their ranks. Their captives consisted of two generals, ten staff-officers, above a hundred other officers, eight thousand infantry, and a thousand cavalry. Throughout the Tyrol, the arms of Bavaria were cast to the ground and all the Bavarian authorities were removed from office. The prisoners were, nevertheless, treated with the greatest humanity, the only instance to the contrary being that of a tax-gatherer, who, having once boasted that he would grind the Tyrolese down until they gladly ate hay, was, in revenge, compelled to swallow a bushel of hay for his dinner.

It was not until after these brilliant achievements on the part of the Tyrolese that Lieutenant Field-Marshal von Chasteler, a Dutchman, and the Baron von Hormayr, the imperial civil intendant, entered Innsbruck with several thousand Austrians, and that Hormayr assumed the reins of government. Two thousand French, under General Lemoine, attempted to make an inroad from Trent, but were repulsed by Hofer and his ally, Colonel Count Leiningen, who had been sent to his aid by Chasteler. The advance of a still stronger force of the enemy under Baraguay d'Hilliers a second time against Botzen called Chasteler in person into the field, and the French, after a smart engagement near Volano, where the Herculean Passeyrers carried the artillery on their shoulders, were forced to retreat. It was on this occasion that Leiningen, who had hastily pushed too far forward, was rescued from captivity by Hofer.[1] The Vorarlberg had, meanwhile, also been raised by Teimer. A Dr. Schneider placed himself at the head of the insurgents, whose forces already extended in this direction as far as Lindau, Kempten, and Memmingen.

Napoleon's success, at this conjuncture, at Ratisbon, enabled him to despatch a division of his army into the Tyrol to quell the insurrection that had broken out to his rear. Wrede, who had been quickly exchanged and set at liberty, speedily found himself at the head of a small Bavarian force, and succeeded in driving the Austrians under Jellachich, after an obstinate and bloody resistance, out of Salzburg, on the 29th of April. Jellachich withdrew to the pass

---

[1] The Austrian general, Marschall, who had been sent to guard the Southern Tyrol, was removed for declaring that he deemed it an insult for the military to make common cause with peasants and for complaining of his being compelled to sit down to table with Hofer.

of Lueg for the purpose of placing himself in communication with the Archduke John, who was on his way from Italy. An attack made upon this position by the Bavarians being repulsed, Napoleon despatched Marshal Lefebvre, duke of Dantzig, from Salzburg with a considerable force to their assistance. Lefebvre spoke German, was a rough soldier, treated the peasants as robbers instead of legitimate foes, shot every leader who fell into his hands, and gave his soldiery license to commit every description of outrage on the villagers. The greater part of the Tyrolese occupying the pass of Strub having quitted their post on Ascension Day in order to attend divine service, the rest were, after a gallant resistance, overpowered and mercilessly butchered. Chasteler, anxious to repair his late negligence, advanced against the Bavarians in the open valley of the Inn and was overwhelmed by superior numbers at Wörgl. Speckbacher, followed by his peasantry, again made head against the enemy, whom, notwithstanding the destruction caused in his ranks by their rapid and well-directed fire, he twice drove out of Schwatz. The Bavarians, nevertheless, succeeded in forcing an entrance into the town, which they set on fire after butchering all the inhabitants, hundreds of whom were hanged to the trees or had their hands nailed to their heads. These cruelties were not, even in a single instance, imitated by the Tyrolese. The proposal to send their numerous Bavarian prisoners home maimed of one ear, as a mode of recognition in case they should again serve against the Tyrol, was rejected by Hofer. The unrelenting rage of the Bavarians was solely roused by the unsparing ridicule of the Tyrolese, by whom they were nicknamed, on account of the general burliness of their figures and their fondness for beer, Bavarian hogs, and who, the moment they came within hearing, would call out to them, as to a herd of pigs, "Tschu, Tschu, Tschu—Natsch, Natsch." The Bavarians, intoxicated with success, advanced further up the country, surrounded the village of Vomp, set it on fire amid the sound of kettledrums and hautboys, and shot the inhabitants as they attempted to escape from the burning houses. Chasteler and Hormayr were, during this robber-campaign, as it was termed by the French, proscribed as chefs de brigands by Napoleon. Count Tannenberg, the descendant of the oldest of the baronial families in the Tyrol, a blind and venerable man, who was also taken prisoner en route, replied with dignity to the censure heaped upon him by Wrede, and at Munich defended his country's cause before the king.[1] The officers, whom he had treated with extreme politeness, rose from his hospitable board to set fire to his castle over his head. The Scharnitz was yielded, and the Bavarians under Arco penetrated also on that side into the country.—Jellachich, upon this, retired upon Carinthia, and was followed through the Pusterthal by Chasteler, who dreaded being cut off. The peasants, incredulous of their abandonment by Austria, implored, entreated him to remain, to which, for the sake of freeing himself from their importunities, he at length consented, but they had no sooner dispersed in order to summon the people again to the conflict than he retired. Hofer, on returning to the spot, merely finding a small body of troops under the command of General Buol, who had received orders to bring up the rear, threw himself in despair on a bed. Eisenstecken, his companion and adjutant, however, instantly declared that the departure of the soldiers must, at all hazards, be prevented. The officers signed a paper by which they bound themselves, even though contrary to the express orders of the general, to remain. Buol, upon this, yielded and remained, but, during the fearful battle that ensued, remained in the post-house on the Brenner, inactively watching the conflict, which terminated in the triumph of the peasantry. Hormayr completely absconded and attempted to escape into Switzerland.

Innsbruck was surrendered by Teimer to the French, on the 19th of May. Napoleon's defeat, about this time, at

---

[1] Proclamation of the emperor Francis to the Tyrolese: "Willingly do I anticipate your wish to be regarded as the most faithful subjects of the Austrian empire. Never again shall the sad fate of being torn from my heart befall you."

Aspern having however compelled Lefebvre to return hastily to the Danube, leaving merely a part of the Bavarians with General Deroy in Innsbruck, the Tyrolese instantly seized the opportunity, and Hofer, Eisenstecken, and the gallant Speckbacher boldly assembled the whole of the peasantry on the mountain of Isel. Peter Thalguter led the brave and gigantic men of Algund. Haspinger, the Capuchin, nicknamed Redbeard, appeared on this occasion for the first time in the guise of a commander and displayed considerable military talent. An incessant struggle was carried on from the 25th to the 29th of May.[1] Deroy, repulsed from the mountain of Isel with a loss of almost three thousand men, simulated an intention to capitulate, and withdrew unheard during the night by muffling the horses' hoofs and the wheels of the artillery carriages and enjoining silence under pain of death. Speckbacher attempted to impede his retreat at Hall, but arrived too late.[2] Teimer was accused of having been remiss in his duty through jealousy of the common peasant leaders. Arco escaped by an artifice similar to that of Deroy and abandoned the Scharnitz. The Vorarlbergers again spread as far as Kempten. Hormayr also returned, retook the reins of government, imposed taxes, flooded the country with useless law-scribbling, and, at the same time, refused to grant the popular demand for the convocation of the Tyrolean diet. After the victory of Aspern, the emperor declared, "My faithful county of Tyrol shall henceforward ever remain incorporated with the Austrian empire, and I will agree to no treaty of peace save one indissolubly uniting the Tyrol with my monarchy." During this happy interval, Speckbacher besieged the fortress of Cuffstein, where he performed many signal acts of valor.[3]

---

1 The Count von Stachelburg from Meran, who fought as a volunteer among the peasantry, fell at that time. He was the last of his race.

2 He was joined here by his son Anderl, a child ten years of age, who collected the enemy's balls in his hat, and so obstinately refused to quit the field of battle that his father was compelled to have him carried by force to a distant alp.

3 He paid a visit, in disguise, to the commandant within the fortress, extinguished a grenade with his hat, crept undiscovered into the fortress and spoiled

The disaster of Wagram followed, and, in the ensuing armistice, the Emperor Francis was compelled to agree to the withdrawal of the whole of his troops from the Tyrol. The Archduke John is said to have given a hint to General Buol to remain in the Tyrol as if retained there by force by the peasantry, instead of which both Buol and Hormayr hurried their retreat, after issuing a miserable proclamation, in which they "recommended the Tyrolese to the care of the duke of Dantzig." Lefebvre actually again advanced at the head of thirty to forty thousand French, Bavarians and Saxons. The courage of the unfortunate peasantry naturally sank. Hofer alone remained unshaken, and said, on bidding Hormayr farewell, "Well, then, I will undertake the government, and, as long as God wills, name myself Andrew Hofer, host of the Sand at Passeyr, Count of the Tyrol." Hormayr laughed.—A general dispersion took place. Hofer alone remained. When, resolute in his determination not to abandon his native soil, he was on his way back to his dwelling, he encountered Speckbacher hurrying away in a carriage in the company of some Austrian officers. "Wilt thou also desert thy country?" was Hofer's sad demand. Buol, in order to cover his retreat, sent back eleven guns and nine hundred Bavarian prisoners to General Rusca, who continued to threaten the Pusterthal.

In the mountains all was tranquil, and the advance of the French columns was totally unopposed. Hofer, concealed in a cavern amid the steep rocks overhanging his native vale, besought Heaven for aid, and, by his enthusiastic entreaties, succeeded in persuading the brave Capuchin,

---

the fire-engines, cut loose the ships moored beneath the walls, etc. Joseph Speckbacher of the Innthal was an open-hearted, fine-spirited fellow, endowed with a giant's strength, and the best marksman in the country. His clear bright eye could, at the distance of half a mile, distinguish the bells on the necks of the cattle. In his youth, he was addicted to poaching, and being, on one occasion, when in the act of roasting a chamois, surprised by four Bavarian Jäger, he unhesitatingly dashed the melted fat of the animal into their faces, and, quick as lightning, dealt each of them a deathblow with the butt-end of his rifle.

Joachim Haspinger, once more to quit the monastery of Seeben, whither he had retired. A conference was held at Brixen between Haspinger, Martin Schenk, the host of the Krug, a jovial man of powerful frame, Kemnater, and a third person of similar calling, Peter Mayer, host of the Mare, who bound themselves again to take up arms in the Eastern Tyrol, while Hofer, in person, raised the Western Tyrol. Speckbacher, to the delight of the three confederates, unexpectedly made his appearance at this conjuncture. Deeply wounded by the reproach contained in the few words addressed to him by Hofer, he had, notwithstanding the urgent entreaties of his companions, quitted them on arriving at the nearest station and hastened to retake his post in defence of his country.

Lefebvre had already entered Innsbruck, and, according to his brutal custom, had plundered the villages and reduced them to ashes; he had also published a proscription-list[1] instead of the amnesty. A desperate resistance now commenced. The whole of the Tyrol again flew to arms; the young men placed in their green hats the bunch of rosemary gathered by the girl of their heart, the more aged a peacock's plume, the symbol of the house of Habsburg, all carried the rifle, so murderous in their hands; they made cannons of larch-wood, bound with iron rings, which did good service; they raised abatis, blew up rocks, piled immense

---

[1] He cited the following names immortal in the Tyrol: A. Hofer, Straub of Hall, Reider of Botzen, Bombardi, postmaster of Salurn, Morandel of Kaltern, Resz of Fleims, Tschöll of Meran, Frischmann of Schlanders, Senn, sheriff of Nauders, Fischer, actuary of Landek, Strehle, burgomaster of Imbst, Plawen, governor of Reutti, Major Dietrich of Lermos, Aschenbacher, governor of the Achenthal, Sieberer of Cuffstein, Wintersteller of Kisbüchl, Kolb of Lienz, Count Sarntheim, Peer, counsellor to the court of appeal. Count Sarntheim was taken prisoner and carried into Bavaria, together with the heroic Baroness of Sternbach, who, mounted on horseback and armed with pistols, accompanied the patriot force and aided in the command. She was seized in her castle of Mühlan, imprisoned in a house of correction at Munich, and afterward carried to Strasburg, was deprived of the whole of her property, ignominiously treated, and threatened with death, but never lost courage.—*Beda, Weber's Tyrol.* Wintersteller was a descendant of the brave host of the same name who, in 1703, adorned his house, which was afterward occupied by Wintersteller, with the trophies won from the Bavarians.

masses of stone on the extreme edges of the precipitous rocks commanding the narrow vales, in order to hurl them upon the advancing foe, and directed the timber-slides in the forest-grown mountains, or those formed of logs by means of which the timber for building was usually run into the valleys, in such a manner upon the most important passes and bridges, as to enable them to shoot enormous trees down upon them with tremendous velocity.

Lefebvre resolved to advance with the main body of his forces across the Brenner to Botzėn, whither another corps under Burscheidt also directed its way through the upper valley of the Inn, the Finstermunz, and Meran, while a third under Rusca came from Carinthia through the Pusterthal, and a fourth under Peyry was on the march from Verona through the vale of the Adige. These various corps d'armée, by which the Tyrol was thus attacked simultaneously on every point, were to concentrate in the heart of the country. Lefebvre found the Brenner open. The Tyrolese, headed by Haspinger, had burned the bridges on the Oberau and awaited the approach of the enemy on the heights commanding the narrow valley of Eisach. The Saxons under Rouyer were sent in advance by Lefebvre to shed their blood for a foreign despot. Rocks and trees hurled by the Tyrolese into the valley crushed numbers of them to death. Rouyer, after being slightly hurt by a rolling mass of rock, retreated after leaving orders to the Saxon regiment, composed of contingents from Weimar, Gotha, Coburg, Hildburghausen, Altenburg, and Meiningen, commanded by Colonel Egloffstein, to retain its position in the Oberau. This action took place on the 4th of August. The Saxons, worn out by the fatigue and danger to which they were exposed, were compelled, on the ensuing day, to make head in the narrow vale against overwhelming numbers of the Tyrolese, whose incessant attacks rendered a moment's repose impossible. Although faint with hunger and with the intensity of the heat, a part of the troops under Colonel Egloffstein succeeded in forcing their way through, though at an immense sacrifice of life,[1] and fell back upon Rouyer, who had taken up a position at Sterzing without fighting a stroke in their aid, and who expressed his astonishment at their escape. The rest of the Saxon troops were taken prisoners, after a desperate resistance, in the dwelling-houses of Oberau.[2] They had lost nearly a thousand men. The other corps d'armée met with no better fate. Burscheidt merely advanced up the valley of the Inn as far as the bridges of Pruz, whence, being repulsed by the Tyrolese and dreading destruction, he retreated during the dark night of the 8th of August. His infantry crept, silent and unheard, across the bridge of Pontlaz, of such fatal celebrity in 1703, which was strictly watched by the Tyrolese. The cavalry cautiously followed, but were betrayed by the sound of one of the horses' feet. Rocks and trees were in an instant hurled upon the bridge, crushing men and horses and blocking up the way. The darkness that veiled the scene but added to its horrors. The whole of the troops shut up beyond the bridge were either killed or taken prisoner. Burscheidt reached Innsbruck with merely a handful of men, completely worn out by the incessant pursuit. Rusca was also repulsed, between the 6th and the 11th of August (particularly at the bridge of Lienz), in the Pusterthal, by brave Antony Steger. Rusca had set two hundred farms on fire. Twelve hundred of his men were killed, and his retreat was accelerated by Steger's threat to roast him, in case he fell

---

[1] When incessantly pursued and ready to drop with fatigue, they found a cask of wine, and a drummer, knocking off its head, stooped down to drink, when he was pierced with a bullet, and his blood mingled with the liquor, which was, nevertheless, greedily swallowed by the famishing soldiery.—*Jacob's Campaign of the Gotha-Altenburgers.*

[2] The Tyrolese aimed at the windows and shot every one who looked out. As soon as the houses were, by this means, filled with the dead and wounded, they stormed them and took the survivors prisoner. Two hundred and thirty men of Weimar and Coburg, commanded by Major Germar, defended themselves to the last; the house in which they were being at length completely surrounded and set on fire by the Tyrolese, they surrendered. This spot was afterward known as the "Sachsenklemme." Seven hundred Saxon prisoners escaped from their guards and took refuge on the Krimmer Tauern, where they were recaptured by the armed women and girls.

into his hands, like a scorpion, within a fiery circle. Peyry did not venture into the country.

Lefebvre, who had followed to the rear of the Saxon troops from Innsbruck, bitterly reproached them with their defeat, but, although he placed himself in advance, did not succeed in penetrating as far as they had up the country. At Mauls, his cavalry were torn from their saddles and killed with clubs, and he escaped, with great difficulty, after losing his cocked hat. His corps, notwithstanding its numerical strength, was unable to advance a step further. The Capuchin harassed his advanced guard from Mauls and was seconded by Speckbacher from Stilfs, while Count Arco was attacked to his rear at Schonberg by multitudes of Tyrolese. The contest was carried on without intermission from the 5th to the 10th of August. Lefebvre was finally compelled to retreat with his thinned and weary troops.[1] On the 11th, Deroy posted himself with the rearguard on the mountain of Isel. The Capuchin, after reading mass under the open sky to his followers, again attacked him on the 13th. A horrible slaughter ensued. Four hundred Bavarians, who had fallen beneath the clubs of their infuriated antagonists, lay in a confused heap. The enemy evacuated Innsbruck and the whole of the Tyrol.[2] Count Arco was one of the last victims of this bloody campaign.

The Sandwirth placed himself at the head of the government at Innsbruck. Although a simple peasant and ever

---

[1] Bartholdy relates that Lefebvre, disguised as a common soldier, mingled with the cavalry in order to escape the balls of the Tyrolese sharpshooters. A man of Passeyr is said to have captured a three-pounder and to have carried it on his shoulders across the mountain. The Tyrolese would even carry their wounded enemies carefully on their shoulders to their villages. A Count Mohr greatly distinguished himself among the people of Vintschgau. The spirit shown by an old man above eighty years of age, who, after shooting a number of the enemy from a rock on which he had posted himself, threw himself, exclaiming "Juhhe! in God's name!" down the precipice, with a Saxon soldier, by whom he had been seized, is worthy of record.

[2] Von Seebach, in his History of the Ducal Saxon Regiment, graphically describes the flight. During the night time, all the mountains around the beautiful valley of Innsbruck were lighted up with watch-fires. Lefebvre ordered his to be kept brightly burning while his troops silently withdrew.

faithful to the habits of his station,[1] he laid down some admirable rules, convoked a national assembly, and raised the confidence of the people of Carinthia, to whom he addressed a proclamation remarkable for dignity. He hoped, at that time, by summoning the whole of the mountain tribes to arms and leading them to Vienna, to compel the enemy to accede to more favorable terms of peace. Speckbacher penetrated into the district of Salzburg, defeated the Bavarians at Lofers and Unken, took one thousand seven hundred prisoners, and advanced as far as Reichenhall and Melek. The Capuchin proposed, in his zeal, to storm Salzburg and invade Carinthia, but was withheld by Speckbacher, who saw the hazard attached to the project, as well as the peril that would attend the departure of the Tyrolese from their country. His plan merely consisted in covering the eastern frontier. His son, Anderle, who had escaped from his secluded alp, unexpectedly joined him and fought at his side. Speckbacher was stationed at Melek, where he drove Major Rummele with his Bavarian battalion into the Salzach, but was shortly afterward surprised by treachery. He had already been deprived of his arms, thrown to the ground, and seriously injured with blows dealt with a club, when, furiously springing to his feet, he struck his opponents to the earth

---

[1] He did not set himself above his equals and followed his former simple mode of life. The emperor of Austria sent him a golden chain and three thousand ducats, the first money received by the Tyrol from Austria; but Hofer's pride was not raised by this mark of favor, and the naiveté of his reply on this occasion has often been a subject of ridicule: "Sirs, I thank you. I have no news for you to-day. I have, it is true, three couriers on the road, the Watscher-Hiesele, the Sixten-Seppele, and the Memmele-Franz, and the Schwanz ought long to have been here; I expect the rascal every hour." The honest fellow permitted no pillage, no disorderly conduct; he even guarded the public morals with such strictness as to publish the following orders against the half-naked mode, imported by the French, at that time followed by the women: "Many of my good fellow-soldiers and defenders of their country have complained that the women of all ranks cover their bosoms and arms too little, or with transparent dresses, and by these means raise sinful desires highly displeasing to God and to all piously-disposed persons. It is hoped that they will, by better behavior, preserve themselves from the punishment of God, and, in case of the contrary, must solely blame themselves should they find themselves disagreeably covered with ——. Andre Hofer, chief in command in the Tyrol."

and escaped with a hundred of his men across a wall of rock unscalable save by the foot of the expert and hardy mountaineer. His young son was torn from his side and taken captive. The king, Maximilian Joseph, touched by his courage and beauty, sent for him and had him well educated.—The Capuchin, who had reached Muhrau in Styria, was also compelled to retire.

The peace of Vienna, in which the Tyrolese were not even mentioned, was meanwhile concluded. The restoration of the Tyrol to Bavaria was tacitly understood, and, in order to reduce the country to obedience, three fresh armies again approached the frontiers, the Italian, Peyry, from the south through the valley of the Adige, and Baraguay d'Hilliers from the west through the Pusterthal; the former suffered a disastrous defeat above Trent, but was rescued from utter destruction by General Vial, who had followed to his rear, and who, as well as Baraguay, advanced as far as Brixen.[1] Drouet d'Erlon, with the main body of the Bavarians, came from the north across the Strub and the Loferpass, and gained forcible possession of the Engpass. Hofer had been persuaded by the priest, Donay, to relinquish the anterior passes into the country and Innsbruck, and to take up a strong position on the fortified mountain of Isel. Speckbacher arrived too late to defend Innsbruck, and, enraged at the ill-laid plan of defence, threw a body of his men into the Zillerthal in order to prevent the Bavarians from falling upon Hofer's rear. He was again twice wounded at the storming of the Kemmberg, which had already been fortified by the Bavarians. On the 25th of October, the Bavarians entered Innsbruck and summoned Hofer to capitulate. During the night of the 30th, Baron Lichtenthurn appeared in the Tyrolese camp, announced the conclusion of peace, and delivered a letter from the Archduke John, in which the Tyrolese were commanded peaceably to disperse and no

---

[1] During the pillage of the monastery of Seeben by the French, a nun, in order to escape from their hands, cast herself from the summit of the rock into the valley.

longer to offer their lives a useless sacrifice. There was no warrant for the future, not a memory of an earlier pledge. The commands of their beloved master were obeyed by the Tyrolese with feelings of bitter regret, and a complete dispersion took place. Speckbacher alone maintained his ground, and repulsed the enemy on the 2d and 3d of November, but, being told, in a letter, by Hofer, "I announce to you that Austria has made peace with France and has forgotten the Tyrol," he gave up all further opposition, and Mayer and Kemnater, who had gallantly made head against General Rusca at the Muhlbacher Klause, followed his example.

The tragedy drew to a close. Hofer returned to his native vale, where the people of Passeyr and Algund, resolved at all hazards not to submit to the depredations of the Italian brigands under Rusca, flocked around him and compelled him to place himself at their head for a last and desperate struggle. Above Meran, the French were thrown in such numbers from the Franzosenbuhl, which still retains its name, that "they fell like a shower of autumnal leaves into the city." The horses belonging to a division of cavalry intended to surround the insurgent peasantry were all that returned; their riders had been shot to a man. Rusca lost five hundred dead and one thousand seven hundred prisoners. The Capuchin was also present, and generously saved the captive Major Doreille, whose men had formerly set fire to a village, from the hands of the infuriated peasantry. But a traitor guided the enemy to the rear of the brave band of patriots; Peter Thalguter fell, and Hofer took refuge amid the highest Alps.—Kolb, who was by some supposed to be an English agent, but who was simply an enthusiast, again summoned the peasantry around Brixen to arms. The peasantry still retained such a degree of courage, as to set up an enormous barn-door as a target for the French artillery, and at every shot up jumped a ludicrous figure. Resistance had, however, ceased to be general; the French pressed in ever-increasing numbers through the valleys, disarmed the people, the majority of whom, obedient to Hofer's first mandate, no longer attempted opposition, and took their leaders captive. Peter Mayer was shot at Botzen. His life was offered to him on condition of his denying all participation in the patriotic struggles of his countrymen, but he disdained a lie and boldly faced death. Those among the peasantry most distinguished for gallantry were either shot or hanged. Baur, a Bavarian author, who had fought against the Tyrolese, and is consequently a trusty witness, remarks that all the Tyrolese patriots, without exception, evinced the greatest contempt of death. The struggle recommenced in the winter, but was merely confined to the Pusterthal. A French division under Broussier was cut off on the snowed-up roads and shot to a man by the peasantry.

Hofer at first took refuge with his wife and child in a narrow rocky hollow in the Kellerlager, afterward in the highest Alpine hut, near the Oetzthaler Firner in the wintry desert. Vainly was he implored to quit the country; his resolution to live or to die on his native soil was unchangeable. A peasant named Raffel, unfortunately descrying the smoke from the distant hut, discovered his place of concealment, and boasted in different places of his possession of the secret of his hiding-place. This came to the ears of Father Donay, a traitor in the pay of France;[1] Raffel was arrested, and, in the night of the 27th of January, 1810, guided one thousand six hundred French and Italian troops to the mountain, while two thousand French were quartered in the circumjacent country. Hofer yielded himself prisoner with calm dignity. The Italians abused him personally, tore out his beard, and dragged him pinioned, half naked and barefoot, in his night-dress, over ice and snow to the valley. He was then put into a carriage and carried into Italy to the fortress of Mantua. No one interceded in his behalf.

---

[1] Donay had devoted himself to the service of the church, but having committed a theft, had been refused ordination. Napoleon rewarded him for his treachery with—ordination and the appointment of chaplain in the Santa Casa at Loretto.

Napoleon sent orders by the Paris telegraph to shoot him within four-and-twenty hours. He prepared cheerfully for death.[1] On being led past the other Tyrolese prisoners, they embraced his knees, weeping. He gave them his blessing. His executioners halted not far from the Porta Chiesa, where, placing himself opposite the twelve riflemen selected for the dreadful office, he refused either to allow himself to be blindfolded or to kneel. "I stand before my Creator," he exclaimed with a firm voice, "and standing will I restore to Him the spirit He gave!" He gave the signal to fire, but the men, it may be, too deeply moved by the scene, missed their aim. The first fire brought him on his knees, the second stretched him on the ground, and a corporal, advancing, terminated his misery by shooting him through the head, February 29, 1810.—At a later period, when Mantua again became Austrian, the Tyrolese bore his remains back to his native Alps. A handsome monument of white marble was erected to his memory in the church at Innsbruck; his family was ennobled. Count Alexander of Wurtemberg has poetically described the restoration of his remains to the Tyrol, for which he so nobly fought and died.

"How was the gallant hunter's breast
With mingled feelings torn,
As slowly winding 'mid the Alps,
His hero's corpse was borne!

"The ancient Gletcher, glowing red,
Though cold their wonted mien,
Bright radiance shed o'er Hofer's head,
Loud thundered the lavine!"

Haspinger, the brave Capuchin, escaped unhurt to Vienna, in which Joseph Speckbacher, the greatest hero of this war,

---

[1] Four hours before his execution he wrote to his brother-in-law, Pöhler, "My beloved, the hostess, is to have mass read for my soul at St. Marin by the rosy-colored blood. She is to have prayers read in both parishes, and is to let the sub-landlord give my friends soup, meat, and half a bottle of wine each. The money I had with me I have distributed to the poor; as for the rest, settle my accounts with the people as justly as you can. All in the world adieu, until we all meet in heaven eternally to praise God. Death appears to me so easy that my eyes have not once been wet on that account. Written at five o'clock in the morning, and at nine o'clock I set off with the aid of all the saints on my journey to God."

also succeeded, after unheard-of suffering and peril.—The Bavarians in pursuit of him searched the mountains in troops, and vowed to "cut his skin into boot-straps, if they caught him." Speckbacher attempted to escape into Austria, but was unable to go beyond Dux, the roads being blocked up with snow. At Dux, the Bavarians came upon his trace, and attacking the house in which he had taken refuge, he escaped by leaping through the roof, but again wounded himself. During the ensuing twenty-seven days, he wandered about the snow-clad forests, exposed to the bitter cold and in danger of starvation. During four consecutive days he did not taste food. He at length found an asylum in a hut in a high and exposed situation at Bolderberg, where he by chance fell in with his wife and children, who had also taken refuge there. The watchful Bavarians pursued him even here, and he merely owed his escape to the presence of mind with which, taking a sledge upon his shoulders, he advanced toward them as if he had been the servant of the house. No longer safe in this retreat, he hid himself in a cave on the Gemshaken, whence he was, in the beginning of spring, carried by a snow-lavine a mile and a half into the valley. He contrived to disengage himself from the snow, but one of his legs had been dislocated and rendered it impossible for him to regain his cave. Suffering unspeakable anguish, he crept to the nearest hut, where he found two men, who carried him to his own house at Rinn, whither his wife had returned. But Bavarians were quartered in the house, and his only place of refuge was the cow-shed, where Zoppel, his faithful servant, dug for him a hole beneath the bed of one of the cows, and daily brought him food. The danger of discovery was so great that his wife was not made acquainted with his arrival. He remained in this half-buried state for seven weeks, until rest had so far invigorated his frame as to enable him to escape across the high mountain passes, now freed by the May sun from the snow. He accordingly rose from his grave and bade adieu to his sorrowing wife. He reached Vienna without encountering further mishap, but gained no thanks for his heroism. He was compelled to give up a small estate that he had purchased with the remains of his property, the purchase-money proving insufficient, and he must have been consigned to beggary, had not Hofer's son, who had received a fine estate from the emperor, engaged him as his steward.

CCLVIII. *Napoleon's Supremacy*

Napoleon had, during the great war in Austria, during the intermediate time between the battles of Aspern and Wagram, caused the person of the pope, Pius VII., to be seized, and had incorporated the state of the church with his Italian kingdom. The venerable pope, whose energies were called forth by misfortune, astonished Christendom by his bold opposition to the ruler over the destinies of Europe, before whom he had formerly bent in humble submission, and for whose coronation he had condescended to visit Paris in person. The re-establishment of Catholicism in France by Napoleon had rendered the pope deeply his debtor, but Napoleon's attempt to deprive him of all temporal power, and to render him, as the first bishop of his realm, subordinate to himself, called forth a sturdy opposition. Napoleon no sooner spoke the language of Charlemagne than the pope responded in the words of Gregory VII. and of Innocent IV.: "Time has produced no change in the authority of the pope; now as ever does the pope reign supreme over the emperors and kings of the earth." The diplomatic dispute was carried on for some time, owing to Napoleon's expectation of the final compliance of the pope.[1] But on his continued refusal to submit, the peril with which Napoleon's Italian possessions were threatened by the landing of a British force in Italy and by the war with Austria, induced him, first of all, to

---

[1] The pope, among other things, long refused his consent to the second marriage of the king of Westphalia, although that prince's first wife was merely a Protestant and an American citizen.

throw a garrison into Ancona, and afterward to take possession of Rome, and, as the pope still continued obstinate, finally to seize his person, to carry him off to France, and to annex the Roman territory to his great empire. The anathema hurled by the pope upon Napoleon's head had at least the effect of creating a warmer interest in behalf of the pontiff in the hearts of the Catholic population and of increasing their secret antipathy toward his antagonist.

In 1810, Napoleon annexed Holland and East Friesland "as alluvial lands" to France. His brother Louis, who had vainly labored for the welfare of Holland, selected a foreign residence and scornfully refused to accept the pension settled upon him by Napoleon. The first act of the new sovereign of Holland was the imposition of an income tax of fifty per cent. Instruction in the French language was enforced in all the schools, and all public proclamations and documents were drawn up in both Dutch and French.[1] Holland was formed into two departments, which were vexed by two prefects, the Conte de Celles and Baron Staffart, Belgian renegades and blind tools of the French despot, and was, moreover, harassed by the tyrannical and cruel espionage, under Duvillieres, Duterrage, and Marivaux, which, in 1812, occasioned several ineffectual attempts to throw off the yoke.[2] In 1811, Holland was also deprived of Batavia, her sole remaining colony, by the British.

Lower Saxony, as far as the Baltic, the principalities of Oldenburg, Salm, and Aremberg, the Hanse towns, Hamburg, Bremen, and Lubeck, were, together with a portion of the kingdom of Westphalia, at the same time also incorporated by Napoleon with France, under pretext of putting a stop to the contraband trade carried on on those coasts,

---

[1] Bilderdyk, whom the Dutch consider as their greatest poet, was, nevertheless, at that time, Napoleon's basest flatterer, and ever expressed a hypochondriacal and senseless antipathy to Germany.

[2] At Amsterdam, in 1811; in the district around Leyden, in 1812. Insurrections of a similar character were suppressed in April, 1811, in the country around Liege; in December, 1812, at Aix-la-Chapelle; the East Frieslanders also rebelled against the conscription.

more particularly from the island of Heligoland. He openly aimed at converting the Germans, and they certainly discovered little disinclination to the metamorphosis, into French. He pursued the same policy toward the Italians, and, had he continued to reign, would have followed a similar system toward the Poles. The subjection of the whole of Italy, Germany, and Poland lay within his power, but, to the nations inhabiting those countries he must, notwithstanding their incorporation with his universal empire, have guaranteed the maintenance of their integrity, a point he had resolved at all hazards not to concede. He, consequently, preferred dividing these nations and allowing one-half to be governed by princes inimical to him, but whose power he despised. His sole dread was patriotism, the popular love of liberty. Had he placed himself, as was possible in 1809, on the imperial throne of Germany, the consequent unity of that empire must, even under foreign sway, have endangered the ruler: he preferred gradually to gallicize Germany as she had been formerly romanized by her ancient conquerors. His intention to sever the Rhenish provinces and Lower Saxony entirely from Germany was clear as day. They received French laws, French governors, no German book was allowed to cross their frontiers without previous permission from the police, and in each department but one newspaper, and that subject to the revision of the prefect, was allowed to be published.—In Hamburg, one Baumhauer was arrested for an anti-gallic expression and thrown into the subterranean dungeons of Magdeburg, where he pined to death. The same tyranny was exercised even on the German territory belonging to the Rhenish confederation. Becker, privy-councillor of the duke of Gotha, was transported beyond the seas for having published a pamphlet against France. Several authors were compelled to retire into Sweden and Russia; several booksellers were arrested, numerous books were confiscated. Not the most trifling publication was permitted within the Rhenish confederated states that even remotely opposed the interests of France. The whole of the princes of the Rhenish confederation were, consequently, under the surveillance of French censors and of the literary spies of Germany in the pay of France. Hormayr's Archives contain a pamphlet well worthy of perusal, in which an account is given of all the arrests and persecutions that took place on account of matters connected with the press.—Madame de Staël was exiled for having spoken favorably of the German character in her work "de l'Allemagne," and the work itself was suppressed; Napoleon, on giving these orders, merely said, "Ce livre n'est pas Français."

His treatment of Switzerland was equally unindulgent. The Valais, which, although not forming part of Switzerland, still retained a sort of nominal independence, was formally incorporated with France; the canton of Tessin was, as arbitrarily, occupied by French troops, an immense quantity of British goods was confiscated, the press was placed under the strictest censorship, the *Erzähler* of Muller-Friedeberg, the only remaining Swiss newspaper of liberal tendency, was suppressed, while Zschokke unweariedly lauded Napoleon to the skies as the regenerator of the liberties of Switzerland and as the savior of the world. A humble entreaty of the Swiss for mercy was scornfully refused by Napoleon. Instead of listening to their complaints, he reproached their envoys, who were headed by Reinhard of Zurich, in the most violent terms, charged the Swiss with conspiracy, and said that a certain Sydler had ventured to speak against him in the federal diet, etc.; nor could his assumed anger be pacified save by the instant dissolution of the federal diet, by the extension of the levy of Swiss recruits for the service of France, and by the threat of a terrible punishment to all Swiss who ventured to enter the service of England and Spain. The Swiss merely bound their chains still closer without receiving the slightest alleviation to their sufferings. Reinhard wrote in 1811, the time of this ill-successful attempt on the part of the Swiss, "a petty nation possesses no means of procuring justice." Why then did the great German nation sever itself into so many petty tribes?

The marriage of Napoleon on the 2d of April, 1810, with Maria Louisa, the daughter of the emperor of Austria, surrounded his throne with additional splendor. This marriage had a double object; that of raising an heir to his broad empire, his first wife, Josephine Beauharnais, whom he divorced, having brought him no children, and that of legitimating his authority and of obliterating the stain of low birth by intermingling his blood with that of the ancient race of Habsburg. Strange as it must appear for the child of revolution to deny the very principles to which he owed his being and to embrace the aristocratic ideas of a bygone age, for the proud conqueror of all the sovereigns of Europe anxiously to solicit their recognition of him as their equal in birth, these apparent contradictions are easily explained by the fact that men of liberal ideas were the objects of Napoleon's greatest dread and hatred, and that he was consequently driven to favor the ancient aristocracy, as he had formerly favored the ancient church, and to use them as his tools. Young and rising nations, not the ancient families of Europe, threatened his power, and he therefore sought to confirm it by an alliance against the former with the ancient dynasties.[1] The nuptials were solemnized with extraordinary pomp at Paris. The conflagration of the Austrian ambassador's, Prince von Schwarzenberg's, house during a splendid fete given by him to the newly-wedded pair, and which caused the death of several persons, among others, of the Princess Pauline Schwarzenberg, the ambassador's sister-in-law, who rushed into the flaming building to her daughter's rescue, clouded the festivities with ominous gloom. In the ensuing year, 1811, the youthful empress

---

[1] It was during this year that Napoleon caused the seamless coat of the Saviour, which had, during the Revolution, taken refuge at Augsburg, to be borne in a magnificent procession to Treves and to be exposed for eighteen days to public view. The pilgrims amounted to two hundred and fifty thousand.—Hormayr, who had, during the foregoing year, summoned the Tyrolese to arms against Napoleon, said in his Annual for 1811, "By the marriage of the emperor Napoleon with Maria Louisa, the Revolution may be considered as completely terminated and peace durably settled throughout Europe."

gave birth to a prince, Napoleon Francis, who was laid in a silver cradle, and provisionally entitled "King of Rome," in notification of his future destiny to succeed his father on the throne of the Roman empire.[1]

Austria offered a melancholy contrast to the magnificence of France. Exhausted by her continual exertions for the maintenance of the war, the state could no longer meet its obligations, and, on the 15th of March, 1811, Count Wallis, the minister of finance, lowered the value of one thousand and sixty millions of bank paper to two hundred and twelve millions, and the interest upon the whole of the state debts to half the new paper issue. This fearful state bankruptcy was accompanied by the fall of innumerable private firms; trade was completely at a standstill, and the contributions demanded by Napoleon amounted to a sum almost impossible to realize. Prussia, especially, suffered from the drain upon her resources. The beautiful and high-souled queen, Louisa, destined not to see the day of vengeance and of victory, died in 1810, of a broken heart.[2]

While Germany lay thus exhausted and bleeding in her chains, Napoleon and Alexander put the plans, agreed to between them at Erfurt, into execution. Napoleon threw himself with redoubled violence on luckless Spain, and the Russians invaded Sweden.

The Germans acted a prominent part in the bloody wars in the Peninsula. Four Swiss regiments, that had at an earlier period been in the Spanish service, and the German Legion, composed of Hanoverian refugees to England, upheld the Spanish cause, while all sorts of troops of the Rhenish confederation, those of Bavaria and Wurtemberg ex-

---

[1] His birth was celebrated by numerous German poets and by general public rejoicings, but with the basest adulation in Switzerland. Meyer of Knonau relates, in his History of Switzerland, that the king of Rome was at one of the festivals termed "the blessed infant." Goethe's poem in praise of Napoleon appeared at this time. The clergy also emulated each other in servility.

[2] At that time the noble-hearted poet, Seume, who had formerly been a victim of native tyranny, died of sorrow and disgust at the rule of the foreigner in Germany, at Tœplitz, 1810.

cepted, several Dutch and four Swiss regiments, fought for Napoleon.

The troops of the Rhenish confederation formed two corps. The fate of one of them has been described by Captain Rigel of Baden. The Baden regiment was, in 1808, sent to Biscay and united under Lefebvre with other contingents of the Rhenish confederation, for instance, with the Nassauers under the gallant Von Schäfer, the Dutch under General Chasse, the Hessians, the Primates (Frankforters), and Poles. As early as October, they fought against the Spaniards at Zornoza, and at the pillage of Portugalete first became acquainted with the barbarous customs of this terrible civil war. The most implacable hatred, merciless rage, the assassination of prisoners, plunder, destruction, and incendiarism, equally distinguished both sides. The Germans garrisoned Bilbao, gained some successes at Molinar and Valmaseda, were afterward placed under the command of General Victor, who arrived with a fresh army, were again victorious at Espinosa and Burgos, formed a junction with Soult and finally with Napoleon, and, in December, 1808, entered Madrid in triumph.—In January, 1809, the German troops under Victor again advanced upon the Tagus, and, after a desperate conflict, took the celebrated bridge of Almaraz by storm. This was followed by the horrid sacking of the little town of Arenas, during which a Nassauer named Hornung, not only, like a second Scipio, generously released a beautiful girl who had fallen into his hands, but sword in hand defended her from his fellow-soldiers. In the following March, the Germans were again brought into action, at Mesa de Ibor, where Schäfer's Nassauers drove the enemy from their position, under a fearful fire, which cut down three hundred of their number; and at Medelin, where they were again victorious and massacred numbers of the armed Spanish peasantry. Four hundred prisoners were, after the battle, shot by order of Marshal Victor. Among the wounded on the field of battle there lay, side by side, Preusser, the Nassauer, and a Spanish corporal, both of whom had severely suffered. A dispute arose between them, in the midst of which they discovered that they were brothers. One had entered the French, the other the Spanish service.—A Dutch battalion under Storm de Grave, abandoned at Merida to the vengeance of the enraged people, was furiously assailed, but made a gallant defence and fought its way through the enemy.

In the commencement of 1809, Napoleon had again quitted Spain in order to conduct the war on the Danube in person. His marshals, left by him in different parts of the Peninsula, took Saragossa, drove the British under Sir John Moore out of the country, and penetrated into Portugal, but were ere long again attacked by a fresh English army under the Duke of Wellington. This rendered the junction of the German troops with the main body of the French army necessary, and they consequently shared in the defeats of Talavera and Almoncid. Their losses, more particularly in the latter engagement, were very considerable, amounting in all to two thousand six hundred men; among others, General Porbeck of Baden, an officer of noted talent, fell: five hundred of their wounded were butchered after the battle by the infuriated Spaniards. But Wellington suddenly stopped short in his victorious career. It was in December, 1809, when the news of the fresh peace concluded by Napoleon with Austria arrived. On the Spaniards hazarding a fresh engagement, Wellington left them totally unassisted, and, on the 19th of November, they suffered a dreadful defeat at Ocasia, where they lost twenty-five thousand men. The Rhenish confederated troops were, in reward for the gallantry displayed by them on this occasion, charged with the transport of the prisoners into France, and were exposed to the whole rigor of the climate and to every sort of deprivation while the French withdrew into winter quarters. The fatigues of this service greatly thinned their ranks. The other German regiments were sent into the Sierra Morena, where they were kept ever on the alert guarding that key to Spain, while the French under Soult advanced as far as Cadiz, those under Massena into Portugal; but Soult being unable to take Cadiz, and Massena being forced by the Duke of Wellington to retire, the German troops were also driven from their position, and, in 1812, withdrew to Valencia, but, in the October of the same year, again advanced with Soult upon Madrid.

The second corps of the Rhenish confederated troops was stationed in Catalonia, where they were fully occupied. Their fate has been described by two Saxon officers, Jacobs and Von Seebach. In the commencement of 1809, Reding the Swiss, who had, in 1808, chiefly contributed to the capture of the French army at Baylen, commanded the whole of the Spanish forces in Catalonia, consisting of forty thousand Spaniards and several thousand Swiss; but these guerilla troops, almost invincible in petty warfare, were totally unable to stand in open battle against the veterans of the French emperor, and Reding was completely routed by St. Cyr at Taragona. In St. Cyr's army were eight thousand Westphalians under General Morio, three thousand Berglanders, fifteen hundred Wurzburgers, from eight to nine hundred men of Schwarzburg, Lippe, Waldeck, and Reuss, all of whom were employed in the wearisome siege of Gerona, which was defended by Don Alvarez, one of Spain's greatest heroes. The popular enthusiasm was so intense that even the women took up arms (in the company of St. Barbara) and aided in the defence of the walls. The Germans, ever destined to head the assault, suffered immense losses on each attempt to carry the place by storm. In one attack alone, on the 3d of July, in which they met with a severe repulse, they lost two thousand of their men. Their demand of a truce for the purpose of carrying their wounded off the field of battle was answered by a Spaniard, Colonel Blas das Furnas, "A quarter of an hour hence not one of them will be alive!" and the whole of the wounded men were, in fact, murdered in cold blood by the Spaniards. During a second assault on the 19th of September, sixteen hundred of their number and the gallant Colonel Neuff, an Alsatian, who had served in Egypt, fell. Gerona was finally driven by famine to capitulate, after a sacrifice of twelve thousand men, principally Germans, before her walls. Of the eight thousand Westphalians but one battalion remained. St. Cyr was, in 1810, replaced by Marshal Augereau, but the troops were few in number and worn out with fatigue; a large convoy was lost in an unlucky engagement, in which numbers of the Germans deserted to the Spanish, and Augereau retired to Barcelona, the metropolis of Catalonia, in order to await the arrival of reinforcements, among which was a Nassau regiment, one of Anhalt, and the identical Saxon corps that had so dreadfully suffered in the Tyrol.[1] The Saxon and Nassau troops, two thousand two hundred strong, under the command of General Schwarz, an Alsatian, advanced from Barcelona toward the celebrated mountain of Montserrat, whose hermitages, piled up one above another en amphitheatre, excite the traveller's wonder. Close in its vicinity lay the city of Manresa, the focus of the Catalonian insurrection. The German troops advanced in close column, although surrounded by infuriated multitudes, by whom every straggler was mercilessly butchered. The two regiments, nevertheless, succeeded in making themselves masters of Manresa, where they were instantly shut in, furiously assailed, and threatened with momentary destruction. The Anhalt troops and a French corps, despatched by Augereau to their relief, were repulsed with considerable loss. Schwarz now boldly sallied forth, fought his way through the Spaniards, and, after losing a thousand men, succeeded in reaching Barcelona, but was shortly afterward, after assisting at the taking of Hostalrich, surprised at La Bisbal and taken prisoner with almost all the Saxon troops. The few that remained fell victims to disease.[2] The fate of the prisoners was indeed melancholy.

---

[1] This regiment was merely rewarded by Napoleon for its gallantry with 15 gros (1*s.* 6¼*d.*) per man, in order to drink to his health on his birthday.—*Von Seebach.*

[2] What the feeling among the Germans was is plainly shown by the charge against General Beurmann for general ill-treatment of his countrymen, whom

Several thousand of them died on the Balearic Islands, chiefly on the island of Cabrera, where, naked and houseless, they dug for themselves holes in the sand and died in great numbers of starvation. They often also fell victims to the fury of the inhabitants. The Swiss engaged in the Spanish service, sometimes saved their lives at the hazard of their own.

Opposed to them was the German Legion, composed of the brave Hanoverians, who had preferred exile in Britain to submission to Jerome, and had been sent in British men-of-war to Portugal, whence they had, in conjunction with the troops of England and Spain, penetrated, in 1808, into the interior of Spain.[1] At Benavente, they made a furious charge upon the French and took their long-delayed revenge. Linsingen's cavalry cut down all before them; arms were severed at a blow, heads were split in two; one head was found cut in two across from one ear to the other. A young Hanoverian soldier took General Lefebvre prisoner, but allowed himself to be deprived of his valuable captive by an Englishman.—The Hanoverians served first under Sir John Moore. On the death of that commander at Corunna, the troops under his command returned to England: a ship of the line, with two Hanoverian battalions on board, was lost during the passage. The German Legion afterward served under the Duke of Wellington, and shared the dangers and the glory of the war in the Peninsula. "The admirable accuracy and rapidity of the German artillery under Major Hartmann greatly contributed to the victory of Talavera, and received the personal encomiums of the Duke."

---

he was accused of having allowed to perish in the hospitals, in order to save the expense of their return home. Out of seventy officers and two thousand four hundred and twenty-three privates belonging to the Saxon regiment, but thirty-nine officers and three hundred and nineteen privates returned to their native country. Vide Jacob's Campaigns of the Gotha-Altenburgers and Von Seebach's History of the Campaigns of the Saxony Infantry. Von Seebach, who was taken prisoner on his return from Manresa, has given a particularly detailed and graphic account of the campaign.

[1] Beamish has recounted their exploits in detail. The "Recollections of a Legionary," Hanover, 1826, is also worthy of perusal.

Langwerth's brigade gained equal glory. The German Legion was, however, never in full force in Spain. A division was, in 1809, sent to the island of Walcheren, but shared the ill-success attending all the attempts made in the North Sea during Napoleon's reign. The conquest and demolition of Vliessingen in August was the only result. A pestilence broke out among the troops, and, on Napoleon's successes in Austria, it was compelled to return to England. A third division, consisting of several Hanoverian regiments, was sent to Sicily, accompanied the expedition to Naples in 1809, and afterward guarded the rocks of Sicily. The Hanoverians in Spain were also separated into various divisions, each of which gained great distinction, more particularly so, the corps of General Alten in the storming of Ciudad-Rodrigo. In 1812, the Hanoverian cavalry broke three French squares at Garcia Hernandez.

The Russians had, meanwhile, invaded Sweden. Gustavus Adolphus, hitherto Russia's firmest ally, was suddenly and treacherously attacked. General Buxhovden overran Finland, inciting the people, as he advanced, to revolt against their lawful sovereign. But the brave Finlanders stoutly resisted the attempted imposition of the yoke of the barbarous Russ, and, although ill-supported by Sweden, performed prodigies of valor. Gustavus Adolphus was devoid of military knowledge, and watched, as if sunk in torpor, the ill-planned operations of his generals. While the flower of the Swedish troops was uselessly employed against Denmark and Norway, Finland was allowed to fall into the grasp of Russia.[1] The Russians were already expected to land in Sweden, when a conspiracy broke out among the nobility and officers of the army, which terminated in the seizure of the king's person and his deposition, March, 1809. His son, Gustavus Vasa, the present ex-king of Sweden, was excluded from the succession, and his uncle Charles, the im-

[1] The gallant acts of the Finlanders and the brutality of the Russians are brought forward in Arndt's "Swedish Histories."

becile and unworthy duke of Sudermania,[1] was proclaimed king under the title of Charles XIII. He was put up as a scarecrow by the conspirators. Gustavus Adolphus IV. had, at all events, shown himself incapable of saving Sweden. But the conspirators were no patriots, nor was their object the preservation of their country; they were merely bribed traitors, weak and incapable as the monarch they had dethroned. They were composed of a party among the ancient nobility, impatient of the restrictions of a monarchy, and of the younger officers in the army, who were filled with enthusiasm for Napoleon. The rejoicings on the occasion of the abdication of Gustavus Adolphus were heightened by the news of the victory gained by Napoleon at Ratisbon, which, at the same time, reached Stockholm. The new and wretched Swedish government instantly deferred everything to Napoleon and humbly solicited his favor; but Napoleon, to whom the friendship of Russia was, at that time, of higher importance than the submission of a handful of intriguants in Sweden, received their homage with marked coldness. Finland, shamefully abandoned in her hour of need, was immediately ceded to Russia, in consideration of which Napoleon graciously restored Rugen and Swedish-Pomerania to Sweden. Charles XIII. adopted, as his son and successor, Christian Augustus, prince of Holstein-Augustenburg, who, falling dead off his horse at a review,[2] the aged and childless monarch was compelled to make a second choice, which fell upon the French general, Bernadotte, who had, at one time, been a furious Jacobin and had afterward acted as Napoleon's general and commandant in Swedish-Pomerania, where he had, by his mildness, gained great popularity. The majority in Sweden deemed him merely a creature of Napoleon, whose favor they hoped to gain by

[1] When regent, on the death of Gustavus III., he had spared his murderers and released those criminated in the conspiracy. On the present occasion, he yielded in everything to the aristocracy, and voted for the dethronement of his own house, which, as he had no children, infallibly ensued on the exclusion of the youthful Gustavus.

[2] An extremely suspicious accident, which gave rise to many reports.

this flattering choice; others, it may be, already beheld in him Napoleon's future foe, and knew the value of the sagacity and wisdom with which he was endowed, and of which the want was so deeply felt in Sweden at a period when intrigue and cunning had succeeded to violence. The Freemasons, with whom he had placed himself in close communication, appear to have greatly influenced his election.[1] The unfortunate king, Gustavus Adolphus, after being long kept a close prisoner in the castle of Gripsholm, where his strong religious bias had been strengthened by apparitions,[2] was permitted to retire into Germany; he disdainfully refused to accept of a pension, separated himself from his consort, a princess of Baden, and lived in proud poverty, under the name of Colonel Gustavson, in Switzerland.—Bernadotte, the newly adopted prince, took the title of Charles John, crown prince of Sweden. Napoleon, who was in ignorance of this intrigue, was taken by surprise, but, in the hope of Bernadotte's continued fidelity, presented him with a million *en cadeau;* Bernadotte had, however, been long jealous of Napoleon's fortune, and, solely intent upon gaining the hearts of his future subjects, deceived him and secretly permitted the British to trade with Sweden, although publicly a party in the continental system.

This system was at this period enforced with exaggerated severity by Napoleon. He not only prohibited the importation of all British goods, but seized all already sent to the continent and condemned them to be publicly burned. Millions evaporated in smoke, principally at Amsterdam, Hamburg, Frankfort, and Leipzig. The wealthiest mercantile establishments were made bankrupt.

In addition to the other blows at that time zealously bestowed upon the dead German lion, the king of Denmark

---

[1] Vide Posselt's Sixth Annual.

[2] This castle was haunted by the ghost of King Eric XIV., who had long pined here in close imprisonment, and who had once before, during a sumptuous entertainment given by Gustavus Adolphus IV. to his brother-in-law, the Margrave of Baden, struck the whole court with terror by his shrieks and groans.

attempted to extirpate the German language in Schleswig, but the edict to that effect, published on the 19th of January, 1811, was frustrated by the courage of the clergy, schoolmasters, and peasantry, who obstinately refused to learn Danish.[1]

CCLIX. *The Russian Campaign*

An enormous comet that, during the whole of the hot summer of 1811, hung threatening in the heavens, appeared as the harbinger of great and important vicissitudes to the enslaved inhabitants of the earth, and it was in truth by an act of Divine providence that a dispute arose between the two giant powers intent upon the partition of Europe.

Napoleon was over-reached by Russia, whose avarice, far from being glutted by the possession of Finland, great part of Prussian and Austrian Poland, Moldavia, and Wallachia, still craved for more, and who built her hopes of Napoleon's compliance with her demands on his value for her friendship. Belgrade was seized, Servia demanded, and the whole of Turkey in Europe openly grasped at. Napoleon was, however, little inclined to cede the Mediterranean to his Russian ally, to whose empire he gave the Danube as a boundary. Russia next demanded possession of the duchy of Warsaw, which was refused by Napoleon. The Austrian marriage was meanwhile concluded. Napoleon, prior to his demand for the hand of the archduchess Maria Louisa, had sued for that of the grandduchess Anna, sister to the emperor Alexander, who was then in her sixteenth year, but, being refused by her mother, the empress Maria, a princess of Wurtemberg, and Alexander delaying a decisive answer, he formed an alliance with the Habsburg. This event naturally led Russia to conclude that she would no longer be permitted to aggrandize herself at the expense of Austria, and Alexander consequently assumed a threatening posture and condescended to listen to the complaints, hitherto condemned

---

[1] Wimpfen, History of Schleswig.

to silence, of the agricultural and mercantile classes. No Russian vessel durst venture out to sea, and a Russian fleet had been seized by the British in the harbors of Lisbon. At Riga lay immense stores of grain in want of a foreign market. On the 31st of December, 1810, Alexander published a fresh tariff permitting the importation of colonial products under a neutral flag (several hundred English ships arrived under the American flag), and prohibiting the importation of French manufactured goods. Not many weeks previously, on the 13th of December, Napoleon had annexed Oldenburg to France. The duke, Peter, was nearly related to the emperor of Russia, and Napoleon, notwithstanding his declared readiness to grant a compensation, refused to allow it to consist of the grandduchy of Warsaw, and proposed a duchy of Erfurt, as yet uncreated, which Russia scornfully rejected.

The alliance between Russia, Sweden and England was now speedily concluded. Sweden, who had vainly demanded from Napoleon the possession of Norway and a large supply of money, assumed a tone of indignation, threw open her harbors to the British merchantmen, and so openly carried on a contraband trade in Pomerania that Napoleon, in order to maintain the continental system, was constrained to garrison Swedish-Pomerania and Rugen, and to disarm the Swedish inhabitants. Bernadotte, upon this, ranged himself entirely on the side of his opponents, without, however, coming to an open rupture, for which he awaited a declaration on the part of Russia. The expressions made use of by Napoleon on the birth of the king of Rome at length filled up the measure of provocation. Intoxicated with success, he boasted, in an address to the mercantile classes, that he would in despite of Russia maintain the continental system, for he was lord over the whole of continental Europe; that if Alexander had not concluded a treaty with him at Tilsit, he would have compelled him to do so at Petersburg.—The pride of the haughty Russian was deeply wounded, and a rupture was nigh at hand.

Two secret systems were at this period undermining each other in Prussia, that of the Tugendbund founded by Stein and Scharnhorst, whose object being the liberation of Germany at all hazards from the yoke of Napoleon, consequently favored Russia, and that of Hardenberg, which aimed at a close union with France. Hardenberg, whose position as chancellor of state gave him the upper hand, had compromised Prussia by the servility with which he sued for an alliance long scornfully refused and at length conceded on the most humiliating terms by Napoleon.[1]

Russia had, meanwhile, made preparations for a war unanticipated by Napoleon. As early as 1811, a great Russian army stood ready for the invasion of Poland, and might, as there were at that time but few French troops in Germany, easily have advanced as far as the Elbe. It remained, nevertheless, in a state of inactivity.[2] Napoleon instantly prepared for war and fortified Dantzig. His continual proposals of peace, ever unsatisfactory to the ambition of the czar, remaining at length unanswered, he declared war. The Rhenish confederation followed as usual in his train, and Austria, from an interested motive, the hope of regaining in the East by Napoleon's assistance all she had lost by opposing him in the West, or that of regaining her station as the third European power when the resources of the two ruling powers, whose coalition had threatened her existence, had been exhausted by war. Prussia also followed the eagles of Napoleon: the Hardenberg party, with a view of conciliating him, and, like the Rhenish confederation, from motives of gain: the Tugendbund, which predominated in the army, with silent but implacable hate.

In the spring of 1812, Napoleon, after leaving a sufficient force to prosecute the war with activity in Spain and to

---

[1] Vide Bignon.

[2] From a letter of Count Münster in Hormayr's Sketches of Life, it appears that Russia still cherished the hope of great concessions being made by Napoleon in order to avoid war and was therefore still reserved in her relations with England and the Prussian patriots.

guard France, Italy, and Germany,[1] led half a million men to the Russian frontiers. Before taking the field, he convoked all the princes of Germany to Dresden, where he treated them with such extreme insolence as even to revolt his most favored and warmest partisans. Tears were seen to start in ladies' eyes, while men bit their lips with rage at the petty humiliations and affronts heaped on them by their powerful but momentary lord. The empress of Austria[2] and the king of Prussia[3] appear, on this occasion, to have felt the most acutely.

For the first time—an event unknown in the history of the world—the whole of Germany was reduced to submission. Napoleon, greater than conquering Attila, who took the field at the head of one-half of Germany against the other, dragged the whole of Germany in his train. The army led by him to the steppes of Russia was principally composed of German troops, who were so skilfully mixed up with the French as not to be themselves aware of their numerical superiority. The right wing, composed of thirty thousand Austrians under Schwarzenberg, was destined for the invasion of Volhynia; while the left wing, consisting of twenty thousand Prussians under York and several thousand French, under the command of Marshal Macdonald, was ordered to advance upon the coasts of the Baltic and without loss of time to besiege Riga. The centre or main body consisted of the troops of the Rhenish confederation,

---

[1] French troops garrisoned German fortresses and perpetually passed along the principal roads, which were for that purpose essentially improved by Napoleon. In 1810, a great part of the town of Eisenach was destroyed by the bursting of some French powder-carts that were carelessly brought through, and by which great numbers of people were killed.

[2] Who was far surpassed in splendor by her stepdaughter of France.

[3] Segur relates that he was received politely but with distant coolness by Napoleon. There is said to have been question between them concerning the marriage of the crown prince of Prussia with one of Napoleon's nieces, and of an incorporation of the still unconquered Russian provinces on the Baltic, Livonia, Courland, and Esthonia, with Prussia. All was, however, empty show. Napoleon hoped by the rapidity of his successes to constrain the emperor of Russia to conclude not only peace, but a still closer alliance with France, in which case it was as far from his intention to concede the above mentioned provinces to Prussia as to emancipate the Poles.

more or less mixed up with French; of thirty-eight thousand Bavarians under Wrede and commanded by St. Cyr; of sixteen thousand Wurtembergers under Scheeler, over whom Marshal Ney was allotted the chief command; single regiments, principally cavalry, were drawn off in order more thoroughly to intermix the Germans with the French; of seventeen thousand Saxons under Reynier; of eighteen thousand Westphalians under Vandamme; also of Hessians, Badeners, Frankforters, Wurzburgers, Nassauers, in short, of contingents furnished by each of the confederated states. The Swiss were mostly concentrated under Oudinot. The Dutch, Hanseatic, Flemish, in fine, all the Germans on the left bank of the Rhine, were at that time crammed among the French troops. Upward of two hundred thousand Germans, at the lowest computation, marched against Russia, a number far superior to that of the French in the army, the remainder of which was made up by several thousand Italians, Portuguese, and Spaniards, who had been pressed into the service.[1]

The Prussians found themselves in the most degraded position. Their army, weak as it was in numbers, was placed under the command of a French general. The Prussian fortresses, with the exception of Colberg, Graudenz, Schweidnitz, Neisse, and Glatz, were already garrisoned with French troops, or, like Pillau near Kœnigsberg, newly occupied by them. In Berlin, the French had unlimited sway. Marshal Augereau was stationed with sixty thousand men in Northern Germany for the purpose of keeping that part of the country, and more particularly Prussia, in check to Napoleon's rear; the Danish forces also stood in readiness to support him in case of necessity. Napoleon's entire army moreover marched through Prussia and completely drained that country of its last resources. Napoleon deemed it unnecessary to take measures equal in severity

---

[1] Napoleon said at that time to a Russian, "Si vous perdez cinq Russes, je ne perds qu un Francais et quatre cochons."

toward Austria, where the favor of the court seemed to be secured by his marriage, and the allegiance of the army by the presence of Schwarzenberg, who neither rejected nor returned his confidence. A rich compensation was, by a secret compact, secured to Austria in case the cession of Galicia should be necessitated by the expected restoration of the kingdom of Poland, with which Napoleon had long flattered the Poles, who, misled by his promises, served him with the greatest enthusiasm. But, notwithstanding the removal of the only obstacle, the jealousy of Austria in regard to Galicia, by this secret compact, his promises remained unfulfilled, and he took possession of the whole of Poland without restoring her ancient independence. The petitions addressed to him on this subject by the Poles received dubious replies, and he pursued toward his unfortunate dupes his ancient system of dismembering and intermingling nations, of tolerating no national unity. Napoleon's principal motive, however, was his expectation of compelling the emperor by a well-aimed blow to conclude peace, and of forming with him an alliance upon still more favorable terms against the rest of the European powers. The friendship of Russia was of far more import to him than all the enthusiasm of the Poles.

The deep conviction harbored by Napoleon of his irresistible power led him to repay every service and to regard every antagonist with contempt. Confident of victory, he deviated from the strict military discipline he had at one time enforced and of which he had given an example in his own person, dragged in his train a multitude of useless attendants fitted but for pomp and luxury, permitted his marshals and generals to do the same, and an incredible number of private carriages, servants, women, etc., to follow in the rear of the army, to hamper its movements, create confusion, and aid in consuming the army stores, which being, moreover, merely provided for a short campaign, speedily became insufficient for the maintenance of the enormous mass. Even in Eastern Prussia, numbers of the soldiery were constrained by want to plunder the villages.—On the 24th of June, 1812, Napoleon crossed the Niemen, the Russian frontier, not far from Kowno. The season was already too far advanced. It may be that, deceived by the mildness of the winter of 1806 to 1807, he imagined it possible to protract the campaign without peril to himself until the winter months. No enemy appeared to oppose his progress. Barclay de Tolly,[1] the Russian commander-in-chief, pursued the system followed by the Scythians against Darius, and, perpetually retiring before the enemy, gradually drew him deep into the dreary and deserted steppes. This plan originated with Scharnhorst, by whom General Lieven was advised not to hazard an engagement until the winter, and to turn a deaf ear to every proposal of peace.[2] General Lieven, on reaching Barclay's headquarters, took Colonel Toll, a German, Barclay's right hand, and Lieutenant-Colonel Clausewitz, also a German, afterward noted for his strategical works, into his confidence. General Pfull, another German, at that time high in the emperor's confidence, and almost all the Russian generals opposed Scharnhorst's plan and continued to advance with a view of giving battle; but, on Napoleon's appearance at the head of an army greatly their superior in number before the Russians had been able to concentrate their forces, they were naturally compelled to retire before him, and, on the prevention, for some weeks, of the junction of a newly-levied Russian army under Prince Bragation with the forces under Barclay, owing to the rapidity of Napoleon's advance, Scharnhorst's plan was adopted as the only one feasible.

Napoleon, in the hope of overtaking the Russians and of compelling them to give battle, pushed onward by forced marches; the supplies were unable to follow, and numbers

---

[1] This general, on the opening of the war, published a proclamation to the Germans, summoning them to throw off the yoke of Napoleon.—*Allgemeine Zeitung, No. 327.* Napoleon replied with, "Whom are you addressing? There are no Germans, there are only Austrians, Prussians, Bavarians," etc.—*All. Zeitung, No. 328.*

[2] Vide Clausewitz's Works.

of the men and horses sank from exhaustion owing to over-fatigue, heat, and hunger.[1] On the arrival of Napoleon in Witebst, of Schwarzenberg in Volhynia, of the Prussians before Riga, the army might have halted, reconquered Poland have been organized, the mén put into winter quarters, the army have again taken the field early in the spring, and the conquest of Russia have been slowly but surely completed. But Napoleon had resolved upon terminating the war in one rapid campaign, upon defeating the Russians, seizing their metropolis, and dictating terms of peace, and incessantly pursued his retreating opponent, whose footsteps were marked by the flames of the cities and villages and by the devastated country to their rear. The first serious opposition was made at Smolensko,[2] whence the Russians, however, speedily retreated after setting the city on fire. On the same day, the Bavarians, who had diverged to one side during their advance, had a furious encounter—in which General Deroy, formerly distinguished for his services in the Tyrol, was killed—at Poloczk with a body of Russian troops under Wittgenstein. The Bavarians remained stationary in this part of the country for the purpose of watching the movements of that general, while Napoleon, careless of the peril with which he was threatened by the approach of winter and by the multitude of enemies gathering to his rear, advanced with the main body of the grand army from Smolensko across the wasted country upon Moscow, the ancient metropolis of the Russian empire.

Russia, at that time engaged in a war with Turkey, whose frontiers were watched by an immense army under Kutusow, used her utmost efforts, in which she was aided by England, to conciliate the Porte in order to turn the whole of her forces against Napoleon. By a master-stroke

---

[1] At each encampment the men were left in such numbers in hastily erected hospitals that, of thirty-eight thousand Bavarians, for instance, but ten thousand, of sixteen thousand Würtembergers, but thirteen hundred, reached Smolensko.

[2] The Würtembergers distinguished themselves here by storming the faubourgs and the bridges across the Dnieper.

of political intrigue,[1] the Porte, besides concluding peace at Bucharest on the 28th of May, ceded the province of Bessarabia (not Moldavia and Wallachia) to Russia. A Russian army under Tschitschakow was now enabled to drive the Austrians out of Volhynia, while a considerable force under Kutusow joined Barclay. Had the Russians at this time hazarded an engagement, their defeat was certain. Moscow could not have been saved. Barclay consequently resolved not to come to an engagement, but to husband his forces and to attack the French during the winter. The intended surrender of Moscow without a blow was, nevertheless, deeply resented as a national disgrace; the army and the people[2] raised a clamor, the venerable Kutusow was nominated commander-in-chief, and, taking up a position on the little river Moskwa near Borodino, about two days' journey from Moscow, a bloody engagement took place there on the 7th of September, in which Napoleon, in order to spare his guards, neglected to follow up his advantage with his usual energy and allowed the defeated Russians, whom he might have totally annihilated, to escape. Napoleon triumphed; but at what a price! After a fearful struggle, in which he lost forty thousand men in killed and wounded,[3] the latter of whom perished almost to a man, owing to want and neglect.[4]

---

[1] The Greek prince, Moruzi, who at that time conducted Turkish diplomacy, accepted a bribe, and concluded peace in the expectation of becoming Prince of Moldavia and Wallachia. Sultan Mahmud refusing to ratify this disgraceful treaty, gold was showered upon the Turkish army, which suddenly dispersed, and the deserted sultan was compelled to yield. Moruzi was deprived of his head, but the Russians had gained their object. It must, moreover, be considered that Napoleon was regarded with distrust by the Porte, against which he had fought in Egypt, which he had afterward enticed into a war with Russia, and had, by the alliance formed at Erfurt with that power, abandoned.

[2] Colonel Toll was insulted during the discussion by Prince Bragation for the firmness with which he upheld Scharnhorst's plan, and avoided hazarding a useless engagement. Prince Bragation was killed in the battle.

[3] A Russian redoubt, the key of the field of battle, was taken and again lost. A Würtemberg regiment instantly pushed through the fugitive French, retook the redoubt and retained possession of it. It also, on this occasion, saved the life of the king of Naples and delivered him out of the hands of the Russians, who had already taken him prisoner.—*Ten Campaigns of the Wurtembergers.*

[4] Everything was wanting, lint, linen, even necessary food. The wounded men lay for days and weeks under the open sky and fed upon the carcasses of horses.

Moscow was now both defenceless and void of inhabitants. Napoleon traversed this enormous city, containing two hundred and ninety-five churches and fifteen hundred palaces rising from amid a sea of inferior dwellings, and took possession of the residence of the czars, the 14th of September, 1812. The whole city was, however, deserted, and scarcely had the French army taken up its quarters in it than flames burst from the empty and closely shut-up houses, and, ere long, the whole of the immense city became a sea of fire and was reduced, before Napoleon's eyes, to ashes. Every attempt to extinguish the flames proved unavailing. Rostopchin, the commandant of Moscow, had, previously to his retreat, put combustible materials, which were ignited on the entrance of the French by men secreted for that purpose, into the houses.[1] A violent wind aided the work of destruction. The patriotic sacrifice was performed, nor failed in its object. Napoleon, instead of peace and plenty, merely found ashes in Moscow.

Instead of pursuing the defeated Russians to Kaluga, where, in pursuance of Toll's first laid-plan, they took up a position close upon the flank of the French and threatened to impede their retreat; instead of taking up his winter quarters in the fertile South or of quickly turning and fixing himself in Lithuania in order to collect reinforcements for the ensuing year, Napoleon remained in a state of inaction at Moscow until the 19th of October, in expectation of proposals of peace from Alexander. The terms of peace offered by him on his part to the Russians did not even elicit a reply. His cavalry, already reduced to a great state of exhaustion, were, in the beginning of October, surprised before the city of Tarutino and repulsed with considerable loss. This at length decided Napoleon upon marching upon Kaluga, but the moment for success had already passed. The reinforced and inspirited Russians made such a desperate resistance at

---

[1] This combustible matter had been prepared by Schmid, the Dutchman, under pretext of preparing an enormous balloon from which fire was to be scattered upon the French army.

Malo-Jaroslawez that he resolved to retire by the nearest route, that by which he had penetrated up the country, marked by ashes and pestilential corpses, into Lithuania. Winter had not yet set in, and his ranks were already thinned by famine.[1] Kutusow, with the main body of the Russian army, pursued the retreating French and again overtook them at Wiazma, the 3d November. Napoleon's hopes now rested on the separate corps d'armée left to his rear on his advance upon Moscow, but they were, notwithstanding the defeat of Wittgenstein's corps by the Bavarians under Wrede, kept in check by fresh Russian armies and exposed to all the horrors of winter.[2] In Volhynia, Schwarzenberg had zealously endeavored to—spare his troops,[3] and had, by his retreat toward the grandduchy of Warsaw, left

---

[1] As early as the 2d of November the remainder of the Würtembergers tore off their colors and concealed them in their knapsacks.—*Roos's Memorabilia of 1812.*

[2] On the 18th of October, the Bavarians, who were intermixed with Swiss, performed prodigies of valor, but were so reduced by sufferings of every description as to be unable to maintain Poloczk. Segur says in his History of the War that St. Cyr left Wrede's gallant conduct unmentioned in the military despatches, and that when, on St. Cyr's being disabled by his wounds, Wrede applied for the chief command, which naturally reverted to him, the army being almost entirely composed of Bavarians, Napoleon refused his request. Völderndorf says in his Bavarian Campaigns that St. Cyr faithlessly abandoned the Bavarians in their utmost extremity, and when all peril was over returned to Poland in order to retake the command. During the retreat from Poloczk he had ordered the bridges to be pulled down, leaving on the other side a Bavarian park of artillery with the army chest and two-and-twenty ensigns, which for better security had been packed upon a carriage. The whole of these trophies fell, owing to St. Cyr's negligence or ill-will, into the hands of the Russians. "The Bavarians with difficulty concealed their antipathy toward the French." On St. Cyr's flight, Wrede kept the remainder of the Bavarians together, covered Napoleon's retreat, and, in conjunction with the Westphalians and Hessians, stood another encounter with the Russians at Wilna. Misery and want at length scattered his forces; he, nevertheless, reassembled them in Poland and was able to place four thousand men, on St. Cyr's return, under his command. He returned home to Bavaria sick. Of these four thousand Bavarians but one thousand and fifty were led by Count Rechberg back to their native soil. A great number of Bavarians, however, remained under General Zoller to garrison Thorn, and about fifteen hundred of them returned home.—At the passage of the Beresina, the Würtembergers had still about eighty men under arms, and in Poland about three hundred assembled, the only ones who returned free. Some were afterward liberated from imprisonment in Russia.

[3] This was Austria's natural policy. In the French despatches, Schwarzenberg was charged with having allowed Tschitschakow to escape in order to pursue the inconsiderable force under Sacken.

Tschitschakow at liberty to turn his arms against Napoleon, against whom Wittgenstein also advanced in the design of blocking up his route, while Kutusow incessantly assailed his flank and rear. On the 6th of November, the frost suddenly set in. The horses died by thousands in a single night; the greater part of the cavalry was consequently dismounted, and it was found necessary to abandon part of the booty and artillery. A deep snow shortly afterward fell and obstructed the path of the fugitive army. The frost became more and more rigorous; but few of the men had sufficient strength left to continue to carry their arms and to cover the flight of the rest. Most of the soldiers threw away their arms and merely endeavored to preserve life. Napoleon's grand army was scattered over the boundless snow-covered steppes, whose dreary monotony was solely broken by some desolate half-burned village. Gaunt forms of famine, wan, hollow-eyed, wrapped in strange garments of misery, skins, women's clothes, etc., and with long-grown beards, dragged their faint and weary limbs along, fought for a dead horse whose flesh was greedily torn from the carcass, murdered each other for a morsel of bread, and fell one after the other in the deep snow, never again to rise. Bones of frozen corpses lay each morn around the dead ashes of the night fires.[1] Numbers were seen to spring, with a horrid cry of mad exultation, into the flaming houses. Numbers fell into the hands of the Russian boors, who stripped them naked and chased them through the snow. Smolensko was at length reached, but the loss of the greater part of the cannon, the want of ammunition and provisions, rendered their stay in that deserted and half-consumed city impos-

---

[1] The following anecdote is related of the Hessians commanded by Prince Emilius of Darmstadt. The prince had fallen asleep in the snow, and four Hessian dragoons, in order to screen him from the north wind, held their cloaks as a wall around him and were found next morning in the same position—frozen to death. Dead bodies were seen frozen into the most extraordinary positions, gnawing their own hands, gnawing the torn corpses of their comrades. The dead were often covered with snow, and the number of little heaps lying around alone told that of the victims of a single night.

sible. The flight was continued, the Russians incessantly pursuing and harassing the wornout troops, whose retreat was covered by Ney with all the men still under arms. Cut off at Smolensko, he escaped almost by miracle, by creeping during the night along the banks of the Dnieper and successively repulsing the several Russian corps that threw themselves in his way.[1] A thaw now took place, and the Beresina, which it was necessary to cross, was full of drift-ice, its banks were slippery and impassable, and moreover commanded by Tschitschakow's artillery, while the roar of cannon to the rear announced Wittgenstein's approach. Kutusow had this time failed to advance with sufficient rapidity, and Napoleon, the river to his front and enclosed between the Russian armies, owed his escape to the most extraordinary good luck. The corps d'armée under Oudinot and Victor, that had been left behind on his advance upon Moscow, came at the moment of need with fresh troops to his aid. Tschitschakow quitted the bank at the spot where Napoleon intended to make the passage of the Beresina under an idea of the attempt being made at another point. Napoleon instantly threw two bridges across the stream, and all the able-bodied men crossed in safety. At the moment when the bridges, that had several times given way, were choked up by the countless throng bringing up the rear, Wittgenstein appeared and directed his heavy artillery upon the motionless and unarmed crowd. Some regiments, forming the rearguard, fell, together with all still remaining on the other side of the river, into the hands of the Russians.

The fugitive army was, after this fearful day, relieved, but the temperature again fell to twenty-seven degrees below zero, and the stoutest hearts and frames sank. On the 5th of December, Napoleon, placing himself in a sledge, hurried in advance of his army, nay, preceded the news of his disas-

---

[1] Napoleon said, "There are two hundred millions lying in the cellars of the Tuileries; how willingly would I give them to save Ney!"

ter, in order at all events to insure his personal safety and to pass through Germany before measures could be taken for his capture.[1] His fugitive army shortly afterward reached Wilna, but was too exhausted to maintain that position. Enormous magazines, several prisoners, and the rest of the booty, besides six million francs in silver money, fell here into the hands of the Russians. Part of the fugitives escaped to Dantzig, but few crossed the Oder; the Saxons under Reynier were routed and dispersed in a last engagement at Calisch; Poniatowsky and the Poles retired to Cracow, on the Austrian frontier, as it were, protected by Schwarzenberg, who remained unassailed by the Russians, and whose neutrality was, not long afterward, formally recognized.

The Prussians, who had been, meanwhile, occupied with the unsuccessful siege of Riga, and who, like the Austrians, had comparatively husbanded their strength,[2] were now the only hope of the fugitive French. The troops under Macdonald, accordingly, received orders to cover the retreat of the grand army, but York, instead of obeying, concluded a neutral treaty with the Russians commanded by Diebitsch of Silesia and remained stationary in Eastern Prussia. The king of Prussia, at that time still at Berlin and in the power of the French, publicly[3] disapproved of the step taken by his

---

[1] He passed with extreme rapidity, incognito, through Germany. In Dresden he had a short interview with the king of Saxony, who, had he shut him up in Königstein, would have saved Europe a good deal of trouble.—Napoleon no sooner reached Paris in safety than, in his twenty-ninth bulletin, he, for the first time, acquainted the astonished world, hitherto deceived by his false accounts of victory, with the disastrous termination of the campaign. This bulletin was also replete with falsehood and insolence. In his contempt of humanity he even said, "Merely the cowards in the army were depressed in spirit and *dreamed* of misfortune, the brave were ever cheerful." Thus wrote the man who had both seen and caused all this immeasurable misery! The bulletin concluded with, "His Imperial Majesty never enjoyed better health."

[2] In the French despatches, General Hünerbein was accused of not having pursued the Russians under General Lewis.

[3] The secret history of those days is still not sufficiently brought to light. Bignon speaks of fresh treaties between Hardenberg and Napoleon, in which he is corroborated by Fain. These two Frenchmen, the former of whom was a diplomatist, the other one of Napoleon's private secretaries, admit that Prussia's object at that time was to take advantage of Napoleon's embarrassment and to offer him aid on certain important considerations. Prussian historians are silent

general,[1] who was, on the evacuation of Berlin by the French, as publicly rewarded.

The immense army of the conqueror of the world was totally annihilated. Of those who entered Moscow scarcely twenty thousand, of the half million of men who crossed the Russian frontier but eighty thousand, returned.

CCLX. *The Spring of 1813*

THE king of Prussia had suddenly abandoned Berlin, which was still in the hands of the French, for Breslau, whence he declared war against France. A conference also took place between him and the emperor Alexander at Calisch, and, on the 28th of February, 1813, an offensive and defensive alliance was concluded between them. The hour for vengeance had at length arrived. The whole Prussian nation, eager to throw off the hated yoke of the foreigner, to obliterate their disgrace in 1806, to regain their ancient name, cheerfully hastened to place their lives and property at the service of the impoverished government. The whole of the able-bodied population was put under arms. The standing army was increased: to each regiment were appended troops of volunteers, Jægers, composed of young men belonging to the higher classes, who furnished their own equipments: a numerous Landwehr, a sort of militia,

---

in this matter. In Von Rauschnik's biographical account of Blücher, the great internal schism at that time caused in Prussia by the Hardenberg party and that of the Tugendbund is merely slightly hinted at; the former still managed diplomatic affairs, while York, a member of the latter, had already acted on his own responsibility. Shortly afterward affairs took a different aspect, as if Hardenberg's diplomacy had merely been a mask, and he placed himself at the head of the movement against France. In a memorial of 1811, given by Hormayr in the Sketches from the War of Liberation, Hardenberg declared decisively in favor of the alliance with Russia against France.

[1] Hans Louis David von York, a native of Pomerania, having ventured, when a lieutenant in the Prussian service, indignantly to blame the base conduct of one of his superiors in command, became implicated in a duel, was confined in a fortress, abandoned his country, entered the Dutch service, visited the Cape and Ceylon, fought against the Mahrattas, was wounded, returned home and re-entered the Prussian service in 1794.

was, as in Austria, raised besides the standing army, and measures were even taken to call out, in case of necessity, the heads of families and elderly men remaining at home, under the name of the Landsturm.[1] The enthusiastic people, besides furnishing the customary supplies and paying the taxes, contributed to the full extent of their means toward defraying the immense expense of this general arming. Every heart throbbed high with pride and hope. Who would not wish to have lived at such a period, when man's noblest and highest energies were thus called forth! More loudly than even in 1809 in Austria was the German cause now discussed, the great name of the German empire now invoked in Prussia, for in that name alone could all the races of Germany be united against their hereditary foe. The following celebrated proclamation, promising external and internal liberty to Germany, was, with this view, published at Calisch, by Prussia and Russia, on the 25th of March, 1813. It was signed by Prince Kutusow and drawn up by Baron Rehdiger of Silesia.

"The victorious troops of Russia, together with those of his Majesty the king of Prussia, having set foot on German soil, the emperor of Russia and his Majesty the king of Prussia announce simultaneously the return of liberty and independence to the princes and nations of Germany. They come with the sole and sacred purpose of aiding them to regain the hereditary and inalienable national rights of which they have been deprived, to afford potent protection and to secure durability to a newly-restored empire. This great object, free from every interested motive and therefore alone worthy of their Majesties, has solely induced the advance and solely guides the movements of their armies.—These armies, led by generals under the eyes of both monarchs, trust in an omnipotent, just God, and hope to free the whole world and Germany irrevocably from the disgraceful yoke they have so gloriously thrown off. They press for-

---

[1] Literally, the general levy of the people.—*Trans.*

ward animated by enthusiasm. Their watchword is, Honor and Liberty. May every German, desirous of proving himself worthy of the name, speedily and spiritedly join their ranks: may every individual, whether prince, noble, or citizen, aid the plans of liberation, formed by Russia and Prussia, with heart and soul, with person and property, to the last drop of his blood!—The expectation cherished by their Majesties of meeting with these sentiments, this zeal, in every German heart, they deem warranted by the spirit so clearly betokened by the victories gained by Russia over the enslaver of the world.—They therefore demand faithful co-operation, more especially from every German prince, and willingly presuppose that none among them will be found, who, by being and remaining apostate to the German cause, will prove himself deserving of annihilation by the power of public opinion and of just arms. The Rhenish alliance, that deceitful chain lately cast by the breeder of universal discord around ruined Germany to the destruction of her ancient name, can, as the effect of foreign tyranny and the tool of foreign influence, be no longer tolerated. Their Majesties believe that the declaration of the dissolution of this alliance being their fixed intention will meet the long-harbored and universal desire with difficulty retained within the sorrowing hearts of the people.—The relation in which it is the intention of his majesty, the emperor of all the Russias, to stand toward Germany and toward her constitution is, at the same time, here declared. From his desire to see the influence of the foreigner destroyed, it can be no other than that of placing a protecting hand on a work whose form is committed to the free, unbiased will of the princes and people of Germany. The more closely this work, in principle, features and outline, coincides with the once distinct character of the German nation, the more surely will united Germany retake her place with renovated and redoubled vigor among the empires of Europe.—His Majesty and his ally, between whom there reigns a perfect accordance in the sentiments and views hereby explained, are at all times ready to exert their utmost power in pursuance of their sacred aim, the liberation of Germany from a foreign yoke.—May France, strong and beauteous in herself, henceforward seek to consolidate her internal prosperity! No external power will disturb her internal peace, no enemy will encroach upon her rightful frontiers.—But may France also learn that the other powers of Europe aspire to the attainment of durable repose for their subjects, and will not lay down their arms until the independence of every state in Europe shall have been firmly secured."

Nor was the appeal vain. It found an echo in every German heart, and such plain demonstrations of the state of the popular feeling on this side the Rhine were made that Davoust sent serious warning to Napoleon, who contemptuously replied, "Pah! Germans never can become Spaniards!" With his customary rapidity, he levied in France a fresh army three hundred thousand strong, with which he so completely awed the Rhenish confederation as to compel it once more to take the field with thousands of Germans against their brother Germans. The troops, however, reluctantly obeyed, and even the traitors were but lukewarm, for they doubted of success. Mecklenburg alone cided with Prussia. Austria remained neutral.

A Russian corps under General Tettenborn had preceded the rest of the troops and reached the coasts of the Baltic. As early as the 24th of March, 1813, it appeared in Hamburg and expelled the French authorities from the city. The heavily oppressed people of Hamburg,[1] whose com-

[1] The exasperation of the people had risen to the utmost pitch. The French rascals in office, especially the custom-house officers, set no bounds to their tyranny and license. No woman of whatever rank was allow to pass the gates without being subjected to the most indecent inquisition. Goods that had long been redeemed were continually taken from the tradesmen's shops and confiscated. The arbitrary enrolment of a number of young men as conscripts at length produced an insurrection, in which the guard-houses, etc., were destroyed. It was, however, quelled by General St. Cyr, and six of the citizens were executed. On the approach of the Russians, St. Cyr fled with the whole of his troops. The bookseller Perthes, Prell, and von Hess, formed a civic guard.—*Von Hess's Agonies.*

merce had been totally annihilated by the continental system, gave way to the utmost demonstrations of delight, received their deliverers with open arms, revived their ancient rights, and immediately raised a Hanseatic corps, destined to take the field against Napoleon. Dornberg, the ancient foe to France, with another flying squadron took the French division under Morand prisoner, and the Prussian, Major Hellwig (the same who, in 1806, liberated the garrison of Erfurt), dispersed, with merely one hundred and twenty hussars, a Bavarian regiment one thousand three hundred strong and captured five pieces of artillery. In January, the peasantry of the upper country had already revolted against the conscription,[1] and, in February, patriotic proclamations had been disseminated throughout Westphalia under the signature of the Baron von Stein. In this month, also, Captain Maas and two other patriots, who had attempted to raise a rebellion, were executed. As the army advanced, Stein was nominated chief of the provisional government of the still unconquered provinces of Western Germany.

The first Russian army, seventeen thousand strong, under Wittgenstein, pushed forward to Magdeburg, and, at Mokern, repulsed forty thousand French, who were advancing upon Berlin. The Prussians, under their veteran general, Blucher, entered Saxony and garrisoned Dresden, on the 27th of March, 1813; an arch of the fine bridge across the Elbe having been uselessly blown up by the French. Blucher, whose gallantry in the former wars had gained for him the general esteem, and whose kind and generous disposition had won the affection of the soldiery, was nominated generalissimo of the Prussian forces, but subordinate in command to Wittgenstein, who replaced Kutusow as generalissimo of the united forces of Russia and Prussia. The

[1] The people rose *en masse* at Ronsdorf, Solingen, and Barmen, and marched tumultuously to Elberfeld, the great manufacturing town, but were dispersed by the French troops. The French authorities afterward declared that the sole object of the revolt was to smuggle in English goods, and, under this pretext, seized all the foreign goods in Elberfeld.

[2] Kutusow had, just at that conjuncture, expired at Bautzen.

emperor of Russia and the king of Prussia accompanied the army and were received with loud acclamations by the people of Dresden and Leipzig. The allied army was merely seventy thousand strong, and Blucher had not formed a junction with Wittgenstein when Napoleon invaded the country by Erfurt and Merseburg at the head of one hundred and sixty thousand men. Ney attacked, with forty thousand men, the Russian vanguard under Winzingerode, which, after gallantly defending a defile near Weissenfels, made an orderly retreat before forces far their superior in number. The French, on this occasion, lost Marshal Bessieres. Napoleon, incredulous of attack, marched in long columns upon Leipzig, and Wittgenstein, falling upon his right flank, committed great havoc among the forty thousand men under Ney, which he had first of all encountered, at Gross-Gorschen. This place was alternately lost and regained owing to his ill-judged plan of attack by single brigades, instead of breaking Napoleon's lines by charging them at once with the whole of his forces. The young Prussian volunteers here measured their strength in a murderous conflict, hand to hand, with the young French conscripts, and excited by their martial spirit the astonishment of the veterans. Wittgenstein's delay and Blucher's too late arrival on the field[1] gave Napoleon time to wheel his long lines round and to encircle the allied forces, which immediately retired. On the eve of the bloody engagement of the 2d of May, the allied cavalry attempted a general attack in the dark, which was also unsuccessful on account of the superiority of the enemy's forces. The allies had, nevertheless, captured some cannons, the French, none. The most painful loss was that of the noble Scharnhorst, who was mortally wounded. Bulow had, on the same day, stormed Halle with a Prussian corps, but was now compelled to resolve upon a retreat,

---

[1] The nature of the ground rendered a night march impossible. The Russian, Michaelofski Danilefski, however, throws the blame upon an officer in Blücher's headquarters, who laid the important orders committed to his charge under his pillow and overslept himself.

which was conducted in the most orderly manner by the allies. At Koldiz, the Prussian rearguard repulsed the French van in a bloody engagement on the 5th of May. The allies marched through Dresden[1] and took up a firm position in and about Bautzen, after being joined by a reinforcement of eighty thousand Bavarians. Napoleon was also reinforced by a number of French, Bavarian, Wurtemberg, and Saxon troops,[2] and despatched Lauriston and Ney toward Berlin; but the former encountering the Russians under Barclay de Tolly at Konigswartha, and the latter the Prussians under York at Weissig, both were constrained to retreat. Napoleon attacked the position at Bautzen from the 19th to the 21st of May, but was gloriously repulsed by the Prussians under Kleist, while Blucher, who was in danger of being completely surrounded, undauntedly defended himself on three sides. The allies lost not a cannon, not a single prisoner, although again compelled to retire before the superior forces of the enemy. The French had suffered an immense loss; eighteen thousand of their wounded were sent to Dresden. Napoleon's favorite, Marshal Duroc, and General Kirchner, a native of Alsace, were killed, close to his side, by a cannon ball. The allied troops, forced to retire after an obstinate encounter, neither fled nor dispersed, but withdrew in close column and repelling each successive attack.[3] The French avant-garde under Maison was, when

---

[1] It may here be mentioned as a remarkable characteristic of those times that Goethe, Ernest Maurice Arndt, and Theodore Körner at that period met at Dresden. The youthful Körner, a volunteer Jæger, was the Tyrtæus of those days: his military songs were universally sung: his father also expressed great enthusiasm. Goethe said almost angrily, "Well, well, shake your chains, the man (Napoleon) is too strong for you, you will not break them!"—*E. M. Arndt's Reminiscences.*

[2] "Unfortunately there were German princes who, even this time, again sent their troops to swell the ranks of the oppressor; Austria had, unfortunately, not yet concluded her preparations; consequently, it was only possible to clog the advance of the conqueror by a gallant resistance."—*Clausewitz.* The Bavarians stood under Raglowich, the Würtembergers under Franquemont, the Saxons under Reynier. There was also a contingent of Westphalians and Badeners.

[3] Blücher exclaimed on this occasion: "He's a rascally fellow that dares to say we fly." Even Fain, the Frenchman, confesses in his manuscript of 1813, in which he certainly does not favor the Germans: "The best Marshals, as it were, killed by spent balls. Great victories without trophies. All the villages

in close pursuit of the allied force, almost entirely cut to pieces by the Prussian cavalry, which unexpectedly fell upon it at Heinau. The main body of the Russo-Prussian army, on entering Silesia, took a slanting direction toward the Riesengebirge and retired behind the fortress of Schweidnitz. In this strong position they were at once partially secure from attack, and, by their vicinity to the Bohemian frontier, enabled to keep up a communication, and, if necessary, to form a junction with the Austrian forces. The whole of the lowlands of Silesia lay open to the French, who entered Breslau on the 1st of June.[1] Berlin was also merely covered by a comparatively weak army under General Bulow,[2] who, notwithstanding the check given by him to Marshal Oudinot in the battles of Hoyerswerda and Luckau, was not in sufficient force to offer resistance to the main body of the French in case Napoleon chose to pass through Berlin on his way to Poland. Napoleon, however, did not as yet venture to make use of his advantage. By the seizure of Prussia and Poland, both of which lay open to him, the main body of the allied army and the Austrians, who had not yet declared themselves, would have been left to the rear of his right flank and could easily have cut off his retreat. His troops, principally young conscripts, were moreover worn out with fatigue, nor had the whole of his reinforcements arrived. To his rear was a multitude of bold partisans, Tettenborn, the Hanseatic legion, Czernitscheff, who, at Halberstadt, captured General Ochs together with

---

on our route in flames which obstructed our advance. 'What a war! We shall all fall victims to it!' are the disgraceful expressions uttered by many, for the iron hearts of the warriors of France are rust-grown." Napoleon exclaimed after the battle, "How! no result after such a massacre? No prisoners? They leave me not even a nail!" Duroc's death added to the catastrophe. Napoleon was so struck that for the first time in his life he could give no orders, but deferred everything until the morrow.

[1] But they merely encamped in the streets, showed themselves more anxious than threatening, and were seized with a terrible panic on a sudden conflagration breaking out during the night, which they mistook for a signal to bring the Landsturm upon them. And yet there were thirty thousand French in the city. How different to their spirit in 1807!

[2] Brother to the unfortunate Henry von Bülow.

the whole of the Westphalian corps and fourteen pieces of artillery, Colomb, the Herculean captain of horse, who took a convoy and twenty-four guns at Zwickau, and the Black Prussian squadron under Lutzow. Napoleon consequently remained stationary, and, with a view of completing his preparations and of awaiting the decision of Austria, demanded an armistice, to which the allies, whose force was still incomplete and to whom the decision of Austria was of equal importance, gladly assented.

On this celebrated armistice, concluded on the 4th of June, 1813, at the village of Pleisswitz, the fate of Europe was to depend. To the side that could raise the most powerful force, that on which Austria ranged herself, numerical superiority insured success. Napoleon's power was still terrible; fresh victory had obliterated the disgrace of his flight from Russia; he stood once more an invincible leader on German soil. The French were animated by success and blindly devoted to their emperor. Italy and Denmark were prostrate at his feet. The Rhenish confederation was also faithful to his standard. Councillor Crome published at Giessen, in obedience to Napoleon's mandate and with the knowledge of the government at Darmstadt, a pamphlet entitled "Germany's Crisis and Salvation," in which he declared that Germany was saved by the fresh victories of Napoleon, and promised mountains of gold to the Germans if they remained true to him.[1] Crome was at that time graciously thanked in autograph letters by the sovereigns of Bavaria and Wurtemberg. Lutzow's volunteer corps was, during the armistice, surprised at Kitzen by a superior corps

---

[1] Crome was afterward barefaced enough to boast of this work in his Autobiography, published in 1833. Napoleon dictated the fundamental ideas of this work to him from his headquarters. His object was to pacify the Germans. He promised them henceforward to desist from enforcing his continental system, to restore liberty to commerce, no longer to force the laws and language of France upon Germany. L'empereur se fera aimer des Allemands. The Germans were, on the other hand, warned that the allies had no intention to render Germany free and independent, they being much more interested in retaining Germany in a state of division and subjection. The unity of Germany, it was also declared, was alone possible under Napoleon, etc.

of Wurtembergers under Normann and cut to pieces. Germans at that period opposed Germans without any feeling for their common fatherland.[1] The king of Saxony, who had already repaired to Prague under the protection of Austria, also returned thence, was received at Dresden with extreme magnificence by Napoleon, and, in fresh token of amity, ceded the fortress of Torgau to the French.[2] These occurrences caused the Saxon minister, Senfft von Pilsach, and the Saxon general, Thielmann, who had already devoted themselves to the German cause, to resign office. The Polish army under Prince Poniatowsky (vassal to the king of Saxony, who was also grandduke of Warsaw) received permission (it had at an earlier period fallen back upon Schwarzenberg) to march, unarmed, through the Austrian territory to Dresden, in order to join the main body of the French under Napoleon. The declaration of the emperor of Austria in favor of his son-in-law, who, moreover, was lavish of his promises, and, among other things, offered to restore Silesia, was, consequently, at the opening of the armistice, deemed certain.

The armistice was, meanwhile, still more beneficial to the allies. The Russians had time to concentrate their scattered troops, the Prussians completed the equipment of their numerous Landwehren, and the Swedes also took the field. Bernadotte landed on the 18th of May in Pomerania, and advanced with his troops into Brandenburg for the purpose, in conjunction with Bulow, of covering Berlin. A German auxiliary corps, in the pay of England, was also formed, under Wallmoden, on the Baltic. The defence of Hamburg was extremely easy; but the base intrigues of foreigners,

---

[1] This arose from hatred to the party that dared to uphold the German cause instead of a Prussian, Saxon, etc., one, and by no means by chance, but, as Manso remarks, intentionally, "through low cunning and injustice."

[2] The king of Saxony was, in return, insulted by Napoleon, in an address to the ministers was termed *une veille hête*, and compelled to countenance immoral theatrical performances by his presence, a sin for which he each evening received absolution from his confessor. Vide Stein's Letter to Münster in the Sketches of the War of Liberation.

who, as during the time of the thirty years' war, paid themselves for their aid by the seizure of German provinces and towns, delivered that splendid city into the hands of the French. Bernadotte had sold himself to Russia for the price of Norway, which Denmark refused to cede unless Hamburg and Lubeck were given in exchange. This agreement had already been made by Prince Dolgorucki in the name of the emperor Alexander, and Tettenborn yielded Hamburg to the Danes, who marched in under pretext of protecting the city and were received with delight by the unsuspecting citizens. The non-advance of the Swedes proceeded from the same cause. The increase of the Danish marine by means of the Hanse towns, however, proved displeasing to England; the whole of the commerce was broken up, and the Danes, hastily resolving to maintain faith with Napoleon, delivered luckless Hamburg to the French, who instantly took a most terrible revenge. Davoust, as he himself boasted, merely sent twelve German patriots to execution,[1] but expelled twenty-five thousand of the inhabitants from the city, while he pulled down their houses and converted them into fortifications, at which the principal citizens were compelled to work in person. Dissatisfied, moreover, with a contribution of eighteen millions, he robbed the great Hamburg bank, treading underfoot every private and national right, all, as he, miserable slave as he was,[2] declared, in obedience to the mandate of his lord.

Austria, at first, instead of aiding the allies, allowed the Poles[3] to range themselves beneath the standard of Napoleon, whom she overwhelmed with protestations of friend-

---

[1] He also said, like his master, "I know of no Germans, I only know of Bavarians, Würtembergers, Westphalians," etc.

[2] His written defence, in which he so lyingly, so humbly and mournfully exculpates himself that one really "compassionates the devil," is a sort of satisfaction for the Germans.

[3] Poniatowsky's dismissal with the Polish army from Poland was apparently a service rendered to Napoleon, but was in reality done with a view of disarming Poland. Poniatowsky might have organized an insurrection to the rear of the allies, and would in that case have been far more dangerous to them than when ranged beneath the standard of Napoleon.

ship, which served to mask her real intentions, and meanwhile gave her time to arm herself to the teeth and to make the allies sensible of the fact of their utter impotency against Napoleon unless aided by her. The interests of Austria favored her alliance with France, but Napoleon, instead of confidence, inspired mistrust. Austria, notwithstanding the marriage between him and Maria Louisa, was, as had been shown at the congress of Dresden, merely treated as a tributary to France, and Napoleon's ambition offered no guarantee to the ancient imperial dynasty. There was no security that the provinces bestowed in momentary reward for her alliance must not, on the first occasion, be restored. Nor was public opinion entirely without weight.[1] Napoleon's star was on the wane, whole nations stood like to a dark and ominous cloud threatening on the horizon, and Count Metternich prudently chose rather to attempt to guide the storm ere it burst than trust to a falling star. Austria had, as early as the 27th of June, 1813, signed a treaty, at Reichenbach in Silesia, with Russia and Prussia, by which she bound herself to declare war against France, in case Napoleon had not, before the 20th of July, accepted the terms of peace about to be proposed to him. Already had the sovereigns and generals of Russia and Prussia sketched, during a conference held with the crown prince of Sweden, the 11th July, at Trachenberg, the plan for the approaching

---

[1] The people in Austria fully sympathized with passing events. How could those be apathetic who had such a burden of disgrace to redeem, such deep revenge to satisfy? An extremely popular song contained the following lines:

"Awake, Franciscus! Hark! thy people call!
Awake! acknowledge the avenger's hand!
Still groans beneath the foreign courser's hoof
The soil of Germany, our fatherland.

"To arms! so long as sacred Germany
Feels but a finger of Napoleon.
Franciscus! up! Cast off each private tie!
The patriot has no kindred, has no son."

All the able-bodied men, as in Prussia, crowded beneath the imperial standard and the whole empire made the most patriotic sacrifices. Hungary summoned the whole of her male population, the insurrection, as it was termed, to the field.

campaign, and, with the permission of Austria, assigned to her the part she was to take as one of the allies against Napoleon, when Metternich again visited Dresden in person for the purpose of repeating his assurances of amity, for the armistice had but just commenced, to Napoleon. The French emperor had an indistinct idea of the transactions then passing, and bluntly said to the Count, "As you wish to mediate, you are no longer on my side." He hoped partly to win Austria over by redoubling his promises, partly to terrify her by the dread of the future ascendency of Russia, but, perceiving how Metternich evaded him by his artful diplomacy, he suddenly asked him, "Well, Metternich, how much has England given you in order to engage you to play this part toward me?" This trait of insolence toward an antagonist of whose superiority he felt conscious, and of the most deadly hatred masked by contempt, was peculiarly characteristic of the Corsican, who, besides the qualities of the lion, fully possessed those of the cat. Napoleon let his hat drop in order to see whether Metternich would raise it. He did not, and war was resolved upon. A pretended congress for the conclusion of peace was again arranged by both sides; by Napoleon, in order to elude the reproach cast upon him of an insurmountable and eternal desire for war, and by the allies, in order to prove to the whole world their desire for peace. Each side was, however, fully aware that the palm of peace was alone to be found on the other side of the battlefield. Napoleon was generous in his concessions, but delayed granting full powers to his envoy, an opportune circumstance for the allies, who were by this means able to charge him with the whole blame of procrastination. Napoleon, in all his concessions, merely included Russia and Austria to the exclusion of Prussia.[1] But neither Russia

[1] Russia was to receive the whole of Poland, the grandduchy of Warsaw was to be annihilated. Such was Napoleon's gratitude toward the Poles!—Illyria was to be restored to Austria. Prussia, however, was not only to be excluded from all participation in the spoil, but the Rhenish confederation was to be extended as far as the Oder. Prussia would have been compelled to pay the expenses of the alliance between France, Russia, and Austria.

nor Austria trusted to his promises, and the negotiations were broken off on the termination of the armistice, when Napoleon sent full powers to his plenipotentiary. Now, was it said, it is too late. The art with which Metternich passed from the alliance with Napoleon to neutrality, to mediation, and finally to the coalition against him, will, in every age, be acknowledged a master-piece of diplomacy. Austria, while coalescing with Russia and Prussia, in a certain degree assumed a rank conventionally superior to both. The whole of the allied armies was placed under the command of an Austrian general, Prince von Schwarzenberg, and if the proclamation published at Calisch had merely summoned the people of Germany to assert their independence, the manifesto of Count Metternich spoke already in the tone of the future regulator of the affairs of Europe.[1] Austria declared herself on the 12th of August, 1813, two days after the termination of the armistice.

---

[1] "Everywhere," said this manifesto, "do the impatient wishes of the people anticipate the regular proceedings of the government. On all sides, the desire for independence under separate laws, the feeling of insulted nationality, rage against the heavy abuses inflicted by a foreign tyrant, burst simultaneously forth. His Majesty the emperor, too clear-sighted not to view this turn in affairs as the natural and necessary result of a preceding and violent state of exaggeration, and too just to view it with displeasure, had rendered it his principal object to turn it to the general advantage, and, by well-weighed and well-combined measures, to promote the true and lasting interests of the whole commonwealth of Europe."

CCLXI. *The Battle of Leipzig*

Immediately after this—for all had been previously arranged—the monarchs of Russia and Prussia passed the Riesengebirge with a division of their forces into Bohemia, and joined the emperor Francis and the great Austrian army at Prague. The celebrated general, Moreau, who had returned from America, where he had hitherto dwelt incognito, in order to take up arms against Napoleon, was in the train of the czar. His example, it was hoped, would induce many of his countrymen to abandon Napoleon. The plan of the allies was to advance, with their main body under Schwarzenberg, consisting of one hundred and twenty thousand Austrians and seventy thousand Russians and Prussians, through the Erzgebirge to Napoleon's rear. A lesser Prussian force, principally Silesian Landwehr, under Blucher, eighty thousand strong, besides a small Russian corps, was, meanwhile, to cover Silesia, or, in case of an attack by Napoleon's main body, to retire before it and draw it further eastward. A third division, under the crown prince of Sweden, principally Swedes, with some Prussian troops, mostly Pomeranian and Brandenburg Landwehr under Bulow, and some Russians, in all ninety thousand men, was destined to cover Berlin, and in case of a victory to form a junction to Napoleon's rear with the main body of the allied army. A still lesser and equally mixed division under Wallmoden, thirty thousand strong, was destined to watch Davoust in Hamburg, while an Austrian corps of twenty-five thousand men under Prince Reuss watched the movements of the Bavarians, and another Austrian force of forty thousand, under Hiller, those of the viceroy Eugene in Italy.

Napoleon had concentrated his main body, that still consisted of two hundred and fifty thousand men, in and around

Dresden. Davoust received orders to advance with thirty thousand men from Hamburg upon Berlin; in Bavaria, there were thirty thousand men under Wrede; in Italy, forty thousand under Eugene. The German fortresses were, moreover, strongly garrisoned with French troops. Napoleon had it in his power to throw himself with his main body, which neither Blucher nor the Swedes could have withstood, into Poland, to levy the people en masse and render that country the theatre of war, but the dread of the defection of the Rhenish confederation and of a part of the French themselves, were the country to his rear to be left open to the allies and to Moreau, coupled with his disinclination to declare the independence of Poland, owing to a lingering hope of being still able to bring about a reconciliation with Russia and Austria by the sacrifice of that country and of Prussia, caused that idea to be renounced, and he accordingly took up a defensive position with his main body at Dresden, whence he could watch the proceedings and take advantage of any indiscretion on the part of his opponents. A body of ninety thousand men under Oudinot meantime acted on the offensive, being directed to advance, simultaneously with Davoust from Hamburg and with Girard from Magdeburg, upon Berlin, and to take possession of that metropolis. Napoleon hoped, when master of the ancient Prussian provinces, to be able to suppress German enthusiasm at its source and to induce Russia and Austria to conclude a separate peace at the expense of Prussia.

In August, 1813, the tempest of war broke loose on every side, and all Europe prepared for a decisive struggle. About this time, the whole of Northern Germany was visited for some weeks, as was the case on the defeat of Varus in the Teutoburg forest, with heavy rains and violent storms. The elements seemed to combine, as in Russia, their efforts with those of man against Napoleon. There his soldiers fell victims to frost and snow, here they sank into the boggy soil and were carried away by the swollen rivers. In the midst of the uproar of the elements, bloody engagements continually took place, in which the bayonet and the butt-end of the firelock were almost alone used, the muskets being rendered unserviceable by the wet. The first engagement of importance was that of the 21st of August between Wallmoden and Davoust at Vellahn. A few days afterward, Theodore Korner, the youthful poet and hero, fell in a skirmish between the French and Wallmoden's outpost at Gadebusch.—Oudinot advanced close upon Berlin, which was protected by the crown prince of Sweden. A murderous conflict took place, on the 23d of August, at Gross-Beeren between the Prussian division under General von Bulow and the French. The Swedes, a troop of horse artillery alone excepted, were not brought into action, and the Prussians, unaided, repulsed the greatly superior forces of the French. The almost untrained peasantry comprising the Landwehr of the Mark and of Pomerania rushed upon the enemy, and, unhabituated to the use of the bayonet and firelock, beat down entire battalions of the French with the butt-end of their muskets. After a frightful massacre, the French were utterly routed and fled in wild disorder, but the gallant Prussians vainly expected the Swedes to aid in the pursuit. The crown prince, partly from a desire to spare his troops and partly from a feeling of shame—he was also a Frenchman—remained motionless. Oudinot, nevertheless, lost two thousand four hundred prisoners. Davoust, from this disaster, returned once more to Hamburg. Girard, who had advanced with eight thousand men from Magdeburg, was, on the 27th, put to flight by the Prussian Landwehr under General Hirschfeld.

Napoleon's plan of attack against Prussia had completely failed, and his sole alternative was to act on the defensive. But on perceiving that the main body of the allied forces under Schwarzenberg was advancing to his rear, while Blucher was stationed with merely a weak division in Silesia, he took the field with immensely superior forces against the latter, under an idea of being able easily to vanquish his weak antagonist and to fall back again in time upon Dresden.

Blucher cauti^usly retired, but, unable to restrain the martial spirit of the soldiery, who obstinately defended every position whence they were driven, lost two thousand of his men on the 21st of August. The news of Napoleon's advance upon Silesia and of the numerical weakness of the garrison left at Dresden reached Schwarzenberg just as he had crossed the Erzgebirge, and induced him and the allied sovereigns assembled within his camp to change their plan of operations and to march straight upon the Saxon capital. Napoleon, who had pursued Blucher as far as the Katzbach near Goldberg, instantly returned and boldly resolved to cross the Elbe above Dresden, to seize the passes of the Bohemian mountains, and to fall upon the rear of the main body of the allied army. Vandamme's corps d'armee had already set forward with this design, when Napoleon learned that Dresden could no longer hold out unless he returned thither with a division of his army, and, in order to preserve that city and the centre of his position, he hastily returned thither in the hope of defeating the allied army and of bringing it between two fires, as Vandamme must meanwhile have occupied the narrow outlets of the Erzgebirge with thirty thousand men and by that means have cut off the retreat of the allied army. The plan was on a grand scale, and, as far as related to Napoleon in person, was executed, to the extreme discomfiture of the allies, with his usual success. Schwarzenberg had, with true Austrian procrastination, allowed the 25th of August, when, as the French themselves confess, Dresden, in her then ill-defended state, might have been taken almost without a stroke, to pass in inaction, and when he attempted to storm the city on the 26th, Napoleon, who had meanwhile arrived, calmly awaited the onset of the thick masses of the enemy in order to open a murderous discharge of grape upon them on every side. They were repulsed after suffering a frightful loss. On the following day, destined to end in still more terrible bloodshed, Napoleon assumed the offensive, separated the retiring allied army by well-combined sallies, cut off its left wing, and made an immense number of prisoners, chiefly Austrians. The unfortunate Moreau had both his legs shot off in the very first encounter. His death was an act of justice, for he had taken up arms against his fellow-countrymen, and was moreover a gain for the Germans, the Russians merely making use of him in order to obscure the fame of the German leaders, and, it may be, with a view of placing the future destinies of France in his hands. The main body of the allied army retreated on every side; part of the troops disbanded, the rest were exposed to extreme hardship owing to the torrents of rain that fell without intermission and the scarcity of provisions. Their annihilation must have inevitably followed had Vandamme executed Napoleon's commands and blocked up the mountain passes, in which he was unsuccessful, owing to the gallantry with which he was held in check at Culm by eight thousand Russian guards, headed by Ostermann,[1] who, although merely amounting in number to a fourth of his army, fought during a whole day without receding a step, though almost the whole of them were cut to pieces and Ostermann was deprived of an arm, until the first corps of the main body, in full retreat, reached the mountains. Vandamme was now in turn overwhelmed by superior numbers. One way of escape, a still unoccupied height, on which he hastened to post himself, alone remained, but Kleist's corps, also in full retreat, unexpectedly but opportunely appeared above his head and took him and the whole of his corps prisoners, the 29th of August, 1813.[2]

At the same time, the 26th of August, a most glorious victory was gained by Blucher in Silesia. After having drawn Macdonald across the Katzbach and the foaming Neisse, he drove him, after a desperate and bloody engage-

---

[1] This general belonged to a German family long naturalized in Russia.

[2] He was led through Silesia, which he had once so shamefully plundered, and, although no physical punishment was inflicted upon him, he was often compelled to hear the voice of public opinion, and was exposed to the view of the people to whom he had once said, "Nothing shall be left to you except your eyes, that you may be able to weep over your wretchedness."—*Manso's History of Prussia.*

ment, into those rivers, which were greatly swollen by the incessant rains. The muskets of the soldiery had been rendered unserviceable by the wet, and Blucher, drawing his sabre from beneath his cloak, dashed forward exclaiming, "Forward!" Several thousand of the French were drowned or fell by the bayonet, or beneath the heavy blows dealt by the Landwehr with the butt-end of their firelocks. It was on this battlefield that the Silesians had formerly opposed the Tartars, and the monastery of Wahlstatt, erected in memory of that heroic day,[1] was still standing. Blucher was rewarded with the title of Prince von der Wahlstatt, but his soldiers surnamed him Marshal Vorwarts. On the decline of the floods, the banks of the rivers were strewn with corpses sticking in horrid distortion out of the mud. A part of the French fled for a couple of days in terrible disorder along the right bank and were then taken prisoner together with their general, Puthod.[2] The French lost one hundred and three guns, eighteen thousand prisoners, and a still greater number in killed; the loss on the side of the Prussians merely amounted to one thousand men. Macdonald returned almost totally unattended to Dresden and brought the melancholy intelligence to Napoleon, "Votre armée du Bobre n'existe plus."

The crown prince of Sweden and Bulow had meanwhile pursued Oudinot's retreating corps in the direction of the Elbe. Napoleon despatched Ney against them, but he met with the fate of his predecessor, at Dennewitz, on the 6th of September. The Prussians, on this occasion, again triumphed, unaided by their confederates.[3] Bulow and Tauen-

---

[1] An ancient battle-axe of serpentine stone was found on the site fixed upon for the erection of a fresh monument in honor of the present victory.—*Allgemenie Zeitung, 1817*

[2] This piece of good fortune befell Langeron, the Russian general, who belonged to the diplomatic party at that time attempting to spare the forces of Russia, Austria, and Sweden at the expense of Prussia, and, at the same time, to deprive Prussia of her well-won laurels. Langeron had not obeyed Blücher's orders, had remained behind on his own responsibility, and the scattered French troops fell into his hands.

[3] The proud armies of Russia and Sweden (forty-six battalions, forty squad-

zien, with twenty thousand men, defeated the French army, seventy thousand strong. The crown prince of Sweden not only remained to the rear with the whole of his troops, but gave perfectly useless orders to the advancing Prussian squadron under General Borstel, who, without attending to them, hurried on to Bulow's assistance, and the French were, notwithstanding their numerical superiority, completely driven off the field, which the crown prince reached just in time to witness the dispersion of his countrymen. The French lost eighteen thousand men and eighty guns. The rout was complete. The rearguard, consisting of the Wurtembergers under Franquemont, was again overtaken at the head of the bridge at Zwettau, and, after a frightful carnage, driven in wild confusion across the dam to Torgau. The Bavarians under Raglowich, who, probably owing to secret orders, had remained, during the battle, almost in a state of inactivity, withdrew in another direction and escaped.[1] Davoust also again retired upon Hamburg, and his rearguard under Pecheux was attacked by Wallmoden, on the 16th of September, on the Gorde, and suffered a trifling loss. On the 29th of September, eight thousand French were also defeated by Platow, the Hetman of the Cossacks, at Zeitz; on the 30th, Czernitscheff penetrated into Cassel and expelled Jerome. Thielemann, the Saxon general, also infested the country to Napoleon's rear, intercepted his convoys at Leipzig, and at Weissenfels took one thousand two hundred, at Merseburg two thousand, French prisoners; he was, however, deprived of his booty by a strong force under Lefebvre-Desnouettes, by whom he was incessantly harassed until Platow's arrival with the Cossacks, who, in conjunction with Thielemann, repulsed Lefebvre with great slaughter at Altenburg. On this occasion,

---

rons, and one hundred and fifty guns) followed to the rear of the Prussians without firing a shot and remained inactive spectators of the action.—*Plotho.*

[1] In order to avoid being carried along by the fugitive French, they fired upon them whenever their confused masses came too close upon them.—*Bölderndorf.*

a Baden battalion, that had been drawn up apart from the French, turned their fire upon their unnatural confederates and aided in their dispersion.[1]

Napoleon's generals had been thrown back in every quarter, with immense loss, upon Dresden, toward which the allies now advanced, threatening to enclose it on every side. Napoleon manœuvred until the beginning of October with the view of executing a coup de main against Schwarzenberg and Blucher; the allies were, however, on their guard, and he was constantly reduced to the necessity of recalling his troops, sent for that purpose into the field, to Dresden. The danger in which he now stood of being completely surrounded and cut off from the Rhine at length rendered retreat his sole alternative. Blucher had already crossed the Elbe on the 5th of October, and, in conjunction with the crown prince of Sweden, had approached the head of the main body of the allied army under Schwarzenberg, which was advancing from the Erzgebirge. On the 7th of October, Napoleon quitted Dresden, leaving a garrison of thirty thousand French under St. Cyr, and removed his headquarters to Duben, on the road leading from Leipzig to Berlin, in the hope of drawing Blucher and the Swedes once more on the right side of the Elbe, in which case he intended to turn unexpectedly upon the Austrians; Blucher, however, eluded him, without quitting the left bank. Napoleon's plan was to take advantage of the absence of Blucher and of the Swedes from Berlin in order to hasten across the defenceless country, for the purpose of inflicting punishment upon Prussia, of raising Poland, etc. But his plan met with opposition in his own military council. His ill success had caused those who had hitherto followed his fortunes to waver. The king of Bavaria declared against him on the 8th of October,[2] and

---

[1] Vide Wagner's Chronicle of Altenburg.

[2] Maximilian Joseph declared in an open manifesto; Bavaria was compelled to furnish thirty-eight thousand men for the Russian campaign, and, on her expressing a hope that such an immense sacrifice would not be requested, France instantly declared the princes of the Rhenish confederation her vassals, who were commanded "under punishment of felony" unconditionally to obey each

the Bavarian army under Wrede united with instead of opposing the Austrian army and was sent to the Maine in order to cut off Napoleon's retreat. The news of this defection speedily reached the French camp and caused the rest of the troops of the Rhenish confederation to waver in their allegiance; while the French, wearied with useless manœuvres, beaten in every quarter, opposed by an enemy greatly their superior in number and glowing with revenge, despaired of the event and sighed for peace and their quiet homes. All refused to march upon Berlin, nay, the very idea of removing further from Paris almost produced a mutiny in the camp.[1] Four days, from the 11th to the 14th of October, were passed by Napoleon in a state of melancholy irresolution, when he appeared as if suddenly inspired by the idea of there still being time to execute a coup de main upon the main body of the allied army under Schwarzenberg before its junction with Blucher and the Swedes. Schwarzenberg was slowly advancing from Bohemia and had already allowed himself to be defeated before Dresden. Napoleon intended to fall upon him on his arrival in the vicinity of

---

of Napoleon's demands. The allies would, on the contrary, have acceded to all the desires of Bavaria and have guaranteed that kingdom. Even the Austrian troops, that stood opposed to Bavaria, were placed under Wrede's command.—Raglowich received permission from Napoleon, before the battle of Leipzig, to return to Bavaria; but his corps was retained in the vicinity of Leipzig without taking part in the action, and retired, in the general confusion, under the command of General Maillot, upon Torgau, whence it returned home.—*Bölderndorf.* In the Tyrol, the brave mountaineers were on the eve of revolt. As early as September, Speckbacher, sick and wasted from his wounds, but endued with all his former fire and energy, reappeared in the Tyrol, where he was commissioned by Austria to organize a revolt. An unexpected reconciliation, however, taking place between Bavaria and Austria, counter orders arrived, and Speckbacher furiously dashed his bullet-worn hat to the ground.—*Brockhaus, 1814.* The restoration of the Tyrol to Austria being delayed, a multitude of Tyrolese forced their way into Innsbruck and deposed the Bavarian authorities; their leader, Kluibenspedel, was, however, persuaded by Austria to submit. Speckbacher was, in 1816, raised by the emperor Francis to the rank of major; he died in 1820, and was buried at Hall by the south wall of the parish church. His son, Andre, who grew up a fine, handsome man, died in 1835, at Jenbach (not Zenbach, as Mercy has it in his attacks upon the Tyrol), in the Tyrol, where he was employed as superintendent of the mines. Mercy's Travels and his account of Speckbacher in the Milan Revista Europea, 1838, are replete with falsehood.

[1] According to Fain and Coulaincourt.

Leipzig, but it was already too late.—Blucher was at hand. On the 14th of October,[1] the flower of the French cavalry, headed by the king of Naples, encountered Blucher's and Wittgenstein's cavalry at Wachau, not far from Leipzig. The contest was broken off, both sides being desirous of husbanding their strength, but terminated to the disadvantage of the French, notwithstanding their numerical superiority, besides proving the vicinity of the Prussians. This was the most important cavalry fight that took place during this war.

On the 16th of October, while Napoleon was merely awaiting the arrival of Macdonald's corps, that had remained behind, before proceeding to attack Schwarzenberg's Bohemian army, he was unexpectedly attacked on the right bank of the Pleisse, at Liebert-wolkwitz, by the Austrians, who were, however, compelled to retire before a superior force. The French cavalry under Latour-Maubourg pressed so closely upon the emperor of Russia and the king of Prussia that they merely owed their escape to the gallantry of the Russian, Orlow Denisow, and to Latour's fall. Napoleon had already ordered all the bells in Leipzig to be rung, had sent the news of his victory to Paris, and seems to have expected a complete triumph when joyfully exclaiming, "Le monde tourne pour nous!" But his victory had been only partial, and he had been unable to follow up his advantage, another division of the Austrian army, under General Meerveldt, having simultaneously occupied him and compelled him to cross the Pleisse at Dolnitz; and, although Meerveldt had been in his turn repulsed with severe loss and been himself taken prisoner, the diversion proved of service to the Austrians by keeping Napoleon in check until the arrival of Blucher, who threw himself upon the division of the French army opposed to him at

---

[1] On the evening of the 14th of October (the anniversary of the battle of Jena), a hurricane raged in the neighborhood of Leipzig, where the French lay, carried away roofs and uprooted trees, while, during the whole night, the rain fell in violent floods.

Möckern by Marshal Marmont. Napoleon, while thus occupied with the Austrians, was unable to meet the attack of the Prussians with sufficient force. Marmont, after a massacre of some hours' duration in and around Möckern, was compelled to retire with a loss of forty guns. The second Prussian brigade lost, either in killed or wounded, all its officers except one.

The battle had, on the 16th of October, raged around Leipzig; Napoleon had triumphed over the Austrians, whom he had solely intended to attack, but had, at the same time, been attacked and defeated by the Prussians, and now found himself opposed and almost surrounded—one road for retreat alone remaining open—by the whole allied force. He instantly gave orders to General Bertrand to occupy Weissenfels during the night, in order to secure his retreat through Thuringia; but, during the following day, the 17th of October, neither seized that opportunity in order to effect a retreat or to make a last and energetic attack upon the allies, whose forces were not yet completely concentrated, ere the circle had been fully drawn around him. The Swedes, the Russians under Bennigsen, and a large Austrian division under Colloredo, had not yet arrived. Napoleon might with advantage have again attacked the defeated Austrians under Schwarzenberg or have thrown himself with the whole of his forces upon Blucher. He had still an opportunity of making an orderly retreat without any great exposure to danger. But he did neither. He remained motionless during the whole day, which was also passed in tranquillity by the allies, who thus gained time to receive fresh reinforcements. Napoleon's inactivity was caused by his having sent his prisoner, General Meerveldt, to the emperor of Austria, whom he still hoped to induce, by means of great assurances, to secede from the coalition and to make peace. Not even a reply was vouchsafed. On the very day, thus futilely lost by Napoleon, the allied army was reintegrated by the arrival of the masses commanded by the crown prince, by Bennigsen and Colloredo, and was consequently raised to double the strength of that of France, which now merely amounted to one hundred and fifty thousand men. On the 18th, a murderous conflict began on both sides. Napoleon long and skilfully opposed the fierce onset of the allied troops, but was at length driven off the field by their superior weight and persevering efforts. The Austrians, stationed on the left wing of the allied army, were opposed by Oudinot, Augereau, and Poniatowsky; the Prussians, stationed on the right wing, by Marmont and Ney; the Russians and Swedes in the centre, by Murat and Regnier. In the hottest of the battle, two Saxon cavalry regiments went over to Blücher, and General Normann, when about to be charged at Taucha by the Prussian cavalry under Bülow, also deserted to him with two Würtemberg cavalry regiments, in order to avoid an unpleasant reminiscence of the treacherous ill-treatment of Lützow's corps. The whole of the Saxon infantry, commanded by Regnier, shortly afterward went, with thirty-eight guns, over to the Swedes, five hundred men and General Zeschau alone remaining true to Napoleon. The Saxons stationed themselves behind the lines of the allies, but their guns were instantly turned upon the enemy.[1]

In the evening of this terrible day, the French were driven back close upon the walls of Leipzig.[2] On the certainty of victory being announced by Schwarzenberg to the three monarchs, who had watched the progress of the battle, they knelt on the open field and returned thanks to God. Napoleon, before nightfall, gave orders for full retreat; but,

---

[1] Not so the Badeners and Hessians. The Baden corps was captured almost to a man; among others, Prince Emilius of Darmstadt. Baden had been governed, since the death of the popular grandduke, Charles Frederick, in 1811, by his grandson, Charles.—Franquemont, with the Würtemberg infantry, eight to nine thousand strong, acted independently of Normann's cavalry. But one thousand of their number remained after the battle of Leipzig, and, without going over to the allies, returned to Würtemberg. Normann was punished by his sovereign.

[2] The city was in a state of utter confusion. "The noise caused by the passage of the cavalry, carriages, etc., by the cries of the fugitives through the streets, exceeded that of the most terrific storm. The earth shook, the windows clattered with the thunder of artillery," etc.—*The Terrors of Leipzig, 1813.*

on the morning of the 19th, recommenced the battle and sacrificed some of his corps d'armee in order to save the remainder. He had, however, foolishly left but one bridge across the Elster open, and the retreat was consequently retarded. Leipzig was stormed by the Prussians, and, while the French rearguard was still battling on that side of the bridge, Napoleon fled, and had no sooner crossed the bridge than it was blown up with a tremendous explosion, owing to the inadvertence of a subaltern, who is said to have fired the train too hastily. The troops engaged on the opposite bank were irremediably lost. Prince Poniatowsky plunged on horseback into the Elster in order to swim across, but sank in the deep mud. The king of Saxony, who to the last had remained true to Napoleon, was among the prisoners. The loss during this battle, which raged for four days, and in which almost every nation in Europe stood opposed to each other, was immense on both sides. The total loss in dead was computed at eighty thousand. The French lost, moreover, three hundred guns and a multitude of prisoners; in the city of Leipzig alone twenty-three thousand sick, without reckoning the innumerable wounded. Numbers of these unfortunates lay bleeding and starving to death during the cold October nights on the field of battle, it being found impossible to erect a sufficient number of lazaretti for their accommodation. Napoleon made a hasty and disorderly retreat with the remainder of his troops, but was overtaken at Freiburg on the Unstrutt, where the bridge broke, and a repetition of the disastrous passage of the Beresina occurred. The fugitives collected into a dense mass, upon which the Prussian artillery played with murderous effect. The French lost forty of their guns. At Hanau, Wrede, Napoleon's former favorite, after taking Würzburg, watched the movements of his ancient patron, and, had he occupied the pass at Gelnhausen, might have annihilated him. Napoleon, however, furiously charged his flank, and, on the 20th of October, succeeded in forcing a passage and in sending seventy thousand men across the Rhine. Wrede was dangerously wounded.[1] On the 9th of November, the last French corps was defeated at Hochheim and driven back upon Mayence.

In the November of this ever memorable year, 1813, Germany, as far as the Rhine, was completely freed from the French.[2] Above a hundred thousand French troops, still shut up in the fortresses and cut off from all communication with France, gradually surrendered. In October, the allies took Bremen; in November, Stettin, Zamosk, Modlin, and those two important points, Dresden and Dantzig. In Dresden, Gouvion St. Cyr capitulated to Count Klenau, who granted him free egress on condition of the delivery of the whole of the army stores. St. Cyr, however, infringed the terms of capitulation by destroying several of the guns and sinking the gunpowder in the Elbe; consequently, on the non-recognition of the capitulation by the generalissimo, Schwarzenberg, he found himself without means of defence and was compelled to surrender at discretion with a garrison thirty-five thousand strong. Rapp, the Alsatian, commanded in Dantzig. This city had already fearfully suffered from the commercial interdiction, from the exactions and the scandalous license of its French protectors, whom the ravages of famine and pestilence finally compelled to yield.[3] Lubeck and Torgau fell in December; the typhus, which had never ceased to accompany the armies, raged there in the crowded hospitals, carrying off thousands, and greater numbers fell victims to this pestilential disease than to the war, not only among the troops, but in every part of the country through which they passed. Wittenberg, whose

---

[1] The king of Würtemberg, who had fifteen hundred men close at hand, did not send them to the aid of the Bavarians, nor did he go over to the allies until the 2d of November.

[2] In November, one hundred and forty thousand French prisoners and seven hundred and ninety-one guns were in the hands of the allies.

[3] Dantzig had formerly sixty thousand inhabitants, the population was now reduced to thirteen thousand. Numbers died of hunger, Rapp having merely stored the magazines for his troops. Fifteen thousand of the French garrison died, and yet fourteen generals, upward of a thousand officers, and about as many controllers belonging to the grand army, who had taken refuge in that city, were, on the capitulation of the fortress, made prisoners of war.

inhabitants had been shamefully abused by the French under Lapoype, Custrin, Glogau, Wesel, Erfurt, fell in the beginning of 1814; Magdeburg and Bremen, after the conclusion of the war.

The Rhenish confederation was dissolved, each of the princes securing his hereditary possessions by a timely secession. The kings of Westphalia and Saxony, Dalberg, grand-duke of Frankfort, and the princes of Isenburg and von der Leyen, who had too heavily sinned against Germany, were alone excluded from pardon. The king of Saxony was at first carried prisoner to Berlin, and afterward, under the protection of Austria, to Prague. Denmark also concluded peace at Kiel and ceded Norway to Sweden, upon which the Swedes, *quasi re bene gesta*, returned home.[1]

CCLXII. *Napoleon's Fall*

NAPOLEON was no sooner driven across the Rhine, than the defection of the whole of the Rhenish confederation, of Holland, Switzerland, and Italy ensued. The whole of the confederated German princes followed the example of Bavaria and united their troops with those of the allies. Jerome had fled; the kingdom of Westphalia had ceased to exist, and the exiled princes of Hesse, Brunswick, and Oldenburg returned to their respective territories. The Rhenish provinces were instantly occupied by Prussian troops and placed under the patriotic administration of Justus Gruner, who was joined by Görres of Coblentz, whose Rhenish Mercury so powerfully influenced public opinion that Napoleon termed him the fifth great European power.[2] The Dutch revolted and took the few French still remaining in the country prisoner. Hogendorp was placed at the head of a provis-

---

[1] The injustice thus favored by the first peace was loudly complained of.—*Manso*

[2] His principal thesis consisted of "We are not Prussians, Westphalians, Saxons, etc., but Germans."

ional government in the name of William of Orange.[1] The Prussians under Bulow entered the country and were received with great acclamation. The whole of the Dutch fortresses surrendered, the French garrisons flying panic-stricken.

The Swiss remained faithful to Napoleon until the arrival of Schwarzenberg with the allied army on their frontiers.[2] Napoleon would gladly have beheld the Swiss sacrifice themselves for him for the purpose of keeping the allies in check, but Reinhard of Zurich, who was at that time Landammann, prudently resolved not to persevere in the demand for neutrality, to lay aside every manifestation of opposition, and to permit, it being impossible to prevent, the entrance of the troops into the country, by which he, moreover, ingratiated himself with the allies. The majority of his countrymen thanked Heaven for their deliverance from French oppression, and if, in their ancient spirit of egotism, they neglected to aid the great popular movement throughout Germany, they, at all events, sympathized in the general hatred toward France.[3] The ancient aristocrats now naturally reappeared and attempted to re-establish the oligarchical governments of the foregoing century. A Count Senfft von Pilsach, a pretended Austrian envoy, who was speedily disavowed, assumed the authority at Berne with so much assurance as to succeed in deposing the existing government and reinstating the ancient oligarchy. In Zurich, the constitution was also revised and the citizens reassumed their authority over the peasantry. The whole of Switzerland was in a state of ferment. Ancient claims of the most varied

---

[1] This prince took the title not of stadtholder, but of king, to which he had no claim, but in which he was supported by England and Russia, who unwillingly beheld Prussia aggrandized by the possession of Holland.

[2] Even in the May of 1813, an ode given in No. 270 of the Allgemeine Zeitung, appeared in Switzerland, in which it was said, "The brave warriors of Switzerland hasten to reap fresh laurels. With their heroic blood have they dyed the distant shores of barbarous Haiti, the waters of the Ister and Tagus, etc. The deserts of Sarmatia have witnessed the martial glories of the Helvetic legion."

[3] Shortly before this, a report had been spread of the nomination of Marshal Berthier, prince of Neufchatel, as perpetual Landammann of Switzerland.—*Muralt's Reinhard.*

description were asserted. The people of the Grisons took up arms and invaded the Valtelline in order to retake their ancient possession. Pancratius, abbot of St. Gall, demanded the restoration of his princely abbey.—Italy, also, deserted Napoleon. Murat, king of Naples, in order not to lose his crown, joined the allies. Eugene Beauharnais, viceroy of Italy, alone remained true to his imperial stepfather and gallantly opposed the Austrians under Hiller, who, nevertheless, rapidly reduced the whole of Upper Italy to submission.

The allies, when on the point of entering the French territory, solemnly declared that their enmity was directed not against the French nation, but solely against Napoleon. By this generosity they hoped at once to prove the beneficence of their intentions to every nation of Europe and to prejudice the French, more particularly, against their tyrant; but that people, notwithstanding their immense misfortunes, still remained true to Napoleon nor hesitated to sacrifice themselves for the man who had raised them to the highest rank among the nations of the earth, and thousands flocked anew beneath the imperial eagle for the defence of their native soil.

The allies invaded France simultaneously on four sides, Bulow from Holland, Blucher, on New Year's eve, 1814, from Coblentz, and the main body of the allied army under Schwarzenberg, which was also accompanied by the allied sovereigns. A fourth army, consisting of English and Spaniards, had already crossed the Pyrenees and marched up the country. The great wars in Russia and Germany having compelled Napoleon to draw off a considerable number of his forces from Spain, Soult had been consequently unable to keep the field against Wellington, whose army had been gradually increased. King Joseph fled from Madrid. The French hazarded a last engagement at Vittoria, in June, 1813, but suffered a terrible defeat. One of the two Nassau regiments under Colonel Kruse and the Frankfort battalion deserted with their arms and baggage to the English. The other Nassau regiment and that of Baden were disarmed by the French and dragged in chains to France in reward for their long and severe service.[1] The Hanoverians in Wellington's army (the German Legion), particularly the corps of Victor von Alten (Charles's brother), brilliantly distinguished themselves at Vittoria and again at Bayonne, but were forgotten in the despatches, an omission that was loudly complained of by their general, Hinuber. Other divisions of Hanoverians, up to this period stationed in Sicily, had been sent to garrison Leghorn and Genoa.[2]—The crown prince of Sweden followed the Prussian northern army, but merely went as far as Liege, whence he turned back in order to devote his whole attention to the conquest of Norway.

In the midst of the contest a fresh congress was assembled at Chatillon, for the purpose of devising measures for the conclusion of the war without further bloodshed. The whole of ancient France was offered to Napoleon on condition of his restraining his ambition within her limits and of keeping peace, but he refused to cede a foot of land, and resolved to lose all or nothing. This congress was in so far disadvantageous on account of the rapid movements of the armies being checked by its fluctuating diplomacy. Schwarzenberg, for instance, pursued a system of procrastination, separated his corps d'armee at long intervals, advanced with extreme slowness, or remained entirely stationary. Napoleon took advantage of this dilatoriness on the part of his opponents to make an unexpected attack on Blucher's corps at Brienne on the 29th of January, in which Blucher narrowly escaped being made prisoner. The flames of the city, in which Napoleon had received his first military lessons, facilitated Blucher's retreat. Napoleon, however, neglecting to pursue him on the 30th of January, Blucher, reinforced by the crown prince of Wurtemberg and by Wrede, attacked him at La Rothière with such superior forces as to put him completely to the rout. The French left seventy-three guns sticking in the mud. Schwarzenberg, neverthe-

---

[1] Out of two thousand six hundred and fifty-four Badeners but five hundred and six returned from Spain.

[2] Beamisch, History of the Legion.

less, instead of pursuing the retreating enemy with the whole of his forces, again delayed his advance and divided the troops. Blucher, who had meanwhile rapidly pushed forward upon Paris, was again unexpectedly attacked by the main body of the French army, and the whole of his corps were, as they separately advanced, repulsed with considerable loss, the Russians under Olsufief at Champeaubert, those under Sacken at Montmirail, the Prussians under York at Château-Thierry, and, finally, Blucher himself at Beauxchamp, between the 10th and 14th of February. With characteristic rapidity, Napoleon instantly fell upon the scattered corps of the allied army and inflicted a severe punishment upon Schwarzenberg, for the folly of his system. He successively repulsed the Russians under Pahlen at Mormant, Wrede at Villeneuve le Comte, the crown prince of Wurtemberg, who offered the most obstinate resistance, at Montereau, on the 17th and 18th of February.[1] Augereau had meantime, with an army levied in the south of France, driven the Austrians, under Bubna, into Switzerland; and, although the decisive moment had arrived, and Schwarzenberg had simply to form a junction with Blucher in order to bring an overwhelming force against Napoleon, the allied sovereigns and Schwarzenberg resolved, in a council of war held at Troyes, upon a general retreat.

Blucher, upon this, magnanimously resolved to obviate at all hazards the disastrous consequences of the retreat of the allied army, and, in defiance of all commands, pushed forward alone.[2] This movement, far from being rash, was

---

[1] Several regiments sacrificed themselves in order to cover the retreat of the rest. Napoleon ordered a twelve-pounder to be loaded and twice directed the gun with his own hand upon the crown prince.—*Campaigns of the Würtembergers.*

[2] Blücher's conduct simply proceeded from his impatience to obtain by force of arms the most honorable terms of peace for Prussia, while the other allied powers, who were far more indulgently disposed toward France and who began to view the victories gained by Prussia with an apprehension which was further strengthened by the increasing popularity of that power throughout Germany, were more inclined to diplomatize than to fight. Blücher was well aware of these reasons for diplomacy and more than once cut the negotiations short with his sabre. A well-known diplomatist attempting on one occasion to prove to him that Napoleon must, even without the war being continued, "descend from

coolly calculated, Blucher being sufficiently reinforced on the Marne by Winzingerode and Bulow, by whose aid he, on the 9th March, defeated the emperor Napoleon at Laon. The victory was still undecided at fall of night. Napoleon allowed his troops to rest, but Blucher remained under arms and sent York to surprise him during the night. The French were completely dispersed and lost forty-six guns. Napoleon, after this miserable defeat, again tried his fortune against Schwarzenberg (who, put to shame by Blucher's brilliant success, had again halted), and, on the 20th of March, maintained his position at Arcis sur Aube, although the crown prince of Wurtemberg gallantly led his troops five times to the assault. Neither side was victorious.

Napoleon now resorted to a bold ruse de guerre. The peasantry, more particularly in Lorraine, exasperated by the devastation unavoidable during war time, and by the vengeance here and there taken by the foreign soldiery, had risen to the rear of the allied army. Unfortunately, no one had dreamed of treating the German Alsatians and Lothringians as brother Germans. They were treated as French. Long unaccustomed to invasion and to the calamities incidental to war, they made a spirited but ineffectual resistance to the rapine of the soldiery. Whole villages were burned down. The peasantry gathered into troops and massacred the foreign soldiery when not in sufficient numbers to keep them in check. Napoleon confidently expected that his diminished armies would be supported by a general rising en masse and that Augereau, who was at that time guarding Lyons,

---

his throne," a league having been formed within France herself for the restoration of the Bourbons—he answered him to his face, "The rascality of the French is no revenge for us. It is we who must pull him down—we. You will no doubt do wonders in your wisdom!—Patience! You will be led as usual by the nose, and will still go on fawning and diplomatizing until we have the nation again upon us, and the storm bursts over our heads." He went so far as to set the diplomatists actually at defiance. On being, to Napoleon's extreme delight, ordered to retreat, he treated the order with contempt and instantly advanced. —*Rauschnick's Life of Blücher*. "This second disjunction on Blücher's part," observes Clausewitz, the Prussian general, the best commentator on this war, "was of infinite consequence, for it checked and gave a fresh turn to the whole course of political affairs."

would form a junction with him; and, in this expectation, threw himself to the rear of the allied forces and took up a position at Troyes with a view of cutting them off, perhaps of surrounding them by means of the general rising, or, at all events, of drawing them back to the Rhine. But, on the self-same day, the 19th of March, Lyons had fallen and Augereau had retreated southward. The people did not rise en masse, and the allies took advantage of Napoleon's absence to form a grand junction, and, with flying banners, to march unopposed upon Paris, convinced that the possession of the capital of the French empire must inevitably bring the war to a favorable conclusion. In Paris, there were numerous individuals who already regarded Napoleon's fall as *un fait accompli*, and who, ambitious of influencing the future prospects of France, were ready to offer their services to the victors. Both parties speedily came to an understanding. The corps d'armee under Marshals Mortier and Marmont, which were encountered midway, were repulsed, and that under Generals Pacthod and Amey captured, together with seventy pieces of artillery, at La Fère Champenoise. On the 29th of March, the dark columns of the allied army defiled within sight of Paris. On the 30th, they met with a spirited resistance on the heights of Belleville and Montmartre; but the city, in order to escape bombardment, capitulated during the night, and, on the 31st, the allied sovereigns made a peaceful entry. The empress, accompanied by the king of Rome, by Joseph, ex-king of Spain, and by innumerable wagons, laden with the spoil of Europe, had already fled to the south of France.

Napoleon, completely deceived by Winzingerode and Tettenborn, who had remained behind with merely a weak rear guard, first learned the advance of the main body upon Paris when too late to overtake it. After almost annihilating his weak opponents at St. Dizier, he reached Fontainebleau, where he learned the capitulation of Paris, and, giving way to the whole fury of his Corsican temperament, offered to yield the city for two days to the license of his soldiery would they but follow him to the assault. But his own marshals, even his hero, Ney, deserted him, and, on the 10th of April, he was compelled to resign the imperial crown of France and to withdraw to the island of Elba on the coast of Italy, which was placed beneath his sovereignty and assigned to him as a residence. The kingdom of France was re-established on its former footing; and, on the 4th of May, Louis XVIII. entered Paris and mounted the throne of his ancestors.

Davoust was the last to offer resistance. The Russians under Bennigsen besieged him in Hamburg, and, on his final surrender, treated him with the greatest moderation.[1]

On the 30th of May, 1814, peace was concluded at Paris.[2] France was reduced to her limits as in 1792, and consequently retained the provinces of Alsace and Lorraine, of which she had, at an earlier period, deprived Germany. Not a farthing was paid by way of compensation for the ravages suffered by Germany, nay, the French prisoners of war were, on their release, maintained on their way home at the expense of the German population. None of the chefs-d'œuvres of which Europe had been plundered were restored, with the sole exception of the group of horses, taken by Napoleon from the Brandenburg gate at Berlin. The allied troops instantly evacuated the country. France was allowed to regulate her internal affairs without the interference of any of the foreign powers, while paragraphs concerning the internal economy of Germany were not only admitted into the treaty of Paris, and France was on that account not

---

[1] Görres said in the Rhenish Mercury, "It is easy to see how all are inclined to conceal beneath the wide mantle of love the horrors there perpetrated. The Germans have from time immemorial been subjected to this sort of treatment, because ever ready to forgive and forget the past." Davoust was arrested merely for form's sake and then honorably released. He was allowed to retain the booty he had seized. The citizens of Hamburg vainly implored the re-establishment of their bank.

[2] Blücher took no part in these affairs. "I have," said he to the diplomatists, "done my duty, now do yours! You will be responsible both to God and man should your work be done in vain and have to be done over again. I have nothing further to do with the business!"—Experience had, however, taught him not to expect much good from "quill-drivers."

only called upon to guarantee and to participate in the internal affairs of Germany, but also afterward sent to the great Congress of Vienna an ambassador destined to play an important part in the definitive settlement of the affairs of Europe, and, more particularly, of those of Germany.

The patriots, of whom the governments had made use both before and after the war, unable to comprehend that the result of such immense exertions and of such a complete triumph should be to bring greater profit and glory to France than to Germany, and that their patriotism was, on the conclusion of the war, to be renounced, were loud in their complaints.[1] But the revival of the German empire, with which the individual interests of so many princely houses were plainly incompatible, was far from entering into the plans of the allied powers. An attempt made by any one among the princes to place himself at the head of the whole of Germany would have been frustrated by the rest. The policy of the foreign allies was moreover antipathetic to such a scheme. England opposed and sought to hinder unity in Germany, not only for the sake of retaining possession of Hanover and of exercising an influence over the disunited German princes similar to that exercised by her over the princes of India, but more particularly for that of ruling the commerce of Germany. Russia reverted to her Erfurt policy. Her interests, like those of France, led her to promote disunion among the German powers, whose weakness, the result of want of combination, placed them at the mercy of France, and left Poland, Sweden, and the East open to the ambition of Russia. A close alliance was in consequence instantly formed between the emperor Alexander and Louis XVIII., the former negotiating, as the first condition of peace, the continuance of Lorraine and Alsace beneath the sovereignty of France.

Austria assented on condition of Italy being placed exclu-

---

[1] The Rhenish Mercury more than all. It was opposed by the Messenger of the Tyrol, which declared that the victory was gained, not by the "people," as they were termed, but by the princes and their armies.—*July, 1814.*

sively beneath her control. Austria united too many and too diverse nations beneath her sceptre to be able to pursue a policy pre-eminently German, and found it more convenient to round off her territories by the annexation of Upper Italy than by that of distant Lorraine, at all times a possession difficult to maintain. Prussia was too closely connected with Russia, and Hardenberg, unlike Blucher at the head of the Prussian army, was powerless at the head of Prussian diplomacy. The lesser states also exercised no influence upon Germany as a whole, and were merely intent upon preserving their individual integrity or upon gaining some petty advantage. The Germans, some few discontented patriots alone excepted, were more than ever devoted to their ancient princes, both to those who had retained their station and to those who returned to their respective territories on the fall of Napoleon; and the victorious soldiery, adorned with ribbons, medals, and orders (the Prussians, for instance, with the iron cross), evinced the same unreserved attachment to their prince and zeal for his individual interest. This complication of circumstances can alone explain the fact of Germany, although triumphant, having made greater concessions to France by the treaty of Paris than, when humbled, by that of Westphalia.

CCLXIII. *The Congress of Vienna—Napoleon's Return and End*

FROM Paris the sovereigns of Prussia[1] and Russia and the victorious field-marshals proceeded, in June, to London, where they, Blucher most particularly, were received with every demonstration of delight and respect by the English, their oldest and most faithful allies.[2] Toward autumn, a great European congress, to which the settlement of every point in dispute and the restoration of order throughout Eu-

---

[1] From London, Frederick William went to Switzerland and took possession of his ancient hereditary territory, Wälsch-Neuenburg or Neufchâtel, visited the beautiful Bernese Oberland, and then returned to Berlin, where, on the 7th of August, he passed in triumph through the Brandenburg gate, which was again adorned with the car of victory and the fine group of horses, and rode through the lime trees to an altar, around which the clergy belonging to every religious sect were assembled. Here public thanks were given and the whole of the citizens present fell upon their knees.—*Allgemeine Zeitung, 252.* On the 17th of September, the preparation of a new liturgy was announced in a ministerial proclamation, "by which the solemnity of the church service was to be increased, the present one being too little calculated to excite or strike the imagination."

[2] Oxford conferred a doctor's degree upon Blücher, who, upon receiving this strange honor, said, "Make Gneisenau apothecary, for he it was who prepared my pills." On his first reception at Carlton House, the populace pushed their way through the guards and doors as far as the apartments of the prince-regent, who, taking his gray-headed guest by the hand, presented him to them, and publicly hung his portrait set in brilliants around his neck. On his passing through the streets, the horses were taken from his carriage, and he was drawn in triumph by the shouting crowd. One fête succeeded another. During the great races at Ascot, the crowd breaking through the barriers and insisting upon Blücher's showing himself, the prince-regent came forward, and, politely telling them that he had not yet arrived, led forward the emperor Alexander, who was loudly cheered, but Blücher's arrival was greeted with thunders of applause far surpassing those bestowed upon the sovereigns, a circumstance that was afterward blamed by the English papers. In the Freemasons' Lodge, Blücher was received by numbers of ladies, on each of whom he bestowed a salute. At Portsmouth, he drank to the health of the English in the presence of an immense concourse of people assembled beneath his windows.—The general rejoicing was solely clouded by the domestic circumstances of the royal family, by the insanity of the aged and blind king and by the disunion reigning between the prince regent and his thoughtless consort, Caroline of Brunswick.—Although the whole of the allied sovereigns, some of whom were unable to speak English, understood German, French was adopted as the medium of conversation.—*Allgemeine Zeitung, 174.*

rope were to be committed, was convoked at Vienna. At this congress, which, in the November of 1814, was opened at Vienna, the emperors of Austria and Russia, the kings of Prussia, Denmark, Bavaria, Wurtemberg, and the greater part of the petty princes of Germany, were present in person; the other powers were represented by ambassadors extraordinary. The greatest statesmen of that period were here assembled; among others, Metternich, the Austrian minister, Hardenberg and Humboldt, the Prussian ministers, Castlereagh, the English plenipotentiary, Nesselrode, the Russian envoy, Talleyrand and Dalberg, Gagern, Bernstorff, and Wrede, the ambassadors of France, Holland, Denmark, and Bavaria, etc. The negotiations were of the utmost importance, for, although one of the most difficult points, the new regulation of affairs in France, was already settled, many extremely difficult questions still remained to be solved. Talleyrand, who had served under every government, under the republic, under the usurper, Napoleon; who had retaken office under the Bourbons and the Jesuits who had returned in their train, and who, on this occasion, was the representative of the criminal and humbled French nation, ventured, nevertheless, to offer his perfidious advice to the victors, and, with diabolical art, to sow the seed of discord among them. This conduct was the more striking on account of its glaring incongruity with the proclamation of Calisch, which expressly declared that the internal affairs of Germany were wholly and solely to be arranged by the princes and nations of Germany, without foreign, and naturally, least of all, without French interference.[1] Talleyrand's first object was to suppress the popular spirit of liberty

---

[1] "There are moments in the life of nations on which the whole of their future destiny depends. The children are destined to expiate their fathers' errors with their blood. Germany has everything to fear from the foreigner, and yet she cannot arrange her own affairs without calling the foreigner to her aid.—Who, in the congress, chiefly oppose every well-laid plan? Who, with the dagger's point pick out and reopen all our wounds, and rub them with salt and poison? Who promote confusion, provoke, insinuate, and attempt to creep into every committee, to interfere in every discussion? who but those sent thither by France?"—*The Rhenish Mercury*.

throughout Germany, and to rouse against it the jealous apprehensions of the princes. He therefore said, "You wish for constitutions; guard against them. In France, desire for a constitution produced a revolution, and the same will happen to you." He it was who gave to the congress that catchword, legitimacy. The object of the past struggle was not the restoration of the liberties of the people but that of the ancient legitimate dynasties and their absolute sovereignty. The war had been directed, not against Napoleon, but against the Revolution, against the usurpation of the people. By means of this legitimacy the king of Saxony was to be re-established on his throne, and Prussia was on no account to be permitted to incorporate Saxony with her dominions. Prussia appealed to her services toward Germany, to her enormous sacrifices, to the support given to her by public opinion; but the power of public opinion was itself questioned. The seeds of discord quickly sprang up, and, on the 3d of January, 1815, a secret league against Prussia was already formed for the purpose of again humbling the state that had sacrificed all for the honor Germany, of frustrating her schemes of aggrandizement, and of quenching the patriotic spirit of German idealists and enthusiasts.[1]

The want of unanimity amid the members of the congress had at the same time a bad effect upon the ancient Rhenish confederated states. In Nassau, the Landwehr was, on its return home after the campaign, received with marks of dissatisfaction. In Baden and Hesse, many of the officers belonging to the army openly espoused Napoleon's cause. In Baden, the volunteer corps was deprived of its horses and sent home on foot.[2] In Wurtemberg, King Fred-

---

[1] Fate willed that Stein should not be called upon to act with firmness, but Hardenberg to make concessions. Stein disappeared from the theatre of events and was degraded to a lower sphere. Hardenburg was created prince.

[2] Napoleon had such good friends among the Rhenish confederated princes that Augustus, duke of Gotha, for instance, even after the second occupation of Paris, on the return of his troops in the November of 1815, prohibited any demonstrations of triumph and even deprived the Landwehr of their uniforms, so that the poor fellows had to return in their shirt-sleeves to their native villages during the hard winter.—*Jacob's Campaigns.*

erick refused to allow the foreign troops and convoys a passage along the highroad through Cannstadt and Ludwigsburg, and forbade the attendance of civil surgeons upon the wounded belonging to the allied army. In Wurtemberg and Bavaria, the Rhenish Mercury was suppressed on account of its patriotic and German tendency. At Stuttgard, the festival in commemoration of the battle of Leipzig was disallowed; and in Frankfort on the Maine, the editor of a French journal ventured, unreprimanded, to turn this festival into ridicule.

Switzerland was in a high state of ferment. The people of the Grisons, who had taken possession of the Valtelline, and the people of Uri, who had seized the Livinenthal, had been respectively driven out of those territories by the Austrians. The Valais, Geneva, Neufchatel, and Pruntrut were, on the other hand, desirous of joining the confederation. The democratic peasantry were almost everywhere at war with the aristocratic burghers. Berne revived her claim upon Vaud and Aargau, which armed in self-defence.[1] Reinhard of Zurich, the Swiss Landammann, went, meanwhile, at the head of an embassy to Vienna, for the purpose of settling in the congress the future destinies of Switzerland by means of the intervention of the great powers. Talleyrand, with unparalleled impudence, also interfered in this affair, threatened to refuse his recognition to every measure passed without his concurrence, and compelled the Swiss to entreat him to honor the deliberations with his presence. On Austria's demanding a right of conscription in the Grisons alone, France having enjoyed that right throughout the whole of Switzerland at an earlier period, Talleyrand advised the Swiss to make a most violent opposition against an at-

---

[1] An attack upon Berne had already been concerted. Colonel Bär marched with the people of Aargau in the night time upon Aarburg, but his confederates failing to make their appearance, he caused the nearest Bernese governor to be alarmed and hastily retraced his steps. The Bernese instantly sent an armed force to the frontier, where, finding all tranquil, the charge of aggression was thrown upon their shoulders.

tempt that placed their independence at stake. "Cry out," he exclaimed, "cry out, as loud as you can!"[1]

The disputes in the congress raised Napoleon's hopes. In France, his party was still powerful, almost the whole of the population being blindly devoted to him, and an extensive conspiracy for his restoration to the imperial throne was secretly set on foot. Several thousands of his veteran soldiery had been released from foreign durance; the whole of the military stores, the spoil of Europe, still remained in the possession of France; the fortresses were solely garrisoned with French troops; Elba was close at hand, and the emperor was guarded with criminal negligence. Heavy, indeed, is the responsibility of those who, by thus neglecting their charge, once more let loose this scourge upon the earth![2] Napoleon quitted his island, and, on the 1st of March, 1815, again set foot on the coast of France. He was merely accompanied by one thousand five hundred men, but the whole of the troops sent against him by Louis XVIII. ranged themselves beneath his eagle. He passed, as if in triumph, through his former empire. The whole nation received him with acclamations of delight. Not a single Frenchman shed a drop of blood for the Bourbon, who fled hastily to Ghent; and, on the 20th of March, Napoleon entered Paris unopposed. His brother-in-law, Murat, at the same time revolted at Naples and advanced into Upper Italy against the Austrians. But all the rest of Napoleon's ancient allies, persuaded that he must again fall, either remained tranquil or formed a close alliance with the combined powers. The Swiss, in particular, showed excessive zeal on this occasion, and took up arms against France, in the hope of rendering the allied sovereigns favorable to their new constitution. The Swiss regiments, which had passed from Napoleon's service to that of Louis XVIII., also remained unmoved by

---

[1] Vide Muralt's Life of Reinhard.

[2] Blücher was at Berlin at the moment when the news of Napoleon's escape arrived. He instantly roused the English ambassador from his sleep by shouting in his ear, "Have the English a fleet in the Mediterranean?"

Napoleon's blandishments, were deprived of their arms and returned separately to Switzerland.

The allied sovereigns were still assembled at Vienna, and at once allowed every dispute to drop in order to form a fresh and closer coalition. They declared Napoleon an outlaw, a robber, proscribed by all Europe, and bound themselves to bring a force more than a million strong into the field against him. All Napoleon's cunning attempts to bribe and set them at variance were treated with scorn, and the combined powers speedily came to an understanding on the points hitherto so strongly contested. Saxony was partitioned between her ancient sovereign and Prussia, and a revolt that broke out in Liege among the Saxon troops, who were by command of Prussia to be divided before they had been released from their oath of allegiance to their king, is easily explained by the hurry and pressure of the times, which caused all minor considerations to be forgotten.[1] Napoleon exclusively occupied the mind of every diplomatist, and all agreed in the necessity, at all hazards, of his utter annihilation. The lion, thus driven at bay, turned upon his pursuers for a last and desperate struggle. The French were still faithful to Napoleon, who, with a view of reinspiring them with the enthusiastic spirit that had rendered them invincible in the first days of the republic, again called forth the old republicans, nominated them to the highest appointments, re-established several republican institutions, and, on the 1st of June, pre-

---

[1] The blame was entirely upon the Prussian side. The Saxons, as good soldiers, naturally revolted at the idea that they would at once be faithless to their oath and mutinied. General Müffling was insulted for having spoken of "Saxon hounds." Blücher even was compelled secretly to take his departure. The Saxon troops were, however, reduced to obedience by superior numbers of Prussians, and their colors were burned. The whole corps was about to be decimated, when Colonel Römer came forward and demanded that the sentence of death should be first executed on him. Milder measures were in consequence reverted to, and a few of the men were condemned to death by drawing lots. Kanitz, the drummer, a youth of sixteen, however, threw away the dice, exclaiming, "It is I who beat the summons for revolt, and I will be the first to die." He and six others were shot. Borstel, the Prussian general, the hero of Dennewitz, who had steadily refused to burn the Saxon colors, was compelled to quit the service.

sented to his dazzled subjects the magnificent spectacle of a field of May, as in the times of Charlemagne and in the commencement of the Revolution, and then led a numerous and spirited army to the Dutch frontiers against the enemy.

Here stood a Prussian army under Blucher, and an Anglo-German one under Wellington, comprehending the Dutch under the Prince of Orange, the Brunswickers under their duke, the recruited Hanoverian Legion under Wallmoden. These corps d'armée most imminently threatened Paris. The main body of the allied army, under Schwarzenberg, then advancing from the south, was still distant. Napoleon consequently directed his first attack against the two former. His army had gained immensely in strength and spirit by the return of his veteran troops from foreign imprisonment. Wellington, ignorant at what point Napoleon might cross the frontier, had followed the old and ill-judged plan of dividing his forces; an incredible error, the allies having simply to unite their forces and to take up a firm position in order to draw Napoleon to any given spot. Wellington, moreover, never imagined that Napoleon was so near at hand, and was amusing himself at a ball at Brussels, when Blucher, who was stationed in and around Namur, was attacked on the 14th of June, 1815.[1] Napoleon afterward observed in his memoirs that he had attacked Blucher first because he well knew that Blucher would not be supported by the over-prudent and egotistical English commander, but that Wellington, had he been first attacked, would have received every aid from his high-spirited and faithful ally. Wellington, after being repeatedly urged by Blucher, collected his scattered corps, but neither completely nor with sufficient rapidity; and on Blucher's announcement

[1] For a refutation of Menzel's absurdly perverted relation of these great events the reader is referred not only to the Duke of Wellington's despatches and to Colonel Siborne's well-established account of the battles of Ligny, Wavre, Quatre Bras, and Waterloo, but also to those of his countrymen, Müffling, the Prussian general, and Wagner.—*Trans.*

of Napoleon's arrival, exerted himself on the following morning so far as to make a reconnoissance. The duke of Brunswick, with impatience equalling that of Blucher, was the only one who had quitted the ball during the night and had hurried forward against the enemy. Napoleon, owing to Wellington's negligence, gained time to throw himself between him and Blucher and to prevent their junction; for he knew the spirit of his opponents. He consequently opposed merely a small division of his army under Ney to the English and turned with the whole of his main body against the Prussians. The veteran Blucher perceived his intentions[1] and in consequence urgently demanded aid from the Duke of Wellington, who promised to send him a reinforcement of twenty thousand men by four o'clock on the 16th. But this aid never arrived, Wellington, although Ney was too weak to obstruct the movement, making no attempt to perform his promise. Wellington retired with superior forces before Ney at Quatre Bras, and allowed the gallant and unfortunate Duke William of Brunswick to fall a futile sacrifice. Blucher meanwhile yielded to the overwhelming force brought against him by Napoleon at Ligny, also on the 16th of June. Vainly did the Prussians rush to the attack beneath the murderous fire of the French, vainly did Blucher in person head the assault and for five hours continue the combat hand to hand in the village of Ligny. Numbers prevailed, and Wellington sent no relief. The infantry being at length driven back, Blucher led the cavalry once more to the charge, but was repulsed and fell senseless beneath his horse, which was shot dead. His adjutant, Count Nostitz, alone remained at his side. The French cavalry passed close by without perceiving them, twilight and a misty rain having begun to fall. The Prussians fortunately missed their leader, repulsed the French cavalry, which again galloped past him as he lay on the ground, and he was at length drawn from beneath his

---

[1] Shortly before the battle, Bourmont, the French general, set up the white cockade (the symbol of Bourbon) and deserted to Blücher, who merely said, "It is all one what symbol the fellows set up, rascals are ever rascals!"

horse. He still lived, but only to behold the complete defeat of his army.

Blucher, although a veteran of seventy-three, and wounded and shattered by his fall, was not for a moment discouraged.[1] Ever vigilant, he assembled his scattered troops with wonderful rapidity, inspirited them by his cheerful words, and had the generosity to promise aid, by the afternoon of the 18th of June, to Wellington, who was now in his turn attacked by the main body of the French under Napoleon. What Wellington on the 16th, with a fresh army, could not perform, Blucher now effected with troops dejected by defeat, and put the English leader to the deepest shame by—keeping his word.[2] He consequently fell back upon Wavre in order to remain as close as possible in Wellington's vicinity, and also sent orders to Bulow's corps, that was then on the advance, to join the English army, while Napoleon, in the idea that Blucher was falling back upon the Meuse, sent Grouchy in pursuit with a body of thirty-five thousand men.[3]

Napoleon, far from imagining that the Prussians, after having been, as he supposed, completely annihilated or panic-stricken by Grouchy, could aid the British, wasted the precious moments, and, instead of hastily attacking Wellington, spent the whole of the morning of the 18th in uselessly parading his troops, possibly with a view of intimidating his opponents and of inducing them to retreat without hazarding an engagement. His well-dressed lines glittered in the sunbeams; the infantry raised their tschakos on their bayonet points, the cavalry their helmets on their

---

[1] The surgeon, when about to rub him with some liquid, was asked by him what it was, and being told that it was spirits, "Ah," said he, "the thing is of no use externally!" and snatching the glass from the hand of his attendant, he drank it off.

[2] Against all expectation to aid an ally who on the previous day had against all expectation been unable to give him aid, evinced at once magnanimity, sense, and good feeling.—*Clausewitz.*

[3] A Prussian battery, that on its way from Namur turned back on receiving news of this disaster and was taken by the French, is said to have chiefly led to the commission of this immense blunder by Napoleon.

sabres, and gave a general cheer for their emperor. The English, however, preserved an undaunted aspect. At length, about midday, Napoleon gave orders for the attack, and, furiously charging the British left wing, drove it from the village of Hougumont. He then sent orders to Ney to charge the British centre. At that moment a dark spot was seen in the direction of St. Lambert. Was it Grouchy? A reconnoitring party was despatched and returned with the news of its being the Prussians under Bulow. The attack upon the British centre was consequently remanded, and Ney was despatched with a considerable portion of his troops against Bulow. Wellington now ventured to charge the enemy with his right wing, but was repulsed and lost the farm of La Haye Sainte, which commanded his position on this side as Hougumont did on his right. His centre, however, remained unattacked, the French exerting their utmost strength to keep Bulow's gallant troops back at the village of Planchenoit, where the battle raged with the greatest fury, and a dreadful conflict of some hours' duration ensued hand to hand. But about five o'clock, the left wing of the British being completely thrown into confusion by a fresh attack on the enemy's side, the whole of the French cavalry, twelve thousand strong, made a furious charge upon the British centre, bore down all before them, and took a great number of guns. The Prince of Orange was wounded. The road to Brussels was already thronged with the fugitive English troops, and Wellington, scarcely able to keep his weakened lines together,[1] was apparently on the brink of destruction, when the thunder of artillery was suddenly heard in the direction of Wavre. "It is Grouchy!" joyfully exclaimed Napoleon, who had repeatedly sent orders

---

[1] The Hanoverian legion again covered itself with glory by the steadiness with which it opposed the enemy. It lost three thousand five hundred men, the Dutch eight thousand; the German troops consequently lost collectively as many as the English, whose loss was computed at eleven or twelve thousand men. The Prussians, whose loss at Ligny and Waterloo exceeded that of their allies, behaved with even greater gallantry.

to that general to push forward with all possible speed. But it was not Grouchy, it was Blucher.

The faithful troops of the veteran marshal (the old Silesian army) were completely worn out by the battle, by their retreat in the heavy rain over deep roads, and by the want of food. The distance from Wavre, whence they had been driven, to Waterloo, where Wellington was then in action, was not great, but was rendered arduous owing to these circumstances. The men sometimes fell down from extreme weariness, and the guns stuck fast in the deep mud. But Blucher was everywhere present, and notwithstanding his bodily pain ever cheered his men forward, with "indescribable pathos," saying to his disheartened soldiers, "My children, we must advance; I have promised it, do not cause me to break my word!" While still distant from the scene of action, he ordered the guns to be fired in order to keep up the courage of the English, and at length, between six and seven in the evening, the first Prussian corps in advance, that of Ziethen, fell furiously upon the enemy: "Bravo!" cried Blucher, "I know you, my Silesians; to-day we shall see the backs of these French rascals!" Ziethen filled up the space still intervening between Wellington and Bulow. Exactly at that moment, Napoleon had sent his old guard forward in four massive squares in order to make a last attempt to break the British lines, when Ziethen fell upon their flank and dealt fearful havoc among their close masses with his artillery. Bulow's troops, inspirited by this success, now pressed gallantly forward and finally regained the long-contested village of Planchenoit from the enemy. The whole of the Prussian army, advancing at the double and with drums beating, had already driven back the right wing of the French, when the English, regaining courage, advanced, Napoleon was surrounded on two sides, and the whole of his troops, the old guard under General Cambronno alone excepted, were totally dispersed and fled in complete disorder. The old guard, surrounded by Bulow's cavalry, nobly replied, when challenged to surrender, "La garde ne se rend pas"; and in a few minutes the veteran conquerors of Europe fell beneath the righteous and avenging blows of their antagonists. At the farm of La Belle Alliance, Blucher offered his hand to Wellington. "I will sleep to-night in Bonaparte's last night's quarters," said Wellington. "And I will drive him out of his present ones!" replied Blucher. The Prussians, fired by enthusiasm, forgot the fatigues they had for four days endured, and, favored by a moonlight night, so zealously pursued the French that an immense number of prisoners and a vast amount of booty fell into their hands and Napoleon narrowly escaped being taken prisoner. At Genappe, where the bridge was blocked by fugitives, the pursuit was so close that he was compelled to abandon his carriage leaving his sword and hat behind him. Blucher, who reached the spot a moment afterward, took possession of the booty, sent Napoleon's hat, sword, and star to the king of Prussia, retained his cloak, telescope and carriage for his own use, and gave up everything else, including a quantity of the most valuable jewelry, gold, and money, to his brave soldiery. The whole of the army stores, two hundred and forty guns, and an innumerable quantity of arms thrown away by the fugitives, fell into his hands.

The Prussian general, Thielemann, who, with a few troops, had remained behind at Wavre in order, at great hazard, to deceive Grouchy into the belief that he was still opposed by Blucher's entire force, acted a lesser, but equally honorable part on this great day. He fulfilled his commission with great skill, and so completely deceived Grouchy as to hinder his making a single attempt to throw himself in the way of the Prussians on the Paris road.

Blucher pushed forward without a moment's delay, and, on the 29th of June, stood before Paris. Napoleon had, meanwhile, a second time abdicated, and had fled from Paris in the hope of escaping across the seas. Davoust, the ancient instrument of his tyranny, who commanded in Paris, attempting to make terms of capitulation with Blucher, was sharply answered, "You want to make a defence?

Take care what you do. You well know what license the irritated soldiery will take if your city must be taken by storm. Do you wish to add the sack of Paris to that of Hamburg, already loading your conscience?"[1] Paris surrendered after a severe engagement at Issy, and Muffling, the Prussian general, was placed in command of the city, July the 7th, 1815. It was on the occasion of a grand banquet given by Wellington shortly after the occupation of Paris by the allied troops that Blucher gave the celebrated toast, "May the pens of diplomatists not again spoil all that the swords of our gallant armies have so nobly won!"

Schwarzenberg had in the interim also penetrated into France, and the crown prince of Wurtemberg had defeated General Rapp at Strasburg and had surrounded that fortress. The Swiss, under General Bachmann, who had, although fully equipped for the field, hitherto prudently watched the turn of events, invaded France immediately after the battle of Waterloo, pillaged Burgundy, besieged and took the fortress of Huningen, which, with the permission of the allies, they justly razed to the ground, the insolent French having thence fired upon the bridges of Basel which lay close in its vicinity. A fresh Austrian army under Frimont advanced from Italy as far as Lyons. On the 17th of July, Napoleon surrendered himself in the bay of Rochefort to the English, whose ships prevented his escape; he moreover preferred falling into their hands than into those of the Prussians. The whole of France submitted to the triumphant allies, and Louis XVIII. was reinstated on his throne. Murat had also been simultaneously defeated at Tolentino in Italy by the Austrians under Bianchi, and Ferdinand IV. had been restored to the throne of Naples. Murat fled to Corsica, but his retreat to France was prevented by the success of the allies, and in his despair he,

---

[1] The French were extremely affronted on account of this communication being made in German instead of French, and even at the present day German historians are generally struck with deeper astonishment at this sample of Blücher's bold spirit than at any other.

with native rashness, yielded to the advice of secret intriguants and returned to Italy with a design of raising a popular insurrection, but was seized on landing and shot on the 13th of October.[1]

Blucher was greatly inclined to give full vent to his justly roused rage against Paris. The bridge of Jena, one of the numerous bridges across the Seine, the principal object of his displeasure, was, curiously enough, saved from destruction (he had already attempted to blow it up) by the arrival of the king of Prussia.[2] His proposal to punish France by partitioning the country and thus placing it on a par with Germany, was far more practical in its tendency.

This honest veteran had in fact a deeper insight into affairs than the most wary diplomatists.[3] In 1815, the same persons, as in 1814, met in Paris, and similar interests were

---

[1] Ney, "the bravest of the brave," who dishonored his bravery by the basest treachery, met with an equally melancholy fate. Immediately after having, for instance, kissed the gouty fingers of Louis XVIII. and boasting that he would imprison Napoleon within an iron cage, he went over to the latter. He was sentenced to death and shot, after vainly imploring the allied monarchs and personally petitioning Wellington for mercy.—Alexander Berthier, prince of Neufchatel, Napoleon's chief confidant, had, even before the outbreak of war, thrown himself out of a window in a fit of hypochondriasis and been killed.

[2] Talleyrand begged Count von der Goltz to use his influence for its preservation with Blücher, who replied to his entreaties, "I will blow up the bridge, and should very much like to have Talleyrand sitting upon it at the time!" An attempt to blow it up was actually made, but failed.

[3] Many of whom were in fact wilfully blind. Hardenberg, by whom the noble-spirited Stein was so ill replaced, and who, with all possible decency, ever succeeded in losing in the cabinet the advantages gained by Blücher in the field, the diplomatic bird of ill omen by whom the peace of Basel had formerly been concluded, was thus addressed by Blücher: "I should like you gentlemen of the quill to be for once in a way exposed to a smart platoon fire, just to teach you what perils we soldiers have to run in order to repair the blunders you so thoughtlessly commit." An instructive commentary upon these events is to be met with in Stein's letters to Gagern. The light in which Stein viewed the Saxons may be gathered from the following passages in his letters: "My desire for the aggrandizement of Prussia proceeded not from a blind partiality to that state, but from the conviction that Germany is weakened by a system of partition ruinous alike to her national learning and national feelings."—"It is not for Prussia but for Germany that I desire a closer, a firmer internal combination, a wish that will accompany me to the grave: the division of our national strength may be gratifying to others, it never can be so to me." This truly German policy mainly distinguished Stein from Hardenberg, who, thoroughly Prussian in his ideas, was incapable of perceiving that Prussia's best-understood policy ever will be to identify herself with Germany.

agitated. Foreign jealousy again effected the conclusion of this peace at the expense of Germany and in favor of France. Blucher's influence at first reigned supreme. The king of Prussia, who, together with the emperors of Russia and Austria, revisited Paris, took Stein and Gruner into his council. The crown prince of Wurtemberg also zealously exerted himself in favor of the reunion of Lorraine and Alsace with Germany.[1] But Russia and England beholding the reintegration of Germany with displeasure, Austria,[2] and finally Prussia, against whose patriots all were in league, yielded.[3] The future destinies of Europe were settled on the side of England by Wellington and Castlereagh; on that of Russia by Prince John Razumowsky, Nesselrode, and Capo d'Istria; on that of Austria by Metternich and Wessenberg; on that of Prussia by Hardenberg and William von Humboldt. The German patriots were excluded from the discussion,[4] and a result extremely unfavorable to Germany naturally followed:[5] Alsace and Lorraine remained annexed to

---

[1] Allgemeine Zeitung, No. 285.

[2] It was proposed that Lorraine and Alsace should be bestowed upon the Archduke Charles, who at that period wedded the Princess Henrietta of Nassau. The proposition, however, quickly fell to the ground.

[3] Even in July, their organ, Görres' Rhenish Mercury, was placed beneath the censor. In August, it was said that the men, desirous of giving a constitution to Prussia, had fallen into disgrace.—*Allgemeine Zeitung, No. 249.* In September, Schmalz, in Berlin, unveiled the presumed revolutionary intrigues of the Tugendbund and declared "the unity of Germany is something to which the spirit of every nation in Germany has ever been antipathetic." He received a Prussian and a Würtemberg order, besides an extremely gracious autograph letter from the king of Prussia, although his base calumnies against the friends of his country were thrown back upon him by the historians Niebuhr and Rühs, who were then in a high position, by Schleiermacher, the theologian, and by others. The nobility also began to stir, attempted to regain their ancient privileges in Prussia, and intrigued against the men who, during the time of need, had made concessions to the citizens.—*Allgemeine Zeitung, No. 276.*

[4] The Allgemeine Zeitung, No. 349, laughs at the report of their having withdrawn from the discussion, and says that they were no longer invited to take part in it.

[5] On the loud complaints of the Rhenish Mercury, of the gazettes of Bremen and Hanau, and even of the Allgemeine Zeitung, the Austrian Observer, edited by Gentz, declared that "to demand a better peace would be to demand the ruin of France."—*Allgemeine Zeitung, Nos. 345, 365.* On Görres' repeated demand for the reannexation of Alsace and Lorraine, of which Germany had been so unwarrantably deprived, the Austrian Observer declared in the beginning of 1816, "who would believe that Görres would lend his pen to such miserable argu-

France. By the second treaty of Paris, which was definitively concluded on the 20th of November, 1815, France was merely compelled to give up the fortresses of Philippeville, Marienburg, Sarlouis, and Landau, to demolish Huningen, and to allow eighteen other fortresses on the German frontier to be occupied by the allies until the new government had taken firm footing in France. Until then, one hundred and fifty thousand of the allied troops were also to remain within the French territory and to be maintained at the expense of the people. France was, moreover, condemned to pay seven hundred millions of francs toward the expenses of the war and to restore the chefs-d'œuvre of which she had deprived every capital in Europe. The sword of Frederick the Great was not refound: Marshal Serrurier declared that he had burned it.[1] On the other hand, however, almost all the famous old German manuscripts, which had formerly been carried from Heidelberg to Rome, and thence by Napoleon to Paris, were sent back to Heidelberg. One of the most valuable, the Manessian Code of the Swabian Minnesingers, was left in Paris, where it had been concealed. Blucher expired, in 1819, on his estate in Silesia.[2]

The French were now sufficiently humbled to remain in tranquillity, and designedly displayed such submission that

---

ments. Alsace and Lorraine are guaranteed to France. To demand their restoration would be contrary to every notion of honor and justice." In this manner was Germany a second time robbed of these provinces. Washington Paine denominated Strasburg, "a melancholy sentry, of which unwary Germany has allowed herself to be deprived, and which now, accoutred in an incongruous uniform, does duty against his own country."

[1] The Invalids had in the same spirit cast the triumphal monument of the field of Rossbach into the Seine, in order to prevent its restoration. The alarum formerly belonging to Frederick the Great was also missing. Napoleon had it on his person during his flight and made use of it at St. Helena, where it struck his death-hour.

[2] He was descended from a noble race, which at a very early period enjoyed high repute in Mecklenburg and Pomerania. In 1271, an Ulric von Blücher was bishop of Ratzeburg. A legend relates that, during a time of dearth, an empty barn was, on his petitioning Heaven, instantly filled with corn. In 1356, Wipertus von Blücher also became bishop of Ratzeburg, and, on the pope's refusal to confirm him in his diocese on account of his youth, his hair turned gray in one night. Vide Klüwer's Description of Mecklenburg, 1728.

the allied sovereigns resolved, at a congress held at Aix-la-Chapelle, in the autumn of 1818, to withdraw their troops. Napoleon was, with the concurrence of the assembled powers, taken to the island of St. Helena, where, surrounded by the dreary ocean, several hundred miles from any inhabited spot, and guarded with petty severity by the English, he was at length deprived of every means of disturbing the peace of Europe. Inactivity and the unhealthiness of the climate speedily dissolved the earthly abode of this giant spirit. He expired on the 5th of May, 1821. His consort, Maria Louisa, was created Duchess of Parma; and his son lived, under the title of Duke of Reichstadt, with his imperial grandfather at Vienna, until his death in 1832. Napoleon's stepson, Eugene Beauharnais, the former viceroy of Italy, the son-in-law to the king of Bavaria, received the newly-created mediatized principality of Eichstadt, which was dependent upon Bavaria, and the title of Duke of Leuchtenberg. Jerome, the former king of Westphalia, became Count de Montfort;[1] Louis, ex-king of Holland, Count de St. Leu.

---

[1] His wife, Catherine of Würtemberg, was, in 1814, attacked during her flight, on her way through France, and robbed of her jewels.—*Allgemeine Zeitung, No. 130.*

PART XXIII

THE LATEST TIMES

CCLXIV. *The German Confederation*

THUS terminated the terrible storms that, not without benefit, had convulsed Europe. Every description of political crime had been fearfully avenged and presumption had been chastised by the unerring hand of Providence. At that solemn period, the sovereigns of Russia, Austria, and Prussia concluded a treaty by which they bound themselves to follow, not the ruinous policy they had hitherto pursued, but the undoubted will of the King of kings, and, as the viceroys of God upon the earth, to maintain peace, to uphold virtue and justice. This Holy Alliance was concluded on the 26th of September, 1815. All the European powers took part in it; England, who excused herself, the pope, and the sultan, whose accession was not demanded, alone excepted.

The new partition of Europe, nevertheless, retained almost all the unnatural conditions introduced by the more ancient and godless policy of Louis XIV. and of Catherine II. Germany, Poland, and Italy remained partitioned among rulers partly foreign. Everywhere were countries exchanged or freshly partitioned and rendered subject to foreign rule. England retained possession of Hanover, which was elevated into a German kingdom, of the Ionian islands, and of Malta in the Mediterranean. Russia received the grand-duchy of Warsaw, which was raised to a kingdom of Poland, but was not united with Lithuania, Volhynia, Podolia, and the Ulraine, the ancient provinces of Poland standing beneath the sovereignty of Russia, and Finland, for which Sweden received in exchange Norway, of which Denmark was forcibly dispossessed. Holland was annexed to the old Austrian Netherlands and elevated to a kingdom under William of Orange.[1] Switzerland remained a confederation of twenty-two cantons,[2] externally independent and neutral, internally somewhat aristocratic in tendency, the ancient oligarchy everywhere regaining their power. The Jesuits were reinstated by the pope. In Spain, Portugal, and Naples, the form of government prior to the Revolution was re-established by the ancient sovereigns on their restoration to their thrones.

Alsace and Lorraine, Switzerland and the new kingdom of the Netherlands, the provinces of Luxemburg excepted, were no longer regarded as forming part of Germany. Austria received Milan and Venice under the title of a Lombardo-Venetian kingdom, the Illyrian provinces also as a kingdom, Venetian Dalmatia, the Tyrol,[3] Vorarlberg, Salzburg, the Inn, and Hausruckviertel, and the part of Galicia ceded by her at an earlier period. The grandduchy of Tuscany and the duchies of Modena, Parma, and Placentia were,

---

[1] William V., the expelled hereditary stadtholder, died in obscurity at Brunswick in 1806. His son, William, had, in 1802, received Fulda in compensation, but afterward served Prussia, was, in 1806, taken prisoner with Möllendorf at Erfurt and afterward set at liberty, served again, in 1809, under Austria, and then retired to England, whence he returned on the expulsion of the French to receive a crown, which he accepted with a good deal of assurance, complaining, at the same time, of the loss of his former possession, Fulda, a circumstance strongly commented upon by Stein in his letters to Gagern. William, in return for his elevation to a throne by the arms of Germany, closed the mouths of the Rhine against her.

[2] Zurich, Berne, Lucerne, Uri, Schwyz, Unterwalden, Glarus, Zug, Freiburg, Solothurn, Basel, Schaffhausen, Appenzell, St. Gall, the Grisons, Aargau, Constance, Tessin, the Vaud, Valais, Neuenburg (Neufchatel), Geneva. The nineteen cantons of 1805 remained *in statu quo*, only those of Valais, Neufchatel, and Geneva were confederated with them, and Pruntrut with the ancient bishopric of Basel were restored to Berne.

[3] The deed of possession of the 26th June, 1814, runs as follows: "Not by an arbitrary, despotic encroachment upon the order of things, but by the hands of the Providence that blessed the arms of your emperor and of the allied princes and by a holy alliance are you restored to the house of Austria."

moreover, restored to the collateral branches of the house of Habsburg.[1]—Prussia received half of Saxony, the grand-duchy of Posen, Swedish-Pomerania,[2] a great portion of Westphalia, and almost the whole of the Lower Rhine from Mayence as far as Aix-la-Chapelle.[3] Since this period Prussia is that one which, among all the states of Germany, possesses the greatest number of German subjects, Austria, although more considerable in extent, containing a population of which by far the greater proportion is not German. Bavaria, in exchange for the provinces again ceded by her to Austria, received the province of Wurzburg together with Aschaffenburg and the Upper Rhenish Pfalz under the title of Rhenish-Bavaria. Hanover received East Friesland, which had hitherto been dependent upon Prussia. Out of this important province, which opened the North Sea to Prussia, was Hardenberg cajoled by the wily English. The electorates of Hesse, Brunswick, and Oldenburg were restored. Everything else was allowed to subsist as at the time of the Rhenish confederation. All the petty princes and counts, then mediatized, continued to be so.

The ancient empire, instead of being re-established, was, on the 8th of June, 1815, replaced by a German confederation, composed of the thirty-nine German states that had escaped the general ruin; Austria, Prussia, Bavaria, Saxony, Hanover, Wurtemberg, Baden, electoral Hesse, Darmstadt, Denmark on account of Holstein,[4] the Netherlands on account of Luxemburg, Brunswick, Mecklenburg-Schwerin,

---

[1] Tuscany fell to Ferdinand, the former grandduke of Würzburg; Modena to Francis, son of the deceased duke, Ferdinand; Parma and Placentia to Maria Louisa, the wife and widow of Napoleon.

[2] Not long before, in the treaty of Kiel, there had been question of bestowing Swedish-Pomerania upon Denmark; to this Prussia refused to accede and Denmark agreed to take 2,600,000 dollars in compensation. Prussia was also compelled to pay 3,500,000 dollars to Sweden.

[3] Rehfues, the director of the circle, a Würtemberg Protestant, published a circular at Bonn, in which he promised full religious security to the Catholic inhabitants, whom he reminded of Prussia's having been "the last supporter of the order of Jesus."—*Allgemeine Zeitung of 1814, No. 234.*

[4] Holstein alone, not Schleswig, was enumerated as belonging to the German confederation, although both duchies were long ago closely united by the *nexus socialis*, more particularly in the representation at the diet.

Nassau, Saxe-Weimar, Saxe-Gotha (where the reigning dynasty became extinct, and the duchy was partitioned among the other Saxon houses of the Ernestine line), Saxe-Coburg, Saxe-Meiningen, Saxe-Hildburghausen, Mecklenburg-Strelitz, Holstein-Oldenburg, Anhalt-Dessau, Anhalt-Bernburg, Anhalt-Kothen, Schwarzburg-Sondershausen, Schwarzburg-Rudolstadt, Hohenzollern-Hechingen, Lichtenstein, Hohenzollern-Sigmaringen, Waldeck, Reuss the elder, and Reuss the younger branch,[1] Schaumburg-Lippe, Lippe-Detmold, Hesse-Homburg: finally, the free towns, Lubeck, Frankfort on the Maine, Bremen, and Hamburg.[2] At Frankfort on the Maine a permanent diet, consisting of plenipotentiaries from the thirty-nine states, was to hold its session. The votes were, however, so regulated that the eleven states of first rank alone held a full vote, the secondary states merely holding a half or a fourth part of a vote, as, for instance, all the Saxon duchies collectively, one vote; Brunswick and Nassau, one; the two Mecklenburgs, one; Oldenburg, Anhalt, and Schwarzburg, one; the petty princes of Hohenzollern, Lichtenstein, Reuss, Lippe, and Waldeck, one; all the free towns, one; forming altogether in the diet seventeen votes. In constitutional questions relating to regulations of the confederation the plenum was to be allowed, that is, the six states of the highest rank were to have each four votes, the next five states each three, Brunswick, Schwerin, and Nassau, each two, and all the remaining princes without distinction, each one vote.[3]—Austria held the permanent

---

[1] The Reusses, formerly imperial governors of Plauen, diverged into so many branches that, as early as 1664, they agreed to distinguish themselves by numbers, which at first amounted to thirty, but at a later period to a hundred, afterward recommencing at number one. The family took the name of Reuss from the Russian wife of its founder, in the beginning of the fourteenth century.

[2] Hamburg had vainly petitioned for the restitution of her bank, of which she had been deprived by Davoust. She received merely a small portion of the general war tax levied upon France.

[3] Austria and Prussia contain forty-two million inhabitants; the rest of Germany merely twelve million; the power of the two former stands consequently in proportion to that of the rest of Germany as forty-two to twelve or seven to two, while their votes in the diet stood not contrariwise, as two to seven, but as two to seventeen in the plenary assembly, and as two to fifteen in the lesser one.

presidency. In all resolutions relating to the fundamental laws, the organic regulations of the confederation, the jura singulorum and matters of religion, unanimity was required. All the members of the confederation bound themselves neither to enter into war nor into any foreign alliance against the confederation or any of its members. The thirteenth article declared, "Each of the confederated states will grant a constitution to the people." The sixteenth placed all Christian sects throughout the German confederation on an equality. The eighteenth granted freedom of settlement within the limits of the confederation, and promised "uniformity of regulation concerning the liberty of the press." The fortresses of Luxemburg, Mayence, and Landau were declared the common property of the confederation and occupied in common by their troops. A fourth fortress was to have been raised on the Upper Rhine with twenty millions of the French contribution money. It has not yet been erected.

This was the new constitution given to Germany. According to the treaty of Paris it could not be otherwise modelled, and it is explained by the foreign influence that then prevailed. The diet assembled at Frankfort on the Maine, and was opened by Count Buol-Schauenstein with a solemn address, which excited no enthusiasm. An orator in the American assembly at that time observed, "The non-development of the seed contained in Germany appears to be the common aim of a resolute policy."

All now united for the complete suppression of the German patriotic party. In the former Rhenish confederated states, it had been treated with open contempt[1] ever since Gentz had given the signal for persecution in Austria. Prussia, however, also drove all those who had most faithfully

---

[1] Aretin, who, at the time of the Rhenish confederation, insolently mocked and had denounced every indication of German patriotism, ventured to say in his "Alemannia," in the beginning of 1817, " 'The patriotic colors,' 'the voice of the people,' 'nationality,' 'the extirpation of foreign influence,' are words now forgotten, magic sounds that have lost their power."

served her in her hour of need from her bosom. Stein was compelled to withdraw to Kappenberg, his country estate. Gruner was removed from office and sent as ambassador to Switzerland, where he died. The Rhenish Mercury, that had performed such great services to Prussia, was prohibited, and Gorres was threatened with the house of correction.[1] All other papers of a patriotic tendency were also suppressed. In Jena, Oken and Luden, in Weimar, Wieland the younger, alone ventured for some time to give utterance to their liberal opinions, but were finally also reduced to silence.

Patriotic enthusiasm was, however, not so speedily suppressed amid the youthful students in the academies and universities. Jahn's gymnastic schools (Turnschulen), the members of which were distinguished by the German costume, a short black frock coat, a black cap, linen trousers, a bare neck with turned-over shirt-collar, extended far and wide and were in close connection with the Burschenschaften of the universities. The prescribed object of these Turnschulen was the promotion of Christian, moral, German manners, the universal fraternization of all German students, the complete eradication of the provincialism and license inherent in the various associations formed at the universities. They wore Jahn's German costume and always acted publicly, until their suppression, when the remaining members formed secret associations. On the 18th of October, 1817, the students of Jena, Halle, and Leipzig, and those of some of the more distant universities, assembled in order to solemnize the jubilee of the three hundredth anniversary of the Reformation, on the Wartburg, where, in imitation of Luther, they committed a number of servile works, inimical to the German cause, to the flames, as Gorres at that time said, "filled with anger that the same reformation required

---

[1] By Sack, the government commissary, who even confiscated the Rhenish Mercury, an earlier and unprohibited paper, and arrested the printer, against which Görres violently protested in a letter addressed to Sack. Görres made a triumphant defence before the tribunal at Treves, and observed, "Strange that the most violent enemy to France should seek the protection of French courts!"

of the church by Luther should be sanctioned, but at the same time refused, by the state." The black, red, and yellow tricolor was hoisted for the first time on this occasion. These were in reality the ancient colors of the empire and were regarded as such by the patriotic students, but were purposely looked upon by the French and their adherents in Germany as an imitation of the tricolored flag of the French republic. The festival solemnized on the Wartburg was speedily succeeded by others. The Turner, more particularly at Berlin and Breslau, rendered themselves conspicuous not only by their dress but by their insolence, boys even of the tenderest years putting themselves forward as reformers of the government and of society, and singing the most bloodthirsty songs of liberty. The Prussian government interfered, and the gymnastic exercises, so well suited to the subjects of a warlike state, were once more prohibited.

At the congress of Aix-la-Chapelle, Stourdza, the Russian councillor of state, a Wallachian by birth, presented a memorial in which the spirit of the German universities was described as revolutionary. The Burschenschaft of Jena sent him a challenge. Kotzebue, the Russian councillor of state and celebrated dramatist, at length published a weekly paper in which he turned every indication of German patriotism to ridicule, and exercised his wit upon the individual eccentricities of the students affecting the old German costume, of precocious boys and doting professors. The rage of the galled universities rose to a still higher pitch on the discovery, made and incontestably proved by Luden, that Kotzebue sent secret bulletins, filled with invective and suspicion, to St. Petersburg. To execrate Kotzebue had become so habitual at the universities that a young man, Sand from Wunsiedel, a theological student of Jena, noted for piety and industry, took the fanatical resolution to free, or at least to wipe off a blot from his country, by the assassination of an enemy whose importance he, in the delusion of hatred, vastly overrated; and he accordingly went, in 1819, to Mannheim, plunged his dagger into Kotzebue's heart, and then attempted his own life, but only succeeded in inflicting a slight wound. He was beheaded in the ensuing year. Loning, the apothecary, probably excited by Sand's example, also attempted the life of the president of Nassau, Ibell, who, however, seized him, and he committed suicide in prison.

These events occasioned a congress at Carlsbad in 1819, which took the state of Germany into deliberation, placed each of the universities under the supervision of a government officer, suppressed the Burschenschaft, prohibited their colors, and fixed a central board of scrutiny at Mayence,[1] which acted on the presupposition of the existence of a secret and general conspiracy for the purposes of assassination and revolution, and of Sand's having acted not from personal fanaticism and religious aberration, but as the agent of some unknown superiors in some new and mysterious tribunal. This inquisition was carried on for years and a crowd of students peopled the prisons; conspiracies perilous to the state were, however, nowhere discovered, but simply a great deal of ideal enthusiasm. The elder men in the universities, who, either in their capacity as tutors or authors, had fed the enthusiasm of the youthful students, were also removed from their situations. Jahn was arrested, Arndt was suspended at Bonn and Fries at Jena; Gorres, who had perseveringly published the most violent pamphlets, was compelled to take refuge in Switzerland, which also offered an asylum to Dewette, the Berlin professor of theology, who had been deprived of his chair on account of a letter addressed by him to Sand's mother. Oken, the great naturalist, who refused to give up "Isis," a periodical publication, also withdrew to Switzerland. Numbers of the younger professors went to America.[2] The solemnization of the

[1] The names of these inquisitors were Schwarz, Grano, Hörmann, Bar, Pfister, Preusschen, Moussel.

[2] Charles Follen, brother to the poet Louis Adolphus Follen, private teacher of law at Jena, a young man of great spirit and talent, who at that period exercised great influence over the youth of Germany, was wrecked, in 1840, in a steamer on the coast of North America and drowned.

October festival was also prohibited, and the triumphal monument on the field of Leipzig was demolished.

CCLXV. *The New Constitutions*

GERMANY had, notwithstanding her triumph, regained neither her ancient unity nor her former power, but still continued to be merely a confederation of states, bound together by no firm tie and regarded with contempt by their more powerful neighbors. The German confederation did not even include the whole of the provinces whose population was distinguished as German by the use of the German language. Several of the provinces of Germany were still beneath a foreign sceptre; Switzerland and the Netherlands had declared themselves distinct from the rest of Germany, which, hitherto submissive to France, was in danger of falling beneath the influence of Russia, who ceaselessly sought to entangle her by diplomatic wiles.

There were still, however, men existing in Germany who hoped to compensate the loss of the external power of their country by the internal freedom that had been so lavishly promised to the people on the general summons to the field. The proclamation of Calisch and the German federative act guaranteed the grant of constitutions. The former Rhenish confederated princes, nevertheless, alone found it to their interest to carry this promise into effect, and, in a manner, formed a second alliance with France by their imitation of the newly introduced French code and by the establishment, in their own territories, of two chambers, one of peers, the other of deputies, similar to those of France; measures by which, at that period of popular excitement, they also regained the popularity deservedly lost by them at an earlier period throughout the rest of Germany, the more so, the less the inclination manifested by Austria and Prussia to grant the promised constitutions. Enslaved Illuminatism characterizes this new zeal in favor of internal liberty and constitutional governments, to denote which the novel term of

Liberalism was borrowed from France. Liberty was ever on the tongues—of the most devoted servants of the state. The ancient church and the nobility were attacked with incredible mettle—in order to suit the purposes of ministerial caprice. Prussia and Austria were loudly blamed for not keeping pace with the times—with the intent of favorably contrasting the ancient policy of the Rhenish confederation. None, at that period, surpassed the ministers belonging to the old school of Illuminatism and Napoleonism in liberalism, but no sooner did the deputies of the people attempt to realize their liberal ideas than they started back in dismay.

The first example of this kind was given by Frederick Augustus, duke of Nassau, as early as the September of 1814. Ibell, the president, who reigned with unlimited power over Nassau, drew up a constitution which has been termed a model of "despotism under a constitutional form." The whole of the property of the state still continuing to be the private property of the duke, and his right arbitrarily to increase the number of members belonging to the first chamber, and by their votes to annul every resolution passed by the second chamber, rendered the whole constitution illusory. Trombetta, one of the deputies, voluntarily renounced his seat, an example that was followed by several others.—The second constitution granted was that bestowed upon the Netherlands in 1815, by King William, who established such an unequal representation in the chambers between the Belgians and Dutch as to create great dissatisfaction among the former, who, in revenge, again affected the French party. This was succeeded, in 1816, by the petty constitutions of Waldeck, Weimar, and Frankfort on the Maine.—Maximilian, king of Bavaria, seemed, in 1817, to announce another system by the dismissal of his minister, Montgelas, and, in 1818, bestowed a new constitution upon Bavaria; but the old abuses in the administration remained uneradicated; a civil and military state unproportioned to the revenue, the petty despotism of government officers and heavy imposts, still weighed upon the people, and the constitution itself was quickly proved illusory, the veto of the first chamber annulling the first resolution passed by the second chamber. Professor Behr of Wurzburg, upon this, energetically protested against the first chamber, and, on the refusal of the second chamber to vote for the maintenance of the army on so high a footing, unless the soldiery were obliged to take the oath on the constitution, it was speedily dissolved.—In Baden the Grandduke Charles expired, in 1818, after having caused a constitution to be drawn up, which Louis, his uncle and successor, carried into effect. Louis having, however, previously, and without the consent of the people, entered into a stipulation with the nobility, to whom he had granted an edict extremely favorable to their interests, Winter, the Heidelberg bookseller, a member of the second chamber, demanded its abrogation. The answer was, the dissolution of the chamber, personal inquisition and intimidation, and the publication of an extremely severe edict of censure, against which, in 1820, Professor von Rotteck of Freiburg, supported by the poet Hebel and by the Freiherr von Wessenberg, administrator of the bishopric of Constance, protested, but in vain.—At the same time, that is, in 1818, Hildburghausen, and even the petty principality of Lichtenstein, which merely contains two square miles and a population amounting to five thousand souls, also received a constitution, which not a little contributed to turn the whole affair into ridicule.—To these succeeded, in 1819, the constitutions of Hanover and Lippe-Detmold, the former as aristocratic as possible, completely in the spirit of olden times, solely dictated and carried into effect by the nobility and government officers. The sittings of the chambers, consequently, continued to be held in secret.—The dukes of Mecklenburg abolished feudal servitude, which existed in no other part of Germany, in 1820.—In Darmstadt, the constitution was granted by the good-natured, venerable Grandduke Louis (whose attention was chiefly devoted to the opera), after the impatient advocates, who had collected subscriptions in the Odenwald to petitions praying for the speedy bestowal of the promised constitution, had been arrested, and an insurrection that consequently ensued among the peasantry had been quelled by force.—Petty constitutions were, moreover, granted, in 1821, to Coburg, and, in 1829, to Meiningen. The Gotha-Altenburg branch of the ducal house of Saxony became extinct in 1825 in the person of Frederick, the last duke, the brother of Duke Augustus Emilius, a great patron of the arts and sciences, deceased 1822. Gotha, consequently, lapsed to Coburg, Altenburg to Hildburghausen, and Hildburghausen to Meiningen.

In Wurtemberg, the dissatisfaction produced by the ancient despotism of the government was also to be speedily appeased by the grant of a constitutional charter. The king, Frederick, convoked the Estates, to whom he, on the 15th of March, 1815, solemnly delivered the newly enacted constitution. But here, as elsewhere, was the government inclined to grant a mere illusory boon. The Estates rejected the constitution, without reference to its contents, simply owing to the formal reason of its being bestowed by the prince and being consequently binding on one side alone, instead of being a stipulation between the prince and the people, and moreover because the ancient constitution of Wurtemberg, which had been abrogated by force and in direct opposition to the will of the Estates, was still in legal force. The old Wurtemberg party alone could naturally take their footing upon their ancient rights, but the new Wurtemberg party, the mediatized princes of the empire, the counts and barons of the empire, and the imperial free towns, nay, even the Agnati of the reigning house,[1] all of whom had suffered more or less under Napoleon's iron rule, ranged themselves on their side. The deputy, Zahn of Calw, drew a masterly picture of the state of affairs at that period, in which he pitilessly disclosed every reigning abuse. The king, thus vigorously and unanimously opposed, was con-

[1] The king bitterly reproached his brother Henry, to whom he said, "You have accused me to my peasantry."—*Pfister, History of the Constitution of Würtemberg.*

strained to yield, and the most prolix negotiations, in which the citizen deputies, headed by the advocate, Weisshaar, were supported by the nobility against the government, commenced.

The affair was, it may be designedly, dragged on ad infinitum until the death of the king in 1816, when his son and successor, William, who had gained a high reputation as a military commander and had rendered himself extremely popular, zealously began the work of conciliation. He not only instantly abolished the abuses of the former government, as, for instance, in the game law,[1] but, in 1817, delivered a new constitution to the Estates. Article 337 was somewhat artfully drawn up, but in every point the constitution was as liberal as a constitutional charter could possibly be. But the Estates refused to accept of liberty as a boon, and rejected this constitution on the same formal grounds upon which they had rejected the preceding one. The Estates were again upheld by a grateful public, and the few deputies, more particularly Cotta and Griesinger, who had defended the new constitution on account of its liberality and who regarded form as immaterial, became the objects of public animadversion. The populace broke the windows of the house inhabited by the liberal-minded minister, von Wangenheim. The poet Uhland greatly distinguished himself as a warm upholder of the ancient rights of the people.[2] The king instantly dissolved the Estates, but at the same time declared his intention to guarantee to the people, with-

---

[1] Pfister mentions in his History of the Constitution of Würtemberg that merely in the superior bailiwick of Heidenheim the game duties amounted, in 1814, to twenty thousand florins, and five thousand two hundred and ninety-three acres of taxed ground lay uncultivated on account of the damage done by the game, and that in march, 1815, one bailiwick was obliged to furnish twenty-one thousand five hundred and eighty-four men and three thousand two hundred and thirty-seven horses for a single hunt.

[2] Colonel von Massenbach, of the Prussian service, who has so miserably described the battle of Jena and the surrender of the Prentzlow in which he acted so miserable a part, and who had in his native Würtemberg embraced the aristocratic party, was delivered by the free town of Frankfort, within whose walls he resided, up to the Prussian government, which he threatened to compromise by the publication of some letters. He died within the fortress of Cüstrin.

out a constitution, the rights he had intended constitutionally to confer upon them; to establish an equal system of taxation, and "to eradicate bureaucracy, that curse upon the country." The good-will displayed on both sides led to fresh negotiations, and a third constitution was at length drawn up by a committee, composed partly of members of the government, partly of members belonging to the Estates, and, in 1819, was taken into deliberation and passed by the reassembled Estates. This constitution, nevertheless, fell far below the mark to which it had been raised by public expectation, partly on account of the retention, owing to ancient prejudice, of the permanent committee and its oligarchical influence, partly on account of the too great and permanent concessions made to the nobility in return for their momentary aid,[1] partly on account of the extreme haste that marked the concluding deliberations of the Estates, occasioned by their partly unfounded dread of interference on the part of the congress then assembled at Carlsbad.

In Wurtemberg, however, as elsewhere, the policy of the government was deeply imbued with the general characteristics of the time. Notwithstanding the constitution, notwithstanding the guarantee given by the federative act, liberty of the press did not exist. List, the deputy from Reutlingen, was, for having ventured to collect subscriptions to petitions, brought before the criminal court, expelled the chamber by his intimidated brother-deputies, took refuge in Switzerland, whence he returned to be imprisoned for some time in the fortress of Asberg, and was finally permitted to emigrate to North America, whence he returned at a later period, 1825, in the capacity of consul. Liesching, the editor of the German Guardian, whose liberty of speech was si-

---

[1] The mediatized princes and counts of the empire sat in the first chamber, the barons of the empire in the second. The prelates, once so powerful, lost, on the other hand, together with the church property, in the possession of which they were not reinstated, also most of their influence. Instead of the fourteen aristocratic and independent prelates, six only were appointed by the monarch to seats in the second chamber. Government officers were also eligible in this chamber, which ere long fell entirely under their influence.

lenced by command of the German confederation, also became an inmate of the fortress of Asberg.

In Hesse and Brunswick, all the old abuses practiced in the petty courts in the eighteenth century were revived. William of Hesse-Cassel returned, on the fall of Napoleon, to his domains. True to his whimsical saying, "I have slept during the last seven years," he insisted upon replacing everything in Hesse exactly on its former footing. In one particular alone was his vanity inconsistent: notwithstanding his hatred toward Napoleon, he retained the title of Prince Elector, bestowed upon him by Napoleon's favor, although it had lost all significance, there being no longer any emperor to elect.[1] He turned the hand of time back seven years, degraded the councillors raised to that dignity by Jerome to their former station as clerks, captains to lieutenants, etc., all, in fact, to the station they had formerly occupied, even reintroduced into the army the fashion of wearing powder and queues, prohibited all those not bearing an official title to be addressed as "Herr," and re-established the socage dues abolished by Jerome. This attachment to old abuses was associated with the most insatiable avarice. He reduced the government bonds to one-third, retook possession of the lands sold during Jerome's reign, without granting any compensation to the holders, compelled the country to pay his son's debts to the amount of two hundred thousand rix-dollars, lowered the amount of pay to such a degree that a lieutenant received but five rix-dollars per mensem, and offered to sell a new constitution to the Estates at the low price of four million rix-dollars, which he afterward lowered to two millions and a tax for ten years upon liquors. This shameful bargain being rejected by the Estates, the constitution fell to the ground, and the prince elector practiced the most unlimited despotism. Discontent was stifled by imprisonment. Two officers, Huth and Rots-

---

[1] He endeavored, but in vain, to persuade the allied powers to bestow upon him the royal dignity.

mann, who had got up a petition in favor of their class, and the Herr von Gohr, who by chance gave a private fete while the prince was suffering from a sudden attack of illness, were among the victims. The purchasers of the crown lands vainly appealed to the federative assembly for redress, for the prince elector "refused the mediation of the federative assembly until it had been authorized by an organic law drawn up with the co-operation of the prince elector himself."—This prince expired in 1821, and was succeeded by his son, William II., who abolished the use of hair-powder and queues, but none of the existing abuses, and demonstrated no inclination to grant a constitution. He was, moreover, the slave of his mistress, Countess Reichenbach, and on ill terms with his consort, a sister of the king of Prussia, and with his son. Anonymous and threatening letters being addressed to this prince with a view of inducing him to favor the designs of the writer, he had recourse to the severest measures for the discovery of the guilty party; numbers of persons were arrested, and travellers instinctively avoided Cassel. It was at length discovered that Manger, the head of the police, a court favorite, was the author of the letters.

Similar abuses were revived by the house of Brunswick. It is unhappily impossible to leave unmentioned the conduct of Caroline, princess of Brunswick, consort to the Prince of Wales, afterward George IV., king of England. Although this German princess had the good fortune to be protected by the Whig party and by the people against the king and the Tory ministry, she proved a disgrace to her supporters by the scandalous familiarity in which she lived in Italy with her chamberlain, the Italian, Pergami. The sympathy with which she was treated at the time of the congress was designedly exaggerated by the Whigs for the purpose of giving the greatest possible publicity to the errors of the monarch. Caroline of Brunswick was declared innocent and expired shortly after her trial, in 1821.

Charles, the hereditary duke of Brunswick, son to the

duke who had so gallantly fallen at Quatre Bras, was under the guardianship of the king of England. A constitution was bestowed in 1820 upon this petty territory, which was governed by the minister, Von Schmidt-Phiseldek. The youthful duke took the reins of government in his nineteenth year. Of a rash and violent disposition and misled by evil associates, he imagined that he had been too long restricted from assuming the government, accused his well-deserving minister of having attempted to prolong his minority, posted handbills for his apprehension as a common delinquent, denied all his good offices, and subverted the constitution. He was surrounded by base intriguers in the person of Bosse, the councillor of state, formerly the servile tool of Napoleon's despotism, of Frike, the Aulic councillor, "whose pliant quill was equal to any task when injustice had to be glossed over," of the adventurer, Klindworth, and of Bitter, the head of the chancery, who conducted the financial speculations. Frike, in contempt of justice, tore up the judgment passed by the court of justice in favor of the venerable Herr von Sierstorff, whom he had accused of high treason. Herr von Cramm, by whom Frike was, in the name of the Estates, accused of this misdemeanor before the federative assembly, was banished, a surgeon, who attended him, was put upon his defence, and an accoucheur, named Grimm, who had basely refused to attend upon Cramm's wife, was presented with a hundred dollars. Hâberlin, the novelist, who had been justly condemned to twenty years' imprisonment with hard labor for his civil misdemeanors, was, on the other hand, liberated for publishing something in the duke's favor. Bitter conducted himself with the most open profligacy, sold all the demesnes, appropriated the sum destined for the redemption of the public debt, and at the same time levied the heavy imposts with unrelenting severity. The federative assembly passed judgment against the duke solely in reference to his attacks upon the king of England.

CCLXVI. *The European Congress—The German Customs' Union*

THE great political drama enacting in Europe excited at this time the deepest attention throughout Germany. In almost every country a struggle commenced between liberalism and the measures introduced on the fall of Napoleon. In France more particularly it systematically and gradually undermined the government of the Bourbons, and the cry of liberty that resounded throughout France once more found an echo in Germany.

The terrible war was forgotten. The French again became the objects of the admiration and sympathy of the radical party in Germany, and the spirit of opposition, here and there demonstrated in the German chambers, gave rise, notwithstanding its impotence, to precautionary measures on the part of the federative governments. In the winter of 1819, a German federative congress, of which Prince Metternich was the grand motor, assembled at Vienna for the purpose, after the utter annihilation of the patriots, of finally checking the future movements of the liberals, principally in the provincial diets. The Viennese Act of 1820 contains closer definitions of the Federative Act, of which the more essential object was the exclusion of the various provincial diets from all positive interference in the general affairs of Germany, and the increase of the power of the different princes vis-à-vis to their provincial diets by a guarantee of aid on the part of the confederates.

During the sitting of this congress, on New Year's Day, 1820, the liberal party in Spain revolted against their ungrateful sovereign, Ferdinand VII., who exercised the most fearful tyranny over the nation that had so unhesitatingly shed its blood in defence of his throne. This example was shortly afterward followed by the Neapolitans, who were also dissatisfied with the conduct of their sovereign. Prince Metternich instantly brought about a congress at Troppau. The czar, Alexander, who had views upon the East and was no stranger to the heterarchical party which, under the guidance of Prince Ypsilanti, prepared a revolution in Greece (which actually broke out) against the Turks, was at first unwilling to give his assent unconditionally to the interference of Austria, but on being, in 1821, to his great surprise, informed by Prince Metternich of the existence of a revolutionary spirit in one of the regiments of the Russian guard, freely assented to all the measures proposed by that minister.[1] The new congress held at Laibach, in 1821, was followed by the entrance of the Austrians under Frimont into Italy. The cowardly Neapolitans fled without firing a shot, and the Piedmontese, who unexpectedly revolted to Frimont's rear, were, after a short encounter with the Austrians under Bubna at Novara, defeated and reduced to submission. The Greeks, whom Russia now no longer ventured openly to uphold, had, in the meantime, also risen in open insurrection. The affairs of Spain were still in an unsettled state. The new congress held at Verona, in 1822, however, decided the fate of both these countries. Prince Hardenberg, the Prussian minister, expired at Genoa on his return home, and Lord Castlereagh, the English ambassador, cut his throat with his penknife, in a fit of frenzy, supposed to have been induced by the sense of his heavy responsibility. At this congress the principle of legitimacy was maintained with such strictness that even the revolt of the Greeks against the long and cruel tyranny of the Turks was, notwithstanding the *Christian spirit of the Holy Alliance* and the political advantage secured to Russia and Austria by the subversion of the Turkish empire, treated as rebellion against the legitimate authority of the Porte and strongly discouraged. A French army was, on the same grounds, despatched with the consent of the Bourbon into Spain, and

---

[1] Vide Binder's Prince Metternich.

Ferdinand was reinstated in his legitimate tyranny in 1823. Russia, in a note addressed to the whole of the confederated states of Germany, demanded at the same time a declaration on their parts to the effect that the late proceedings of the great European powers at Verona "were in accordance with the well-understood interests of the people." Every member of the federative assembly at Frankfort gave his assent, with the exception of the Freiherr von Wangenheim, the envoy from Wurtemberg, who declaring that his instructions did not warrant his voting upon the question, the ambassadors from the two Hesses made a similar declaration. This occasioned the dismissal of the Freiherr von Wangenheim; and the illegal publication of a Wurtemberg despatch, in which the non-participation of the German confederation in the resolutions passed by the congresses, to which their assent was afterward demanded, was treated of, occasioned a second dismissal, that of Count Winzingerode, the Wurtemberg minister. In the July of 1824, the federal diet resolved to give its support to the monarchical principle in the constitutional states, and to maintain the Carlsbad resolutions referring to censorship and to the universities. The Mayence committee remained sitting until 1828.

On the sudden decease of Alexander, the czar of all the Russias, amid the southern steppes, a revolution induced by the nobility broke out at Petersburg, but was suppressed by Alexander's brother and successor, the emperor Nicholas I. Nicholas had wedded Charlotte, the eldest daughter of the king of Prussia. This energetic sovereign instantly invaded Persia and rendered that country dependent upon his empire without any attempt being made by the Tory party in England and Austria to hinder the aggrandizement of Russia, every attack directed against her being regarded as an encouragement to liberalism. Russia consequently seized this opportunity to turn her arms against Turkey, and, in the ensuing year, a Russian force under Count Diebitsch, a Silesian, crossed the Balkan (Hæmus) and penetrated as far as Adrianople; while another corps d'armée, under Count Paskiewicz, advanced from the Caucasus into Asia Minor and took Erzerum. The fall of Constantinople seemed near at hand, when Austria and England for the first time intervened and declared that, notwithstanding their sympathy with the absolute principles on which Russia rested, they would not permit the seizure of Constantinople. France expressed her readiness to unite with Russia and to fall upon the Austrian rear in case troops were sent against the Russians.[1] Prussia, however, intervened, and General Muffling was despatched to Adrianople, where, in 1829, a treaty was concluded, by which Russia, although for the time compelled to restore the booty already accumulated, gained several considerable advantages, being granted possession of the most important mountain strongholds and passes of Asia Minor, a right to occupy and fortify the mouths of the Danube so important to Austria, and to extend her ægis over Moldavia and Wallachia.

In the midst of this wretched period, which brought fame to Russia and deep dishonor upon Germany, there still gleamed one ray of hope; the Customs' Union was proposed by some of the German princes for the more intimate union of German interests.

Maximilian of Bavaria, a prince whose amiable manners and character rendered him universally beloved, expired in 1825. His son, Louis, the foe to French despotism, a German patriot and a zealous patron of the arts, declared himself, on his coronation, the warm and sincere upholder of the constitutional principle and excited general enthusiasm. His first measures on assuming the government were the reduction of the royal household and of the army with a view to the relief of the country from the heavy imposts, the removal of the university of Landshut to Munich, and the enrichment on an extensive scale of the institutions of art. The union

---

[1] Official report of the Russian ambassador, Count Pozzo di Borgo, from Paris, of the 14th of December, 1828.

of the galleries of Dusseldorf and Mannheim with that of Munich, the collection of valuable antiques and pictures, for instance, that of the old German paintings collected by the brothers Boisserée in Cologne during the French usurpation, the academy of painting under the direction of the celebrated Cornelius, the new public buildings raised by Klenze, among which the Glyptothek, the Pinakothek, the great Königsbau or royal residence, the Ludwigschurch, the Auerchurch, the Arcades, etc., may be more particularly designated, rendered Munich the centre of German art. This sovereign also founded at Ratisbon the Walhalla, a building destined for the reception of the busts of all the celebrated men to whom Germany has given birth. The predilection of this royal amateur for classic antiquity excited within his bosom the warmest sympathy with the fate of the modern Greeks, then in open insurrection against their Turkish oppressors, and whom he alone, among all the princes of Germany, aided in the hour of their extremest need.—With the same spirit that dictated his poems, in which he so repeatedly lamented the want of unity in Germany, he was the first to propose the union of her material interests. Germany unhappily resembled, and indeed immediately after the war of liberation, as De Pradt, the French writer, maliciously observed, even in a mercantile point of view, a menagerie whose inhabitants watched each other through a grating. Vainly had the commercial class of Frankfort on the Maine presented a petition, in 1819, to the confederation, praying for free trade, for the fulfilment of the nineteenth article of the federal act. Their well-grounded complaint remained unheard. The non-fulfilment of the treaty relating to the free navigation of the Rhine to the sea was most deeply felt. In the first treaty concluded at Paris, the royal dignity and the extension of the Dutch territory had been generously granted to the king of the Netherlands under the express proviso of the free navigation of the Rhine to the sea. The papers relating to this transaction had been drawn up in French, and the ungrateful Dutch perfidiously gave the words "jusqu' à la mer" their most literal construction, merely "as far as the sea," and as the French, moreover, possessed a voice in the matter on account of the Upper Rhine, and the German federal states were unable to give a unanimous verdict, innumerable committees were held and acts were drawn up without producing any result favorable to the trade of Germany.

Affairs stood thus, when, shortly after Louis's accession to the throne of Bavaria, negotiations having for object the settlement of a commercial treaty took place between him and William, king of Wurtemberg. This example was imitated by Prussia, which at first merely formed a union with Darmstadt; afterward by Hesse, Hanover, Saxony, etc., by which a central German union was projected. This union was, however, unable to stand between that of Wurtemberg and Bavaria, and that of Prussia and Darmstadt. The German Customs' Union was carried into effect in 1828. An annual meeting of German naturalists had at that time been arranged under the auspices of Oken, the great naturalist, and at the meeting held at Berlin, in 1828, the Freiherr von Cotta, by whom the moral and material interests of Germany have been greatly promoted, drew up the first plan for a junction of the commercial union of Southern Germany with that of the North, as the first step to the future liberation of Germany from all internal commercial restrictions. The zeal with which he carried this great plan into effect gained the confidence of the different governments, and he not only succeeded in combining the two older unions, but also in gradually embodying with them the rest of the German states.

The attachment of King Louis to ancient Catholicism was extremely remarkable. He began to restore some of the monasteries, and several professors inclined to Ultramontanism and to Catholic mysticism, the most distinguished among whom was Görres, the Prussian exile, assembled at the new university at Munich. Here and there appeared a pious enthusiast. Shortly after the restoration, a peasant from the Pfalz named Adam Muller began to prophesy, and

Madame von Krudener, a Hanoverian, to preach the necessity of public penance; both these persons gained the ear of exalted personages, and Madame von Krudener more particularly is said not a little to have conduced to the piety displayed by the emperor Alexander during the latter years of his life. At Bamberg, Prince Alexander von Hohenlohe, then a young man, had the folly to attempt the performance of miracles, until the police interfered, and he received a high ecclesiastical office in Hungary. In Austria, the Ligorians, followers in the footsteps of the Jesuits, haunted the vicinity of the throne. The conversion of Count Stolberg and of the Swiss, Von Haller, to the Catholic church, created the greatest sensation. The former, a celebrated poet, simple and amiable, in no way merited the shameless outbursts of rage of his old friend, Voss; Haller, on the other hand, brought forward in his "Restoration of Political Science" such a decided theory in favor of secession as to inspire a sentiment of dread at his consistency. The conversion of Ferdinand, prince of Anhalt-Köthen, to the Catholic church, in 1825, excited far less attention.

In France, where the Bourbons were completely guided by the Jesuits, by whose aid they could alone hope to suppress the revolutionary spirit of their subjects, the reaction in favor of Catholicism had assumed a more decided character than in Germany. Louis XVIII. was succeeded by his brother, the Count d'Artois, under the name of Charles X., a venerable man seventy years of age, who, notwithstanding his great reverses, had "neither learned nor forgotten anything." Polignac, his incapable and imperious minister, the tool of the Jesuits, had, since 1829, impugned every national right, and at length ventured, by the ordinances of the 25th July, 1830, to subvert the constitution. During three days, from the 27th to the 30th of July, the greatest confusion reigned in Paris; the people rose in thousands; murderous conflicts took place in the streets between them and the royal troops, who were driven from every quarter, and the king was expelled. The chambers met, declared the elder branch of the house of Bourbon (Charles X., his son, the Dauphin, Duke d'Angouleme, and his grandson, the youthful Duke de Bordeaux, the son of the murdered Duke de Berri) to have forfeited the throne, but at the same time allowed them unopposed to seek an asylum in England, and elected Louis Philippe, Duke of Orleans, the son of the notorious Jacobin, the head of the younger line of the house of Bourbon and the grand-master of the society of Freemasons, king of the French. The rights of the chambers and of the people were also extended by an appendix to the charta signed by Louis XVIII.

The revolution of July was the signal for all discontented subjects throughout Europe to gain, either by force or by legal opposition, their lost or sighed-for rights. In October, the constitutional party in Spain attempted to overturn the despotic rule of Ferdinand VII. In November, the prime minister of England, the renowned Duke of Wellington, was compelled by the people to yield his seat to Earl Grey, a man of more liberal principles, who commenced the great work of reform in the constitution and administration of Great Britain. During this month, a general insurrection took place in Poland: the grandduke, Constantine, was driven out of Warsaw, and Poland declared herself independent. A great part of Germany was also convulsed: and a part of the ill-raised fabric, erected by the statesmen of 1815, fell tottering to the ground.

CCLXVII. *The Belgian Revolution*

A NATION'S self-forgetfulness is ever productive of national disgrace. The Netherlands were torn from the empire and placed partly beneath the tyranny of Spain, partly beneath the ægis of France; the dominion of Austria, at a later period, merely served to rouse their provincial spirit, and, during their subsequent annexation to France, the French element decidedly gained the ascendency among the population. When, in 1815, these provinces fell under the rule of Holland, it was hoped that the German element would again rise. But Holland is not Germany. Estranged provinces are alone to be regained by means of their incorporation with an empire imbued with one distinct national spirit; the subordination of one province to another but increases national antipathy and estrangement. Holland, by an ungrateful, inimical policy, unfortunately strove to separate herself from Germany.[1] And yet Holland owes her whole prosperity to Germany. There is her market; thence does she draw her immense wealth; the loss of that market for her colonial productions would prove her irredeemable ruin. Her sovereign, driven into distant exile, was restored to her by the arms of Germany and generously endowed with royalty. Holland, in return for all these benefits, deceitfully deprived Germany of the free navigation of the Rhine to the sea guaranteed to her by the federal act and assumed the right of fixing the price of all goods, whether imported to or exported from Germany. The whole of Germany was, in this unprecedented manner, rendered doubly tributary to the petty state of Holland.

---

[1] "The Netherlands formed, nevertheless, but a weak bulwark to Germany. Internal disunion, superfluous fortresses, a weak army. On the one side, a witless, wealthy, haughty aristocracy, an influential and ignorant clergy; on the other, civic pride, capelocratic pettiness, Calvinistic *brusquerie*. The policy pursued by the king was inimical to Germany."—*Stein's Letters.*

Belgium, annexed to this secondary state instead of being incorporated with great and liberal Germany, necessarily remained a stranger to any influence calculated to excite her sympathy with the general interests of Germany. Cut off, as heretofore, from German influence, she retained, in opposition to the Dutch, a preponderance of the old Spanish and modern French element in her population. Priests and liberals, belonging to the French school, formed an opposition party against the king, who, on his side, rested his sole support upon the Dutch, whom he favored in every respect. Count Broglio, archbishop of Ghent, first began the contest by refusing to take the oath on the constitution. Violence was resorted to and he fled the country. The impolicy of the government in affixing his name to the pillory merely served to increase the exasperation of the Catholics. Hence their acquiescence with the designs of the Jesuits, their opposition to the foundation of a philosophical academy, independent of the clergy, at Louvain. The fact of the population of Belgium being to that of Holland as three to two and the number of its representatives in the states-general being as four to seven, of few, if any, Belgians being allowed to enter the service of the state, the army or the navy, still further added to the popular discontent. The gross manners of the minister, Van Maanen, also increased the evil. As early as January, 1830, eight liberal Belgian deputies were deprived of their offices, and De Potter, with some others, who had ventured to defend them by means of the press, were banished the kingdom under a charge of high treason.

The Dutch majority in the states-general, notwithstanding its devotion to the king, rejected the ten years' budget on the ground of its affording too long a respite to ministerial responsibility, and protested against the levy of Swiss troops. Slave-trade in the colonies was also abolished in 1818.

The position of the Netherlands, which, Luxemburg excepted, did not appertain to the German confederation, continually exposed her, on account of Belgium, to be attacked on the land side by France, on that of the sea by her ancient commercial foe, England, and had induced the king to form a close alliance with Russia. His son, William of Orange, married a sister of the emperor Alexander.

The colonies did not regain their former prosperity. The Dutch settlement at Batavia with difficulty defended itself against the rebellious natives of Sumatra and Java.

The revolution in Paris had an electric effect upon the irritated Belgians. On the 25th of August, 1830, Auber's opera, "The Dumb Girl of Portici," the revolt of Masaniello in Naples, was performed at the Brussels theatre and inflamed the passions of the audience to such a degree, that, on quitting the theatre, they proceeded to the house of Libry, the servile newspaper editor, and entirely destroyed it: the palace of the minister, Van Maanen, shared the same fate. The citizens placed themselves under arms, and sent a deputation to The Hague to lay their grievances before the king. The entire population meanwhile rose in open insurrection, and the whole of the fortresses, Maestricht and the citadel of Antwerp alone excepted, fell into their hands. William of Orange, the crown prince, ventured unattended among the insurgents at Brussels and proposed, as a medium of peace, the separation of Belgium from Holland in a legislative and administrative sense. The king also made an apparent concession to the wishes of the people by the dismissal of Van Maanen, but shortly afterward declared his intention not to yield, disavowed the step taken by his son, and allowed some Belgian deputies to be insulted at The Hague. A fanatical commotion instantly took place at Brussels; the moderate party in the civic guard was disarmed, and the populace made preparations for desperate resistance. On the 25th of September, Prince Frederick, second son to the king of Holland, entered Brussels with a large body of troops, but encountered barricades and a heavy fire in the Park, the Place Royal, and along the Boulevards. An immense crowd, chiefly composed of the people of Liege and of peasants dressed in the blue smock of the country, had assembled for the purpose of aiding in the defence of the city. The contest, accompanied by destruction of the dwelling-houses and by pillage, lasted five days. The Dutch were accused of practicing the most horrid cruelties upon the defenceless inhabitants and of thereby heightening the popular exasperation. At length, on the 27th of September, the prince was compelled to abandon the city. On the 5th of October, Belgium declared herself independent. De Potter returned and placed himself at the head of the provisional government. The Prince of Orange recognized the absolute separation of Belgium from Holland in a proclamation published at Antwerp, but was, nevertheless, constrained to quit the country. Antwerp fell into the hands of the insurgents; the citadel, however, refused to surrender, and Chassé, the Dutch commandant, caused the magnificent city to be bombarded, and the well-stored entrepot, the arsenal, and about sixty or seventy houses, to be set on fire, during the night of the 27th of October, 1830.[1] The cruelties perpetrated by the Dutch were bitterly retaliated upon them by the Belgian populace. On the 10th of November, however, a national Belgian congress met, in which the moderate party gained the upper hand, principally owing to the influence of the clergy. De Potter's plan for the formation of a Belgian commonwealth fell to the ground. The congress decided in favor of the maintenance of the kingdom, drew up a new constitution, and offered the crown to the Prince de Nemours, second son of the king of the French. It was, however, refused by Louis Philippe in the name of his son, in order to avoid war with the other great European powers. Surlet de Chokier, the leader of the liberal party, hereupon undertook the provisional government of the country, and negotiations were entered into with Prince Leopold of Coburg.

---

[1] So bitter was the enmity existing between the Belgians and the Dutch that the Dutch lieutenant, Van Speyk, when driven by a storm before Antwerp, blew up his gunboat in the middle of the Scheldt rather than allow it to fall into the hands of the Belgians.

On the 4th of November, a congress, composed of the ministers of England, Russia, Austria, and Prussia, met at London for the purpose of settling the Belgian question without disturbing the peace of Europe, and it was decided that Prince Leopold of Coburg, the widower of the princess royal of England, a man entirely under British influence, and who had refused the throne of Greece, should accept that of Belgium. Eighteen articles favorable to Belgium were granted to him by the London congress. Scarcely, however, had he reached Brussels, on the 31st July, 1831, than the fetes given upon that occasion were disturbed by the unexpected invasion of Belgium by a numerous and powerful Dutch force. At Hasselt, the Prince of Orange defeated the Belgians under General Daine, and, immediately advancing against Leopold, utterly routed him at Tirlemont, on the 12th August. The threats of France and England, and the appearance of a French army in Belgium, saved Brussels and compelled the Dutch to withdraw. The eighteen articles in favor of Belgium were, on the other hand, replaced by twenty-four others, more favorable to the Dutch, which Leopold was compelled to accept. The king of Holland, however, refusing to accept these twenty-four articles, with which, notwithstanding the concessions therein contained, he was dissatisfied, the Belgian government took advantage of the undecided state of the question not to undertake, for the time being, half of the public debt of Holland, which, by the twenty-four articles, was laid upon Belgium.

Negotiations dragged on their weary length, and protocol after protocol followed in endless succession from London. In 1832, Leopold espoused Louisa, one of the daughters of the king of the French, and was not only finally recognized by the northern powers, but, by means of the intervention of England, being backed by a fleet, and by means of that of France, being backed by an army, compelled Holland to accept of terms of peace. The French troops under Gerard, unassisted by the Belgians and watched by a Prussian army stationed on the Meuse, regularly besieged and took the citadel of Antwerp, on Christmas eve, 1832, gave it up to the Belgians as pertaining to their territory, and evacuated the country. King William, however, again rejecting the twenty-four articles, all the other points, the division of the public debt, the navigation of the Scheldt, and, more than all, the future destiny of the province of Luxemburg —which formed part of the confederated states of Germany, had been declared hereditary in the house of Nassau-Orange, and which, by its geographical position and the character of its inhabitants, was more nearly connected with Belgium— remained for the present unsettled. In 1839, Holland was induced by a fresh demonstration on the part of the great powers to accept the twenty-four articles, against which Belgium in her turn protested, on the ground of the procrastination on the part of Holland having rendered her earlier accession to these terms null and void. Belgium was, however, also compelled to yield. By this fresh agreement it was settled that the western part of Luxemburg, which had in the interim fallen away from the German confederation, should be annexed to Belgium, and that Holland (and the German confederation) should receive the eastern part of Limburg in indemnity; and that Belgium, instead of taking upon herself one-half of the public debt of the Netherlands, should annually pay the sum of five million Dutch guldens toward defraying the interest of that debt.

The period of the independence of Belgium, brief as it was, was made use of, particularly under the Nothomb ministry, for the development of great industrial activity, and, more especially, for the creation of a system of railroads, until now without its parallel on the continent. Unfortunately but little was done in favor of the interests of Germany. The French language had already become so prevalent throughout Belgium that, in 1840, the provincial councillors of Ghent were constrained to pass a resolution to the effect that the offices dependent upon them should, at all events, solely be intrusted to persons acquainted with the

Flemish dialect, and that their rescripts should be drawn up in that language.—Holland immensely increased her public debt in consequence of her extraordinary exertions. In 1841, the king, William I., voluntarily abdicated the throne and retired into private life, in the enjoyment of an enormous revenue, with a Catholic countess whom he had wedded. He was succeeded by his son, William II.

CCLXVIII. *The Swiss Revolution*

THE restoration of 1814 had replaced the ancient aristocracy more or less on their former footing throughout Switzerland. In this country the greatest tranquillity prevailed; the oppression of the aristocracy was felt, but not so heavily as to be insupportable. Many benefits, as, for instance, the draining of the swampy Linththal by Escher of Zurich, were, moreover, conferred upon the country. Mercenaries were also continually furnished to the king of France, to the pope, and, for some time, to the king of the Netherlands. France, nevertheless, imposed such heavy commercial duties that several of the cantons leagued together for the purpose of taking reprisals. This misunderstanding between Switzerland and France unfortunately did not teach wisdom to the states belonging to the German confederation, and the Rhine was also barricaded with custom-houses, those graves of commerce. The Jesuits settled at Freiburg in the Uechtland, where they founded a large seminary and whence they finally succeeded in expelling Peter Girard, a man of high merit, noted for the liberality of his views on education.[1]

The Paris revolution of July also gave rise to a democratic reaction throughout Switzerland. Berne, by a circular published September 22, 1830, called upon the other

[1] In Lucerne, the disorderly trial of a numerous band of robbers, which had been headed by an extremely beautiful and talented girl, named Clara Wendel, made the more noise on account of its bringing the bandit-like murder of Keller, the aged mayor, and intrigues, in which the name of the nuncio was mixed up, before the public. 1825.

Swiss governments to suppress the revolutionary spirit by force, and, by so doing, fired the train. The government of Zurich wisely opposed the circular and made a voluntary reform. In all the other cantons popular societies sprang up, and, either by violence or by threats, subverted the ancient governments. New constitutions were everywhere granted. The immense majority of the people was in favor of reform, and the aristocracy offered but faint resistance. Little towns or villages became the centre of the movements against the capitals. Fischer, an innkeeper from Merischwanden, seized the city of Aarau; the village of Burgdorf revolutionized the canton of Berne, the village of Murten the canton of Freiburg, the village of Weinfelden the canton of Constance; this example was followed by the peasantry of Solothurn and Vaud; the government of St. Gall imitated that of Zurich.

Basel was also attempted to be revolutionized by Liestal, but the wealthy and haughty citizens, principally at the instigation of the family of Wieland, made head against the peasantry, who were led by one Gutzwyler. The contest that had taken place in Belgium was here reacted on a smaller scale. A dispute concerning privileges commencing between the citizens and the peasantry, bloody excesses ensued and a complete separation was the result. The peasantry, superior in number, asserted their right to send a greater number of deputies to the great council than the cities, and the latter, dreading the danger to which their civic interests would be thereby exposed, obstinately refused to comply. Party rage ran high; the Baselese insulted some of the deputies sent by the peasantry, and the latter, in retaliation, began to blockade the town. Colonel Wieland made some sallies; the federal diet interfered, and the peasantry, being dispersed by the federal troops, revenged themselves during their retreat by plundering the vale of Reigoldswyler, which had remained true to Basel. In Schwyz, the Old-Schwyzers and the inhabitants of the outer circles, who, although for centuries in possession of the rights of citizenship, were still regarded by the former as their vassals, also fell at variance, and the latter demanded equal rights or complete separation. In Neufchatel, Bourguin attempted a revolution against the Prussian party and took the city, but succumbed to the vigorous measures adopted by General Pfuel, 1831.

The conduct of the federal diet, which followed in the footsteps of European policy, and which, by winking at the opposing party and checking that in favor of progression, sought to preserve the balance, but served to increase party spirit. In September, 1831, the Radicals founded, at Langenthal, the Schutzverein or protective union, which embraced all the liberal clubs throughout Switzerland and was intended to counteract the impending aristocratic counter-revolution. Men like Schnell of Berne, Troxler the philosopher, etc., stood at its head. They demanded the abolition of the constitution of 1815 as too aristocratic and federal, and the foundation of a new one in a democratic and independent sense for the increase of the external power and unity of Switzerland, and for her internal security from petty aristocratic and local views and intrigues. In March, 1832, Lucerne, Zurich, Berne, Solothurn, St. Gall, Aargau, and Constance formed a Concordat for the mutual maintenance of their democratic constitutions until the completion of the revisal of the confederation. The aristocratic party, Schwyz, Uri, Unterwalden (actuated by ancient pride and led by the clergy), Basel, and Neufchatel meanwhile formed the Sarner confederation. In August, the deposed Bernese aristocracy, headed by Major Fischer, made a futile attempt to produce a counter-revolution. In the federal diet, the envoys of the Concordat and the threatening language of the clubs compelled the members to bring a new federal constitution under deliberation, but opinions were too divided, and the constitution projected in 1833 fell to the ground for want of sufficient support. At the moment of this defeat of the liberal party, Alt-Schwyz, led by Abyberg, took up arms, took possession of Küssnacht, and threatened the Concordat, the Baselese at the same time taking the field with one thousand two hundred men and fourteen pieces of ordnance. The people were, however, inimical to their cause; Abyberg fled; the Baselese were encountered by the peasantry in the Hartwald and repulsed with considerable loss. The federal diet demonstrated the greatest energy in order to prevent the Concordat and the Schutzverein from acting in its stead. Schwyz and Basel were occupied with soldiery; the former was compelled to accept a new constitution drawn up with a view of pacifying both parties, the latter to accede to a complete separation between the town and country. The Sarner confederation was dissolved, and all discontented cantons were compelled, under pain of the infliction of martial law, to send envoys to the federal diet. Intrigues, having for object the alienation of the city of Basel, of Neufchatel, and Valais from the confederation, were discovered and frustrated by the diet, not without the approbation of France, the Valais and the road over the Simplon being thereby prevented from falling beneath the influence of Austria.

In 1833, five hundred Polish refugees, suspected of supporting the Frankfort attempt in Germany, quitted France for Switzerland, and soon afterward unsuccessfully invaded Savoy in conjunction with some Italian refugees. Crowds of refugees from every quarter joined them and formed a central association, Young Europe, whence branched others, Young France, Young Poland, Young Germany, and Young Italy. The principal object of this association was to draw the German journeymen apprentices (Handwerksbursche) into its interests, and for this purpose a banquet was given by it to these apprentices in the Steinbrölzle near Berne. These intrigues produced serious threats on the side of the great powers, and Switzerland yielded. The greater part of the refugees were compelled to emigrate through France to England and America. Napoleon's nephew was, at a later period, also expelled Switzerland. His mother, Queen Hortense, consort to Louis, ex-king of Holland, daughter to Josephine Beauharnais, consequently both stepdaughter and sister-in-law to Napoleon, possessed the beautiful estate of Arenenberg on the Lake of Constance. On her death it was inherited by her son, Louis, who, during his residence there, occupied himself with intrigues directed against the throne of Louis Philippe. In concert with a couple of military madmen, he introduced himself into Strasburg, where, with a little hat, in imitation of that worn by Napoleon, on his head, he proclaimed himself emperor in the open streets. He was easily arrested. This act was generously viewed by Louis Philippe as that of a senseless boy, and he was restored to liberty upon condition of emigrating to America. No sooner, however, was he once more free, than, returning to Switzerland, he set fresh intrigues on foot. Louis Philippe, upon this, demanded his expulsion. Constance would willingly have extended to him the protection due to one of her citizens, but how were the claims of a Swiss citizen to be rendered compatible with those of a pretender to the throne of France? French troops already threatened the frontiers of Switzerland, where, as in 1793, the people, instead of making preparations for defence, were at strife among themselves. Louis at length voluntarily abandoned the country in 1838.

In the beginning of 1839, Dr. Strauss, who, in 1835, had, in his work entitled "The Life of Jesus," declared the Gospels a cleverly devised fable, and had, at great pains, sought to refute the historical proofs of the truth of Christianity, was, on that account, appointed, by the council of education and of government at Zurich, professor of divinity to the new Zurich academy. Burgomaster Hirzel (nicknamed "the tree of liberty" on account of his uncommon height) stood at the head of the enthusiastic government party by which this extraordinary appointment had been effected; the people, however, rose en masse, the great council was compelled to meet, and the anti-Christian party suffered a most disgraceful defeat. Strauss, who had not ventured to appear in person on the scene of action, was offered and accepted a pension. The Christian party, concentrated into a committee of faith, under the presidency of Hurliman, behaved with extreme moderation, although greatly superior in number to their opponents. The radical government, ashamed and perplexed, committed blunder after blunder, and at length threatened violence. Upon this, Hirzel, the youthful priest of Pfäffikon, rang the alarm from his parish church, and, on the 6th of September, 1839, led his parishioners into the city of Zurich. This example was imitated by another crowd of peasantry, headed by a physician named Rahn. The government troops attacked the people and killed nine men. On the fall of the tenth, Hegetschwiler, the councillor of state, a distinguished savant and physician, while attempting to restore harmony between the contending parties, the civic guard turned against the troops and dispersed them. The radical government and the Strauss faction also fled. Immense masses of peasantry from around the lake entered the city. A provisional government, headed by Hiesz and Muralt, and a fresh election, insured tranquillity.

In the canton of Schwyz, a lengthy dispute, similar to that between the Vettkoper and Schieringer in Friesland, was carried on between the Horn and Hoof-men (the wealthy in possession of cattle and the poor who only possessed a cow or two) concerning their privileges. In 1839, a violent opposition, similar in nature, was made by the people of Vaud against the oligarchical power assumed by a few families.

The closing of the monasteries in the Aargau in 1840 gave rise to a dispute of such importance as to disturb the whole of the confederation. In the Aargau the church and state had long and strenuously battled, when the monastery of Muri was suddenly invested as the seat of a conspiracy, and, on symptoms of uneasiness becoming perceptible among the Catholic population, the whole country was flooded with twenty thousand militia raised on the spur of the moment, and the closing of the monastery of Muri and of all the monasteries in the Aargau was proclaimed and carried into execution. The rest of the Catholic cantons and Rome vehemently protested against this measure, and even some of the Reformed cantons, for the sake of peace, voted at the diet for the maintenance of the monasteries: the Aargau, nevertheless, steadily refused compliance.

CCLXIX. *The Revolution in Brunswick, Saxony, Hesse, Etc.*

THE Belgian revolution spread into Germany. Liege infected her neighbor, Aix-la-Chapelle, where, on the 30th of August, 1830, the workmen belonging to the manufactories raised a senseless tumult which was a few days afterward repeated by their fellow-workmen at Elberfeld, Wetzlar, and even by the populace of Berlin and Breslau, but which solely took a serious character in Brunswick, Saxony, Hanover and Hesse.

Charles, duke of Brunswick, was at Paris, squandering the revenue derived from his territories, on the outburst of the July revolution, which drove him back to his native country, where he behaved with increased insolence. His obstinate refusal to abolish the heavy taxes, to refrain from disgraceful sales, to recommence the erection of public buildings, and to recognize the provincial Estates, added to his threat to fire upon the people and his boast that he knew how to defend his throne better than Charles X. of France, so maddened the excitable blood of his subjects that, after throwing stones at the duke's carriage and at an actress on whom he publicly bestowed his favors, they stormed his palace and set fire to it over his head, September 7, 1830. Charles escaped through the garden. His brother, William, supported by Hanover and Prussia, replaced him, recognized the provincial Estates, granted a new constitution, built a new palace, and re-established tranquillity. The conduct of the expelled duke, who, from his asylum in the Harzgebirge, made a futile attempt to regain possession of Brunswick by means of popular agitation and by the proclamation of democratical opinions, added to the contempt with which he treated the admonitions of his superiors, induced the federal diet to recognize his brother's authority. The ex-duke has, since this period, wandered over England, France, and Spain, sometimes engaged in intrigues with Carlists, at others with republicans. In 1836, he accompanied a celebrated female aeronaut in one of her excursions from London. The balloon accidentally upset and the duke and his companion fell to the ground. He was, however, as in his other adventures, more frightened than hurt.

In Saxony, the progress of enlightenment had long rendered the people sensible of the errors committed by the old and etiquettish aristocracy of the court and diet. As early as 1829, all the grievances had been recapitulated in an anonymous printed address, and, in the beginning of 1830, on the venerable king, Antony (brother to Frederick Augustus, deceased 1827), declaring invalid the settlement of his affairs by the Estates, which evinced a more liberal spirit than they had hitherto done, and on the prohibition of the festivities on the 25th of June, the anniversary of the Augsburg Confession, by the town council of Dresden and by the government commissioner of the university of Leipzig from devotion to the Catholic court, a popular tumult ensued in both cities, which was quelled but to be, a few weeks later, after the revolution of July, more disastrously renewed. The tumult commenced at Leipzig on the 2d of September and lasted several days, and, during the night of the 9th, Dresden was stormed from without by two immense crowds of populace, by whom the police buildings and the town-house were ransacked and set on fire. Disturbances of a similar nature broke out at Chemnitz and Bautzen. The king, upon this, nominated his nephew, Prince Frederick, who was greatly beloved by the people, co-regent; the civic guard restored tranquillity, the most crying abuses, particularly those in the city administration, were abolished, and the constitution was revised. The popular minister, Lindenau, replaced Einsiedel, who had excited universal detestation.

In the electorate of Hesse, the period of terror occasioned by the threatening letters addressed to the elector was succeeded by the agitation characteristic of the times. On the 6th of September, 1830, a tumultuous rising took place at Cassel; on the 24th, the people of Hanau destroyed every custom-house stationed on the frontier. The public was so unanimous and decided in opinion that the elector not only agreed to abolish the abuses, to convoke the Estates, and to grant a new constitution, but even placed the reins of government provisionally in the hands of his son, Prince William, in order to follow the Countess Reichenbach, who had been driven from Cassel by the insults of the populace. Prince William was, however, as little inclined as his father to make concessions; and violent collisions speedily ensued. He wedded Madame Lehmann, the wife of a Prussian officer, under the name of the Countess von Schaumburg, and closed the theatre against his mother, the electress, for refusing to place herself at her side in public. The citizens sided with the electress, and when, after some time had elapsed, she again ventured to visit the theatre, the doors were no longer closed against her, and, on her entrance, she found the house completely filled. On the close of the evening's entertainment, however, while the audience were peaceably dispersing, they were charged by a troop of cavalry, who cut down the defenceless multitude without distinction of age or sex, December 7, 1830. The Estates, headed by Professor Jordan, vainly demanded redress; Giesler, the head of the police, was alone designated as the criminal; the scrutiny was drawn to an interminable length and produced no other result than Giesler's decoration with an order by the prince.

In Hesse-Darmstadt, where the poll-tax amounted to 6fls. 12krs. (10s. 4d.) a head, the Estates ventured, even prior to the revolution of July, to refuse to vote 2,000,000fls. (£166,666 13s. 4d.) to the new grandduke, Louis II. (who had just succeeded his aged father, the patron of the arts), for the defrayment of debts contracted by him before his accession to the ducal chair. In September, the peasantry of Upper Hesse rose en masse on account of the imposition of the sum of 100,000fls. (£8,333 6s. 8d.) upon the poverty-stricken communes in order to meet the outlay occasioned by the festivities given in the grandduke's honor on his route through the country; the burdens laid upon the peasantry in the mediatized principalities, more particularly in that of Ysenburg, had also become unbearable. The insurgents took Budingen by storm and were guilty of some excesses toward the public officers and the foresters, but deprived no one of life. Ere long convinced of their utter impotence, they dispersed before the arrival of Prince Emilius at the head of a body of military, who, blinded by rage, unfortunately killed a number of persons in the village of Södel, whom they mistook for insurgents owing to the circumstance of their being armed, but who had in reality been assembled by a forester for the purpose of keeping the insurgents in check.

In this month, September, 1830, popular disturbances, but of minor import, broke out also at Jena and Kahla, Altenburg, and Gera.

In Hanover, the first symptoms of revolution appeared in January, 1831. Dr. König was at that time at the head of the university of Osterode, Dr. Rauschenplatt of that of Göttingen.[1] The abolition of the glaring ancient abuses and the removal of the minister, Count Munster, the sole object of whose policy appeared to be the eternalization of every administrative and juridical antiquity in the state, were demanded. The petty insurrections were quelled by the military. König was taken prisoner; most of the other demagogues escaped to France. The Duke of Cambridge, the king's brother, mediated. Count Munster was dismissed, and Hanover received a new and more liberal constitution.

While these events were passing in Germany, the Poles carried on a contest against the whole power of Russia as glorious and as unfortunate as their former one under their leader, Kosciuszko. Louis Philippe, king of the French, in

---

[1] Also the unfortunate Dr. Plath, to whom science is indebted for an excellent historical work upon China. He became implicated in this affair and remained in confinement until 1836, when he was sentenced to fifteen years' further imprisonment.

the hope of gaining favor with the Northern powers by the abandonment of the Polish cause, dealt not a stroke in their aid. Austria, notwithstanding her natural rivalry to Russia, beheld the Polish revolution merely through the veil of legitimacy and refused her aid to rebels. A Hungarian address in favor of Poland produced no result. Prussia was closely united by family ties to Russia. The Poles were consequently left without external aid, and their spirit was internally damped by diplomatic arts. Aid was promised by France, if they would wait. They accordingly waited: and in the interim, after the failure of Diebitsch's attempt upon Warsaw and his sudden death, Paskewitch, the Russian general, unexpectedly crossed the Vistula close to the Prussian fortress of Thorn and seized the city of Warsaw while each party was still in a state of indecision. Immense masses of fugitive Polish soldiery sought shelter in Austria and Prussia. The officers and a few thousand private soldiers were permitted to pass onward to France: they found a warm welcome in Southern Germany, whence they had during the campaign been supplied with surgeons and every necessary for the supply of the hospitals. The rest were compelled to return to Russia.

The Russian troops drawn from the distant provinces, the same that had been employed in the war with Persia, overran Poland as far as the Prussian frontier, bringing with them a fearful pestilence, Asiatic cholera. This dire malady, which had, since 1817, crept steadily onward from the banks of the Ganges, reached Russia in 1830, and, in the autumn of 1831, spread across the frontiers of Germany. It chiefly visited populous cities and generally spared districts less densely populated, passing from one great city to another whither infection could not have been communicated. *Cordons de sante* and quarantine regulations were of no avail. The pestilence appeared to spread like miasma through the air and to kindle like gas wherever the assemblage of numbers disposed the atmosphere to its reception. The patients were seized with vomiting and diarrhœa, accompanied with violent convulsions, and often expired instantaneously or after an agony of a few hours' duration. Medicinal art was powerless against this disease, and, as in the 14th century, the ignorant populace ascribed its prevalence to poison. Suspicion fell this time upon the physicians and the public authorities and spread in the most incredible manner from St. Petersburg to Paris. The idea that the physicians had been charged to poison the people *en masse* occasioned dreadful tumults, in which numbers of physicians fell victims and every drug used in medicine was destroyed as poisonous. Similar scenes occurred in Russia and in Hungary. In the latter country a great insurrection of the peasants took place, in August, 1831, in which not only the physicians, but also numbers of the nobility and public officers who had provided themselves with drugs fell victims, and the most inhuman atrocities were perpetrated. In Vienna, where the cholera raged with extreme virulence, the people behaved more reasonably.

In Prussia, the cholera occasioned several disturbances at Kœnigsberg, Stettin, and Breslau. At Kœnigsberg the movement was not occasioned by the disease being attributed to poison. The strict quarantine regulations enforced by the government had produced a complete commercial stagnation, notwithstanding which permission had been given to the Russian troops, when hard pushed by the insurgent Poles, to provide themselves with provisions and ammunition from Prussia, so that not only Russian agents and commissaries, but whole convoys from Russia crossed the Prussian frontier. The appearance of cholera was ascribed to this circumstance, and the public discontent was evinced both by a popular outbreak and in an address from the chief magistrate of Kœnigsberg to the throne. The Prussian army, under the command of Field-Marshal Gneisenau, stationed in Posen for the purpose of watching the movements of the Poles, was also attacked by the cholera, to which the field-marshal fell victim. It speedily reached Berlin, spread through the north of Germany to France, England, and North America, returned thence to the south of Europe, and, in 1836, crept steadily on from Italy through the Tyrol to Bavaria.

The veil had been torn from many an old and deep-rooted evil by the disturbances of 1830. The press now emulated the provincial diets and some of the governments that sought to meet the demands of the age in exposing to public view all the political wants of Germany. Party spirit, however, still ran too high, and the moderate constitutionalists, who aimed at the gradual introduction of reforms by legal means, found themselves ere long outflanked by two extreme parties. While Gentz at Vienna, Jarcke at Berlin, etc., refused to make the slightest concession and in that spirit conducted the press, Rotteck's petty constitutional reforms in Baden were treated with contempt by Wirth and Siebenpfeiffer, by whom a German republic was with tolerable publicity proclaimed in Rhenish Bavaria. Nor were attempts at mediation wanting. In Darmstadt, Schulz proposed the retention of the present distribution of the states of Germany and the association of a second chamber, composed of deputies elected by the people from every part of the German confederation, with the federal assembly at Frankfort.

The Tribune, edited by Dr. Wirth, and the Westboten, edited by Dr. Siebenpfeiffer, were prohibited by the federal diet, March 2, 1832. Schuler, Savoie, and Geib opposed this measure by the foundation of a club in Rhenish Bavaria for the promotion of liberty of the press, ramifications of which were intended by the founders to be extended throughout Germany. The approaching celebration of the festival in commemoration of the Bavarian constitution afforded the malcontents a long-wished-for opportunity for the convocation of a monster meeting at the ancient castle of Hambach, on the 27th of May. Although the black, red and gold flag waved on this occasion high above the rest, the tendency to French liberalism predominated over that to German patriotism. Numbers of French being also present, Dr. Wirth deemed himself called upon to observe that the festival they had met to celebrate was intrinsically German, that he despised liberty as a French boon, and that the patriot's first thoughts were for his country, his second for liberty. These observations greatly displeased the numerous advocates for French republicanism among his audience, and one Rey, a Strasburg citizen, read him a severe lecture in the Mayence style of 1793.[1] There were also a number of Poles present, toward whom no demonstrations of jealousy were evinced. This meeting peaceably dissolved, but no means were for the future neglected for the purpose of crushing the spirit manifested by it. Marshal Wrede occupied Spires, Landau, Neustadt, etc., with Bavarian troops; the clubs for the promotion of liberty of the press were strictly prohibited, their original founders, as well as the orators of Hambach and the boldest of the newspaper editors, were either arrested or compelled to quit the country. Siebenpfeiffer took refuge in Switzerland; Wirth might have effected his escape, but refused. Some provocations in Neustadt, on the anniversary of the Hambach festival in 1833, were brought by the military to a tragical close. Some newspaper editors, printers, etc., were also arrested at Munich, Wurzburg, Augsburg, etc. The most celebrated among the accused was Professor Behr, court-councillor of Wurzburg, the burgomaster and former deputy of that city, who at the time of the meeting at Hambach made a public speech at Gaibach. On account of the revolutionary tendency manifested in it he was arrested, and, in 1836, sentenced to ask pardon on his knees before the

---

[1] All national distinctions must cease and be fused in universal liberty and equality; this was the sole aim of the noble French people, and for this cause should we meet them with a fraternal embrace, etc. Paul Pfizer well observed in a pamphlet on German liberalism, published at that period, "What epithet would the majority of the French people bestow upon a liberty which a part of their nation would purchase by placing themselves beneath the protection of a foreign and superior power, called to their aid against their fellow-citizens? If the cause of German liberalism is to remain pure and unspotted, we must not, like Coriolanus, arm the foreign foe against our country. The egotistical tendency of the age is, unhappily, too much inclined (by a coalition with France) to prefer personal liberty and independence to the liberty and independence (thereby infallibly forfeited) of the whole community. The supposed fellowship with France would be subjection to her. France will support the German liberals as Richelieu did the German Protestants."

king's portrait and to imprisonment, a punishment to which the greater part of the political offenders were condemned.

The federal diet had for some time been occupied with measures for the internal tranquillity of Germany. The Hambach festival both brought them to a conclusion and increased their severity. Under the date of the 28th of June, 1832, the resolutions of the federal assembly, by which first of all the provincial Estates, then the popular clubs, and finally the press, were to be deprived of every means of opposing in any the slightest degree the joint will of the princes, were published. The governments were bound not to tolerate within their jurisdiction aught contrary to the resolutions passed by the federal assembly, and to call the whole power of the confederation to their aid if unable to enforce obedience; nay, in cases of urgency, the confederation reserved to itself the right of armed intervention, undemanded by the governments. Taxes, to meet the expenses of the confederation, were to be voted submissively by the provincial Estates. Finally, all popular associations and assemblies were also prohibited, and all newspapers, still remaining, of a liberal tendency, were suppressed.

The youthful revolutionists, prinicipally students, assembled secretly at Frankfort on the Maine, during the night of the 3d of April, 1833, attacked the town-watch for the purpose of liberating some political prisoners, and possibly intended to have carried the federal assembly by a *coup-de-main* had they not been dispersed. These excesses had merely the effect of increasing the severity of the scrutiny and of crowding the prisons with suspected persons.

CCLX X.—*The Struggles of the Provincial Diets*

THE Estates of the different constitutional states sought for constitutional reform by legal means and separated themselves from the revolutionists. But, during periods of great political agitation, it is difficult to draw a distinctive line, and any opposition, however moderate, appears as dangerous as the most intemperate rebellion. It was, consequently, impossible for the governments and the Estates to come to an understanding during these stormy times. The result of the deliberations, whenever the opposition was in the majority, was protestations on both sides in defence of right; and, whenever the opposition was or fell in the minority, the chambers were the mere echo of the minister.

In Bavaria, in 1831, the second chamber raised a violent storm against the minister, von Schenk, principally on account of the restoration of some monasteries and of the enormous expense attending the erection of the splendid public buildings at Munich. A law of censorship had, moreover, been published, and a number of civil officers elected by the people been refused permission to take their seats in the chamber. Schwindel, von Closen, Cullmann, Seyffert, etc., were the leaders of the opposition. Schenk resigned office; the law of censorship was repealed, and the Estates struck two millions from the civil list. The first chamber, however, refused its assent to these resolutions, the law of censorship was retained, and the saving in the expenditure of the crown was reduced to an extremely insignificant amount. In the autumn of 1832, Prince Otto, the king's second son, was, with the consent of the sultan, elected king of Greece by the great maritime powers intrusted with the decision of the Greek question, and Count Armansperg, formerly minister of Bavaria, was placed at the head of the regency during the minority of the youthful monarch. Steps having to be taken for the levy of troops for the Greek service, some regiments were sent into Greece in order to carry the new regulations into effect. The Bavarian chambers were at a later period almost entirely purged from the opposition and granted every demand made by the government. The appearance of the Bavarians in ancient Greece forms one of the most interesting episodes in modern history. The jealousy of the great powers explains the election of a sovereign independent of them all: the noble sympathy displayed for the Grecian cause by King Louis, who, shortly after the congress of Verona, sent considerable sums of money and Colonel von Heideck to the aid of the Greeks, and, it may be, also the wish to bring the first among the second-rate powers of Germany into closer connection with the common interests of the first-rate powers, more particularly explains that of the youthful Otto.[1] The task of organizing a nation, noble, indeed, but debased by long slavery and still reeking with the blood of late rebellion, under the influence of a powerful and mutually jealous diplomacy, on a European and German footing, was, however, extremely difficult. Hence the opposite views entertained by the regency, the resignation of the councillors of state, von Maurer and von Abel, who were more inclined to administrate, and the retention of office by Count Armansperg, who was more inclined to diplomatize. Hence the ceaseless intrigues of party, the daily increasing contumacy, and the revolts, sometimes quenched in blood, of the wild mountain tribes and ancient robber-chiefs, to whom European institutions were still an insupportable yoke. King Otto received, on his accession to the throne, in 1835, a visit

---

[1] Thiersch, the Bavarian court-councillor, one of the most distinguished connoisseurs of Grecian antiquity, who visited Greece shortly after Heideck and before the arrival of the king, was received by the modern Greeks with touching demonstrations of delight. No nation has so deeply studied, so deeply become imbued with Grecian lore, as that of Germany, and the close connection formed, on the accession of the Bavarian Otto to the throne of Greece, between her sons and the children of that classic land, justifies the proudest expectations.

from his royal parent; and, in the ensuing year, conducted the Princess of Oldenburg to Athens as his bride.

In Wurtemberg, the chambers first met in 1833, and were, two months later, again dissolved on account of the refusal of the second chamber to reject "with indignation" Pfizer's protestation against the resolutions of the confederation. In the newly-elected second chamber, the opposition, at whose head stood the celebrated poet, Uhland, brought forward numerous propositions for reform, but remained in the minority, and it was not until the new diet, held in 1836, that the aristocratic first chamber was induced to diminish socage service and other feudal dues twenty-two and one-half per cent in amount. The literary piracy that had hitherto continued to exist solely in Wurtemberg was also provisionally abolished, the system of national education was improved, and several other useful projects were carried into execution or prepared. A new criminal code, published in 1838, again bore traces of political caution. The old opposition lost power.

In Baden, the venerable grandduke, Louis, expired in 1830, and was succeeded by Leopold, a descendant of the collateral branch of the counts of Hochberg. Bavaria had, at an earlier period, stipulated, in case of the extinction of the elder and legitimate line, for the restoration of the Pfalz (Heidelberg and Mannheim), which had, in 1816, been secured to her by a treaty with Austria. The grandduke, Louis, had protested against this measure and had, in 1817, declared Baden indivisible. Bavaria finally relinquished her claims on the payment of two million florins (£166,666 13*s.* 4*d.*) and the cession of the bailiwick of Steinfeld, to which Austria moreover added the county of Geroldseck. The new grandduke, who was surnamed "the citizen's friend," behaved with extreme liberality and consequently went hand in hand with the first chamber, of which Wessenberg and Prince von Furstenberg were active members, and with the second, at the head of which stood Professors Rotteck, Welcker, and von Itzstein. Rotteck proposed and carried through the abolition of capital punishment as alone worthy of feudal times, and, on Welcker's motion, censorship was abolished and a law for the press was passed. The federal assembly, however, speedily checked these reforms. The grandduke was compelled to repeal the law for the press, the Freiburg university was for some time closed, Professors Rotteck and Welcker were suspended, and their newspaper, the "Freisinnige" or Liberal, was suppressed in 1832. Rotteck was, notwithstanding, at feud with the Hambachers, and had raised the Baden flag above that of Germany at a national fete at Badenweiler. This extremely popular deputy, who had been presented with thirteen silver cups in testimony of the affection with which he was regarded by the people, afterward protested against the resolutions of the confederation, but his motion was violently suppressed by the minister, Winter. The Baden chamber, nevertheless, still retained a good deal of energy, and, after the death of Rotteck, in 1841, a violent contest was carried on concerning the rights of election.

In Hesse-Darmstadt, the Estates again met in 1832; the liberal majority in the second chamber, led by von Gagern, E. E. Hoffmann, Hallwachs, etc., protested against the resolutions of the confederation, and the chamber was dissolved. A fresh election took place, notwithstanding which the chamber was again dissolved in 1834, on account of the government being charged with party spirit by von Gagern and the refusal of the chamber to call him to order. The people afterward elected a majority of submissive members.

In Hesse-Cassel the popular demonstrations were instantly followed by the convocation of the Estates and the proposal of a new and stipulated constitution, which received the sanction of the chambers as early as January, 1831; but, amid the continual disturbances, and on account of the disinclination of the prince co-regent to the liberal reforms, the chamber, of which the talented professor, Jordan of Marburg, was the most distinguished member, yielded, notwithstanding its perseverance, after two rapidly successive dissolutions, in 1832 and 1833, to the influence of the (once liberal) minister, Hassenpflug, and Jordan quitted the scene of contest. Hassenpflug's tyrannical behavior and the lapse of Hesse-Rotenburg (the mediatized collateral line, which became extinct with the Landgrave Victor in 1834), the revenues of which were appropriated as personal property by the prince elector instead of being declared state property, fed the opposition in the chambers, which was, notwithstanding the menaces of the prince elector, carried on until 1838. Hassenpflug threw up office.

In Nassau, the duke, William, fell into a violent dispute with the Estates. The second chamber, after vainly soliciting the restitution of the rich demesnes, appropriated by the duke as private property, on the ground of their being state property, and the application of their revenue to the payment of the state debts, refused, in the autumn of 1831, to vote the taxes. The first chamber, in which the duke had the power of raising at will a majority in his favor by the creation of fresh members, protested against the conduct of the second, which in return protested against that of the first and suspended its proceedings until their constitutional rights should have received full recognition; five of the deputies, however, again protested against the suspension of the proceedings of the chamber and voted the taxes during the absence of the majority. The majority again protested, but became entangled in a political lawsuit, and Herber, the gray-headed president, was confined in the fortress of Marxburg.

In Brunswick, a good understanding prevailed between William, the new duke, and the Estates, which were, however, accused of having an aristocratic tendency by the democratic party. Their sittings continued to be held in secret.

In Saxony, the long-wished-for reforms, above all, the grant of a new constitution, were realized, owing to the influence of the popular co-regent, added to that of Lindenau, the highly-esteemed minister, and of the newly-elected Estates, in 1831. The law of censorship, nevertheless, continued to be enforced with extreme severity, which also marked the treatment of the political prisoners. Count Hohenthal and Baron Watzdorf, who seized every opportunity to put in protestations, even against the resolutions of the confederation, evinced the most liberal spirit. On the demise of the aged king, Antony, in 1835, and the accession of the co-regent, Frederick, to the throne, the political movements totally ceased.

Holstein and Schleswig had also, as early as 1823, solicited the restitution of their ancient constitutional rights, which the king, Frederick IV., delayed to grant. Lornsen, the councillor of chancery, was arrested in 1830, for attempting to agitate the people. Separate provincial diets were, notwithstanding, decreed, in 1831, for Holstein and Schleswig, although both provinces urgently demanded their union. Frederick IV. expired in 1839 and was succeeded by his cousin, Christian.

Immediately after the revolution of July, the princes of Oldenburg, Altenburg, Coburg, Meiningen, and Schwarzburg-Sondershausen made a public appeal to the confidence of their subjects, whom they called upon to lay before them their grievances, etc. Augustus, duke of Oldenburg, who had assumed the title of grandduke, proclaimed a constitution, but shortly afterward withdrew his promise and strictly forbade his subjects to annoy him by recalling it to his remembrance. The prince von Sondershausen also refused the hoped-for constitution. In Sigmaringen, Altenburg, and Meiningen the constitutional movement was, on the contrary, countenanced and encouraged by the princes. Pauline, the liberal-minded princess of Lippe-Detmold, had already drawn up a constitution for her petty territory with her own hand, when the nobility rose against it, and, aided by the federal assembly, compelled her to withdraw it.

In the autumn of 1833, the emperor of Russia held a conference with the king of Prussia at Munchen-Gratz, whither the emperor of Austria also repaired. A German ministerial congress assembled immediately afterward at Vienna, and the first of its resolutions was made public late in the autumn of 1834. It announced the establishment of a court of arbitration, empowered, as the highest court of appeal, to decide all disputes between the governments and their provincial Estates. The whole of the members of this court were to be nominated by the governments, but the disputing parties were free to select their arbitrators from among the number.

A fresh and violent constitutional battle was, notwithstanding these precautions, fought in Hanover, where Adolphus Frederick, duke of Cambridge, had, in the name of his brother, William IV., king of England, established a new constitution, which had received many ameliorations notwithstanding the inefficiency of the liberals, Christiani, Luntzel, etc., to counteract the overpowering influence of the monarchical and aristocratic party. William IV., king of England and Hanover, expired in 1837 and was succeeded on the throne of Great Britain by Victoria Alexandrina, the daughter of his younger and deceased brother, Edward, duke of Kent, and of the Princess Victoria of Saxe-Coburg; and on that of Hanover, which was solely heritable in the male line, by his second brother, Ernest, duke of Cumberland, the leader of the Tory party in England. No sooner had this new sovereign set his foot on German soil[1] than he repealed the constitution granted to Hanover in 1833 and ordained the restoration of the former one of 1819, drawn up in a less liberal but more monarchical and aristocratic spirit. Among the protestations made against this *coup d'état*, that of the seven Gottingen professors, the two brothers Grimm, to whom the German language and antiquarian research are so deeply indebted, Dahlmann, Gervinus, Ewald, Weber, and

---

[1] He did not restore the whole of the crown property that had, at an earlier period, been carried away to England. A considerable portion of the crown jewels had been taken away by George I., and when, in 1802, the French occupied Hanover, the whole of the movable crown property, even the great stud, was sent to England. On the demise of George III., the crown jewels were divided among the princes of the English house.—*Copied from the Courier of August, 1838.*

Albrecht, is most worthy of record. Their instant dismission produced an insurrection among the students, which was, after a good deal of bloodshed, quelled by the military. In the beginning of 1838, the Estates were convoked according to the articles of the constitution of 1819 for the purpose of taking a constitution, drawn up under the dictation of the king, under deliberation. Many of the towns refused to elect deputies, and some of those elected were not permitted to take their seats. The city of Osnabruck protested in the federal assembly. Notwithstanding this, the Estates meanwhile assembled, but declared themselves incompetent, regarding themselves simply in the light of an arbitrative committee, and, as such, threw out the constitution presented by the king, June, 1838. The federal assembly remained passive.[1] In 1839, Schele, the minister, finally succeeded, by means of menaces and bribery, and by arbitrarily calling into the chamber the ministerial candidates who had received the minority of votes during the elections, in collecting as many deputies devoted to his party as were requisite in order to form the chamber and to pass resolutions. The city of Hanover hereupon brought before the federal assembly a petition for redress and a list of grievances in which Schele's chamber was described as "unworthy of the name of a constitutional representative assembly, void of confidence, unpossessed of the public esteem, and unrecognized by the country." The king instantly divested Rumann, the city director, of his office, but so far yielded to the magistrate, to whom he gave audience in the palace and who was followed by crowds of the populace, as to revoke the nomination, already declared illegal, of Rumann's successor, and to promise that the matter at issue should be brought before the common tribunal instead of the council of state, July

[1] The Darmstadt government declared to the second chamber, on its bringing forward a motion for the intercession of Darmstadt with the federal assembly in favor of the legality of the ancient constitution then in force in Hanover, that the grandduke would never tolerate any co-operation on the part of the Estates with his vote in the federal assembly.

17th. Numerous other cities, corporations of landed proprietors, etc., also followed the example set by Hanover and laid their complaints before the federal assembly, which hereupon declared that, according to the laws of the confederation, it found no cause for interference, but at the same time advised the king to come to an understanding consistent with the rights of the crown and of the Estates, with the "present" Estates (unrecognized by the democratic party), concerning the form of the constitution. In the federal assembly, Wurtemberg and Bavaria, most particularly, voted in favor of the Hanoverians. Professor Ewald was appointed to the university of Tubingen; Albrecht, at a later period, to that of Leipzig; the brothers Grimm, to that of Berlin; Dahlmann, to that of Bonn. Among the assembled Estates, those of Baden, Wurtemberg, and Saxony most warmly espoused the cause of the people of Hanover, but, as was natural, without result.[1]

In 1840, the king convoked a fresh diet. The people refused to elect members, and it was solely by means of intrigue that a small number of deputies (not half the number fixed by law) were assembled, creatures of the minister, Schele, who were disowned by the people in addresses couched in the most energetic terms (the address presented by the citizens of Osnabruck was the most remarkable) and their proceedings were protested against. This petty assembly, nevertheless, took under deliberation and passed a new constitution, against which the cities and the country again protested. The king also declared his only son, George, who was afflicted with blindness, capable of governing and of succeeding to the throne.

---

[1] "This defeat is, however, not to be lamented: the battle for the separate constitutions has not been fought in vain if German nationality spring from the wreck of German separatism, if we are taught that without a liberal federal constitution liberal provincial constitutions are impossible in Germany."—*Pfizer.*

CCLXXI. *Austria and Prince Metternich*

Austria might, on the fall of Napoleon, have maintained Alsace, Lorraine, the Breisgau, and the whole of the territory of the Upper Rhine in the same manner in which Prussia had maintained that of the Lower Rhine, had she not preferred the preservation of her rule in Italy and rendered her position in Germany subordinate to her station as a European power. This policy is explained by the peculiar circumstances of the Austrian state, which had for centuries comprised within itself nations of the most distinct character, and the population of whose provinces were by far the greater part Slavonian, Hungarian, and Italian, the great minority German. By this policy she lost, as the Prussian Customs' Union has also again proved, much of her influence over Germany, while, on the other hand, she secured it the more firmly in Southern and Eastern Europe. Austria has long made a gradual and almost unperceived advance from the northwest in a southeasterly direction. In Germany she has continually lost ground. Switzerland, the Netherlands, Alsace, Lorraine, the Swabian counties, Lusatia, Silesia, have one by one been severed from her, while her non-German possessions have as continually been increased, by the addition of Hungary, Transylvania, Galicia, Dalmatia, and Upper Italy.

The contest carried on between Austria, the French Revolution, and Napoleon, has at all events left deep and still visible traces; the characters of the emperor Francis and of his chancellor of state, Prince Metternich, that perfect representative of the aristocracy of Europe, sympathize also as closely with the Austrian system as the character of the emperor Joseph was antipathetical to it. This system dates, however, earlier than those revolutionary struggles, and has already outlived at least one of its supporters.

Austria is the only great state in Europe that comprises so many diverse but well-poised nationalities within its bosom; in all the other great states, one nation bears the preponderance. To this circumstance may be ascribed her peaceful policy, every great war threatening her with revolt of some one of the foreign nations subordinate to her sceptre. To this may, moreover, be ascribed the tenacity with which she upholds the principle of legitimacy. The historical hereditary right of the reigning dynasty forms the sole but ideal tie by which the diverse and naturally inimical nations beneath her rule are linked together. For the same reason, the concentration of talent in the government contrasts, in Austria, more violently with the obscurantism of the provinces than in any other state. Not only does the overpowering intelligence of the chancery of state awe the nations beneath its rule, but the proverbial good nature and patriarchal cordiality of the imperial family win every heart. The army is a mere machine in the hands of the government; a standing army, in which the soldier serves for life or for the period of twenty years, during which he necessarily loses all sympathy with his fellow-citizens, and which is solely reintegrated from militia whom this privilege renders still more devoted to the government. The pretorian spirit usually prevalent in standing armies has been guarded against in Austria by there being no guards, and all sympathy between the military and the citizens of the various provinces whence they were drawn is at once prevented by the Hungarian troops being sent into Italy, the Italian troops into Galicia, etc., etc. The nationality of the private soldier is checked by the Germanism of the subalterns and by the Austrianism of the staff. Besides the power thus everywhere visible, there exists another partially invisible, that of the police, in connection with a censorship of the severest description, which keeps a guard over the inadvertencies of the tongue as well as over those of the press. The people are, on the other hand, closely bound up with the government and interested in the maintenance of the existing state of affairs by the paper currency, on the value of which the welfare of every subject in the state depends.

To a government thus strong in concentrated power and intelligence stands opposed the mass of nations subject to the Austrian sceptre whose natural antipathies have been artfully fostered and strengthened. In Austria the distinctions of class, characteristic of the Middle Ages, are still preserved. The aristocracy and the clergy possess an influence almost unknown in Germany, but solely over the people, not over the government. As corporative bodies they still are, as in the days of Charles VI., convoked for the purpose of holding postulate diets, whose power, with the exception of that of the Hungarian diet, is merely nominal. The nobility, even in Hungary, as everywhere else throughout the Austrian states (more particularly since the Spanish system adopted by Ferdinand II.), is split into two inimical classes, those of the higher and lower aristocracy. Even in Galicia, where the Polish nobility formed, at an earlier period and according to earlier usage, but one body, the distinction of a higher and lower class has been introduced since the occupation of that country by Austria. The high aristocracy are either bound by favors, coincident with their origin, to the court, the great majority among them consisting of families on whom nobility was conferred by Ferdinand II., or they are, if families belonging to the more powerful and more ancient national aristocracy, as, for instance, that of Esterhazy in Hungary, brought by the bestowal of fresh favors into closer affinity with the court and drawn within its sphere. The greater proportion of the aristocracy consequently reside at Vienna. The lower nobility make their way chiefly by talent and perseverance in the army and the civil offices, and are therefore naturally devoted to the government, on which all their hopes in life depend. The clergy, although permitted to retain the whole of their ancient pomp and their influence over the minds of the people, have been rendered dependent upon the government, a point easily gained, the pope being principally protected by Austria.

The care of the government for the material welfare of the people cannot be denied; it is, however, frustrated by two obstacles raised by its own system. The maintenance of the high aristocracy is, for instance, antipathetic to the welfare of the subject, and, although comfort and plenty abound in the immediate vicinity of Vienna, the population on the enormous estates of the magnates in the provinces often present a lamentable contrast. The Austrian government moreover prohibits all free intercourse with foreign parts, and the old-fashioned system of taxation, senseless as many other existing regulations, entirely puts a stop to all free trade between Hungary and Austria. Consequently, the new and grand modes of communication, the Franzen Canal, that unites the Danube and the Thiess, the Louisenstrasse, between Carlstadt and Fiume, the magnificent road to Trieste, the admirable road across the rocks of the Stilfser Jock, and, more than all, the steam navigation as far as the mouths of the Danube and the railroads, will be unavailing to scatter the blessings of commerce and industry so long as these wretched prohibitions continue to be enforced.

Austria has, in regard to her foreign policy, left the increasing influence of Russia in Poland, Persia, and Turkey unopposed, and even allowed the mouths of the Danube to be guarded by Russian fortresses, while she has, on the other hand, energetically repelled the interference of France in the affairs of Italy. The July revolution induced a popular insurrection in the dominions of the Church, and the French threw a garrison into the citadel of Ancona; the Austrians, however, instantly entered the country and enforced the restoration of the ancien régime. In Lombardy, many ameliorations were introduced and the prosperity of the country promoted by the Austrian administration, notwithstanding the national jealousy of the inhabitants. Venice, with her choked-up harbor, could, it is true, no longer compete with Trieste. The German element has gained ground in Galicia by means of the public authorities and the immigration of agriculturists and artificers. The Hungarians endeavored to render their language the common medium throughout Hungary, and to expel the German element, but their apprehension of the numerous Slavonian population of Hungary, whom religious sympathy renders subject to Russian influence, has speedily reconciled them with the Germans. Slavonism has, on the other hand, also gained ground in Bohemia.

The emperor, Francis I., expired in 1835, and was succeeded by his son, Ferdinand I., without a change taking place in the system of the government, of which Prince Metternich continued to be the directing principle.

The decease of some of the heads of foreign royal families and the marriages of their successors again placed several German princes on foreign thrones. The last of the Guelphs on the throne of Great Britain expired with William IV., whose niece and successor, Victoria Alexandrina, wedded, 1840, Albert of Saxe-Coburg, second son of Ernest, the reigning duke. That the descendant of the steadfast elector should, after such adverse fortune, be thus destined to occupy the highest position in the reformed world, is of itself remarkable. One of this prince's uncles, Leopold, is seated on the throne of Belgium, and one of his cousins, Ferdinand, on that of Portugal, in right of his consort, Donna Maria da Gloria, the daughter of Dom Pedro, king of Portugal and emperor of the Brazils, to whom, on the expulsion of the usurper, Dom Miguel, he was wedded in 1835. These princes of Coburg are remarkable for manly beauty.

The antipathy with which the new dynasty on the throne of France was generally viewed rendered Ferdinand, Duke of Orleans, Louis Philippe's eldest son, for some time an unsuccessful suitor for the hand of a German princess; he at length conducted Helena, princess of Mecklenburg-Schwerin, although against the consent of her stepfather, Paul Frederick, the reigning duke, to Paris in 1837, as future queen of the French. He was killed in 1842, by a fall from his carriage, and left two infant sons, the Count of Paris and the

Duke of Chartres. The Czarowitz, Alexander, espoused Maria, Princess of Darmstadt.

The French chambers and journals have reassumed toward Germany the tone formerly affected by Napoleon, and, with incessant cries for war, in which, in 1840, the voice of the prime minister Thiers joined, demand the restoration of the left bank of the Rhine. Thiers was, however, compelled to resign office, and the close alliance between Austria, Prussia, and the whole of the confederated princes, as well as the feeling universally displayed throughout Germany, demonstrated the energy with which an attack on the side of France would be repelled. The erection of the long-forgotten federal fortresses on the Upper Rhine was also taken at length under consideration, and it was resolved to fortify both Rastadt and Ulm without further delay.

Nor have the statesmen of France failed to threaten Germany with a Russo-Gallic alliance in the spirit of the Erfurt congress of 1808; while Russia preseveres in the prohibitory system so prejudicial to German commerce, attempts to suppress every spark of German nationality in Livonia, Courland, and Esthonia, and fosters Panslavism, or the union of all the Slavonic nations for the subjection of the world, among the Slavonian subjects of Austria in Hungaria and Bohemia. The extension of the Greek church is also connected with this idea. "The European Pentarchy," a work that attracted much attention in 1839, insolently boasts how Russia, in defiance of Austria, has seized the mouths of the Danube, has wedged herself, as it were, by means of Poland, between Austria and Prussia, in a position equally threatening to both, recommends the minor states of Germany to seek the protection of Russia, and darkly hints at the alliance between that power and France.

Nor are the prospects of Germany alone threatened by France and Russia; disturbances, like a fantastic renewal of the horrors of the Middle Age, are ready to burst forth on the other side of the Alps, as though, according to the ancient saga of Germany, the dead were about to rise in order to mingle in the last great contest between the gods and mankind.

CCLXXII. *Prussia and Rome*

WHILE Austria remains stationary, Prussia progresses. While Austria relies for support upon the aristocracy of the Estates, Prussia relies for hers upon the people, that is to say, upon the public officers taken from the mass of the population, upon the citizens emancipated by the city regulation, upon the peasantry emancipated by the abolition of servitude, of all the other agricultural imposts, and by the division of property, and upon the enrolment of both classes in the Landwehr. While Austria, in fine, renders her German policy subordinate to her European diplomacy, the influence exercised by Prussia upon Europe depends, on the contrary, solely upon that possessed by her in Germany.

Prussia's leading principle appears to be, "All for the people, nothing through the people!" Hence the greatest solicitude for the instruction of the people, whether in the meanest schools or the universities, but under strict political control, under the severest censorship; hence the emancipation of the peasantry, civic self-administration, freedom of trade, the general arming of the people, and, with all these, mere nameless provincial diets, the most complete popular liberty on the widest basis without a representation worthy of the name; hence, finally, the greatest solicitude for the promotion of trade on a grand scale, for the revival of the commerce of Germany, which has lain prostrate since the great wars of the Reformation, for the mercantile unity of Germany, while it is exactly in Prussia that political Unitarians are the most severely punished.

The greatest measures were commenced in Prussia immediately after the disaster of 1806: first, the reorganization of the army and the abolition of the privileges of the aristocracy in respect to appointments and the possession of landed property; these were, in 1808, succeeded by the celebrated civic regulation which placed the civic administration in the hands of the city deputies freely elected by the citizens; in 1810, by freedom of trade and by the foundation of the new universities of Berlin (instead of Halle), of Breslau (instead of Frankfort on the Oder), and, in 1819, of Bonn, by which means the libraries, museums, and scientific institutions of every description were centralized; in 1814, by the common duty imposed upon every individual of every class, without exception, to bear arms and to do service in the Landwehr up to his thirty-ninth year; in 1821, by the regulation for the division of communes; and, in 1822, by the extra post.

In respect to the popular representation guaranteed by the federal act, Prussia announced, on the 22d of May, 1815, her intention to form provincial diets, from among whose members the general representation or imperial diet, which was to be held at Berlin, was to be elected. When the Rhenish provinces urged the fulfilment of this promise in the Coblentz address of 1817, the reply was, "Those who admonish the king are guilty of doubting the inviolability of his word." Prussia afterward declared that the new regulations would be in readiness by the February of 1819. On the 20th of January, 1820, an edict was published by the government, the first paragraph of which fixed the public debt at $180,091,720,[1] and the second one rendered the contraction of every fresh debt dependent upon the will of the future imperial diet.[2] The definitive regulations in respect to the provincial Estates were finally published on the 5th of June, 1823, but the convocation of a general diet was passed over in silence.

The prosperity of the nations of Germany, wrecked by the great wars of the Reformation, must and will gradually return. Prussia has inherited all the claims upon, and consequently all the duties owing to Germany. Still the general position of Germany is not sufficiently favorable to

---

[1] £26,263,375 16*s.* 8*d.*

[2] The Maritime Commercial Company, meanwhile, entered into a contract.

render the renovation of her ancient Hanseatic commerce possible.[1] It is to be deplored that the attachment of the Prussian cabinet to Russian policy has not at all events modified the commercial restrictions along the whole of the eastern frontier of Prussia,[2] and that Prussia has not been able to effect more with Holland in regard to the question concerning the free navigation of the Rhine.[3] Prussia has, on the other hand, deserved the gratitude of Germany for the zeal with which she promoted the settlement of the Customs' Union, which has, at least in the interior of Germany, removed the greater part of the restrictions upon commercial intercourse, and has a tendency to spread still further. Throughout the last transactions, partly of the Customs' Union, partly of Prussia alone, with England and Holland, a vain struggle against those maritime powers is perceptible. England trades with Germany from every harbor and in every kind of commodity, while German vessels are restricted to home produce and are only free to trade with England from their own ports. Holland finds a market for her colonial wares in Germany, and, instead of taking German manufactured goods in exchange, provides herself from England, throws English goods into Germany, and, in lieu of being, as she ought to be, the great emporium of Germany, is content to remain a mere huge English factory.

---

[1] "We have long since lost all our maritime power. The only guns now fired by us at sea are as signals of distress. Who now remembers that it was the German Hansa that first made use of cannons at sea, that it was from Germans that the English learned to build men-of-war?"—*Jahn's Nationality.*

[2] Prussia, of late, greatly contributed toward the aggrandizement of the power of Russia by solemnly declaring in 1828, when Russia extended her influence over Turkey, that she would not on that account prevent Russia from asserting her "just claims," a declaration that elicited bitter complaints from the British government; and again in 1831, by countenancing the entry of the Russians into Poland, at that time in a state of insurrection.

[3] The reason of the backwardness displayed from the commencement by Prussia to act as the bulwark of Germany on the Lower Rhine is explained by Stein in his letters: "Hanoverian jealousy, by which the narrow-minded Castlereagh was guided, and, generally speaking, jealousy of the German ministerial clauses, as if the existence of a Mecklenburg were of greater importance to Germany than that of a powerful warlike population, alike famous in time of peace or war, presided over the settlement of the relation in which Belgium was to stand to Prussia."

The Hanse towns have also been converted into mercantile depots for English goods on German soil.

The misery consequent on the great wars, and the powerful reaction against Gallicism throughout Germany, once more caused despised religion to be reverenced in the age of philosophy. Prussia deemed herself called upon, as the inheritor of the Reformation brought about by Luther, as the principal Protestant power of Germany, to assume a prominent position in the religious movement of the time. Frederick William III., a sovereign distinguished for piety, appears, immediately after the great wars, to have deemed the conciliation of the various sects of Christians within his kingdom feasible. He, nevertheless, merely succeeded in effecting a union between the Lutherans and Calvinists. He also bestowed a new liturgy upon this united church, which was censured as partial, as proceeding too directly from the cabinet without being sanctioned by the concurrence of the assembled clergy and of the people. Some Lutherans, who refused compliance, were treated with extreme severity and compelled to emigrate; the utility of a union which, two centuries earlier, would have saved Germany from ruin, was, however, generally acknowledged. It nevertheless was not productive of unity in the Protestant world. In the universities and among the clergy, two parties, the Rationalists and the Supernaturalists, stood opposed to one another. The former, the disciples of the old Neologians, still followed the philosophy of Kant, merely regarded Christianity as a code of moral philosophy, denominated Christ a wise teacher, and explained away his miracles by means of physics. The latter, the followers of the old orthodox Lutherans, sought to confirm the truths of the gospel also by philosophical means, and were denominated Supernaturalists, as believers in a mystery surpassing the reasoning powers of man. The celebrated Schleiermacher of Berlin mediated for some time between both parties. But it was in Prussia more particularly that both parties stood more rigidly opposed to one another and fell into the greatest extremes.

The Rationalists were supplanted by the Pantheists, the disciples of Hegel, the Berlin philosopher, who at length formally declared war against Christianity; the Supernaturalists were here and there outdone by the Pietists, whose enthusiasm degenerated into licentiousness.[1] The king had, notwithstanding his piety, been led to believe that Hegel merely taught the students unconditioned obedience to the state, and that Pantheist was consequently permitted to spread, under the protection of Prussia, his senseless doctrine of deified humanity, the same formerly proclaimed by Anacharsis Cloots in the French Convention. When too late, the gross deception practiced by this sophist was perceived: his disciples threw off their troublesome mask, with Dr. Strauss, who had been implicated in the Zurich disturbances, at their head, openly renounced Christianity, and, at Halle, led by Ruge, the journalist, embraced the social revolutionary ideas of "Young France," to which almost the whole of the younger journalists of literary "Young Germany" acceded; nor was this Gallic reaction, this retrogression toward the philosophical ideas of the foregoing century, without its cause, German patriotism, which, from 1815 to 1819, had predominated in every university throughout Prussia, having been forcibly suppressed. Hegel, on his appearance in Berlin, was generally regarded as the man on whom the task of diverting the enthusiasm of the rising generation for Germany into another channel devolved.[2] Everything German had been treated with ridicule.[3] French fashions and French ideas had once more come into vogue.

While Protestant Germany was thus torn, weakened, and

---

[1] At Königsberg, in Prussia, a secret society was discovered which was partly composed of people of rank, who, under pretence of meeting for the exercise of religious duties, gave way to the most wanton license.

[2] The police, while attempting to lead science, was unwittingly led by it. The students were driven in crowds into Hegel's colleges, his pupils were preferred to all appointments, etc., and every measure was taken to render that otherwise almost unnoted sophist as dangerous as possible.

[3] In this the Jews essentially aided: Börne more in an anti-German, Heine more in an anti-Christian, spirit, and were highly applauded by the simple and infatuated German youth.

degraded by schism, the religious movement throughout Catholic Germany insensibly increased in strength and unity. The adverse fate of the pope had, on his deliverance from the hands of Napoleon, excited a feeling of sympathy and reverence so universal as to be participated in by even the Protestant powers of Europe. He had, as early as 1814, reinstated the Jesuits without a remonstrance on the part of the sovereign by whom they had formerly been condemned. The ancient spirit of the Romish church had revived. A new edifice was to be raised on the thick-strewn ruins of the past. In 1817, Bavaria concluded a concordat with the pope for the foundation of the archbishopric of Munich with the three bishoprics of Augsburg, Passau, and Ratisbon, and of the archbishopric of Bamberg, with the three bishoprics of Wurzburg, Eichstadt, and Spires. The king retained the right of presentation. In 1821, Prussia concluded a treaty by which the archbishopric of Cologne with the three bishoprics of Treves, Munster, and Paderborn, the archbishopric of Posen with Culm, and two independent bishoprics in Breslau and Ermeland were established. The bishoprics of Holdesheim and Osnabruck were re-established in 1824 by the concordat with Hanover. In southwestern Germany, the archbishopric of Freiburg in the Breisgau with the bishoprics of Rotenburg on the Neckar, Limburg on the Lahn, Mayence, and Fulda arose. In Switzerland there remained four bishoprics, Freiburg in the Uechtland, Solothurn, Coire, and St. Gall; in Alsace, Strasburg and Colmar. In the Netherlands, the archbishopric of Malines with the bishoprics of Ghent, Liege, and Namur. In Holland, three Jansenist bishoprics, Utrecht, Deventer, and Haarlem, are remarkable for having retained their independence of Rome.

The renovated body of the church was inspired with fresh energy. On the fall of the Jesuits, the other extreme, Illuminatism, had raised its head, but had been compelled to yield before a higher power and before the moral force of Germany. The majority of the German Catholics now clung to the idea that the regeneration of the abused and despised church was best to be attained by the practice of evangelical simplicity and morality, that Jesuitism and Illuminatism were, consequently, to be equally avoided, and the better disposed among the Protestants to be imitated. Sailer, the great teacher of the German clergy, and Wessenberg, whom Rome on this account refused to raise to the bishopric of Constance, acted upon this idea. In Silesia, a number of youthful priests, headed by Theimer, impatient for the realization of the union, apparently approaching, of this moderate party with the equally moderately disposed party among the Protestants into one great German church, took, in 1825, the bold step of renouncing celibacy. This party was however instantly suppressed by force by the king of Prussia. Theimer, in revenge, turned Jesuit and wrote against Prussia. Professors inclined to Ultramontanism were, meanwhile, installed in the universities, more particularly at Bonn, Munster and Tubingen, by the Protestant as well as the Catholic governments; by them the clerical students were industriously taught that they were not Germans but subjects of Rome, and were flattered with the hope of one day participating in the supremacy about to be regained by the pontiff. Every priest inspired with patriotic sentiments, or evincing any degree of tolerance toward his Protestant fellow citizens, was regarded as guilty of betraying the interests of the church to the state and the tenets of the only true church to heretics. Gorres, once Germany's most spirited champion against France, now appeared as the champion of Rome in Germany. The scandalous schisms in the Protestant church and the no less scandalous controversies carried on in the Protestant literary world rendered both contemptible, and, as in the commencement of the seventeenth century, appeared to offer a favorable opportunity for an attack on the part of the Catholics.

A long-forgotten point in dispute was suddenly revived. Marriages between Catholics and Protestants had hitherto been unhesitatingly sanctioned by the Catholic priesthood. The Prussian ordinance of 1803, by which the father was empowered to decide the faith in which the children were to be brought up, had, on account of its conformity with nature and reason, never been disputed. Numberless mixed marriages had taken place among all classes from the highest to the lowest without the slightest suspicion of wrong attaching thereto. A papal brief of 1830 now called to mind that the church tolerated, it was true, although she disapproved of mixed marriages, which she permitted to take place solely on condition of the children being brought up in the Catholic faith. Prussia had acted with little foresight. Instead of, in 1814, on taking possession of the Rhenish provinces and of Westphalia, concluding a treaty with the then newly-restored pope, Hardenberg had, as late as 1820, during a visit to Rome, merely entered upon a transient agreement, by which Rome was bound to no concessions. The war openly declared by Rome was now attempted to be turned aside by means of petty and secret artifices. Several bishops, in imitation of the precedent given by Count von Spiegel, the peace-loving archbishop of Cologne, secretly bound themselves to interpret the brief in the sense of the government and to adhere to the ordinance of 1803. On Spiegel's decease in 1835, his successor, the Baron Clement Augustus Droste, promised at Vischering, prior to his presentation, strictly to adhere to this secret compact; but, scarcely had he mounted the archiepiscopal seat, than his conscience forbade the fulfilment of his oath; God was to be obeyed rather than man! He prohibited the solemnization of mixed marriages within his diocese without the primary assurance of the education of the children in the Catholic faith, compelled his clergy strictly to obey the commands of Rome in points under dispute, and suppressed the Hermesian[1] doctrine in the university of Bonn. The warnings secretly given by the government proved unavailing, and he was, in consequence, unexpectedly deprived of his office in

[1] Hermes, it is true, recognized the tenets of the church, not, however, on account of their being taught by the church, but because he had arrived at similar conclusions in the course of his philosophical researches.

the November of 1837, arrested, and imprisoned in the fortress of Minden. This arbitrary measure caused great excitement among the Catholic population; and the ancient dislike of the Rhenish provinces to the rule of Prussia, and the discontent of the Westphalian nobility on account of the emancipation of the peasantry, again broke forth on this occasion. Gorres, in Munich, industriously fed the flame by means of his pamphlet, "Athanasius." Dunin, archbishop of Gnesen and bishop of Thorn, followed the example of his brother of Cologne, was openly upheld by Prussian Poland, was cited to Berlin, fled thence, was recaptured and detained for some time within the fortress of Colberg, in 1839.—The pope, Gregory XVI., solemnly declared his approbation of the conduct of these archbishops and rejected every offer of negotiation until their reinstallation in their dioceses. A crowd of hastily established journals, more especially in Bavaria, maintained their cause, and were opposed by numberless Protestant publications, which generally proved injurious to the cause they strove to uphold, being chiefly remarkable for base servility, frivolity, and infidelity.

On the demise of Frederick William III., on the 7th of June, 1840, and the succession of his son, Frederick William IV., the church question was momentarily cast into the shade by that relating to the constitution. Constitutional Germany demanded from the new sovereign the convocation of the imperial diet promised by his father. The Catholic party, however, conscious that it would merely form the minority in the diet, did not participate in the demand.[1] The constitution was solely demanded by Protestant Eastern Prussia; but the king declared, during the ceremony of fealty at Kœnigsberg, that "he would never do homage to the idea of a general popular representation and would pursue a course based upon historical progression, suitable to German nationality." The provincial Estates were shortly

---

[1] Görres even advised against it, although, in 1817, he had acted the principal part on the presentation of the Cologne address.

afterward instituted, and separate diets were opened in each of the provinces. This attracted little attention, and the dispute with the church once more became the sole subject of interest. It terminated in the complete triumph of the Catholic party. In consequence of an agreement with the pope, the brief of 1820 remained in force, Dunin was reinstated, Droste received personal satisfaction by a public royal letter and a representative in Cologne in von Geissel, hitherto bishop of Spires. The disputed election of the bishop of Treves was also decided in favor of Arnoldi, the ultramontane candidate.

Late in the autumn of 1842, the king of Prussia for the first time convoked the deputies selected from the provincial diets to Berlin. He had, but a short time before, laid the foundation-stone to the completion of the Cologne cathedral, and on that occasion, moreover, spoken words of deep import to the people, admonitory of unity to the whole of Germany.

CCLXXIII. *The Progress of Science, Art, and Practical Knowledge in Germany*

In the midst of the misery entailed by war and amid the passions roused by party strife the sciences had attained to a height hitherto unknown. The schools had never been neglected, and immense improvements, equally affecting the lowest of the popular schools and the colleges, had been constantly introduced. Pestalozzi chiefly encouraged the proper education of the lower classes and improved the method of instruction. The humanism of the learned academies (the study of the dead languages) went hand in hand with the realism of the professional institutions. The universities, although often subjected to an overrigid system of surveillance and compelled to adopt a partial, servile bias, were, nevertheless, generally free from a political tendency and incredibly promoted the study of all the sciences. The mass of celebrated savants and of their works is too great to permit of more than a sketch of the principal features of modern German science.

The study of the classics, predominant since the time of the Reformation, has been cast into the shade by the German studies, by the deeper investigation of the language, the law, the history of our forefathers and of the romantic Middle Age, by the great Catholic reaction, and, at the same time, by the immense advance made in natural history, geography, and universal history. The human mind, hitherto enclosed within a narrow sphere, has burst its trammels to revel in immeasurable space. The philosophy and empty speculations of the foregoing century have also disappeared before the mass of practical knowledge, and arrogant man, convinced by science, once more bends his reasoning faculties in humble adoration of their Creator.

The aristocracy of talent and learned professional pride have been overbalanced by a democratic press. The whole nation writes, and the individual writer is either swallowed up in the mass or gains but ephemeral fame. Every writer, almost without exception, affects a popular style. But, in this rich literary field, all springs up freely without connection or guidance. No party is concentrated or represented by any reigning journal, but each individual writes for himself, and the immense number of journals published destroy each other's efficiency. Many questions of paramount importance are consequently lost in heaps of paper, and the interest they at first excited speedily becomes weakened by endless recurrence.

Theology shared in the movement above mentioned in the church. The Rationalists were most profuse in their publications, Paulus at Heidelberg, and, more particularly, the Saxon authors, Tschirner, Bretschneider, etc. Ancient Lutheran vigor degenerated to shallow subtleties and a sort of coquettish tattling upon morality, in which Zschokke's "Hours of Devotion" carried away the palm. Neander, Gieseler, Gfrörer and others greatly promoted the study of the history of the church. The propounders of the Gospels, however, snatched them, after a lamentable fashion, out of each other's hands, now doubting the authenticity of the whole, now that of most or of some of the chapters, and were unable to agree upon the number that ought to be retained. They, at the same time, outvied one another in political servility, while the Lutherans who, true to their ancient faith, protested against the Prussian liturgy, were too few in number for remark. This frivolous class of theologians at length entirely rejected the Gospels, embraced the doctrine of Hegel and Judaism, and renounced Christianity. Still, although the Supernaturalists, the orthodox party, and the Pietists triumphantly repelled these attacks, and the majority of the elder Rationalists timidly seceded from the antichristian party, the Protestant literary world was reduced to a state of enervation and confusion, affording but too good occasion for an energetic demonstration on the part of the Catholics.

Philosophy also assumed the character of the age. Fichte of Berlin still upheld, in 1814, the passion for liberty and right in their nobler sense that had been roused by the French Revolution, but, as he went yet further than Kant in setting limits to the sources of perception and denied the existence of conscience, his system proved merely of short duration. To him succeeded Schelling, with whom the return of philosophy to religion and that of abstract studies to nature and history commenced, and in whom the renovated spirit of the nineteenth century became manifest. His pupils were partly natural philosophers, who, like Oken, sought to comprehend all nature, her breathing unity, her hidden mysteries, in religion; partly mystics, who, like Eschenmaier, Schubert, Steffens, in a Protestant spirit, or, like Gorres and Baader, in a Catholic one, sought also to comprehend everything bearing reference to both nature and history in religion. It was a revival of the ancient mysticism of Hugo de St. Victoire, of Honorius, and of Rupert in another and a scientific age; nor was it unopposed: in the place of the foreign scholasticism formerly so repugnant to its doctrines, those of Schelling were opposed by a reaction of the superficial mock-enlightenment and sophistical scepticism predominant in the foregoing century, more particularly of the sympathy with France, which had been rendered more than ever powerful in Germany by the forcible suppression of patriotism. Abstract philosophy, despising nature and history, mocking Christianity, once more revived and set itself up as an absolute principle in Hegel. None of the other philosophers attained the notoriety gained by Schelling and Hegel, the representatives of the antitheses of the age.

An incredible advance, of which we shall merely record the most important facts, took place in the study of the physical sciences. Three new planets were discovered, Pallas, in 1802, and Vesta, in 1807, by Olbers; Juno, in 1824, by Harding. Enke and Biela first fixed the regular return and brief revolution of the two comets named after them. Schröter and Mädler minutely examined the moon and planets; Struve, the fixed stars. Fraunhofer improved the telescope. Chladni first investigated the nature of fiery meteors and brought the study of acoustics to perfection. Alexander von Humboldt immensely promoted the observation of the changes of the atmosphere and the general knowledge of the nature of the earth. Werner and Leopold von Buch also distinguished themselves among the investigators of the construction of the earth and mountains. Scheele, Gmelin, Liebig, etc., were noted chemists. Oken, upon the whole, chiefly promoted the study of natural history, and numberless researches were made separately in mineralogy, the study of fossils, botany, and zoölogy by the most celebrated scientific men of the day. While the travellers visited every quarter of the globe in search of plants and animals as yet unknown and regulated them by classes, other men of science were engaged at home in the investigation of their internal construction, their uses and habits, in which they were greatly assisted by the improved microscope, by means of which Ehrenberg discovered a completely new class of animalculæ. The discoveries of science were also zealously applied for practical uses. Agriculture, cattle-breeding, manufactures received a fresh impulse and immense improvements as knowledge advanced. Commerce by water and by land experienced a thorough revolution on the discovery of the properties of steam, by the use of steamers and railroads.—Medical science also progressed, notwithstanding the number of contradictory and extravagant theories. The medical practitioners of Germany took precedence throughout Europe. Animal magnetism was practiced by Eschenmaier, Kieser, and Justin Kerner, by means of whose female seer, von Prevorst, the seeing of visions and the belief in ghosts were once more brought forward. Hahnemann excited the greatest opposition by his system of homœopathy, which cured diseases by the administration of homogeneous substances in the minutest doses. He was superseded by the cold-water cure. During the last twenty years the naturalists and medical men of Germany have held an annual meeting in one or other of their native cities.

The philologists and savants have for some years past also been in the habit of holding a similar meeting. The classics no longer form the predominant study among philologists. Even literati, whose tastes, like that of Creuzer, are decidedly classic, have acknowledged that the knowledge of the Oriental tongues is requisite for the attainment of a thorough acquaintance with classic antiquity. A great school for the study of the Eastern languages has been especially established under the precedence of the brothers Schlegel, Bopp, and others. The study of the ancient language of Germany and of her venerable monuments has, finally, been promoted by Jacob Grimm and by his widely diffused school.

The study of history became more profound and was extended over a wider field. A mass of archives hitherto secret were rendered public and spread new light on many of the remarkable characters and events in the history of Germany. Historians also learned to compile with less party spirit and on more solid grounds. History, at first compiled in a Protestant spirit, afterward inclined as partially to Catholicism, and the majority of the higher order of historical writers were consequently rendered the more careful in their search after truth. Among the universal historians, Rotteck gained the greatest popularity on account of the extreme liberality of his opinions, and Heeren and Schlosser acquired great note for depth of learning. Von Hammer, who rendered us acquainted with the history of the Mahometan East, takes precedence among the historical writers upon foreign nations. Niebuhr's Roman History, Wilken's History of the Crusades, Leo's History of Italy, Ranke's History of the Popes, etc., have attained well-merited fame.—The history of Germany as a whole, which Germany neither was nor is, was little studied, but an immense mass of facts connected with or referring to Germany was furnished by the numberless and excellent single histories and biographies that poured through the press. All the more ancient collections of script. rerum were, according to the plan of Stein, the celebrated Prussian minister, to be surpassed by a critical work on the sources of German history, conducted by Pertz, which could, however, be but slowly carried out. Grimm, Mone, and Barth threw immense light upon German heathen antiquity, Zeusz upon the genealogy of nations. The best account of the Ostrogoths was written by Manso, of the Visigoths by Aschbach, of the Anglo-Saxons by Lappenberg, of the more ancient Franks by Mannert, Pertz, and Löbell, of Charlemagne by Diebold and Ideler, of Louis the Pious by Funk, of the Saxon emperors by Ranke and his friends, Wachter and Leutsch, of the Salic emperors by Stenzel, of the German popes of those times by Höfler, of the Hohenstaufen by Raumer, Kortum, and Hurter, of the emperor Richard by Gebauer, of Henry VII. of Luxemburg by Barthold, of King John by Lenz, of Charles IV. by Pelzel and Schottky, of Wenzel by Pelzel, of Sigismund by Aschbach, of the Habsburgs by Kurz, Prince Lichnowsky, and Hormayr, of Louis the Bavarian by Mannert, of Ferdinand I. by Buchholz, of the Reformation by C. A. Menzel and Ranke, of the Peasant War by Sartorius, Oechsle, and Bensen, of the Thirty Years' War by Barthold, of Gustavus Adolphus by Gfrörer, of Wallenstein by Förster, of Bernhard of Weimar by Röse, of George of Lüneburg by von der Decken. Of the ensuing period by Förster and Guhrauer, of the Eighteenth Century by Schlosser, of the Wars with France by Clausewitz, of Modern Times by Hormayr.

Coxe, Schneller, Mailàth, Chmel, and Gervay also wrote histories of Austria, Schottky and Palacky of Bohemia, Beda, Weber, and Hormayr of the Tyrol, Voigt of the Teutonic Order, Manso, Stenzel, Förster, Dohm, Massenbach, Colln, Preusz, etc., of the Kingdom of Prussia, Stenzel of Anhalt, Kobbe of Lauenburg, Lützow of Mecklenburg, Barthold of Pomerania, Kobbe of Holstein, Wimpfen of Schleswig, Sartorius and Lappenberg of the Hansa, Hanssen of the Ditmarses, Spittler, Havemann, and Strombeck of Brunswick and Hanover, van Kampen of Holland, Warnkonig of Flanders, Rommel of Hesse, Lang of Eastern Franconia, Wachter and Langenn of Thuringia and Saxony, Lang, Wolf, Mannert, Zschokke, Volderndorf of Bavaria, Pfister, Pfaff, and Stälin of Swabia, Glutz-Blotzheim, Hottinger, Meyer von Knonau, Zschokke, Haller, Schuler, etc., of Switzerland. The most remarkable among the histories of celebrated cities are those of St. Gall by Arx, of Vienna by Mailath, of Frankfort on the Maine by Kirchner, of Ulm and Heilbronn by Jæger, of Rotenburg on the Tauber by Bensen, etc.

Ritter, and, next to him, Berghaus, greatly extended the knowledge of geography. Maps were drawn out on a greatly improved scale. Alexander von Humboldt, who ruled the world with his scientific as Napoleon with his eagle glance, attained the highest repute among travellers of every nation. Krusenstern, Langsdorf, and Kotzebue, Germans in the service of Russia, circumnavigated the globe. Meyen, the noted botanist, did the same in a Prussian ship. Baron von Hügel explored India. Gützlaff acted as a missionary in China. Ermann and Ledebur explored Siberia; Klaproth, Kupfer, Parrot, and Eichwald, the Caucasian provinces; Burckhardt, Rüppell, Ehrenberg, and Russegger, Syria and Egypt; the Prince von Neuwied and Paul William, duke of Würtemberg, North America; Becher, Mexico; Schomburg, Guiana; the Prince von Neuwied and Martius, the Brazils; Poppig, the banks of the Amazon; Rengger, Paraguay. The Missionary Society for the conversion of the heathen in distant parts and that for the propagation of the gospel, founded at Basel, 1816, have gained well-merited repute.

At the commencement of the present century, amid the storms of war, German taste took a fresh bias. French frivolity had increased immorality to a degree hitherto unknown. Licentiousness reigned unrestrained on the stage and pervaded the lighter productions of the day. If Iffland had, not unsuccessfully, represented the honest citizens and peasantry of Germany struggling against the unnatural customs of modern public life, Augustus von Kotzebue, who, after him, ruled the German stage, sought, on the contrary, to render honor despicable and to encourage the license of the day. In the numerous romances, a tone of lewd sentimentality took the place of the strict propriety for which they had formerly been remarkable, and the general diffusion of these immoral productions, among which the romances of Lafontaine may be more particularly mentioned, contributed in no slight degree to the moral perversion of the age.

Jean Paul Friedrich Richter stands completely alone. He shared the weaknesses of his times, which, like Goethe and Kotzebue, he both admired and ridiculed, passing with extraordinary versatility, almost in the same breath, from the most moving pathos to the bitterest satire. His clever but too deeply metaphysical romances are not only full of domestic sentimentality and domestic scenes, but they also imitate the over-refinement and effeminacy of Goethe, and yet his sound understanding and warm patriotic feelings led him to condemn all the artificial follies of fashion, all that was unnatural as well as all that was unjust.

Modern philosophy had no sooner triumphed over ancient religion and France over Germany than an extraordinary reaction, inaptly termed the romantic, took place in poetry. Although Ultramontanism might be traced even in Friedrich Schlegel, this school of poetry nevertheless solely owes its immense importance to its resuscitation of the older poetry of Germany, and to the success with which it opposed Germanism to Gallicism. Ludwig Tieck exclusively devoted himself to the German and romantic Middle Ages, to the Minnesingers, to Shakespeare, Cervantes, and Calderon, and modelled his own on their immortal works. The eyes of his contemporaries were by him first completely opened to the long-misunderstood beauties of the Middle Ages. His kindred spirit, Novalis (Hardenberg), destined to a too brief career, gave proofs of signal talent. Heinrich von Kleist, who committed suicide, left the finest-spirited and most delightful dramas. Ludwig Achim von Arnim, like Tieck, cultivated the older German Saga; his only fault was that, led away by the richness of his imagination, he overcolored his descriptions. Aided by Brentano, he collected the finest of the popular ballads of Germany in "des Knaben Wunderhorn." At Berlin, Fouque, with true old German taste, revived the romances of chivalry and, shortly before 1813, met the military spirit once more rising in Prussia with a number of romances in which figured battle-steeds and coats of mail, German faith and bravery, valiant knights and chaste dames, intermixed, it must be confessed, with a good deal of affectation. On the discovery being made that many of the ancient German ballads were still preserved among the lower classes, chiefly among the mountaineers, they were also sought for, and some poets tuned their lyres on the naive popular tone, etc., first, Hebel, in the partly extremely natural, partly extremely affected, Alemannic songs, which have found frequent imitators. Zacharia Werner and Hoffman, on the other hand, exclusively devoted themselves to the darker side of days of yore, to their magic and superstition, and filled the world, already terror-stricken by the war, with supernatural stories. Still, throughout one and all of these productions, curiously as they contrasted, the same inclination to return to and to revive a purely German style was evident. At that moment the great crisis suddenly took place. Before even the poets could predict the event, Germany cast off the yoke of Napoleon, and the German "Sturm and Freiheitslieder" of Theodor Körner, Arndt, Schenkendorf, etc., chimed in like a fearfully beautiful Allegro with the Adagio of their predecessors.

This was in a manner also the finale of the German notes that so strangely resounded in that Gallic time; the restoration suppressed every further outburst of patriotism, and the patriotic spirit that had begun to breathe forth in verse once more gave place to cosmopolitism and Gallicism. The lyric school, founded by Ludwig Uhland, alone preserved a German spirit and a connection with the ancient Minnelider of Swabia.

The new cosmopolitic tendency of the poetry of these times is chiefly due to the influence exercised by Goethe. The quick comprehension and ready adoption of every novelty is a faculty of, not a fault in, the German character, and alone becomes reprehensible when the German, forgetful of himself and of his own peculiar characteristics, adopts a medley of foreign incongruities and falsifies whatever ought to be preserved special and true. Goethe and his school, however, not content with imitating singly the style of every nation and of every period, have interwoven the most diverse strains, antique and romantic, old German and modern French, Grecian and Chinese, in one and the same poem. This unnatural style, itself destructive of the very peculiarity at which it aims, has infected both modern poetry and modern art; the architect intermixes the Grecian and the Gothic in his creations, while the painter seeks to unite the styles of the Flemish and Italian schools in his productions, and the poet those of Persia, Scandinavia, and Spain, in his strains. —Those are indeed deserving of gratitude who have comprehended and preserved the character peculiar to the productions of foreign art, in which the brothers Friedrich and August Wilhelm Schlegel have been so eminently successful. Hammer and, after him, Ruckert have also opened the Eastern world to our view. Count Platen, on the other hand, hung fluctuating between the antique Persian and German. —Cosmopolitism was greatly strengthened by the historical romances in vogue in England, descriptive of olden time, and which found innumerable imitators in Germany. They were, at all events, thus far beneficial; they led us from the parlor into the world.

But no sooner was genuine German taste neglected for that of foreign nations than Gallomania revived; all were compelled to pay homage to the spirit and the tone prevalent throughout Europe. The witty aristocratic médisance and grim spirit of rebellion emulating each other in France, were, in Germany, represented by Prince Püchler, the most spirituel drawing-room satirist, and by the Jew, Börne, the most spirited Jacobin of the day. The open infidelity again demonstrated in France, also led to its introduction into Germany by the Jew, Heine, while the immoral romances with which that country was deluged speedily became known to us through the medium of the translations and imitations of "Young Germany," and were incredibly increased by our literary industry; all the lying memoirs, in which the French falsify history, view Napoleon as a demigod, and treat the enthusiasm with which the Germans were animated in 1813 with derision, were also diligently translated. This tendency to view everything German with French eyes and to ridicule German honor and German manners was especially promoted by the light literature and numerous journals of the day, and was, in the universities, in close connection with the anti-christian tendency of the school of Hegel.—The late Catholic reaction, too exclusively political, has as yet exercised no influence over the literary world, and would scarcely succeed in gaining any, being less German than Roman.

While German poetry follows so false a course, it naturally follows that art also must be deprived of its natural character. Architecture has, it is true, abandoned the periwig style of France, but the purer antique or Byzantine taste to which it has returned is generally insipidly simple, while the attempts at Gothic and Moorish are truly miserable. A more elevated feeling than the present generation (which, in Goethe's manner, delights in trifling alternately with every style, or is completely enslaved by the modes imposed by France) is fitted to comprehend, is requisite for the revival of German or Gothic architecture. Still it may be, as is hoped, that the intention to complete the building of the Cologne cathedral will not be entirely without a beneficial influence.

The art of painting aspires far more energetically toward national emancipation. In the present century, the modern French style affecting the antique presented a complete contrast with the German romantic school, which, in harmony with the simultaneous romantic reaction in the poetical world, returned to the sacred simplicity of the ancient German and Italian masters. Overbeck was in this our greatest master. Since this period, the two great schools at Munich and Dusseldorf, founded by Peter Cornelius, and whose greatest masters are Peter Hesz, Bendemann, Lessing, Kaulbach, etc., have sought a middle path, and with earnest zeal well and skilfully opposed the too narrow imitation of, and the medley of style produced by the study of, the numerous old masters on the one hand, and, on the other, the search for effect, that Gallic innovation so generally in vogue. Were the church again to require pictures, or the state to employ the pencil of the patriot artist in recording the great deeds of past or present times or in the adornment of public edifices, painting would be elevated to its proper sphere.—Germany has also produced many celebrated engravers, among whom Muller holds precedence. Lithography, now an art of so much importance, was invented by the Bavarian, Senefelder. The art of painting on glass has also been revived.

In music, the Germans have retained their ancient fame. After Mozart, Beethoven, Weber, etc., have gained immense celebrity as composers. Still, much that is unnatural, affected, bizarre, and licentious has crept into the compositions of the German masters, more particularly in the operas, owing to the imitation of the modern Italian and French composers. A popular reaction has, however, again taken place, and, as before, in choral music, by means of the "singing clubs," which become more and more general among the people.

The stage has most deeply degenerated. At the commencement of the present century, its mimic scenes afforded a species of consolation for the sad realities of life, and formed the Lethe in whose waters oblivion was gladly sought. The public afterward became so practical in its tastes, so sober in its desires, that neither the spirit of the actor nor the coquetry of the actress had power to attract an audience. The taste and love for art were superseded by criticism and low intrigues, the theatre became a mere political engine, intended to divert the thoughts of the population of the great cities from the discussion of topics dangerous to the state by the all-engrossing charms of actresses and ballet-dancers.

The Germans, although much more practical in the present than in the past century, are still far from having freed themselves from the unjust, unfitting, and inconvenient situation into which they have fallen as time and events rolled on.

A mutual understanding in regard to the external position of the German in reference to the Slavonian nation has scarcely begun to dawn upon us. Scarcely have we become sensible to the ignominious restrictions imposed upon German commerce by the prohibitory regulations of Russia, by the customs levied in the Sound, on the Elbe, and Rhine. Scarcely has the policy that made such immense concessions to Russian diplomacy, and scarcely has the party spirit that looked for salvation for Germany from France, yielded to a more elevated feeling of self-respect. And yet, whoever should say to the people of Alsace, Switzerland, and Holland, "Ye are Germans," would reap but derision and insult. Germany is on the point of being once more divided into Catholic and Protestant Germany, and no one can explain how the German Customs' Union is to extend to the German Ocean, on account of the restrictions mutually imposed by the Germans. Could we but view ourselves as the great nation we in reality are, attain to a consciousness of the immeasurable strength we in reality possess, and make use of it in order to satisfy our wants, the Germans would be thoroughly a practical nation, instead of lying like a dead lion among the nations of Europe, and unresistingly suffering them to mock, tread underfoot, nay, deprive him of his limbs, as though he were a miserable, helpless worm.

More, far more has been done for the better regulation of the internal economy of Germany than for her external protection and power. The reforms suited to the age, commenced by the philosophical princes and ministers of the past century, have been carried on by Prussia in her hour of need, by constitutional Germany by constitutional means. Everywhere have the public administration been better regulated, despotism been restrained by laws, financial affairs been settled even under the heavy pressure of the national debts. Commerce, manufactured industry, and agriculture have been greatly promoted by the Customs' Union, by government aid and model institutions, by the improvements in the post-offices, by the laying of roads and railways. The public burdens and public debts, nevertheless, still remain disproportionately heavy on account of the enormous military force which the great states are compelled to maintain for the preservation of their authority, and on account of the polyarchical state of Germany, which renders the maintenance of an enormous number of courts, governments, general staffs and chambers necessary.

The popular sense of justice and legality, never entirely suppressed throughout Germany, also gave fresh proof of its existence under the new state of affairs, partly in the endlessly drawn-out proceedings in the chambers, partly in the incredible number of new laws and regulations in the different states. Still, industriously as these laws have been compiled, no real, essential, German law, neither public nor private, has been discovered. The Roman and French codes battled with each other and left no room for the establishment of a code fundamentally and thoroughly German. The most distinguished champions of the common rights of the people against cabinet-justice, the tyranny of the police and of the censor, were principally advocates and savants. The Estates, as corporations, were scarcely any longer represented. The majority of governments, ruled by the principle of absolute monarchy and the chambers, ruled by that of democracy, had, since the age of philosophy, been unanimous in setting the ancient Estates aside. The nobility alone preserved certain privileges, and the Catholic clergy alone regained some of those they had formerly enjoyed; all the Estates were, in every other respect, placed on a level. The ancient and national legal rights of the people were consequently widely trenched upon.

The emancipation of the peasant from the oppressive feudal dues, and the abolition of the restraint imposed by the laws of the city corporations, which had so flagrantly been abused, were indubitably well intended, but, instead of stopping there, good old customs, that ought only to have been freed from the weeds with which they had been overgrown, were totally eradicated. The peasant received a freehold, but was, by means of his enfranchisement, generally laden with debts, and, while pride whispered in his ear that he was now a lord of the soil and might assume the costume of his superiors, the land, whence he had to derive his sustenance, was gradually diminished in extent by the systematic division of property. His pretensions increased exactly in the ratio in which the means for satisfying them decreased; and the necessity of raising money placed him in the hands of Jews. The smaller the property by reason of subdivision, the more frequently is land put up for sale, the deeper is the misery of the homeless outcast. The restoration of the inalienable, indivisible allod and of the federal rights of the peasant, as in olden times, would have been far more to the purpose.—Professional liberty and the introduction of mechanism and manufactural industry have annihilated every warrant formerly afforded by the artificer as master and member of a city corporation, and, at the same time, every warrant afforded to him by the community of his being able to subsist by means of his industry. Manufactures on an extensive scale that export their produce must at all events be left unrestricted, but the small trades carried on within a petty community, their only market, excite, when free, a degree of competition which is necessarily productive both of bad workmanship and poverty, and the superfluous artificers, unaided by their professional freedom, fall bankrupt and become slaves in the establishments of their wealthier[1] competitors. The restoration of the city guilds under restrictions suitable to the times would have been far more judicious.

The maintenance of a healthy, contented class of citizens and peasants ought to be one of the principal aims of every German statesman. The fusion of these ancient and powerful classes into one common mass whence but a few wealthy individuals rise to eminence would be fatal to progression in Germany. By far the greater part of the people have already lost the means of subsistence formerly secured to all, nay, even to the serf, by the privileges of his class. The insecure possession, the endless division and alienation of property, an anxious dread of loss, and a rapacious love of gain, have become universal. Care for the means of daily existence, like creeping poison, unnerves the population. The anxious solicitude to which this gives rise has a deeply demoralizing effect. Even offices under government are less sought for from motives of ambition than as a means of subsistence; the arts and sciences have been degraded to mere sources of profit, envious trade decides questions of the highest importance, the torch of Hymen is lit by Plutus, not at the shrine of Love; and in the bosom of the careworn father of a family, whose scanty subsistence depends upon a patron's smile, the words "fatherland" and "glory" find no responsive echo.

Among the educated classes this state of poverty is allied with the most inconsistent luxury. Each and all, however poor, are anxious to preserve an appearance of wealth or to raise credit by that means. All, however needy, must be fashionable. The petty tradesman and the peasant ape their superiors in rank, and the old-fashioned but comfortable and picturesque national costume is being gradually thrown aside for the ever-varying modes prescribed by Paris to the world. The inordinate love of amusements in which the lower classes and the proletariat, ever increasing in

---

[1] Because more skilful.—*Trans.*

number, seek more particularly to drown the sense of misery, is another and a still greater source of public demoralization. The general habit of indulging in the use of spirituous liquors has been rightfully designated the brandy pest, owing to its lamentable moral and physical effect upon the population. This pest was encouraged not alone by private individuals, who gain their livelihood by disseminating it among the people, but also by governments, which raised a large revenue by its means; and the temperance societies, lately founded, but slightly stem the evil.

The public authorities throughout Germany have, it must be confessed, displayed extraordinary solicitude for the poor by the foundation of charitable institutions of every description, but they have contented themselves with merely alleviating misery instead of removing its causes; and the benevolence that raised houses of correction, poor-houses, and hospitals is rendered null by the laxity of the legislation. No measures are taken by the governments to provide means for emigration, to secure to the peasant his freehold, to the artificer the guarantee he ought to receive and to give, and the maintenance of the public morals. The punishment awarded for immorality and theft is so mild as to deprive them of the character of crime, pamphlets and works of the most immoral description are dispersed by means of the circulating libraries among all classes, and the bold infidelity preached even from the universities is left unchecked. But —is not the thief taught morality in the house of correction? and are not diseases, the result of license, cured in the hospitals with unheard-of humanity?

Private morality, so long preserved free from contamination, although all has for so long conspired against the liberty and unity of Germany, is greatly endangered. Much may, however, be hoped for from the sound national sense. The memory of the strength displayed by Germany in 1813 has been eradicated neither by the contempt of France or Russia, by any reactionary measure within Germany herself, by social and literary corruption, nor by the late contest between church and state. The Customs' Union has, notwithstanding the difference in political principle, brought despotic Prussia and constitutional Germany one step nearer. The influence of Russia on the one hand, of that of France on the other, has sensibly decreased. The irreligious and immoral tendencies now visible will, as has ever been the case in Germany, produce a reaction, and, when the necessity is more urgently felt, fitting measures will be adopted for the prevention of pauperism. The dangers with which Germany is externally threatened will also compel governments, however egotistical and indifferent, to seek their safety in unity, and even should the long neglect of this truth be productive of fresh calamity and draw upon Germany a fresh attack from abroad, that very circumstance will but strengthen our union and accelerate the regeneration of our great fatherland, already anticipated by the people on the fall of the Hohenstaufen.

CCLXXIV. *German Emigrants*

THE overplus population of Germany has ever emigrated; in ancient times, for the purpose of conquering foreign powers; in modern times, for that of serving under them. In the days of German heroism, our conquering hordes spread toward the west and south, over Italy, Gaul, Spain, Africa, England, and Iceland; during the Middle Ages, our mail-clad warriors took an easterly direction and overran the Slavonian countries, besides Prussia, Transylvania, and Palestine; in modern times, our religious and political refugees have emigrated in scarcely less considerable numbers to countries far more distant, but in the humble garb of artificers and beggars, the Pariahs of the world. Our ancient warriors gained undying fame and long maintained the influence and the rule of Germany in foreign lands. Our modern emigrants have, unnoted, quitted their native country, and, as early as the second generation, intermixed with the people among whom they settled. Hundreds of thousands of Germans have in this manner aided to aggrandize the British colonies, and Germany has derived no benefit from the emigration of her sons.

The first great mass of religious refugees threw itself into Holland and into the Dutch colonies, the greater part of which have since passed into the hands of the British. The illiberality of the Dutch caused the second great mass to bend its steps to British North America, within whose wilds every sect found an asylum. William Penn, the celebrated Quaker, visited Germany, and, in 1683, gave permission to some Germans to settle in the province named, after him, Pennsylvania, where they founded the city of Germantown.[1]

---

[1] The abolition of negro slavery was first mooted by Germans in 1688, at the great Quaker meeting in North America.

These fortunate emigrants were annually followed by thousands of exiled Protestants, principally from Alsace and the Palatinate. The industry and honesty for which the German workmen were remarkable caused some Englishmen to enter into a speculation to procure their services as white slaves. The greatest encouragement was accordingly given by them to emigration from Germany, but the promises so richly lavished were withdrawn on the unexpected emigration of thirty-three thousand of the inhabitants of the Palatinate, comprising entire communes headed by their preachers, evidently an unlooked and unwished for multitude. These emigrants reached London abandoned by their patrons and disavowed by the government. A fearful fate awaited them. After losing considerable numbers from starvation in England, the greater part of the survivors were compelled to work like slaves in the mines and in the cultivation of uninhabited islands; three thousand six hundred of them were sent over to Ireland, where they swelled the number of beggars; numbers were lost at sea, and seven thousand of them returned in despair, in a state of utter destitution, to their native country. A small number of them, however, actually sailed for New York, where they were allotted portions of the primitive forests, which they cleared and cultivated; but they had no sooner raised flourishing villages in the midst of rich cornfields and gardens, than they were informed that the ground belonged to the state and were driven from the home they had so lately found. Pennsylvania opened a place of refuge to the wanderers.[1]

The religious persecution and the increasing despotism of the governments in Germany meanwhile incessantly drove fresh emigrants to America, where, as they were generally sent to the extreme verge of the provinces in order to clear the ground and drive away the aborigines, numbers of them were murdered by the Indians. Switzerland also sent forth

[1] Account of the United States by Eggerling.

many emigrants, who settled principally in North Carolina. The people of Salzburg, whose expulsion has been detailed above, colonized Georgia in 1732. In 1742, there were no fewer than a hundred thousand Germans in North America, and, since that period, their number has been continually on the increase. Thousands annually arrived; for instance, in the years 1749 and 1750, seven thousand; in 1754, as many as twenty-two thousand; in 1797, six thousand Swabians. The famine of 1770, the participation of German mercenaries in the wars of the British in North America, at first against the French colonies, afterward against the English colonists (the German prisoners generally settled in the country), induced the Germans to emigrate in such great numbers that, from 1770 to 1791, twenty-four emigrant ships on an average arrived annually at Philadelphia, without reckoning those that landed in the other harbors.[1]

The passage by sea to the west being continually closed during the great wars with France, the stream of emigration took an easterly direction overland. Russia had extended her conquests toward Persia and Turkey. The necessity of fixing colonies in the broad steppes as in the primitive forests of America, to serve as a barrier against the wild frontier tribes, was plainly perceived by the Russian government, and Germans were once more made use of for this purpose. Extensive colonies, which at the present date contain hundreds of thousands of German inhabitants, but whose history is as yet unknown, were accordingly formed northward of the Black and Caspian Seas. Swabian villages were also built on the most southern frontier of Russia toward

---

[1] One of the most distinguished Germans in America was a person named John Jacob Astor, the son of a bailiff at Walldorf near Heidelberg, who was brought up as a furrier, emigrated to America, where he gradually became the wealthiest of all furriers, founded at his own expense the colony of Astoria, on the northwestern coast of North America, so interestingly described by Washington Irving, and the Astor fund, intended as a protection to German emigrants to America from the frauds practiced on the unwary. He resided at New York. He possessed an immense fortune and was highly and deservedly esteemed for his extraordinary philanthropy.

Persia, and in 1826 suffered severely from an inroad of the Persians.

The fall of Napoleon had no sooner reopened the passage by sea than the tide of emigration again turned toward North America. These emigrants, the majority of whom consisted of political malcontents, preferred the land of liberty to the steppes of Russia, whither sectarians and those whom the demoralization and irreligion of the Gallomanic period had filled with disgust had chiefly resorted. The Russo-Teuto colonies are proverbial for purity and strictness of morals. One Wurtemberg sectarian alone, the celebrated Rapp, succeeded during the period of the triumph of France in emigrating to Pennsylvania, where he founded the Harmony, a petty religious community. An inconsiderable number of Swiss, dissatisfied with Napoleon's supremacy, also emigrated in 1805 and built New Vevay. But it was not until after the wars, more particularly during the famine in 1816 and 1817, that emigration across the sea was again carried on to a considerable extent. In 1817, thirty thousand Swiss, Wurtembergers, Hessians, and inhabitants of the Palatinate emigrated, and about an equal number were compelled to retrace their steps from the sea-coast in a state of extreme destitution on account of their inability to pay their passage and of the complete want of interest in their behalf displayed by the governments. Political discontent increased in 1818 and 1819, and each succeeding spring thirty thousand Germans sailed down the Rhine to the land of liberty in the far west. In 1820, a society was set on foot at Berne for the protection of the Swiss emigrants from the frauds practiced upon the unwary. The union of the Archduchess Leopoldine, daughter to the emperor Francis, with Dom Pedro, the emperor of the Brazils, had, since 1817, attracted public attention to South America. Dom Pedro took German mercenaries into his service for the purpose of keeping his wild subjects within bounds, and the fruitful land offered infinite advantages to the German agriculturist; but colonization was rendered impracticable by the revolutionary disorders and by the ill-will of the natives toward the settlers, and the Germans who had been induced to emigrate either enlisted as soldiers or perished. Several among them, who have published their adventures in the Brazils, bitterly complained of the conduct of Major Schäfer, who had been engaged in collecting recruits at Hamburg for the Brazils. They even accused him of having allowed numbers of their fellow-countrymen to starve to death from motives of gain, so much a head being paid to him on his arrival in the Brazils for the men shipped from Europe whether they arrived dead or alive. The publication of these circumstances completely checked the emigration to the Brazils, and North America was again annually, particularly in 1827 and after the July revolution, overrun with Germans, and they have even begun to take part in the polity of the United States. The peasants, who had been settled for a considerable period, and who have insensibly acquired great wealth and have retained the language and customs of their native country, form the flower of the German colonists in the West.[1]

[1] The Allgemeine Zeitung of September, 1837, reports that there were at that time one hundred and fifty-seven thousand Germans in North America who were still unnaturalized, consequently had emigrated thither within the last two or three years. In Philadelphia alone there were seventy-five thousand Germans. Grund says in his work, "The Americans in 1837," "The peaceable disposition of the Germans prevents their interfering with politics, although their number is already considerable enough for the formation of a powerful party. They possess, notwithstanding, great weight in the government of Pennsylvania, in which State the governors have since the revolution always been Germans. This is in fact so well understood on all sides that even during the last election, when two democrats and a Whig candidate contended for the dignity of governor, they were all three Germans by birth and no other would have had the slightest chance of success. In the State of Ohio there are at the present date, although that province was first colonized by New-English, no fewer than forty-five thousand Germans possessed of the right of voting. The State of New York, although originally colonized by Dutch, contains a numerous German population in several of its provinces, particularly in that of Columbia, the birthplace of Martin Van Buren, the present Vice-President and future President of the republic. The State of Maryland numbers twenty-five thousand Germans possessed of votes; almost one-third of the population of Illinois is German, and thousands of fresh emigrants are settling in the valley of the Mississippi. I believe that the number of German voters or of voters of German descent may, without exaggeration, be reckoned on an average annually at four hundred thou-

In the Cape colonies, the Dutch peasants, the boors, feeling themselves oppressed by the English government, emigrated en masse, in 1837, to the north, where they settled with the Caffres, and, under their captain, Prætorius, founded an independent society, in 1839, at Port Natal, where they again suffered a violent aggression on the part of the British.

Thus are Germans fruitlessly scattered far and wide over the face of the globe, while on the very frontiers of Germany nature has designated the Danube as the near and broad path for emigration and colonization to her overplus population, which, by settling in her vicinity, would at once increase her external strength and extend her influence.

---

sand, and certainly in less than twenty years hence at a million. In the city of New York, the Germans greatly influence the election of the burgomaster and other city authorities by holding no fewer than three thousand five hundred votes. These circumstances naturally render the German vote an object of zealous contention for politicians of every party, and there is accordingly no dearth of German newspapers in any of the German settlements. In Pennsylvania, upward of thirty German (principally weekly) papers are in circulation, and about an equal number are printed and published in the State of Ohio. A scarcely lower number are also in circulation in Maryland."

SUPPLEMENTARY CHAPTER

FROM THE FALL OF NAPOLEON TO THE PRESENT DAY

THE Confederation of the Rhine, wounded to the death by the campaign of 1812, was killed by the fall of Napoleon. From that event to the present time the accompanying pages must be restricted to a consideration of those matters which have been of capital importance to the German people. These matters may be summarized as consisting in the formation of the German Confederation, the Danish war, the Austro-Prussian war, the Franco-Prussian war, and the refounding of the empire.

As the fall of Sennacherib was sung by the Hebrews, so was the fall of Napoleon sung by the Germans. They had been at his mercy. He had deposed their sovereigns, dismembered their states, crippled their trade, and exhausted their resources. Yet in 1814, by the Peace of Paris, they had restored to them all they had possessed in 1792, but as a reconstruction of the former empire was impracticable, those states which still maintained their sovereignty coalesced.

This was in 1815. At the time there remained of the three hundred states into which the empire had originally been divided but thirty-nine, a number afterward reduced, through the extinction of four minor dynasties, to thirty-five. A diet, recognized as the legislative and executive organ of the Confederation, was instituted at Frankfort. Instead, however, of satisfying the expectations of the nation, it degenerated into a political tool, which princes manipulated, which they made subservient to their inherent conservatism, and with which they oppressed their subjects. The French revolution of 1830 influenced to a certain extent their attitude, and a few of them were induced to accord constitutions to their people, but the effect was transient. Reforms which had been stipulated they managed to ignore. It took the insurrectionary movements of 1848 to shake them on their thrones. Forced then to admit the inefficiency of the diet, and attempting by hasty concessions to check the progress of republican principles, they consented to the convocation of a national assembly. Over this body the Archduke John of Austria was elected to preside. The choice was not happy. Measures which he failed to facilitate he succeeded in frustrating. As a consequence, matters went from bad to worse, until, after the refusal of the king of Prussia to accept the imperial crown which was offered to him in 1849 and the election of a provisional regency which ensued, the assembly lapsed into a condition of impotence which terminated in its dissolution.

Meanwhile republican demonstrations having been forcibly suppressed, there arose between Prussia and Austria a feeling of jealousy, if not of ill-will, which more than once indicated war, and which, though resulting in the restoration of the diet and temporarily diverted by a joint attack on Denmark, culminated in the battle of Sadowa.

Into the details of this attack it is unnecessary to enter. The casus belli was apparently an entirely virtuous endeavor to settle the respective claims of the king of Denmark and the duke of Augustenburg to the sovereignty of Schleswig-Holstein. The fashion in which the claims were settled consisted in wiping them out. The direction not merely of Schleswig-Holstein but of Lauenberg was assumed by Austria and Prussia, who, by virtue of a treaty signed October 30, 1864, took upon themselves their civil and military administration.

The administration which then ensued was announced as being but a temporary trusteeship, and throughout Europe was generally so regarded. But Prussia had other views.

In the chambers Bismarck declared that the crown had no intention of resigning the booty, that, come what might, never would it give up Kiel. Bismarck was seldom wrong. In this instance he was right. In the month of August following the treaty the Emperor Francis of Austria and King William of Prussia met at Gastein and concluded a convention by which it was agreed that Schleswig should belong to Prussia, Holstein to Austria, with Kiel as a free port under Prussian rule.

These proceedings, as might have been expected, created the greatest indignation in England, France, and among the minor states. Earl Russell declared that all rights, old and new, had been trodden under by the Gastein Convention, and that violence and force had been the only bases on which this convention had been established, while utter disregard of all public laws had been shown throughout all these transactions. On the part of France, her minister said that the Austrian and Prussian governments were guilty in the eyes of Europe of dividing between themselves territories they were bound to give up to the claimants who seemed to have the best title, and that modern Europe was not accustomed to deeds fit only for the dark ages; such principles, he added, can only overthrow the past without building up anything new. The Frankfort Diet declared the two powers to have violated all principles of right, especially that of the duchies to direct their own affairs as they pleased, provided they did not interfere with the general interests of the German nation. Nevertheless, a Prussian governor was appointed over Schleswig, and an Austrian over Holstein, both assuming these duchies to be parts of their respective empires.

Early in 1866, it was evident that no real friendship could long continue between Prussia and Austria, and that these two great robbers would surely fall out over the division of the plunder; making it the ostensible cause for dispute, which was in reality their rivalry for the leadership in Germany. In June, the Prussians crossed the Eyder, and took possession of Holstein, appointed a supreme president over the two duchies which passed under Prussian rule, and settled, after a summary fashion, the vexed question. There were also other causes which tended to war. The weak side of Austria, weaker far than Hungary, was her Italian province of Venetia, one, indeed, that few can say she had any real or natural right to hold, beyond having acquired it by the treaty of 1813. To recover this from German rule had been the incessant desire of Italy, and grievous was her disappointment when the emperor of the French thought fit to stop immediately after the battles of Magenta and Solferino, instead of pushing on, as it was hoped he would have done, to the conquest of Venetia.

In the spring of 1866, Italy was making active preparations for war, and Austria, on the other hand, increased largely the number of her troops, Prussia choosing, in defiance of all fair dealing, to assume that all these armaments were directed against herself; and, on this supposition, sent a circular to the minor states to tell them they must decide which side to take in the impending struggle. A secret treaty was made between Prussia and Italy: that Italy should be ready to take up arms the moment Prussia gave the signal, and that Prussia should go on with the war until Venetia was ceded to Italy. Angry discussions took place in the diet between Austria and Prussia, which ended in Prussia declaring the Germanic Confederation to be broken up, and both sides preparing for war.

Austria began early to arm, for she required longer time to mobilize her army. Prussia, on the contrary, was in readiness for action. Every Prussian who is twenty years old, without distinction of rank, has to serve in the army, three years with the colors, five more in the reserve, after which he is placed for eleven years in the Landwehr, and liable to be called out when occasion requires. In peace everything is kept ready for the mobilization of its army. In a wonderfully short time the organization was complete, and 260,000 men brought into the field in Bohemia. In arms, they had the advantage of the needle-gun. The Prussian forces were in three divisions, the "First Army" under the command of Prince Frederick Charles; the "Second Army" under that of the crown prince; and the "Army of the Elbe," under General Herwarth. The supreme command of the Austrian army of the north was given to Feldzeugmeister von Benedek, that of the south to the Archduke Albert.

On June 14, Prussia sent a telegraphic summons to Hanover, Hesse-Cassel, and Saxony, demanding them to reduce their armies to the peace establishment, and to concur with Prussia respecting the Germanic confederation; and that if they did not send their consent within twelve hours, war would be declared. The states did not reply, Prussia declared war, and on the 16th invaded their territories. The occupation and disarmament of Hanover and Hesse were necessary to Prussia for a free communication with her Rhenish provinces, and she effected her purpose by means of well-planned combinations, so that in the course of a few days these states were overrun by Prussian troops, and their sovereigns expelled.

The rapid progress of events, and the Prussian declaration of war, had taken Hanover by surprise. Her army was not yet mobilized; Austria had evacuated Holstein, or she could have looked to her for support. To attempt to defend the capital was hopeless; so King George, suffering from blindness, moved with his army to Gottingen, with a view of joining the Bavarians. Prussia entered by the north, and, assisted by her navy on the Elbe, was by the 22d in possession of the whole of Hanover. Closed round on all sides by the Prussians, unassisted by Prince Charles of Bavaria, Gotha having declared for Prussia, the king of Hanover, with his little army, crossed the frontier of his kingdom, and at Langensalza, fifteen miles north of Gotha, encountered the Prussians, and remained master of the battlefield. But victory was of little avail; surrounded by 40,000 Prussians, the king was forced to capitulate. The arms and military stores were handed over to the enemy, and the king and his soldiers allowed to depart. Thus, through the supineness of

Prince Charles of Bavaria, a whole army was made captive, and Hanover erased from the roll of independent states.

More fortunate than his neighbor, the elector of Hesse-Cassel saved his army, though not his territory, from the invader. His troops retired toward the Maine, where they secured a communication with the federal army at Frankfort. The elector remained in Hesse, and was sent a state prisoner to the Prussian fortress of Stettin, on the Oder. The Prussians overran his territory, declaring they were not at war against "peoples, but against governments."

Two bodies of Prussian troops entered Saxony—the First Army and the Army of the Elbe—and the Saxon army retired into Bohemia to effect a junction with the Austrians. On the 20th, Leipzig was seized, and the whole of Saxony was in undisturbed possession of the Prussians; Prince Frederick Charles issuing a most stringent order that private property should be respected, and every regard shown to the comfort of the inhabitants. His order was strictly observed, and every measure taken to prevent the miseries attendant on the occupation of a country by a foreign army.

The invasion of Saxony brought immediately open war between Prussia and Austria, and on the 23d the Prussian army crossed the Bohemian frontier—only a week since it had entered Saxony. It is needless here to detail the battles which immediately followed; suffice it to say, the Prussians were victorious in all—at Podoll, where the needle-gun did such terrible work; Munchengratz, which gave them the whole line of the Iser; Trautenan, Gitschen, and others. On the 1st of July, the king of Prussia arrived from Berlin and took the supreme command of the army. The following day brought news from the crown prince that he was hastening from Silesia with the Second Army, whereby the whole of the Prussian forces would be concentrated. On the 3d of July was fought the decisive battle of Koniggratz, or Sadowa, as it is sometimes called, from the village of that name, a cluster of pine-wood cottages, enclosed by orchards, with a wood-crowned hill at the back, which was fiercely disputed by the contending parties.

On that day, General von Benedek had taken his position with the Austrian army in front of the frontier fortress of Koniggratz, on the right bank of the Elbe, about fifty-five miles east of Prague, to oppose the passage of the crown prince from Silesia. In his front lay the marshy stream of Bistritz, upon which Sadowa and a few other villages are situated. At half-past seven in the morning the battle began, and continued with great slaughter without any marked advantage on either side till the arrival of the crown prince decided, like the advance of Blücher at Waterloo, the fortune of the day. The Austrians were completely routed, and fled across the Elbe to save the capital. They lost 40,000 men in this sanguinary conflict, the Prussians 10,000. The forces in the field were 200,000 Austrians and Saxons, and 260,000 Prussians.

Immediately after her crushing defeat, Austria surrendered Venetia to France, and the Emperor Napoleon at once accepted the gift and gave it over to Victor Emmanuel.

On July 26, preliminaries of peace were signed at Nikolsburg, and peace was finally concluded at Prague, August 23, between Prussia and Austria, and about the same time with the South German states. The Prussian House of Deputies voted the annexation of the conquered states, and in October peace was concluded with Saxony. By these arrangements, Hanover, Hesse-Cassel, and Frankfort became provinces of Prussia, as well as the long-disputed duchies of Denmark. All the German states north of the Maine concluded a treaty, offensive and defensive, for the maintenance of the security of their states. Prussia increased her territory by 32,000 square miles and her population 4,000,000; and in October, 1866, the whole of northern Germany was united into a Confederation.

This Confederation, known as the North German, possessed a common parliament elected by universal suffrage, in which each state was represented according to its population. The first or constituent parliament met early in 1867, and adopted, with a few modifications, the constitution proposed by Count Bismarck. The new elections then took place, and the first regular North German parliament met in September, 1867. According to this constitution, there was to be a common army and fleet, under the sole command of Prussia; a common diplomatic representation abroad, of necessity little else than Prussian; and to Prussia also was intrusted the management of the posts and telegraphs in the Confederation.

The Southern German states which up to this point had not joined the Bund, were Bavaria, Baden, Wurtemberg, Hesse-Darmstadt, and Lichtenstein, with a joint area of 43,990 square miles, and a total population (1866) of 8,524,-460. But, though these states were not formally members of the Bund, they were so practically, for they were bound to Prussia by treaties of alliance offensive and defensive, so that in the event of a war the king of Prussia would have at his disposal an armed force of upward of 1,100,000 men.

During the next few years the North German Confederation was employed in consolidating and strengthening itself, and in trying to induce the southern states to join the league. The Zollverein was remodelled and extended, until by the year 1868 every part of Germany was a member of it, with the exception of the cities of Hamburg and Bremen, and a small part of Baden. This paved the way for the formal entrance of the southern states into the confederation; but they still hung back, though the ideal of a united Germany was gradually growing in force and favor.

Meanwhile the terms of the treaty of Prague, together with the complete removal of alien powers from Italy, had wrought a radical change in the political relations of the European States. Excluded from Germany, the dominions of Austria still extended to the verge of Venetia and the Lombard plains, but her future lay eastward and her centre of gravity had been removed to Buda-Pesth. In the South German courts, no doubt, there was a bias toward Vienna, and a dislike of Prussia; yet both the leaning and the repugnance were counterbalanced by a deeper dread of France rooted in the people by the vivid memories of repeated and cruel invasions. Russia, somewhat alarmed by the rapid success of King William, had been soothed by diplomatic reassurances, the tenor of which is not positively known, although a series of subsequent events more than justified the inference made at that time, that promises, bearing on the czar's Eastern designs, were tendered and accepted as a valuable consideration for the coveted boon of benevolent neutrality, if not something more substantial. Like Russia, France had lost nothing by the campaign of 1866; her territories were intact; her ruler had mediated between Austria and Prussia; and he had the honor of protecting the pope, who, as a spiritual and temporal prince, was still in possession of Rome and restricted territorial domains. But the Napoleonic court, and many who looked upon its head as a usurper, experienced, on the morrow of Sadowa, and in a greater degree after the preface to a peace had been signed at Nikolsburg, a sensation of diminished magnitude, a consciousness of lessened prestige, and a painful impression that their political, perhaps even their military place in Europe, as the heirs of Richelieu, Louis XIV., and Napoleon, had been suddenly occupied by a power which they had taught themselves to contemn as an inferior. Until the summer of 1866 the emperor Napoleon fancied that he was strong enough to play with Bismarck a game of diplomatic chess.

In that he erred profoundly. As early as the first week in August, 1866, M. Benedetti, the French ambassador to the court of Berlin, was instructed to claim the left bank of the Rhine as far as and including Mainz. Bismarck replied that "the true interest of France is not to obtain an insignificant increase of territory, but to aid Germany in constituting herself after a fashion which will be most favorable to all concerned." Delphos could not have been more oracular. But Napoleon III. could not or would not heed. A week later Benedetti was instructed to submit a regular scale of concessions—the frontiers of 1814 and the annexation of Belgium, or Luxemburg and Belgium. Benedetti received the most courteous attention and nothing more. This was irritating. The French had been accustomed for more than two hundred years to meddle directly in Germany and find there allies, either against Austria, Prussia, or England; and the habit of centuries had been more than confirmed by the colossal raids, victories, and annexations of Napoleon I. A Germany which should escape from French control and reverse, by its own energetic action, the policy of Henry IV., Richelieu, Louis XIV., his degenerate grandson, Louis XV., and of the great Napoleon himself, was an affront to French pride, and could not be patiently endured. The opposing forces which had grown up were so strong that the wit of man was unable to keep them asunder; and all the control over the issue left to kings and statesmen was restricted to the fabrication of means wherewith to deliver or sustain the shock, and the choice of the hour, if such choice were allowed.

Then presently the opportunity occurred. On July 4, 1870, the throne of Spain was offered to Prince Leopold of Hohenzollern. The fact created the greatest excitement in France. Threatening speeches were made. On July 12 Prince Leopold declined the offer. On the morrow Benedetti was instructed to demand a guarantee that any future offer of the kind would be refused. The king of Prussia would not listen to the proposition. The French minister, through whom the demand had been transmitted, then asked for his passports. War was imminent.

At the prospect Paris grew mad with enthusiasm. Crowds assembled in the streets, shouting "Down with Prussia!" "Long live France!" "To the Rhine!" "To Berlin!" The papers abounded with inflammatory appeals, and, after the impulsive French fashion, glorified beforehand the easy triumphs that were to be won over the Prussians. Men told one another that they would be across the Rhine in a week, and at Berlin in a fortnight. The excitement in Prussia was not less than that in France. The people, with scarcely an exception, declared their readiness for war, and seemed to find a pleasure in the opportunity now presented for settling old quarrels. Like the people of Paris, the Prussians shouted "To the Rhine!" The French cry of "To Berlin!" had its counterpart in the German ejaculation of "To Paris!"

Perhaps a sentence spoken by M. Guyot Montpayroux best illustrates the predominant feeling. "Prussia," he said, "has forgotten the France of Jena, and the fact must be recalled to her memory." Thus was war declared on the night of July 15. Thiers, who desired a war with Prussia "at the proper time," has left on record his judgment that the hour then selected was "detestably ill-chosen." Yet even he and Gambetta were both anxious that "satisfaction" should be obtained for Sadowa; while the thought which animated the court is admirably expressed in the phrase imputed to the empress who, pointing to the prince imperial, said, "This child will never reign unless we repair the misfortunes of Sadowa." Such was the ceaseless refrain. The word haunted French imaginations incessantly, and it was the pivot on which the imperial policy revolved; it exercised a spell scarcely less powerful and disastrous upon monarchists like Thiers and republicans like Gambetta. Long foreseen, the dread shock, like all grave calamities, came nevertheless as a surprise, even upon reflective minds. Statesmen and soldiers who looked on, while they shared in the natural feelings aroused by so tremendous a drama, were also the privileged witnesses of two instructive experiments on a grand scale—the processes whereby mighty armies are brought into the field, and the methods by means of which they are conducted to defeat or victory.

The French field army, called at the outset the "Army of the Rhine," consisted nominally of 336,000 men with 924 guns. It was considered that of these, 300,000 would be available for the initial operations. The infantry of the army was provided with a breech-loading weapon, called after its inventor the Chassepot. The Chassepot was a weapon in all respects superior to the famous needle-gun, which was still the weapon of the Prussian army. Attached likewise to the divisional artillery was a machine gun called the Mitrailleuse, from which great things were expected. But this gun had been manufactured with a secrecy which, while it prevented foreign inspection, had withheld also the knowledge of its mechanism from the soldiers who were to work it. In the field, therefore, it proved a failure.

Since the Crimean and Austrian wars, while the armies of the other European states had advanced in efficiency, the French army had deteriorated. The reason was that favoritism rather than merit had been made the road to court favor. The officers who had pointed to the training of the Prussian soldiers, as indicating the necessity for the adoption of similar modes for the French army, had been laughed at and left in the cold. The consequence was, that for ten years prior to the war of 1870, the French army had received instruction only of the most superficial character. It had been considered sufficient if the soldiers were brought to the point of making a good show on the parade ground. Little more had been required of them. Field training and musketry training had been alike neglected. The officers had ceased to study, and the government had taken no pains to instruct them. What was more vicious still, the alienation between officers and men, which had been noticed even in the war of 1859, had widened. The officers generally had ceased to take the smallest interest in the comfort of the men in camp or in quarters. These matters were left to the non-commissioned officers. Needless to add, they were not always properly attended to. It may be added that the system of drill was so devised as to give no play to the reasoning powers of the officer. He was a machine and nothing more.

Of the artillery of the French army it has to be said, that it was far inferior to that of the Germans, and known to be so by the French war department. In the matter of reserves, France had comparatively nothing.

Far different were the composition and the state of preparation of the Prussian army; far different, also, those of her German allies; far higher the qualities of their general officers; far superior the discipline and morale of their troops; far more ready, in every single particular, to begin a war; far more thoroughly provided to carry that war to a successful issue.

The German infantry had been thoroughly organized on a system which gave to every officer the necessity of exercising independent action, and to the men the faculty of understanding the object of the manœuvre directed. Its cavalry had been specially instructed in duties of reconnoissance, of insuring repose for the infantry, of collecting intelligence, of concealing the march of armies, of acting as a completer of victory, or as a shield in case of defeat. It had profited greatly by the lessons it had learned in the war of 1866.

The German artillery had likewise been greatly improved in efficiency of manœuvre since 1866. It was in all respects superior to that of the French.

Of the Prussian and South German leaders, I will only say that we shall meet again the men from whom we parted on the conclusion of the armistice of Nikolsburg. What was their task and how they executed it will be described in the pages that follow. In mere numbers, the king of Prussia had a great advantage over his enemy. For, while without any assistance from South Germany, and after allowing for three army corps which might be necessary to watch Austria and Denmark, he could begin the campaign with a force of 350,000 men, he was certain of the assistance of Southern Germany, and confident that, unless the French should obtain considerable successes at the outset, neither Austria nor Denmark would stir a hand to aid them.

To counterbalance this superiority of numbers the French emperor had cherished a vague hope that, in a war against Prussia, he might possibly count upon the ancient friendship for France of Bavaria and Saxony, and to a still greater extent upon Austria and Italy. With regard to Bavaria and Saxony he was speedily undeceived. Moreover, contrary to expectation, other German states decided to support Prussia and placed their armies, which were eventually commanded by the crown prince, at the disposal of King William. With regard to Austria and Italy, Colonel Malleson in a work on this subject,[1] to which we are much indebted, states that their co-operation was made dependent on the initial successes of the French troops. Colonel Malleson adds:

"It was not only understood, but was actually drafted in a treaty—the signing of which, however, was prevented by the rapid course of the war—that if, on the 15th of September, France should be holding her own in Southern Germany, then Austria and Italy would jointly declare war against Prussia.

These conditions made it clear that ultimate success in the struggle about to commence would accrue to the power which should obtain the first advantages.

That Germany—for it was Germany and not Prussia only which entered upon this great struggle—would obtain these initial advantages seemed almost certain. Count Moltke had for some time previous been engaged in planning for a war with France. So far back as 1868 all his arrangements for the formation of the armies to be employed, the points to be occupied, the nature of the transport, had been clearly laid down. These instructions had been carefully studied by the several corps commanders and their staff. Not one matter, however apparently trivial, had been neglected. When, then, on the 16th of July, the king of Prussia gave the order for mobilization, it required only to insert the day and the hour on which each body of troops should march. With respect to the armies of the states of Southern Germany, Moltke, anticipating that the French emperor would throw his main army as rapidly as possible into Southern Ger-

[1] G. B. Malleson: The Refounding of the German Empire.

many, had recommended that the contingents from that part of the country should march northward to join those of Prussia on the middle Rhine, to assume there a position which should menace the flank and rear of the invading army. This position would be the more practical, as in the event of the French not invading Southern Germany, the combined force, stretching from Saarbrucken to Landau, would be ready to invade France, and sever the communications with Paris of the French armies on the frontier. Count Moltke had calculated that the German troops intended to cross the French frontier would be in a position to make their forward movement by the 4th of August. Pending the development of the French strategy with respect to Southern Germany, therefore, he thought it prudent to delay the march of the southern contingents, in order that no part of the army might be suddenly overwhelmed by a superior force. On the actual frontier he placed, then, only a few light troops, for the purposes of reconnoitring, and for checking the first advance of the enemy until supports should arrive.

The French emperor had, indeed, been keenly alive to the advantages which would accrue to himself from a prompt invasion of Southern Germany. He designed to concentrate one hundred and fifty thousand men at Metz; one hundred thousand at Strasburg; to cross into Baden with these armies; while a third, assembling at Chalons, should protect the frontier against the German forces. The plan itself was an excellent one had he only been able to execute it, for, as we have seen, early success in Southern Germany would have meant the armed assistance of Austria and Italy. But the French army was in a condition more unready, one might truly say, of greater demoralization, thus early, than its severest critics had imagined. Considerable forces were indeed massed about Metz and Strasburg. But the commissariat and transport departments were in a state of the most hopeless confusion. The army could not move. To remedy these evils time was wanted, and time was the commodity the generals could not command. Every day which evoked some little order out of chaos brought the Germans nearer to positions, the occupation of which would render impossible the contemplated invasion. The emperor had quitted Paris for Metz, accompanied by the prince imperial, on the 28th of July, and had arrived there and taken the supreme command the same day. The day following he met his generals at St. Avoid, and unfolded to them his plans. Since war had been declared he had lost many illusions. It had become clear to him that he was warring against the concentrated might of Germany; that he could not make the inroad into Southern Germany originally contemplated without exposing Paris to an attack from forces already occupying the country between Treves and Mannheim: that he was bound to hold that line. Anxious, however, to assume the offensive, he dictated the following plan to his marshals. Bazaine, with the Second, Third, and Fifth Army Corps, should cross the Saar at Saarbrücken, covered on his left by the Fourth Corps, which should make a show of advancing against Saarlouis, while MacMahon, pushing forward from his position near Strasburg, should cover his right. The emperor had some reason to believe that the Saar was weakly held.

But his own generals showed him that his plan was impossible. They represented to him that instead of the three hundred thousand men whom, in the delirium of the Paris enthusiasm, he believed he would find available for his purposes, he had at the utmost one hundred and eighty-six thousand; that in every requirement for moving the army was deficient; that there was scarcely a department which was not disorganized. He was compelled, therefore, to renounce his plan for decisive offensive action. He came to that resolve most unwillingly, for Paris was behind him, ready to rise unless he should make some show of advancing. It was to reassure the excited spirits of the capital, rather than to effect any military result, that, on the 2d of August, he moved with sixty thousand men in the direction of Saarbrücken. The garrison of that place consisted of something less than four thousand men with six guns. The emperor attacked it with the corps of Frossard, eighteen battalions and four batteries. These compelled the slender German garrison to evacuate the place, but Frossard, though the bridges across the Saar were not defended, made no attempt to cross that river. The soldierly manner in which the Germans had covered their retreat had left on his mind the impression that they were more numerous than they were, and that there was a larger force behind them.

Still, for the only time in the war, the emperor was able to send a reassuring telegram to Paris. The young prince, upon whom the hopes of the nation would, he hoped, rest, had undergone the "baptism of fire." French troops had made the first step in advance.

Soon, however, it became clear to him that the enemy had concentrated along the line of the frontier, and were about to make their spring. Moltke, in fact, from his headquarters at Mayence, was, by means of solitary horsemen employed in profusion, keeping himself thoroughly well acquainted not only with the movements of the French, but with their vacillation, their irresolution, their want of plan. The sudden appearance from unexpected quarters of these horsemen conveyed a marked feeling of insecurity to the minds of the French soldiers, and these feelings were soon shared by their chiefs. It was very clear to them that an attack might at any moment come, though from what quarter and in what force they were absolutely ignorant. This ignorance increased their vacillations, their uncertainties. Orders and counter-orders followed each other with startling rapidity. The soldiers, harassed, began to lose confidence; the leaders became more and more incapable of adopting a plan.

Suddenly, in the midst of their vacillations, of their marchings and counter-marchings, the true report reached them, on the evening of the 3d of August, that a French division, the outpost of MacMahon's army, had been surprised and defeated at Weissenburg by a far superior force. Napoleon at once ordered the Fifth Corps to concentrate at Bitsche, and despatched a division of the Third to Saarguemünd. These orders were followed by others. Those of the 5th of August divided the army of the Rhine into two portions, the troops in Alsace being placed under MacMahon, those in Lorraine under Bazaine, the emperor retaining the Guard. Those of the 7th directed the Second Corps to proceed to Bitsche, the Third to Saarguemund, the Fourth to Haut-Homburg, the Guard to St. Avoid. These instructions plainly signified the making of a flank movement in front of a superior enemy. With such an army as the emperor had, inferior in numbers, many of the regiments as yet incomplete, all his resources behind him, and these becoming daily more unavailable, his one chance was to concentrate in a position commanding the roads behind it, and yet adapted for attack if attack should be necessary. As it was, without certain information as to the movements of the Germans, anxious to move, yet dreading to do so, until his regiments should be completed, the French emperor was confused and helpless. He forgot even to transmit to the generals on one flank the general directions he had issued to those on the other. Bazaine, for instance, was left on the 5th in ignorance of the emperor's intentions with respect to MacMahon; on the 6th none of the subordinate generals knew that the flank march was contemplated. Frossard, who had fallen back to Spicheren, considered his position so insecure that he suggested to Lebœuf that he should be allowed to retire from the Saarbrücken ridge. He was ordered in reply to fall back on Forbach, but no instructions were given him as to the course he should pursue in the event of his being attacked, nor were the contemplated movements of the emperor communicated to him. In every order that was issued there was apparent the confused mind of the issuer.

Turn we now to MacMahon and the movements of himself and his generals. When the war broke out MacMahon was in the vicinity of Strasburg with forty-five thousand men; General Douay with twelve thousand men at Weissenburg. The same confusion prevailed here as at Metz. The orders given to MacMahon were of the vaguest description: Douay had no instructions at all. Yet, in front of him, the German hosts had been gathering. The commander of the left wing of the German army, the crown prince of Prussia, had, in obedience to the instructions he had received, crossed the frontier river, the Lauter, on the 4th of August, with an army composed of the Second Bavarian and Fifth Prussian army, numbering about forty thousand men, and marched on Weissenburg. As his advanced guard approached the town, it was met by a heavy fire from the French garrison. The crown prince resolved at once to storm the place. Douay had placed his troops in a strong position, a portion of his men occupying the town defended by a simple wall; the bulk, formed on the Gaisberg, a hill two miles to the south of it. Against this position the crown prince directed his chief attack. The contest which ensued was most severe, the assailants and the defenders vying with one another in determination and courage. But the odds in favor of the former were too great to permit Douay to hope for ultimate success. After a resistance of five hours' duration the Germans carried the Gaisberg. Douay himself was killed; but his surviving troops, though beaten, were not discouraged. They successfully foiled an attempt made by the Germans to cut off their retreat, and fell back on the corps of MacMahon, which lay about ten miles to the south of Weissenburg.

The same day on which the crown prince had attacked and carried Weissenburg, another German army corps, that of Baden-Wurtemberg, a part of the Third Army, under the command of the crown prince, had advanced on and occupied Lauterburg. That evening the entire Third Army, consisting of one hundred and thirty thousand men, bivouacked on French ground. Meanwhile MacMahon, on hearing of Douay's defeat, had marched to Reichshofen, received there the shattered remnants of Douay's division, and, with the emperor's orders under no circumstances to decline a battle, took up a position on the hills of which Wörth, Fröschweiler, and Elsasshausen form the central points. He had with him forty-seven thousand men, but the Fifth Corps, commanded by De Failly, was at Bitsche, seventeen miles from Reichshofen, and MacMahon had despatched the most pressing instructions to that officer to join him. These orders, however, De Failly did not obey.

The ground on which MacMahon had retired offered many capabilities for defence. The central point was the village of Wörth on the rivulet Sauerbach, which covered the entire front of the position. To the right rear of Wörth, on the road from Gundershofen, was the village of Elsasshausen, covered on its right by the Niederwald, having the village of Eberbach on its further side, and the extreme right of the position, the village of Morsbronn, to its southeast. Behind Wörth, again, distant a little more than two miles on the road to Reichshofen, was the key to the position, the village of Fröschweiler. From this point the French left was thrown back to a mound, covered by a wood, in front of Reichshofen.

On the 5th of August the crown prince had set his army in motion, and had rested for the night at Sulz. There information reached him regarding the position taken by MacMahon. He immediately issued orders for the concentration of his army, and for its march the following morning toward the French position, the village of Preuschdorf, on the direct road to Worth, to be the central point of the movement. But the previous evening General von Walther, with the Fifth Prussian Corps, had reached Gorsdorf, a point whence it was easy for him to cross the Sauerbach, and take Worth in flank. Marching at four o'clock in the morning Walther tried this manœuvre, and at seven o'clock succeeded in driving the French from Worth. MacMahon then changed his front, recovered Worth, and repulsed likewise an attack which had in the meanwhile been directed against Froschweiler by the Eleventh Prussian and Fifth Bavarian Corps.

For a moment it seemed as though he might hold his position. But between eleven and twelve the enemy renewed his attack. While one corps again attacked and carried Worth, the Eleventh Prussian Corps, aided by sixty guns placed upon the heights of Gunstett, assailed his right. They met here a most stubborn resistance, the French cuirassiers charging the advancing infantry with the greatest resolution. So thoroughly did they devote themselves that they left three-fourths of their number dead or dying on the field. But all was in vain. The Prussians steadily advanced, forced their way through the Niederwald, and threatened Elsasshausen. While the French were thus progressing badly on their right, they were faring still worse in the centre.

The Germans, having seized Worth, stormed the hilly slopes between that place and Froschweiler, and made a furious assault upon the latter, now more than ever the key of the French position. For while Froschweiler was their objective centre, their right was thrown back toward Elsasshausen and the Niederwald, their left to Reichshofen. While the Eleventh Prussians were penetrating the Niederwald, preparatory to attacking Elsasshausen on the further side of it, the Fifth Prussian Corps with the Second Bavarians were moving against Froschweiler. It was clear then to MacMahon that further resistance was impossible. Still holding Froschweiler, he evacuated Elsasshausen, and drew back his right to Reichshofen. The safety of his army depended now upon the tenacity with which Froschweiler might be held. It must be admitted, in justice to the French, that they held it with a stubborn valor not surpassed during the war. Attacked by overwhelming numbers, they defended the place, house by house. At length, however, they were overpowered. Then, for the first time, the bonds of discipline loosened, and the French, struck by panic, fled, in wild disorder, in the direction of Saverne. They reached that place by a march across the hills the following evening. On their way they fell in with one of the divisions of the corps of De Failly, and this served to cover the retreat.

Though their defeat, considering the enormous superiority of their assailants, might be glorious, it was doubly disastrous, inasmuch that it followed those perturbations of spirit alluded to in a previous page, which had done so much to discourage the French soldier. A victory at Worth might have done much to redeem past mistakes. A defeat emphasized them enormously. It was calculated that, inclusive of the nine thousand prisoners taken by the Germans, the French lost twenty-four thousand men. The loss of the victors amounted to ten thousand. They captured thirty-three guns, two eagles, and six mitrailleuses.

The emperor was deeply pained by the result of the battle. To keep up, if possible, the spirits of his partisans, he wired on the evening of the 7th to Paris, with the news of the defeat, the words, "tout se peut retablir." He was mistaken. While the crown prince was crushing MacMahon at Worth, the imperial troops were being beaten at Spicheren as well.

Thereafter the German advance was hardly checked for a moment, though the losses on both sides were heavy. On the 18th of August was fought the battle of Gravelotte, in which King William commanded in person, and though his troops suffered immense loss, they were again victorious, and forced Bazaine to shut himself up in Metz, which he subsequently surrendered. In this battle, one of the most decisive of the war, it is worth noting that the Germans outnumbered the French by more than two to one. The exact figures are uncertain, but we shall probably be correct in accepting 230,000 as the strength of the Germans, and in estimating the French outside of Metz at 110,000.

We now come to Sedan. With the army of Bazaine beleaguered, there remained, in the opinion of the German chiefs —an opinion not justified by events—only the army of MacMahon. To remove that army from the path which led to Paris was the task intrusted to the crown prince.

MacMahon, meanwhile, after his defeat at Worth, had fallen back with the disordered remnants of his army on Chalons, there to reorganize and strengthen it. Much progress had been made in both respects, when, after the result of the battle of Gravelotte had been known in Paris, he received instructions from the Count of Palikao to march with the four army corps at his disposal northward toward the Meuse, and to give a hand to the beleaguered Bazaine.

MacMahon prepared to obey. But circumstances ordered otherwise. On the night of August 31st, accompanied by the emperor—who, having transferred his authority to the Empress Eugenie and his command to Bazaine, followed the army as mere spectator—MacMahon reached Sedan, and there ranged his troops so as to meet an attack which he foresaw inevitable, and fatal too. Placing his strongest force to the east, his right wing was at Bazeilles and the left at Illy. The ground in front of his main defence was naturally strong, the entire front being covered by the Givonne rivulet, and the slopes to that rivulet, on the French side of it.

The possibility that the French marshal would accept battle at Sedan had been considered at the German headquarters on the night of the 31st, and arrangements had been made to meet his wishes. The army of the crown prince of Saxony (the Fourth Army) occupied the right of the German forces, the Bavarian Corps formed the centre, and the Prussians the left wing. The advanced troops of the army were ranged in the following order. On the right stood the Twelfth Corps, then the Fourth Prussian Corps, the Prussian Guards, and finally the Fourth Cavalry Division, their backs to Remilly. From this point they were linked to the First and Second Bavarian Corps, opposite Bazeilles; they, in turn, to the Eleventh and Fifth Corps; and they, at Dom-le-Mesnil, to the Würtembergers. The Sixth Prussian Corps was placed in reserve between Attigny and Le Chene.

A word now as to the nature of the ground on which the

impending battle was to be fought. Sedan lies in the most beautiful part of the valley of the Meuse, amid terraced heights, covered with trees, and, within close distance, the villages of Donchery, Iges, Villette, Glaire, Daigny, Bazeilles, and others. Along the Meuse, on the left bank, ran the main road from Donchery through Frenois, crossing the river at the suburb Torcy, and there traversing Sedan. The character of the locality may best be described as a ground covered with fruit gardens and vineyards, narrow streets shut in by stone walls, the roads overhung by forests, the egress from which was in many places steep and abrupt. Such was the ground. One word now as to the troops.

The German army before Sedan counted, all told, 240,000 men; the French 130,000. But the disparity in numbers was the least of the differences between the two armies. The one was flushed with victory, the other dispirited by defeat. The one had absolute confidence in their generals and their officers, the other had the most supreme contempt for theirs. The one had marched from Metz on a settled plan, to be modified according to circumstances, the drift of which was apparent to the meanest soldier; the other had been marched hither and thither, now toward Montmedy, now toward Paris, then again back toward Montmedy, losing much time; the men eager for a pitched battle, then suddenly surprised through the carelessness of their commanders, and compelled at last to take refuge in a town from which there was no issue. There was hardly an officer of rank who knew aught about the country in which he found himself. The men were longing to fight to the death, but they, one and all, distrusted their leaders. It did not tend, moreover, to the encouragement of the army to see the now phantom emperor, without authority to command even a corporal's guard, dragged about the country, more as a pageant than a sovereign. He, poor man, was much to be pitied. He keenly felt his position, and longed for the day when he might, in a great battle, meet the glorious death which France might accept as an atonement for his misfortunes.

The battle began at daybreak on the morning of the 1st of September. Under cover of a brisk artillery fire, the Bavarians advanced, and opened, at six o'clock, a very heavy musketry fire on Bazeilles. The masonry buildings of this village were all armed and occupied, and they were defended very valiantly. The defenders drove back the enemy as they advanced and kept them at bay for two hours. Then the Saxons came up to the aid of the Bavarians, and forced the first position. Still the defence continued, and the clocks were striking ten when the Bavarians succeeded in entering the place. Even then a house-to-house defence prolonged the battle, and it was not until every house but one[1] had been either stormed or burned that the Germans could call the village, or the ruins which remained of it, their own. Meanwhile, on the other points of their defensive position; at Floing, St. Menges, Fleigneux, Illy, and, on the extreme left, at Iges, where a sharp bend of the Meuse forms a peninsula of the ground round which it slowly rolls; the French had been making a gallant struggle. In their ranks, even in advance of them, attended finally by a single aide-de-camp, all the others having been killed, was the emperor, cool, calm, and full of sorrow, earnestly longing for the shell or the bullet which should give a soldier's finish to his career. MacMahon, too, was there, doing all that a general could do to encourage his men. The enemy were, however, gradually but surely making way. To hedge the French within the narrowest compass, the Fifth and Eleventh Corps of the Third Army had crossed the Meuse to the left of Sedan, and were marching now to roll up the French left. But before their attack had been felt, an event had occurred full of significance for the French army.

Early in the day, while yet the Bavarians were fighting to get possession of Bazeilles, Marshal MacMahon was so severely wounded that he had to be carried from the field

---

[1] The house is called "A la derniere Cartouche," and is the subject of De Neuville's splendid painting.

into Sedan. He made over the command of the army to General Ducrot. That general had even before recognized the impossibility of maintaining the position before Sedan against the superior numbers of the German army, and had seen that the one chance of saving his army was to fall back on Mezieres. He at once, then, on assuming command, issued orders to that effect. But it was already too late. The march by the defile of St. Albert had been indeed possible at any time during the night or in the very early morning. But it was now no longer so. The German troops swarmed in the plains of Donchery, and the route by Carignan could only be gained by passing over the bodies of a more numerous and still living foe. Still Ducrot had given the order, and the staff officers did their utmost to cause it to be obeyed. The crowded streets of Sedan were being vacated, when suddenly the orders were countermanded. General Wimpffen had arrived from Paris the previous day to replace the incapable De Failly in command of the Fifth Corps, carrying in his pocket an order from the Minister of War to assume the command-in-chief in the event of any accident to MacMahon. The emperor had no voice in the matter, for, while the regency of the empress existed, he no longer represented the government. The two generals met, and, after a somewhat lively discussion, Ducrot was forced to acknowledge the authority of the minister. Wimpffen then assumed command. His first act was to countermand the order to retreat on Mezieres, and to direct the troops to reassume the positions they had occupied when MacMahon had been wounded. This order was carried out as far as was possible.

Meanwhile the Germans were pressing more and more those positions. About midday the Guards, having made their way step by step, each one bravely contested, gave their hand to the left wing of the Third Army. Then Illy and Floing, which had been defended with extraordinary tenacity, as the keys of the advanced French position, were stormed. The conquest of those heights completed the investment of Sedan. There was now no possible egress for the French. Their soldiers retreated into the town and the suburbs, while five hundred German guns hurled their missiles, their round shot and their shells, against the walls and the crowded masses behind them.

Vainly then did Wimpffen direct an assembly in mass of his men to break through the serried columns of the enemy. In the disordered state of the French army the thing was impossible. The emperor, who had courted death in vain, recognized the truth, and, desirous to spare the sacrifice of life produced by the continued cannonade, ordered, on his own responsibility, the hoisting of a white flag on the highest point of the defences, as a signal of surrender. But the firing still continued, and Wimpffen, still bent on breaking through, would not hear of surrender. Then Napoleon despatched his chief aide-de-camp, General Reille, with a letter to the king of Prussia."

King William early that day had taken his stand on an eminence which commanded an extensive view and which rises a little south of Frenois. There, his staff about him, he watched the progress of the fight. Toward this eminence Reille rode. Walking his horse up the steep, he dismounted, and raising his cap presented the letter. King William, breaking the imperial seal, read these phrases, which, if somewhat dramatic, are striking in their brevity:[1]

"MONSIEUR MON FRÈRE—N'ayant pu mourir au milieu de mes troupes, il ne me reste qu' à remettre mon epée entre les mains de Votre Majeste.

"Je suis de Votre Majeste,
"le bon Frere,
"NAPOLÉON.

"Sédan, le 1er Septembre, 1870."

"Only one half hour earlier," writes Mr. George Hooper in his "Campaign of Sedan," "had the information been

[1] "Not having been able to die in the midst of my troops, nothing remains for me but to place my sword in the hands of your Majesty."

brought that the emperor was in Sedan." Mr. Hooper adds:

"The king conferred with his son, who had been hastily summoned, and with others of his trusty servants, all deeply moved by complex emotions at the grandeur of their victory. What should be done? The emperor spoke for himself only, and his surrender would not settle the great issue. It was necessary to obtain something definite, and the result of a short conference was that Count Hatzfeldt, instructed by the chancellor, retired to draft a reply. 'After some minutes he brought it,' writes Dr. Busch, 'and the king wrote it out, sitting on one chair, while the seat of a second was held up by Major von Alten, who knelt on one knee and supported the chair on the other.' The king's letter, brief and business-like, began and ended with the customary royal forms, and ran as follows:

"'Regretting the circumstances in which we meet, I accept your Majesty's sword, and beg that you will be good enough to name an officer furnished with full powers to treat for the capitulation of the army which has fought so bravely under your orders. On my side I have designated General von Moltke for that purpose.'

"General Reille returned to his master, and as he rode down the hill the astounding purport of his visit flew from lip to lip through the exulting army which now hoped that, after this colossal success, the days of ceaseless marching and fighting would soon end. As a contrast to this natural outburst of joy and hope we may note the provident Moltke, who was always resolved to 'mak siker.' His general order, issued at once, suspending hostilities during the night, declared that they would begin again in the morning should the negotiations produce no result. In that case, he said, the signal for battle would be the reopening of fire by the batteries on the heights east of Frenois.

"The signal was not given. Late on the evening of September 1st a momentous session was held in Donchery, the little town which commands a bridge over the Meuse below Sedan. On one side of a square table covered with red baize sat General von Moltke, having on his right hand the quartermaster-general Von Podbielski, according to one account, and Von Blumenthal according to another, and behind them several officers, while Count von Nostitz stood near the hearth to take notes. Opposite to Von Moltke sat De Wimpffen alone; while in rear, 'almost in the shade,' were General Faure, Count Castelnau, and other Frenchmen, among whom was a cuirassier, Captain d'Orcet, who had observant eyes and a retentive memory. Then there ensued a brief silence, for Von Moltke looked straight before him and said nothing, while De Wimpffen, oppressed by the number present, hesitated to engage in a debate 'with the two men admitted to be the most capable of our age, each in his kind.' But he soon plucked up courage, and frankly accepted the conditions of the combat. What terms, he asked, would the king of Prussia grant to a valiant army which, could he have had his will, would have continued to fight? 'They are very simple,' answered Von Moltke. 'The entire army, with arms and baggage, must surrender as prisoners of war.' 'Very hard,' replied the Frenchman. 'We merit better treatment. Could you not be satisfied with the fortress and the artillery, and allow the army to retire with arms, flags and baggage, on condition of serving no more against Germany during the war?' No. 'Moltke,' said Bismarck, recounting the interview, 'coldly persisted in his demand,' or as the attentive d'Orcet puts it, 'Von Moltke was pitiless.' Then De Wimpffen tried to soften his grim adversary by painting his own position. He had just come from the depths of the African desert; he had an irreproachable military reputation; he had taken command in the midst of a battle, and found himself obliged to set his name to a disastrous capitulation. 'Can you not,' he said, 'sympathize with an officer in such a plight, and soften, for me, the bitterness of my situation by granting more honorable conditions?' He painted in moving terms his own sad case, and described what he might have done; but seeing that his personal pleadings were unheeded, he took a tone of defiance, less likely to prevail. 'If you will not give better terms,' he went on, 'I shall appeal to the honor of the army, and break out, or, at least, defend Sedan.' Then the German general struck in with emphasis, 'I regret that I cannot do what you ask,' he said; 'but as to making a sortie, that is just as impossible as the defence of Sedan. You have some excellent troops, but the greater part of your infantry is demoralized. To-day, during the battle, we captured more than twenty thousand unwounded prisoners. You have only eighty thousand men left. My troops and guns around the town would smash yours before they could make a movement; and as to defending Sedan, you have not provisions for eight-and-forty hours, nor ammunition which would suffice for that period.' Then, says De Wimpffen, he entered into details respecting our situation, which, 'unfortunately, were too true,' and he offered to permit an officer to verify his statements, an offer which the Frenchman did not then accept.

"Beaten off the military ground, De Wimpffen sought refuge in politics. 'It is your interest, from a political standpoint, to grant us honorable conditions,' he said. 'France is generous and chivalric, responsive to generosity, and grateful for consideration. A peace, based on conditions which would flatter the amour-propre of the army, and diminish the bitterness of defeat, would be durable; whereas rigorous measures would awaken bad passions, and, perhaps, bring on an endless war between France and Prussia.' The new ground broken called up Bismarck, 'because the matter seemed to belong to my province,' he observed when telling the story; and he was very outspoken as usual. 'I said to him that we might build on the gratitude of a prince, but certainly not on the gratitude of a people—least of all on the gratitude of the French. That in France neither institutions nor circumstances were enduring; that governments and dynasties were constantly changing, and the one need not carry out what the other had bound itself to do. That if the emperor had been firm on his throne, his gratitude for our granting good conditions might have been counted upon; but as things stood it would be folly if we did not make full use of our success. That the French were a nation full of envy and jealousy, that they had been much mortified by our success at Koniggratz, and could not forgive it, though it in nowise damaged them. How, then, should any magnanimity on our side move them not to bear us a grudge for Sedan?' This Wimpffen would not admit. 'France,' he said, 'had much changed latterly; it had learned under the empire to think more of the interests of peace than of the glory of war. France was ready to proclaim the fraternity of nations;' and more of the same kind. Captain d'Orcet reports that, in addition, Bismarck denied that France had changed, and that to curb her mania for glory, to punish her pride, her aggressive and ambitious character, it was imperative that there should be a glacis between France and Germany. 'We must have territory, fortresses and frontiers which will shelter us forever from an attack on her part.' Further remonstrances from De Wimpffen only drew down fresh showers of rough speech very trying to bear, and when Bismarck said, 'We cannot change our conditions,' De Wimpffen exclaimed, 'Very well; it is equally impossible for me to sign such a capitulation, and we shall renew the battle.'

"Here Count Castelnau interposed meekly to say, on behalf of the emperor, that he had surrendered, personally, in the hope that his self-sacrifice would induce the king to grant the army honorable terms. 'Is that all?' Bismarck inquired. 'Yes,' said the Frenchman. 'But what is the sword surrendered,' asked the chancellor; 'is it his own sword, or the sword of France?' 'It is only the sword of the emperor,' was Castelnau's reply. 'Well, there is no use talking about other conditions,' said Von Moltke, sharply, while a look of contentment and gratification passed over his face, according to Bismarck; one 'almost joyful,' writes the keen Captain d'Orcet. 'After the last words of Von Moltke,' he continues, 'De Wimpffen exclaimed, "We shall renew the battle." "The truce," retorted the German general, "expires to-morrow morning at four o'clock. At four, precisely, I shall open fire." We were all standing. After Von Moltke's words no one spoke a syllable. The silence was icy.' But then Bismarck intervened to soothe excited feelings, and called on his soldier-comrade to show, once more, how impossible resistance had become. The group sat down again at the red baize-covered table, and Von Moltke began his demonstration afresh. 'Ah,' said De Wimpffen, 'your positions are not so strong as you would have us believe them to be.' 'You do not know the topography of the country about Sedan,' was Von Moltke's true and crushing answer. 'Here is a bizarre detail which illustrates the presumptuous and inconsequent character of your people,' he went on, now thoroughly aroused. 'When the war began you supplied your officers with maps of Germany at a time when they could not study the geography of their own country for want of French maps. I tell you that our positions are not only very strong, they are inexpugnable.' It was then that De Wimpffen, unable to reply, wished to accept the offer made but not accepted at an earlier period, and to send an officer to verify these assertions. 'You will send nobody,' exclaimed the iron general. 'It is useless, and you can believe my word. Besides, you have not long to reflect. It is now midnight; the truce ends at four o'clock, and I will grant no delay.' Driven to his last ditch, De Wimpffen pleaded that he must consult his fellow-generals, and he could not obtain their opinions by four o'clock. Once more the diplomatic peacemaker intervened, and Von Moltke agreed to fix the final limit at nine. 'He gave way at last,' says Bismarck, 'when I showed him that it could do no harm.' The conference so dramatic broke up, and each one went his way; but, says the German official narrative, 'as it was not doubtful that the hostile army, completely beaten and nearly surrounded, would be obliged to submit to the clauses already indicated, the great headquarter staff was occupied, that very night, in drawing up the text of the capitulation,' a significant and practical comment, showing what stuff there was behind the severe language which, at the midnight meeting, fell from the Chief of that able and sleepless body of chosen men.

"From this conference General de Wimpffen went straight to the wearied emperor, who had gone to bed. But he received his visitor, who told him that the proposed conditions were hard, and that the sole chance of mitigation lay in the efforts of his Majesty. 'General,' said the emperor, 'I shall start at five o'clock for the German headquarters, and I shall see whether the king will be more favorable;' for he seems to have become possessed of an idea that King William would personally treat with him. The emperor kept his word. Believing that he would be permitted to return to Sedan, he drove forth without bidding farewell to any of his troops; but, as the drawbridge of Torcy was lowered and he passed over, the Zouaves on duty shouted 'Vive l'Empereur!' This cry was 'the last adieu which fell on his ears,' as we read in the narrative given to the world on his behalf. He drove in a drosky toward Donchery, preceded by General Reille, who, before six o'clock, awoke Bismarck from his slumbers, and warned him that the emperor desired to speak with him. 'I went with him directly,' said Bismarck, in a conversation reported by Busch; 'and got on my horse, all dusty and dirty as I was, in an old cap and my great waterproof boots, to ride to Sedan, where I supposed him to be.' But he met him on the highroad near Frenois, 'sitting in a two-horse carriage.' Beside him was the Prince de la Moskowa, and on horseback Castelnau and Reille. 'I gave the military salute,' says Bismarck. 'He took his cap off and the officers did the same; whereupon I took off mine, although it was contrary to rule. He said, "Couvrez-vous, donc." I behaved to him just as if in St. Cloud, and asked his commands.' Naturally, he wanted to see the king, but that could not be allowed. Then Bismarck placed his quarters in Donchery at the emperor's disposal, but he declined the courtesy, and preferred to rest in a house by the wayside.

The cottage of a Belgian weaver unexpectedly became famous; a one-storied house, painted yellow, with white shutters and venetian blinds. He and the chancellor entered the house, and went up to the first floor where there was 'a little room with one window. It was the best in the house, but had only one deal table and two rush-bottomed chairs.' In that lowly abode they talked together of many things for three-quarters of an hour, among others about the origin of the war—which, it seems, neither desired—the emperor asserting, Bismarck reports, that 'he had been driven into it by the pressure of public opinion,' a very inadequate representation of the curious incidents which preceded the fatal decision. But when the emperor began to ask for more favorable terms, he was told that, on a military question, Von Moltke alone could speak. On the other hand, Bismarck's request to know who now had authority to make peace was met by a reference to 'the Government in Paris'; so that no progress was made. Then 'we must stand to our demands with regard to the Army of Sedan,' said Bismarck. General von Moltke was summoned, and 'Napoleon III. demanded that nothing should be decided before he had seen the king, for he hoped to obtain from his Majesty some favorable concessions for the army.' The German official narrative of the war states that the emperor expressed a wish that the army might be permitted to enter Belgium, but that, of course, the chief of the staff could not accept the proposal. General von Moltke forthwith set out for Vendresse, where the king was, to report progress. He met his Majesty on the road, and there 'the king fully approved the proposed conditions of capitulation, and declared that he would not see the emperor until the terms prescribed had been accepted'; a decision which gratified the chancellor as well as the chief of the staff. 'I did not wish them to come together,' observed the count, 'until we had settled the matter of the capitulation'; sparing the feelings of both and leaving the business to the hard military men.

"The emperor lingered about in the garden of the weaver's cottage; he seems to have desired fresh air after his unpleasant talk with the chancellor. Dr. Moritz Busch, who had hurried to the spot, has left a characteristic description of the emperor. He saw there 'a little thick-set man,' wearing jauntily a red cap with a gold border, a black paletôt lined with red, red trousers, and white kid gloves. 'The look in his light gray eyes was somewhat soft and dreamy, like that of people who have lived hard. His whole appearance,' says the irreverent Busch, 'was a little unsoldierlike. The man looked too soft, I might say too shabby, for the uniform he wore.' While one scene in the stupendous drama was performed at the weaver's cottage, another was acted or endured in Sedan, where De Wimpffen had summoned the generals to consider the terms of capitulation. He has given his own account of the incident; but the fullest report is supplied by Lebrun. There were present at this council of war more than thirty generals. With tearful eyes and a voice broken by sobs the unhappy and most ill-starred De Wimpffen described his interview and conflict with Von Moltke and Bismarck, and its dire result—the army to surrender as prisoners of war, the officers alone to retain their arms, and, by way of mitigating the rigor of these conditions, full permission to return home would be given to any officer, provided he would engage in writing and on honor not to serve again during the war. The generals, save one or two, and these finally acquiesced, felt that the conditions could not be refused; but they were indignant at the clause suggesting that the officers might escape the captivity which would befall their soldiers, provided they would engage to become mere spectators of the invasion of their country. In the midst of these mournful deliberations Captain von Zingler, a messenger from Von Moltke, entered, and the scene became still more exciting. 'I am instructed,' he said, 'to remind you how urgent it is that you should come to a decision. At ten o'clock, precisely, if you have not come to a resolution, the German batteries will fire on Sedan. It is now nine, and I shall have barely time to carry your answer to headquarters.' To this sharp summons De Wimpffen answered that he could not decide until he knew 'the result of the interview between the emperor and the king,' 'That interview,' said the stern captain, 'will not in any way affect the military operations, which can only be determined by the generals who have full power to resume or stop the strife.' It was, indeed, as Lebrun remarked, useless to argue with a captain charged to state a fact; and at the general's suggestion De Wimpffen agreed to accompany Captain von Zingler to the German headquarters.

"These were, for the occasion, the Château de Bellevue, where the emperor himself had been induced to take up his abode, and about eleven o'clock, in a room under the imperial chamber, De Wimpffen put his name at the foot of the document drawn up, during the night, by the German staff. Then he sought out the emperor, and, greatly moved, told him that 'all was finished.' His majesty, he writes, 'with tears in his eyes, approached me, pressed my hand, and embraced me,' and 'my sad and painful duty having been accomplished, I remounted my horse and road back to Sedan, "la mort dans l'âme."'

"So soon as the convention was signed, the king arrived, accompanied by the crown prince. Three years before, as the emperor reminds us in the writing attributed to him, the king had been his guest in Paris, where all the sovereigns of Europe had come to behold the marvels of the famous Exhibition. 'Now,' so runs the lamentation, 'betrayed by fortune, Napoleon III. had lost all, and had placed in the hands of his conqueror the sole thing left him—his liberty.' And he goes on to say, in general terms, that the king deeply sympathized with his misfortunes, but nevertheless could not grant better conditions to the army. 'He told the emperor that the castle of Wilhelmshohe had been selected as his residence; the crown prince then entered and cordially shook hands with Napoleon; and at the end of a quarter of an hour the king withdrew. The emperor was permitted to send a telegram in cipher to the empress, to tell her what had happened, and urge her to negotiate a peace.' Such is the bald record of this impressive event. The telegram, which reached the empress at four o'clock on the afternoon of the 3d, was in these words: 'The army is defeated and captive; I myself am a prisoner.'

"For one day more the fallen sovereign rested at Bellevue to meditate on the caprices of fortune or the decrees of fate. But that day, at the head of a splendid company of princes and generals, King William, crossing the bridge of Donchery, rode throughout the whole vast extent of the German lines, to greet his hardy warriors and be greeted by them on the very scene of their victories. And well they deserved regal gratitude, for together with their comrades who surrounded Metz, by dint of long swift marches and steadfast valor, they had overcome two great armies in thirty days.

"During the battle of Sedan, the Germans lost in killed and wounded, 8,924 officers and men. On the other hand, the French lost 3,000 killed, 14,000 wounded, and 21,000 captured in the battle. The number of prisoners by capitulation was 83,000, while 3,000 were disarmed in Belgium, and a few hundreds, more or less, made their way by devious routes near and over the frontier, to Mezières, Recroi, and other places in France. In addition, were taken one eagle and two flags, 419 field guns and mitrailleuses, 139 garrison guns, many wagons, muskets, and horses. On the day after the surrender, the French soldiers, having stacked their arms in Sedan, marched into the peninsula formed by the deep loop of the Meuse—'le Camp de Misère' as they called it—and were sent thence in successive batches, numbered by thousands, to Germany. Such was the astonishing end of the Army of Chalons, which had been impelled to its woful doom by the Comte de Palikao and the Paris politicians."

Here closes the first and most dramatic phase of the war. Thereafter the enemy was smitten hip and thigh. At once hurry orders were given to open the line which led from Nancy to Paris. What followed must be briefly told.

On the 5th of September the king of Prussia entered Rheims. On the 8th Laon surrendered. On the 15th advanced troops halted within three hours of the capital of France, making a half circle round its defences. This investment Ducrot—who had escaped from Sedan—attempted to prevent. His resources consisted in the Thirteenth Corps under General Vinoy, and the Fourteenth under General Renault, and 18,000 marines, excellent soldiers, a total of 88,000 regular troops. He had also in the camps of Vincennes and St. Maur 100,000 Garde-Mobiles, only very imperfectly disciplined; 10,000 volunteers from the provinces, resolute men, prepared to give their lives for their country; the National Guard, composed of sixty old and a hundred and ninety-four new battalions which, with other miscellaneous volunteers of Paris, numbered perhaps 200,000 men, not, however, thoroughly to be depended upon. Altogether the defenders numbered about 400,000, but of these only the 88,000 regular troops and the 10,000 volunteers from the provinces could be reckoned as trustworthy.

Nevertheless, the Third German Army had no difficulty in establishing itself in a position embracing the southern and southeastern front of the city, from Sèvres to the Marne; the Fourth Army faced the northeast and northern front, the cavalry the west front, so far as the windings of the Seine would permit it. On the 5th of October the crown prince took up his headquarters at Versailles, those of the king being at Ferrières, the seat of the Paris Rothschilds. Here took place, on the 19th October, the famous interview between the French foreign minister, Jules Favre, and Bismarck, in which the former made his declaration that France would surrender neither one inch of her territories nor one stone of her fortresses. The interview remained without result.

Meanwhile the fortress of Toul had surrendered. Strasburg, after a siege of six weeks, also surrendered, and, on

October 27, Bazaine handed over Metz and an army consisting of three marshals of France, 6,000 officers, and 173,000 soldiers—an act for which after the conclusion of the war he was court-martialled, declared guilty of treason, and sentenced to death and degradation. The then president of the republic, Marshal MacMahon, commuted the death sentence into one of imprisonment for twenty years. Confined in the fort of the island St. Marguerite, near Cannes, Bazaine escaped, and lived in Spain till his death.

Bazaine's surrender made the Germans masters of one of the strongest fortresses in Europe, with 800 heavy guns, 102 mitrailleuses, 300,000 Chassepots, and placed at the disposal of the king an entire blockading army.

If was at that juncture that Gambetta astonished the world. Reaching Tours in a balloon from Paris, and there assuming the ministry of war, he became practically dictator of France. Thence he issued a proclamation to the people of France, urging them to continue their resistance to the bitter end, and directed that all men, capable of bearing arms, should lend their hands to the work, and should join the troops of the line at Tours. In this way he formed an Army of the North, and an Army of the Loire, and, later, an Army of the East. In all respects he displayed a fertility of resource which astounded. He obtained arms, uniforms, munitions, and other necessaries from foreign countries, especially from England. He bestowed the greatest pains in selecting as generals of the new levies men who should be real soldiers. Under his inspiring influence the war in the provinces assumed a very serious complexion. France had responded nobly to the call he had made upon her people. Early reverses gave vigor to the new levies, and they fought with energy against the Bavarians under Von der Than at Arthenay and Orleans, and against the division of Wittich at Chateaudun and Chartres. But they were fighting against increasing odds. Every day brought reinforcements to the Germans.

With the exception of a momentary gleam of success on

the Loire, France met with nothing but disaster. In Paris matters were critical. Every one of the different sorties made by her defenders had been repulsed; the hope by which the spirits of her defenders had been buoyed was vanishing fast: famine was approaching with giant strides, the strong places outside the circle of her defences were falling one after another; the fire of the enemy was, by the nearer approach of their troops, becoming more concentrated and more severe. Peace must be had. On January 28th, then, there was concluded at Versailles an armistice for three weeks. Then a national assembly was summoned to Bordeaux to consider how peace might be restored. In that assembly Thiers received full administrative powers, including the power of nominating his own ministers. He himself, with Jules Favre, undertook the negotiations with Bismarck. To insure the success of those negotiations the armistice was twice prolonged. This was done at the instance of Thiers, for the conditions insisted upon by Bismarck were hard, and the French statesman struggled with all his energies to induce him to abate his demands. Especially did he strive to save Metz, or, at least, to receive Luxemburg in compensation.

But his endeavors were fruitless. The utmost that Bismarck would do was not to insist upon securing the still unconquered Belfort. Despairing of moving him further, Thiers and Favre gave way on the 24th of February, and signed the preliminaries of peace. They were, first, the transfer to Germany of the northeast portion of Lorraine, with Metz and Diedenhofen, and of Alsace, Belfort excepted; second, the payment to Germany by France of one milliard of francs in 1871, and four milliards in the three years following; third, the Germans to begin to evacuate French territory immediately after the ratification of the treaty; Paris and its forts on the left bank of the Seine and certain departments at once; the forts on the right bank after the ratification and the payment of the first half milliard. After the payment of two milliards the German occupation of the departments Marne, Ardennes, Upper Marne, Meuse, the Vosges, and Meurthe, and the fortress of Belfort should cease. Interest at five per cent to be charged on the milliards remaining unpaid from the date of ratification; fourth, the German troops remaining in France to make no requisitions on the departments in which they were located, but to be fed at the cost of France; fifth, the inhabitants of the sequestered provinces to be allowed a certain fixed time in which to make their choice between the two countries; sixth, all prisoners to be at once restored; seventh, a treaty embodying all these terms to be settled at Brussels. It was further arranged that the German army should not occupy Paris, but should content itself with marching through the city.

Meanwhile, negotiations between the statesmen and governments of Germany resulted in a proposal to King William that, as head of the confederation, he should assume the title of German emperor. A resolution to that effect was passed by the North German Reichstag on the 9th of December, and a deputation proceeded to the royal headquarters at Versailles, where, on the 18th of December, the imperial crown was offered to the brother of the king who had once refused it. Deeply touched, King William accepted, and in the palace of Louis XIV., surrounded by a brilliant assembly of princes, officers, and ministers of state, the venerable monarch was proclaimed Deutscher Kaiser.

Then at last was the dream of centuries realized. At last was the empire restored. Not the holy Roman empire, not the empire of the Middle Ages, but the empire as a national state.

Under the leadership of Bismarck, to whom the restoration of the empire was directly due, the new Reich began its organization as a united federation. Among its earliest difficulties was an ecclesiastical contest with the Church of Rome. Known as the Kulturkampf, this struggle was an effort to vindicate the right of the state to interfere in the affairs of all German religious societies. Another difficulty which demanded government interference was the Judenhetze, or persecution of the Jews, which reached a climax in 1881. A further difficulty was encountered in the quick growth of socialism. Two attempts on the life of the kaiser were attributed to it, and a plot being discovered, which had for object the elimination of the emperor and other German rulers, repressive measures resulted. Meanwhile an alliance offensive and defensive between Germany and Austria had been formed, into which Italy subsequently entered.

On March 9, 1888, the Emperor William I. died. His son, Frederick, at that time suffering from a cancerous affection of the throat, became kaiser. Three months later he also died, and William II. succeeded him.

The latter's first step of any importance was to get in front of half a million bayonets. Coincidently he declared that those bayonets and he—or rather he and those bayonets—were born for one another. Incidentally he announced that he was a monarch, specially conceived, specially created, specially ordained by the Almighty.

The step and the remarks were tantamount to a call to quarters. It would be dramatic to state that the circumjacent territories trembled, but it is exact to affirm that there was a war scare at once, one which by no means diminished when a little later he showed Bismarck the door.

As already noted, the refounding of the empire was Bismarck's work. To achieve his purpose he had—to again quote Colonel Malleson—defied parliaments and people. He had led his master and his country over abysses, in the traversing of which one false step would have been fatal. Aided a great deal by the wretched diplomacy of Austria, by the deterioration of the powers of the French emperor, and by his sublime audacity, he had compelled to his will all the moral difficulties of the undertaking. Von Roon and Moltke had done the rest. No longer, however, was he allowed to put forth his hand to sustain the work which he had created. For him it had been better to die, like Von Roon, like Moltke, keeping to the end the confidence of his sovereign, than to feel himself impelled, dismissed from office, to pour out his grievances to every passing listener, to speak in terms not far removed from treason of the sovereign who had declined to be his pupil. Was it for this, he must have muttered, that I forced on the war which gave Prussia Schleswig and Holstein in 1864; that I compelled unwilling Austria to declare war in 1866; that, by the freest circulation of exaggerated statements, I roused a bitter feeling in Germany against France, and excited the statesmen, and, above all, the mob, of Paris in 1870?—for this, that, the work accomplished, an empire given to the Hohenzollerns, I might be cast aside like a squeezed-out orange? Well might these be his thoughts, for it was he who made possible the task of German unity, though in a manner which will commend itself only to those who argue that the end justifies the means.

A journalist wrote a pamphlet on the subject. In it he compared the kaiser to Caligula. For his pains he was sent to jail. He might better have been sent to school. Caligula was a poet in love with the moon. The kaiser is a poseur in love with himself. One of Caligula's many diversions was killing his people. Such slaughter as the kaiser has effected consists in twenty-five thousand head of game. The career of Caligula is horrible, yet in the horrible is sometimes the sublime. The career of the kaiser has been theatrical, and in the theatrical is always the absurd. The single parallel between the two lies in the fact that all young emperors stand on a peak so lofty that, do they look below, vertigo rises, while from above delirium comes. There is nothing astonishing in that. It would be astonishing were it otherwise. What does astonish is the equilibrium which the kaiser, in spite of his words, his threats and actions, has managed to maintain. Regarded as a firebrand and a menace to the peace of Europe, with the exception of two big blunders—an invitation to King Humbert to promenade with him through Strasburg, and the message which he sent to President Kruger of the Transvaal after the failure of the Jameson raid—with these exceptions he has exhibited a regard for international etiquette entirely immaculate, and not always returned.

In recompense for overtures to France he has been snubbed. In recompense for others to Russia he has been ignored. Neither Austria nor Italy love him. He has weakened the Triple Alliance, alienated England, and lost his place. When he ascended the throne Germany's position on the continent was preponderant. That position is Russia's to-day.

Had he had the power—which he has always denied—to return to France the keys of Metz and Strasburg, and had he had the ability—which others have denied for him—to coalesce with France and Russia he would have been war-lord indeed. As it is, failing in an effort to realize the dream of Napoleon I., he has at present writing subsided into a martinet.

What the future holds for Germany and for him the future will tell. But into the future it is not given to any one, even to an emperor, to look.

THE END

INDEX

A

B

C

D

E

F

H

K

L

O

P

R

S

T

Z